Developmentally Appropriate Practice

in Early Childhood Programs

Serving Children from Birth through Age 8

Third Edition

**Carol Copple and
Sue Bredekamp, editors**

National Association for the Education of Young Children
Washington, DC

naeyc®

National Association for
the Education of
Young Children
1313 L Street NW, Suite 500
Washington, DC 20005-4101
202-232-8777 • 800-424-2460
www.naeyc.org

NAEYC Books
Director, Publications and
Educational Initiatives
Carol Copple

Managing Editor
Bry Pollack

Design and Production
Malini Dominey

Editorial Associate
Melissa Edwards

Editorial Assistant
Elizabeth Wegner

Permissions
Lacy Thompson

Marketing Director
Matt Munroe

Through its publications program, the National Association for the Education of Young Children (NAEYC) provides a forum for discussion of major issues and ideas in the early childhood field, with the hope of provoking thought and promoting professional growth. The views expressed or implied in this book are not necessarily those of the Association or its members.

Permissions

The preschool, kindergarten, and primary overview chapters include material from NCTM's *Curriculum Focal Points*, reprinted with the permission of the National Council of Teachers of Mathematics. To view *Curriculum Focal Points* in its entirety, visit the NCTM website: www. nctm.org/focalpoints.

Excerpts from the National Research Council's *Starting Out Right: A Guide to Promoting Children's Reading Success* (selectively adapted from p. 66–114), edited by M. Susan Burns, Peg Griffin, and Catherine E. Snow (Washington, DC: National Academies Press, 1999), are reprinted with permission. © 1999 by National Academy of Sciences.

Excerpt from *Worms, Shadows, and Whirlpools: Science in the Early Childhood Classroom* (p. 3–7), by Karen Worth and Sharon Grollman (Portsmouth, NH: Heinemann, 2003) is reprinted with permission. © 2003 by Education Development Center, Inc.

Chapter 2 is © ZERO TO THREE (2008), *Caring for Infants and Toddlers in Groups: Developmentally Appropriate Practice* (2d ed.), Washington, DC. Reprinted with permission.

Book credits

Additional text/photo editing: Lisa Cook and Natalie Klein Cavanagh

Indexing: Laura Power

Cover and other design: Reece Quiñones, Design Imprint

Age group montage photographs © by: Cleo Photography—51 (*top right*); Cris M. Kelly—109 (*top right*); Terre Kugler—51 (*top left*); Jean-Claude LeJeune—109 (*top left and bottom right*), 185 (*top right, bottom right, and bottom left*), 255 (*bottom right and bottom left*); Marilyn Nolt—51 (*bottom right and bottom left*), 255 (*top right*); Daniel Raskin—109 (*bottom left*); Ellen B. Senisi—185 (*top left*), 255 (*top left*).

Other photographs are credited on their respective pages.

CD credits

Text and video editing: Gaye Gronlund, project manager for DAP resources for NAEYC, and consultant, ECE Consulting

Design and Flash animation: KINETIK, Inc.

Video technical assistance: Dan Huber/Video Active Productions

Proper citations:

Book

Copple, C., & S. Bredekamp, eds. 2009. *Developmentally Appropriate Practice in Early Childhood Programs Serving Children from Birth through Age 8*. 3d ed. Washington, DC: National Association for the Education of Young Children.

Position statement (pp. 1–31)

National Association for the Education of Young Children. 2009. "Developmentally Appropriate Practice in Early Childhood Programs Serving Children from Birth through Age 8." Position Statement. In *Developmentally Appropriate Practice in Early Childhood Programs Serving Children from Birth through Age 8*. 3d ed., C. Copple & S. Bredekamp, eds., pp. 1–31 Washington, DC: Author. Online: www.naeyc.org/files/naeyc/file/positions/PSDAP.pdf.

Developmentally Appropriate Practice in Early Childhood Programs Serving Children from Birth through Age 8

Library of Congress Control Number: 2008939179
ISBN: 978-1-928896-64-7
NAEYC Item #375

About the Editors

Carol Copple is director of Publications and Initiatives in Educational Practice at NAEYC. She was on the faculty at Louisiana State University and at the New School for Social Research. At the Educational Testing Service she co-developed and directed a research-based model for early childhood education and conducted research on children's cognition. Her previous publications include *Developmentally Appropriate Practice in Early Childhood Programs* (Bredekamp & Copple 1997), *Basics of Developmentally Appropriate Practice: An Introduction for Teachers of Children 3 to 6* (Copple & Bredekamp 2006), and *Educating the Young Thinker: Classroom Strategies for Cognitive Growth* (Copple, Sigel, & Saunders 1984). She received her doctorate from Cornell University.

Sue Bredekamp is an early childhood education consultant in Washington, DC. She has consulted for NAEYC, the Council for Professional Recognition, the Head Start Bureau, and state and local departments of education, and served on the Committee on Early Childhood Mathematics of the National Research Council. She developed a satellite television course on early literacy, HeadsUp! Reading. While director of Accreditation and Professional Development at NAEYC (1981–1998), she was responsible for a number of major NAEYC position statements and publications including those on developmentally appropriate practice, curriculum and assessment, literacy, and accreditation. Currently she is writing a textbook, to be titled *Effective Practices in Early Childhood Education: Becoming an Intentional Teacher.* She received her doctorate from the University of Maryland.

About the Contributors

Heather Biggar Tomlinson is a professional development specialist at NAEYC. She previously worked for Senator Edward Kennedy on issues related to the education of young children, with a particular focus on the reauthorization of Head Start. She was a fellow for the Society for Research on Child Development and the American Association for the Advancement of Science in 2002–2003. Prior to that, she worked at the National Institute of Child Health and Human Development on the Study of Early Child Care and Youth Development. She received her doctorate from the University of Georgia.

Marilou Hyson is a senior consultant with NAEYC and an affiliate faculty member in applied developmental psychology at George Mason University. She was professor and chair of the University of Delaware's Individual and Family Studies department and editor-in-chief of *Early Childhood Research Quarterly.* Among her publications are *The Emotional Development of Young Children: Building an Emotion-Centered Curriculum* (2003) and *Enthusiastic and Engaged Learners: Approaches to Learning in the Early Childhood Classroom* (2008). She received her doctorate from Bryn Mawr College.

Contents

Acknowledgments

This book—and the NAEYC position statement on developmentally appropriate practice it contains and is based on—reflects the expertise and experience of a great many people working in early childhood education over the years. These individuals have deepened our collective knowledge and understanding of young children through their work with young children and study of early childhood teaching and learning.

Three years ago, NAEYC launched a discussion among early childhood professionals to inform the revision of its 1996 position statement. Internet technology made it possible for a wider group of people to participate in the discussion than was ever possible previously. The revision process included a thorough review of current research; open forums at NAEYC conferences; convening of a DAP Working Group to advise on content and to review and revise drafts; input, review, and comment by NAEYC Affiliate Groups and pertinent professional organizations; public invitation to anyone in the field to comment on the draft via NAEYC's website; and finally, consideration and approval by NAEYC's Governing Board.

Space prevents us from acknowledging all of the contributions, but we must mention the following:

The outstanding members of the 2007 DAP Working Group. This delightful, knowledgeable group (Juanita Copley, Carolyn Pope Edwards, Linda Espinosa, Ellen Frede, Mary Louise Hemmeter, Marjorie Kostelnik, and Dorothy Strickland) began their work on the position statement revision in March 2007 and continued to respond to that document and plans for the book as they evolved.

The 2007 group's predecessors, the members of NAEYC's Panel on Revisions to Developmentally Appropriate Practice (1993–1996), who gave tirelessly of their time and wisdom to the conceptualization of the 1996 version of the position statement. And before them, the members of NAEYC's 1985 Commission on Appropriate Education for 4- and 5-Year-Olds, who began the process of codifying the Association's position on quality in early childhood practice that culminated in the first position statements on developmentally appropriate practice in 1985/6.

Members of the NAEYC Governing Board (2006–08) for their useful input and much appreciated support.

The NAEYC State Affiliates, who were valuable partners in our collective thinking about developmentally appropriate practice. The Affiliate Council highlighted DAP during their face-to-face meetings, and State Affiliates engaged

in strategic discussions with their local member communities, forwarding their responses, questions, and suggestions directly to NAEYC. In addition, several State Affiliates hosted regional discussion groups across their states.

Important feedback provided by leaders of the Southern Early Childhood Association (SECA), which shares NAEYC's commitment to developmentally appropriate practice.

Staff and representatives of ZERO TO THREE, for their work on developmentally appropriate practice for infants and toddlers, and their generosity in allowing NAEYC to include in this volume a chapter from their book *Caring for Infants and Toddlers in Groups: Developmentally Appropriate Practice, 2d ed.*

The dozens of early childhood leaders, practitioners, and scholars who reacted to our questions about the position statement revision and then to preliminary drafts. Among the many who helped us in this way, we would like to give special thanks to Elena Bodrova, Barbara Bowman, Mon Cochran, Herb Ginsburg, Deborah Leong, Robert Pianta, Sharon Ritchie, Tom Schultz, Barbara Smith, Dorothy Strickland, Ruby Takanishi, Francis Wardle, and Carol Anne Wien for their thoughtful and detailed comments.

Janet Gonzalez-Mena, who contributed substantively to the book, based on her expertise and wisdom in the areas of infant and toddler care and culture in early care and education.

Gaye Gronlund, project manager for DAP resources and activities for NAEYC, without whom the supplementary CD of readings and video examples would not have been possible.

Of the many supportive colleagues at NAEYC who helped in so many ways . . .

We especially appreciate the contributions of Linda Halgunseth; Marilou Hyson; Adele Robinson; and the resolute Heather Biggar Tomlinson, whose knowledge and writing skill shine in her three chapters, written while parenting a toddler and carrying twins.

The one indispensable person in this effort from start to finish was the incredible Bry Pollack, nominally the managing editor for books but our true partner in every aspect of the work. We are also grateful for the sharp skills, hard work, and unflagging dedication of the other members of the books team, Malini Dominey, Melissa Edwards, and Liz Wegner. And to two of our favorite books department alums, freelance editors Lisa Cook and Natalie Cavanagh.

Thanks to Jerlean Daniel, Mark Ginsberg, Marilyn Smith, and Carol Brunson Day for their personal guidance and consistent support over the years and during our work on this edition.

And finally . . .

Special acknowledgment to Patty Smith Hill, Lois Meek Stolz, and Rose Alschuler for their vision, courage, leadership, and commitment in forming an organization that would one day become NAEYC and for framing as its mission the achievement of developmentally appropriate practice in programs for young children.

Editors' Preface

Young children are born learners. Although individual differences are present at birth, most set out to explore their world with unbridled eagerness and curiosity. Perhaps more than any other time of life, early childhood is a period of never ending possibilities. Similarly, most early childhood educators enthusiastically embrace their work, because every day brings the chance to share in children's excitement of discovery. We enter and stay in the field because we believe that our work can make a significant difference in the lives of children and their families, and so make a profound and lasting contribution to society.

But whether we make that difference in young children's lives is not assured. Children are born learners, but for them to actually learn and develop optimally requires us to provide them with care and education of the highest quality. *Developmentally appropriate practice* is a term that has come to be used within the profession to describe the complex and rewarding work done by excellent early childhood educators.

More than 20 years ago, NAEYC published its first position statements defining and describing developmentally appropriate practice in early childhood programs serving young children. A 1986 statement was expanded and released in book form the next year (see Bredekamp 1986; 1987). The concept of *developmentally appropriate* was certainly not new, having been used by developmental psychologists for more than a century in reference to age-related and individual human variation. NAEYC, however, was motivated by two factors to go on record with more specific guidance for teachers: by the launch of its national program accreditation system, whose standards necessitated clearer interpretation of quality in early childhood practice, and by the growing trend to push down curriculum and teaching methods more appropriate for older children to kindergarten and preschool programs.

A decade later, NAEYC (1996) revisited its position statement on developmentally appropriate practice in response to new knowledge, the changing context, and critiques from within and beyond the profession. Among the major issues reflected in that revised statement and the book containing it (Bredekamp & Copple 1997) were these: the teacher as decision maker; the importance of goals for children being both challenging and achievable; and expanding the basic definition of developmentally appropriate practice to include consideration of social and cultural context. Later, to more clearly communicate the concepts of the 1996 statement, NAEYC published *Basics of*

> We enter and stay in the field because we believe that our work can make a significant difference in the lives of children and their families, and so make a profound and lasting contribution to society.

Developmentally Appropriate Practice, 3d Edition

Developmentally Appropriate Practice: An Introduction for Teachers of Children 3 to 6 (Copple & Bredekamp 2006).

Another decade in the life of the position statement has passed, and once again the Association seeks to offer the best, most current thinking about which practices are most effective in promoting young children's learning and development—that is, which practices are developmentally appropriate.

The current position statement, reproduced in this book and on which the book is based, was propelled less by critiques from within the field than by the infusion of new knowledge to guide practice and by the rapidly changing context in which early childhood programs operate—including the growing role of public schools and the increasing focus on narrowing the achievement gap. Further, in 2005 NAEYC significantly revised its Early Childhood Program Standards that identify key components of quality programs. To ensure the consistency of NAEYC's most influential sets of guidelines for practice—the Early Childhood Program Standards and the Position Statement on Developmentally Appropriate Practice—revisiting the position statement was timely.

This third edition of NAEYC's major book on developmentally appropriate practice, as well as the position statement, builds on the fundamental principles articulated in 1997 and emphasizes several interrelated themes:

Excellence and equity. Achievement gaps—real and present early in life—persist not because children are lacking in any way but because they lack opportunities to learn. Although the current emphasis on accountability and learning gaps has led to inappropriate practices in some classrooms and raised concerns among early childhood educators, the field has long been commited to improving all children's life chances. A prime example, of course, is Head Start. We know that excellent early childhood education can make a difference, and we simply cannot be content with the inequities in early experience that contribute to school failure and lifelong negative consequences for so many of our nation's children.

Intentionality and effectiveness. Good early childhood teachers are purposeful in the decisions they make about their practices, but they also attend to the consequences of those decisions. The current widespread recognition of the value of early education, as well as the explosion in state funding for prekindergarten programs, derives almost exclusively from its effectiveness in producing positive short- and long-term outcomes for children. Holding ourselves accountable for learning and developmental outcomes (as long as they are the right outcomes) is actually evidence of our increased commitment to all children.

Continuity and change. Just as human development through the life span is marked by both continuity and change, so too must be any document that is designed to guide educational practice that reflects knowledge of development. Therefore, the revised statement preserves the enduring values of our field—commitment to the whole child; recognition of the value of play; respect and responsiveness to individual and cultural diversity; and partnerships with families. At the same time, it has responded to the changing and expanding knowledge base about effective practices in addressing these

> We simply cannot be content with the inequities in early experience that contribute to school failure and lifelong negative consequences for so many of our nation's children.

values as well as improving curriculum, teaching, and assessment. Further, the statement challenges our profession to be more precise and clear when advocating for or criticizing practices, from play to structured curriculum.

Joy and learning. In revisiting the position statement in light of new knowledge and the changing context, we were repeatedly reminded of the core value that cuts across all of our work: Certainly an important and legitimate focus of early care and education is helping children toward becoming productive, responsible adults; but we want their childhood years to be full of joy. High-quality early childhood experiences help equip tomorrow's adults, but childhood is and should be its own special time of life. And it is our responsibility to cultivate children's delight in exploring and understanding their world. Early childhood is and should be a time of laughter, love, play, and great fun. While we still believe that fun for fun's sake is an inadequate rationale for planning a program, we also believe strongly that healthy development and learning cannot occur without attention to children's pleasure and interest.

At the same time, we shouldn't forget how much sheer pleasure children obtain from learning something new, mastering a skill after much effort, or solving a challenging problem. Think of the big smile on a baby's face when she pulls herself up for the first time, a preschooler's pride in writing his own name, the glee that accompanies the first independent bike ride, the look of accomplishment when a first-grader reads "a whole book" for the first time, or the "aha" look on a second-grader's face when she finally understands how to add two-digit numbers quickly. Human beings strive for mastery, and we feel both power and pleasure in our own accomplishments.

We conclude with a reminder (though experienced early childhood practitioners will scarcely need it) about why our field values developmentally appropriate practice in the first place. Seeing children joyfully, physically, and intellectually engaged in meaningful learning about their world and everyone and everything in it is the truest measure of our success as early childhood educators.

It is through developmentally appropriate practice that we create a safe, nurturing, and supportive place for young children to experience those unique joys of childhood.

> It is our responsibility to cultivate children's delight in exploring and understanding their world. Early childhood is and should be a time of laughter, love, play, and great fun.

About This Book

This book begins conceptually and literally with NAEYC's **position statement**. It is a consensus document, the product of more than three years of discussion and input from the field. Adopted by the NAEYC Governing Board, the statement has the weight of the world's largest organization of early childhood educators behind it.

NAEYC's position statement places "excellence and equity" at the center of its argument, and **To Be an Excellent Teacher** continues that theme. The chapter describes the kinds of decisions that good teachers make that enact developmentally appropriate practice in their classrooms.

The core of the volume is eight chapters that address the periods of early childhood—**The Infant and Toddler Years (Ages 0–3); The Preschool Years (Ages 3–5), The Kindergarten Year (Ages 5–6),** and **The Primary Grades (Ages 6–8)**. In this third edition, practice for kindergartners gets separate treatment for the first time, reflecting the view of a great many early childhood educators that the kindergarten year is worthy of special focus in its own right, not merely as the last year of preschool or the first of elementary school. For each age group, an **overview chapter** broadly sketches children's development and learning in that period, along with some major implications of those developmental considerations for practice. Following each age group overview is a chapter offering **charts of practice examples** for that age group.

Readers who have used this book in its various iterations over the years will notice in this edition that the column headings in these charts have changed. The labels over the columns—formerly "Developmentally Appropriate/ Inappropriate"—are now "Developmentally Appropriate/In Contrast." The decision was that across all the age groups and all the charts it would be overstating to call every example in a right-hand column a wrong or bad practice. Certainly some of them are harmful (e.g., unsanitary diapering procedures with infants and toddlers); but some practices are merely mediocre or less than optimal. Moreover, as differences in culture can cause people to view the same practice quite differently, it seemed presumptuous to label a practice as "inappropriate" simply because those who favor it may not be in the majority. Hence, the right-hand examples are intended to draw readers' attention to practices that require careful consideration.

To provoke and inform that consideration are "comments" in the charts. Sometimes a comment adds information about cultural factors or individual differences to be considered. In some cases, a comment describes the implications or rationale for using or not using the practices described in the cells above it.

The book concludes with some of the most **frequently asked questions** about developmentally appropriate practice.

For the first time, the book includes a **supplementary CD** of more than 60 readings (pdfs) and video examples of developmentally appropriate practice in action. Additional resources are available on the NAEYC website at www.naeyc.org/dap.

Key Messages
of the Position Statement

The NAEYC position statement on developmentally appropriate practice reflects both continuity and change in the early childhood field. Still central since its last iteration (NAEYC 1996) are our fundamental commitments to **excellence and equity** in educating children and our core understanding of how children learn and develop. At the same time, new knowledge gained over the last decade has deepened that understanding, allowing us to revise and refine our ideas about how to promote every child's optimal development and learning.

What is developmentally appropriate practice?

- Developmentally appropriate practice requires both meeting children where they are—which means that teachers must get to know them well—and enabling them to reach goals that are both challenging and achievable.

- All teaching practices should be appropriate to children's age and developmental status, attuned to them as unique individuals, and responsive to the social and cultural contexts in which they live.

- Developmentally appropriate practice does not mean making things easier for children. Rather, it means ensuring that goals and experiences are suited to their learning and development *and* challenging enough to promote their progress and interest.

- Best practice is based on knowledge—not on assumptions—of how children learn and develop. The research base yields major principles in human development and learning (this position statement articulates 12 such principles). Those principles, along with evidence about curriculum and teaching effectiveness, form a solid basis for decision making in early care and education.

A call to reduce the achievement gap

- Because in the United States children's learning opportunities often differ sharply with family income and education, ethnicity, and language background, sizable achievement gaps exist between demographic groups. Emerging early in life and persisting throughout the school years, these disparities have serious consequences for children and for society as a whole. Narrowing the gaps must be a priority for early childhood educators as well as policy makers.

- When young children have not had the learning opportunities they require in order to succeed in school, early childhood programs need to provide even more extended, enriched, and intensive learning experiences than they do for children who have had a wealth of such experiences outside of the program or school. The earlier in life those experiences are provided, the better the results for children. Parent engagement strategies, health services, and mental health supports are also critical.

Comprehensive, effective curriculum

- All the domains of children's development and learning interrelate. For example, because social factors strongly influence cognitive development and academic competence—and the cognitive domain influences the social domain—teachers must foster learning and development in both, as well as in the emotional and physical domains.

- Effective, developmentally appropriate curriculum is based on what is known about the interrelationships and sequences of ideas, so that children's later abilities and understandings can be built on those already acquired. At the same time, the rate and pattern of each child's learning is unique. An effective teacher must account for all these factors, maintaining high expectations while setting challenging, achievable goals and providing the right amount and type of scaffolding for each child.

- Children's learning experiences across the early childhood years (birth to age 8) need to be far better integrated and aligned, particularly between prekindergarten and K–3. Education quality and outcomes would improve substantially if elementary teachers incorporated the best of preschool's emphases and practices (e.g., attention to the whole child; integrated, meaningful learning; parent engagement) and if preschool teachers made more use of those elementary-grade practices that are valuable for younger children, as well (e.g., robust content, attention to learning progressions in curriculum and teaching).

Improving teaching and learning

- A teacher's moment-by-moment actions and interactions with children are the most powerful determinant of learning outcomes and development. Curriculum is very important, but what the teacher does is paramount.

- Both child-guided and teacher-guided experiences are vital to children's development and learning. Developmentally appropriate programs provide substantial periods of time when children may select activities to pursue from among the rich choices teachers have prepared in various centers in the room. In addition to these activities, children ages 3–8 benefit from planned, teacher-guided, interactive small-group and large-group experiences.

- Rather than diminishing children's learning by reducing the time devoted to academic activities, play promotes key abilities that enable children to learn successfully. In high-level dramatic play, for example, the collaborative planning of roles and scenarios and the impulse control required to stay within the play's constraints develop children's self-regulation, symbolic thinking, memory, and language—capacities critical to later learning, social competence, and school success.

- Because of how they spend their time outside of school, many young children now lack the ability to play at the high level of complexity and engagement that affords so many cognitive, social, and emotional benefits. As a result, it is vital for early childhood settings to provide opportunities for sustained high-level play and for teachers to actively support children's progress toward such play.

- Effective teachers are intentional in their use of a variety of approaches and strategies to support children's interest and ability in each learning domain. Besides embedding significant learning in play, routines, and interest areas, strong programs also provide carefully planned curriculum that focuses children's attention on a particular concept or topic. Further, skilled teachers adapt curriculum to the group they are teaching and to each individual child to promote optimal learning and development.

- To ensure that teachers are able to provide care and education of high quality, they must be well prepared, participate in ongoing professional development, and receive sufficient support and compensation.

NAEYC Position Statement

Developmentally Appropriate Practice in Early Childhood Programs Serving Children from Birth through Age 8

Adopted 2009

The purpose of this position statement is to promote excellence in early childhood education by providing a framework for best practice. Grounded both in the research on child development and learning and in the knowledge base regarding educational effectiveness, the framework outlines practice that promotes young children's optimal learning and development. Since its first adoption in 1986, this framework has been known as *developmentally appropriate practice.*[1]

The profession's responsibility to promote quality in the care and education of young children compels us to revisit regularly the validity and currency of our core knowledge and positions, such as this one on issues of practice. Does the position need modification in light of a changed context? Is there new knowledge to inform the statement? Are there aspects of the existing statement that have given rise to misunderstandings and misconceptions that need correcting?

Over the several years spent in developing this revision, NAEYC invited the comment of early childhood educators with experience and expertise from infancy to the primary grades, including a late 2006 convening of respected leaders in the field. The result of this broad gathering of views is this updated position statement, which addresses the current context and the relevant knowledge base for developmentally appropriate practice and seeks to convey the nature of such practice clearly and usefully.

This statement is intended to complement NAEYC's other position statements on practice, which include *Early Learning Standards* and *Early Childhood Curriculum, Assessment, and Program Evaluation,* as well as the *Code of Ethical Conduct* and *NAEYC Early Childhood Program Standards and Accreditation Criteria.*[2]

Note: Throughout this statement, the terms *teacher, practitioner,* and *educator* are variously used to refer to those working in the early childhood field. The word *teacher* is always intended to refer to any adult responsible for the direct care and education of a group of children in any early childhood setting. Included are not only classroom teachers but also infant/toddler caregivers, family child care providers, and specialists in other disciplines who fulfill the role of teacher. In more instances, the term *practitioners* is intended to also include a program's administrators. *Educators* is intended to also include college and university faculty and other teacher trainers.

Critical issues in the current context

Since the 1996 version of this position statement, the landscape of early childhood education in the United States has changed significantly and a number of issues have grown in importance. Shortage of good care for children in the highly vulnerable infant and toddler years has become critical.[3] Issues of home language and culture, second language learning, and school culture have increased with the steady growth in the number of immigrant families and children in our population.[4] In addition, far more children with special needs (including those with disabilities, those at risk for disabilities, and those with challenging behaviors) participate in typical early childhood settings today than in the past.[5] As for teachers, the nation continues to struggle to develop and maintain a qualified teaching force.[6] This difficulty is especially acute in the under-funded early childhood arena, especially the child care sector, which is losing well prepared teaching staff and administrators at an alarming rate.[7]

Looking forward, demographic trends predict a modest growth in the number of young children in the population, significant increases in the demand for early care and education, dramatic increases in children's cultural and linguistic diversity, and unless conditions change, a greater share of children living in poverty. Among these, the biggest single child-specific demographic change in the United States over the next 20 years is predicted to be an increase in children whose home language is not English.[8]

Also significant is that policy makers and the public are far more aware of the importance of the early childhood years in shaping children's futures. Based on this widespread recognition and the context of early childhood education today, it was decided this statement would highlight three challenges: reducing learning gaps and increasing the achievement of all children; creating improved, better connected education for preschool and elementary children; and recognizing teacher knowledge and decision making as vital to educational effectiveness.

Reducing learning gaps and increasing the achievement of all children

All families, educators, and the larger society hope that children will achieve in school and go on to lead satisfying and productive lives. But that optimistic future is not equally likely for all of the nation's schoolchildren. Most disturbing, low-income and African American and Hispanic students lag significantly behind their peers on standardized comparisons of academic achievement throughout the school years, and they experience more difficulties while in the school setting.[9]

Behind these disparities in school-related performance lie dramatic differences in children's early experiences and access to good programs and schools. Often there is also a mismatch between the "school" culture and children's cultural backgrounds.[10] A prime difference in children's early experience is in their exposure to language, which is fundamental in literacy development and indeed in all areas of thinking and learning. On average, children growing up in low-income families have dramatically less rich experience with language in their homes than do middle-class children:[11] They hear far fewer words and are engaged in fewer extended conversations. By 36 months of age, substantial socioeconomic disparities already exist in vocabulary knowledge,[12] to name one area.

Children from families living in poverty or in households in which parent education is low typically enter school with lower levels of foundational skills, such as those in language, reading, and mathematics.[13] On starting kindergarten, children in the lowest socioeconomic group have average cognitive scores that are 60 percent below those of the most affluent group. Explained largely by socioeconomic differences among ethnic groups, average math achievement is 21 percent lower for African American children than for white children and 19 percent lower for Hispanic children than for non-Hispanic white children.[14] Moreover, due to deep-seated equity issues present in communities and schools, such early achievement gaps tend to *increase* rather than diminish over time.[15]

Concerns over the persistence of achievement gaps between subgroups are part of a larger concern about lagging student achievement in the United States and its impact on American economic competitiveness in an increasingly global economy. In comparisons with students of other industrialized countries, for example, America's students have not consistently fared well on tests of educational achievement.[16]

It is these worries that drive the powerful "standards/accountability" movement. Among the movement's most far-reaching actions has been the 2001 passing of No Child Left Behind (NCLB), which made it national policy to hold schools accountable for eliminating the persistent gaps in achievement between different groups of children. With the aim of ensuring educational equity, the law requires the reporting of scores disaggregated by student group; that is, reported separately for the economically disadvantaged, major racial and ethnic minorities, special education recipients, and English language learners.[17] By requiring the reporting of achievement by student group and requiring all groups to make achievement gains annually, NCLB seeks to make schools accountable for teaching *all* their students effectively.

Whether NCLB and similar "accountability" mandates can deliver that result is hotly debated, and many critics argue that the mandates have unintended negative consequences for children, teachers, and schools, including narrowing the curriculum and testing too much and in the wrong ways. Yet the majority of Americans support the movement's stated goals,[18] among them that *all* children should be achieving at high levels.[19] This public support—for the goals, if not the methods—can be viewed as a demand that educators do something to improve student achievement and close the gaps that all agree are damaging many children's future prospects and wasting their potential.

Learning standards and accountability policies have impinged directly on public education from grade K and up, and they are of growing relevance to preschool education, as well. As of 2007, more than three-quarters of the states had some sort of early learning standards—that is, standards for the years before kindergarten—and the remaining states had begun developing them.[20] Head Start has put in place a "child outcomes framework," which identifies learning expectations in eight domains.[21] National reports and public policy statements have supported the creation of standards-based curriculum as part of a broader effort to build children's school readiness by improving teaching and learning in the early years.[22] For its part, NAEYC has position statements defining the features of high-quality early learning standards, curriculum, and assessment.[23]

So we must close existing learning gaps and enable all children to succeed at higher levels—but *how?* While this question is not a new one, in the current context it is the focus of increased attention. As later outlined in "Applying New Knowledge to Critical Issues," accumulating evidence and innovations in practice now provide guidance as to the knowledge and abilities that teachers must work especially hard to foster in young children, as well as information on how teachers can do so.

Creating improved, better connected education for preschool and elementary children

For many years, preschool education and elementary education—each with its own funding sources, infrastructure, values, and traditions—have remained largely separate. In fact, the education establishment typically has not thought of preschool as a full-fledged part of American public education. Among the chief reasons for this view is that preschool is neither universally funded by the public nor mandatory.[24] Moreover, preschool programs exist within a patchwork quilt of sponsorship and delivery systems and widely varying teacher credentials. Many programs came into being primarily to offer child care for parents who worked. In recent years, however, preschool's educational purpose and potential have been increasingly recognized, and this recognition contributes to the blurring of the preschool-elementary boundary. The two spheres now have substantial reasons to strive for greater continuity and collaboration.

One impetus is that mandated accountability requirements, particularly third grade testing, exert pressures on schools and teachers at K–2,[25] who in turn look to teachers of younger children to help prepare students to demonstrate the required proficiencies later. A related factor is the growth of state-funded prekindergarten, located in schools or other community settings, which collectively serves more than a million 3- and 4-year-olds. Millions more children are in Head Start programs and child care programs that meet state prekindergarten requirements and receive state preK dollars. Head Start, serving more than 900,000 children nationwide, is now required to coordinate with the public schools at the state level.[26] Title I dollars support preschool education and services for some 300,000 children. Nationally, about 35

percent of all 4-year-olds are in publicly supported prekindergarten programs.[27]

For its part, the world of early care and education stands to gain in some respects from a closer relationship with the K–12 system. Given the shortage of affordable, high-quality programs for children under 5 and the low compensation for those staff, advocates see potential benefits to having more 4-year-olds, and perhaps even 3-year-olds, receive services in publicly funded schooling. Proponents also hope that a closer relationship between early-years education and the elementary grades would lead to enhanced alignment and each sphere's learning from the other,[28] thus resulting in greater continuity and coherence across the preK–3 span.

At the same time, however, preschool educators have some fears about the prospect of the K–12 system absorbing or radically reshaping education for 3-, 4-, and 5-year-olds, especially at a time when pressures in public schooling are intense and often run counter to the needs of young children. Many early childhood educators are already quite concerned about the current climate of increased high-stakes testing adversely affecting children in grades K–3, and they fear extension of these effects to even younger children. Even learning standards, though generally supported in principle in the early childhood world,[29] are sometimes questioned in practice because they can have negative effects.

Early learning standards are still relatively new, having been mandated by Good Start, Grow Smart in 2002 for the domains of language, literacy, and mathematics. While some states have taken a fairly comprehensive approach across the domains of learning and development, others focus heavily on the mandated areas, particularly literacy. When state standards are not comprehensive, the curriculum driven by those standards is less likely to be so, and any alignment will likely address only those few curriculum areas identified in the standards.

Such narrowing of curriculum scope is one shortcoming that can characterize a set of standards; there can be other deficiencies, too. To be most beneficial for children, standards need to be not only comprehensive but also address what is important for children to know and be able to do; be aligned across developmental stages and age/grade levels; and be consistent with how children develop and learn. Unfortunately, many state standards focus on superficial learning objectives, at times underestimating young children's competence and at other times requiring understandings and tasks that young children cannot really grasp until they are older.[30] There is also growing concern that most assessments of children's knowledge are exclusively in English, thereby missing important knowledge a child may have but cannot express in English.[31]

Alignment is desirable, indeed critical, for standards to be effective. Yet effective alignment consists of more than simplifying for a younger age group the standards appropriate for older children. Rather than relying on such downward mapping, developers of early learning standards should base them on what we know from research and practice about children from a variety of backgrounds at a given stage/age and about the processes, sequences, variations, and long-term consequences of early learning and development.[32]

As for state-to-state alignment, the current situation is chaotic. Although discussion about establishing some kind of national standards framework is gaining momentum, there is no common set of standards at present. Consequently, publishers competing in the marketplace try to develop curriculum and textbooks that address the standards of all the states. Then teachers feel compelled to cover this large array of topics, teaching each only briefly and often superficially. When such curriculum and materials are in use, children move through the grades encountering a given topic in grade after grade—but only shallowly each time—rather than getting depth and focus on a smaller number of key learning goals and being able to master these before moving on.[33]

Standards overload is overwhelming to teachers and children alike and can lead to potentially problematic teaching practices. At the preschool and K–3 levels particularly, practices of concern include excessive lecturing to the whole group, fragmented teaching of discrete objectives, and insistence that teachers follow rigid, tightly paced schedules. There is also concern that schools are curtailing valuable experiences such as problem solving, rich play, collaboration with peers, opportunities for emotional and social development, outdoor/physical activity, and the arts. In the high-pressure classroom, children are less likely to develop a love of learning and a sense of their own competence and ability to make choices, and

they miss much of the joy and expansive learning of childhood.[34]

Educators across the whole preschool-primary spectrum have perspectives and strengths to bring to a closer collaboration and ongoing dialogue. The point of bringing the two worlds together is *not* for children to learn primary grade skills at an earlier age; it is for their teachers to take the first steps together to ensure that young children develop and learn, to be able to acquire such skills and understandings as they progress in school.

The growing knowledge base can shed light on what an exchanging of best practices might look like,[35] as noted later in "Applying New Knowledge to Critical Issues." Through increased communication and collaboration, both worlds can learn much that can contribute to improving the educational experiences of *all* young children and to making those experiences more coherent.

Recognizing teacher knowledge and decision making as vital to educational effectiveness

The standards/accountability movement has led to states and other stakeholders spelling out what children should know and be able to do at various grade levels. Swift improvement in student achievement across all student subgroups has been demanded. Under that mandate, many policy makers and administrators understandably gravitate toward tools and strategies intended to expedite the education enterprise, including "teacher proofing" curriculum, lessons, and schedules. As a result, in some states and districts, teachers in publicly funded early childhood settings report that they are allowed far less scope in classroom decision making than they were in the past,[36] in some cases getting little to no say in the selection of curriculum and assessments or even in their use of classroom time.

How much directing and scaffolding of teachers' work is helpful, and how much teacher autonomy is necessary to provide the best teaching and learning for children? The answer undoubtedly varies with differences among administrators and teachers themselves and the contexts in which they work.

A great many school administrators (elementary principals, superintendents, district staff) lack a background in early childhood education, and their limited knowledge of young children's development and learning means they are not always aware of what is and is not good practice with children at that age. Teachers who have studied how young children learn and develop and effective ways of teaching them are more likely to have this specialized knowledge. Moreover, it is the teacher who is in the classroom every day with children. So it is the teacher (not administrators or curriculum specialists) who is in the best position to know the particular children in that classroom—their interests and experiences, what they excel in and what they struggle with, what they are eager and ready to learn. Without this particular knowledge, determining what is best for those children's learning, as a group and individually, is impossible.

But it must be said that many teachers themselves lack the current knowledge and skills needed to provide high-quality care and education to young children, at least in some components of the curriculum. Many factors contribute, including the lack of a standard entry-level credential, wide variation in program settings and auspices, low compensation, and high turnover.[37] With workforce parameters such as these, is it reasonable to expect that every teacher in a classroom today is capable of fully meeting the challenges of providing high-quality early care and education?

Expert decision making lies at the heart of effective teaching. The acts of teaching and learning are too complex and individual to prescribe a teacher's every move in advance. Children benefit most from teachers who have the skills, knowledge, and judgment to make good decisions and are given the opportunity to use them.

Recognizing that effective teachers are good decision makers, however, does not mean that they should be expected to make all decisions in isolation. Teachers are not well served when they are stranded without the resources, tools, and supports necessary to make sound instructional decisions, and of course children's learning suffers as well.

Ideally, well conceived standards or learning goals (as described previously) are in place to guide local schools and programs in choosing or developing comprehensive, appropriate curriculum. The curriculum framework is a starting place, then teachers can use their expertise to make adaptations as needed to optimize the fit with the

children. Further, such curricular guidance gives teachers some direction in providing the materials, learning experiences, and teaching strategies that promote learning goals most effectively, allowing them to focus on instructional decision making without having to generate the entire curriculum themselves.

Even well qualified teachers find it challenging to create from scratch a comprehensive curriculum that addresses all the required standards and important learning goals, as well as designing the assessment methods and learning experiences. This daunting task is even less realistic for those teachers with minimal preparation. Hence, there is value in providing teachers a validated curriculum framework and related professional development, as long as teachers have the opportunity to make individual adaptations for the diversity of children they teach.[38]

That good teaching requires expert decision making means that teachers need solid professional preparation, as well as ongoing professional development and regular opportunities to work collaboratively.[39] Since this level of preparation and training does not yet exist for many in the early childhood workforce, the question of how best to equip and support inadequately prepared teachers needs serious investigation. Research on critical factors in good teaching, as described in the next section of this statement, has powerful lessons to offer.

Applying new knowledge to critical issues

Fortunately, a continually expanding early childhood knowledge base enables the field to refine, redirect, or confirm understandings of best practice. The whole of the present position statement reflects fresh evidence of recent years and the perspectives and priorities emerging from these findings. This section looks within that mass of new knowledge to a few lines of research specifically helpful in addressing the three critical issues for the field identified in this position statement.

First, new findings hold promise for reducing learning gaps and barriers and increasing the achievement of all children. More is now known about which early social and emotional, cognitive, physical, and academic competencies enable young children to develop and learn to their full potential. Such findings are useful in determining curriculum content and sequences for all children. But they are especially important in helping those children most likely to begin school with lower levels of the foundational skills needed to succeed and most likely to fall farther behind with time— among whom children of color, children growing up in poverty, and English language learners are overrepresented. Another key aspect is ensuring that children who have learning difficulties or disabilities receive the early intervention services they need to learn and function well in the classroom.

Research continues to confirm the greater efficacy of early action—and in some cases, intensive intervention—as compared with remediation and other "too little" or "too late" approaches. Changing young children's experiences can substantially affect their development and learning, especially when intervention starts early in life and is not an isolated action but a broad-gauged set of strategies.[40] For example, Early Head Start, a comprehensive two-generational program for children under age 3 and their families, has been shown to promote cognitive, language, and social and emotional development.[41] The success of Early Head Start illustrates that high-quality services for infants and toddlers—far too rare in the United States today—have a long-lasting and positive impact on children's development, learning abilities, and capacity to regulate their emotions.[42]

Although high-quality preschool programs benefit children (particularly low-income children) more than mediocre or poor programs do,[43] fewer children living in poverty get to attend high-quality preschool programs than do children from higher-income households.[44] Findings on the impact of teaching quality in the early grades show a similar pattern.[45] In addition to this relationship of overall program and school quality to later school success, research has identified a number of specific predictors of later achievement. Some of these predictors lie in language/literacy and mathematics; others are dimensions of social and emotional competence and cognitive functioning related to how children fare in school.

In the language and literacy domain, vocabulary knowledge and other aspects of oral language are particularly important predictors of children's reading comprehension.[46] Even when children with limited vocabulary manage to acquire basic decoding skills, they still often encounter difficulty around grade 3 or 4 when they begin needing to read more advanced text in various subjects.[47] Their vocabulary deficit impedes comprehension and thus their acquisition of knowledge necessary to succeed across the curriculum.[48] Clearly, children who hear little or no English in the home would have even more initial difficulty with comprehension in English.

To shrink the achievement gap, then, early childhood programs need to start early with proactive vocabulary development to bring young children whose vocabulary and oral language development is lagging—whatever the causes—closer to the developmental trajectory typical of children from educated, affluent families.[49] For these children to gain the vocabulary and the advanced linguistic structures they will need for elementary grade reading, their teachers need to engage in language interactions throughout the day, including reading to them in small groups and talking with them about the stories. Especially rich in linguistic payoff is extended discourse; that is, conversation between child and adult on a given topic sustained over many exchanges.[50]

Compelling evidence has shown that young children's alphabet knowledge and phonological awareness are significant predictors of their later proficiency in reading and writing.[51] A decade ago, many preschool teachers did not perceive it as their role—or even see it as appropriate—to launch young children on early steps toward literacy, including familiarizing them with the world of print and the sounds of language. The early childhood profession now recognizes that gaining literacy foundations is an important facet of children's experience before kindergarten,[52] although the early literacy component still needs substantial improvement in many classrooms.

Like the teaching of early literacy, mathematics education in the early childhood years is key to increasing all children's school readiness and to closing the achievement gap.[53] Within the mathematics arena, preschoolers' knowledge of numbers and their sequence, for example, strongly predicts not only math learning but also literacy skills.[54] Yet mathematics typically gets very little attention before kindergarten.[55] One reason is that early childhood teachers themselves often lack the skills and confidence to substantially and effectively increase their attention to mathematics in the curriculum.[56]

Mathematics and literacy concepts and skills—and, indeed, robust content *across* the curriculum—can be taught to young children in ways that are engaging and developmentally appropriate.[57] It can be, but too often isn't; to achieve such improvements will require considerable strengthening of early-years curriculum and teaching. Failing to meet this challenge to improve all children's readiness and achievement will perpetuate the inequities of achievement gaps and the low performance of the U.S. student population as a whole.

Besides specific predictors in areas such as mathematics and literacy, another major thread in recent research is that children's social and emotional competencies, as well as some capabilities that cut across social and emotional and cognitive functioning, predict their classroom functioning. Of course, children's social, emotional, and behavioral adjustment is important in its own right, both in and out of the classroom. But it now appears that some variables in these domains also relate to and predict school success. For example, studies have linked emotional competence to both enhanced cognitive performance and academic achievement.[58] A number of factors in the emotional and social domain, such as independence, responsibility, self-regulation, and cooperation, predict how well children make the transition to school and how they fare in the early grades.[59]

A particularly powerful variable is self-regulation, which the early childhood field has long emphasized as a prime developmental goal for the early years.[60] Mounting research evidence confirms this importance, indicating that self-regulation in young children predicts their later functioning in areas such as problem solving, planning, focused attention, and metacognition, and thus contributes to their success as learners.[61] Moreover, helping children from difficult life circumstances to develop strong self-regulation has proven to be both feasible and influential in preparing them to succeed in school.[62]

The gains children make as a result of high-quality programs for children under 6 have been

found to diminish in a few years if children do not continue to experience high-quality education in grades K–3.[63] This consistent finding makes clear the importance of improving quality and continuity all along the birth–8 continuum. As previously described, critical to developing a better connected, more coherent preschool-elementary framework is aligning standards, curriculum, and assessment practices within that continuum.[64] (Ideally, such a framework would extend to infant and toddler care as well.)

Further, educators and researchers are beginning to consider how to unite the most important and effective elements of preschool education with those of K–3.[65] In this search for the "best of both worlds," policy makers and educators can look to the expanding body of knowledge on the aspects of early learning and development that enable children to do well in school and the practices that should be more prevalent across the entire preK–3 span.[66]

First, research evidence on the predictors of successful outcomes for children (highlighted earlier) suggests a number of learning goals and experiences that in some form ought to be incorporated across preK–3. These include, for example, robust curriculum content; careful attention to known learning sequences (in literacy, mathematics, science, physical education, and other domains); and emphasis on developing children's self-regulation, engagement, and focused attention. Also proven to yield positive results for children are practices familiar to early childhood educators, such as relationship-based teaching and learning; partnering with families; adapting teaching for children from different backgrounds and for individual children; active, meaningful, and connected learning;[67] and smaller class sizes.[68] Evidence of the benefits of these practices suggests that they should be extended more widely into the elementary grades.

A second source of knowledge about effectively connecting education across the preschool-grade 3 span comes from educational innovations now being piloted. Schools that encompass these grades and thoughtfully consider how to increase continuity, alignment, and coherence are emerging around the country, and some are being studied by researchers.[69]

Expansion of P–16 or P–20 commissions around the country, although not yet giving much attention to prekindergarten,[70] provides one vehicle for the conversations about continuity that need to take place. While there are entrenched practices and structures separating preschool and K–3 education, the current forces noted here provide considerable impetus and opportunity to achieve stronger, more coordinated preK–3 education.

The importance of teachers to high-quality early education, indeed to all of education, cannot be overemphasized. Although wise administrative and curricular decisions made upstream from the individual teacher significantly affect what goes on in the classroom, they are far from ensuring children's learning. Research indicates that the most powerful influences on whether and what children learn occur in the teacher's interactions with them, in the real-time decisions the teacher makes throughout the day.[71] Thus, no educational strategy that fails to recognize the centrality of the teacher's decisions and actions can be successful.

It is the teacher's classroom plans and organization, sensitivity and responsiveness to all the children, and moment-to-moment interactions with them that have the greatest impact on children's development and learning.[72] The way teachers design learning experiences, how they engage children and respond to them, how they adapt their teaching and interactions to children's background, the feedback they give—these matter greatly in children's learning. And none can be fully determined in advance and laid out in a curriculum product or set of lesson plans that every teacher is to follow without deviation. Teachers will always have moment-to-moment decisions to make.

To make these decisions with well-grounded intentionality, teachers need to have knowledge about child development and learning in general, about the individual children in their classrooms, and about the sequences in which a domain's specific concepts and skills are learned. Teachers also need to have at the ready a well developed repertoire of teaching strategies to employ for different purposes.[73]

Directly following from this first lesson is a second: the imperative to make developing teacher quality and effectiveness a top priority. This investment must include excellent preservice preparation, ongoing professional development, and on-the-ground support and mentoring. For example, good curriculum resources are helpful when they specify the key skills and concepts for children and provide a degree of teaching guidance, but

without overscripting. New or inadequately trained teachers and those encountering a new curriculum or set of standards may be particularly in need of such scaffolding.[74]

Another valuable form of scaffolding for teachers is interaction with mentors and peers. Meeting the needs of diverse learners and helping all children to develop and learn require significant time for teachers to collaborate with colleagues, discuss and observe best practices, and participate in meaningful professional development. Most teachers, including novice teachers, get too little time for such activities. While providing time and opportunity for teachers to do these things can be very challenging for administrators, it is critical.[75]

To act on this second "lesson"—the imperative to make teaching quality and effectiveness a top priority—means changing what happens in the classroom. But it also means establishing policies and committing public funds at the federal, state, and local levels, as described in "Policy Considerations," the concluding section of this position statement.

Core considerations in developmentally appropriate practice

Every day, early childhood practitioners make a great many decisions, both long-term and short-term. As they do so, they need to keep in mind the identified goals for children's learning and development and be intentional in helping children achieve these goals. The core of developmentally appropriate practice lies in this intentionality, in the knowledge that practitioners consider when they are making decisions, and in their always aiming for goals that are both challenging and achievable for children.

Knowledge to consider in making decisions

In all aspects of their work with children, early childhood practitioners must consider these three areas of knowledge:

1. What is known about child development and learning—referring to knowledge of age-related characteristics that permits general predictions about what experiences are likely to best promote children's learning and development.

Teachers who are knowledgeable about child development and learning are able to make broad predictions about what children of a particular age group typically will be like, what they typically will and will not be capable of, and what strategies and approaches will most likely promote their optimal learning and development. With this knowledge, teachers can make preliminary decisions with some confidence about environment, materials, interactions, and activities. At the same time, their knowledge also tells them that specific groups of children and the individual children in any group always will be the same in some ways but different in others.

2. What is known about each child as an individual—referring to what practitioners learn about each child that has implications for how best to adapt and be responsive to that individual variation.

To be effective, teachers must get to know each child in the group well. They do this using a variety of methods—such as observation, clinical interview (an extended dialogue in which the adult seeks to discern the child's concepts or strategies), examination of children's work, individual child assessments, and talking with families. From the information and insights gathered, teachers make plans and adjustments to promote each child's individual development and learning as fully as possible. Developmental variation among children is the norm, and any one child's progress also will vary across domains and disciplines, contexts, and time. Children differ in many other respects, too—including in their strengths, interests, and preferences; personalities and approaches to learning; and knowledge, skills, and abilities based on prior experiences. Children may also have special learning needs; sometimes these have been diagnosed and sometimes they have not. Among the factors that teachers need to consider as they seek to optimize a child's school adjustment and learning are circumstances such as living in poverty or homelessness, having to move frequently, and other challenging situations. Responding to each child as an individual is fundamental to developmentally appropriate practice.

3. What is known about the social and cultural contexts in which children live—referring to the values, expectations, and behavioral and linguistic conventions that shape children's lives at home and in their communities that practitioners must strive to understand in order to ensure that learning experiences in the program or school are meaningful, relevant, and respectful for each child and family.

As we grow up in a family and in a broader social and cultural community, we all come to certain understandings about what our group considers appropriate, values, expects, admires. We learn this through direct teaching from our parents and other important people in our lives and through observing those around us. Among these understandings, we absorb "rules" about behaviors—such as how to show respect, how to interact with people we know well and those we have just met, how to regard time and personal space, how to dress, and countless other attitudes and actions. We typically absorb these rules very early and very deeply, so we live by them with little conscious thought. When young children are in a group setting outside the home, what makes sense to them, how they use language to interact, and how they experience this new world depend on the social and cultural contexts to which they are accustomed. A skilled teacher takes such contextual factors into account, along with the children's ages and their individual differences, in shaping all aspects of the learning environment.

To recap this decision-making process: An effective teacher begins by thinking about what children of the age and developmental status represented in the group are typically like. This knowledge provides a general idea of the activities, routines, interactions, and curriculum that will be effective with that group. The teacher also must consider each child, including looking at the child as an individual and within the context of family, community, culture, linguistic norms, social group, past experience (including learning and behavior), and current circumstances. Only then can the teacher see children *as they are* to make decisions that are developmentally appropriate for each of them.

Challenging *and* achievable goals

Meeting children where they are is essential, but no good teacher simply leaves them there. Keeping in mind desired goals and what is known about the children as a group and individually, the teacher plans experiences to promote children's learning and development.

Learning and development are most likely to occur when new experiences build on what a child already knows and is able to do and when those learning experiences also entail the child stretching a reasonable amount in acquiring new skills, abilities, or knowledge. After the child reaches that new level of mastery in skill or understanding, the teacher reflects on what goals should come next; and the cycle continues, advancing children's learning in a developmentally appropriate way.

Clearly, such effective teaching does not happen by chance. A hallmark of developmentally appropriate teaching is intentionality. Good teachers are intentional in everything they do—setting up the classroom, planning curriculum, making use of various teaching strategies, assessing children, interacting with them, and working with their families. Intentional teachers are purposeful and thoughtful about the actions they take, and they direct their teaching toward the goals the program is trying to help children reach.

Principles of child development and learning that inform practice

Developmentally appropriate practice as defined in this position statement is not based on what we think might be true or what we want to believe about young children. Developmentally appropriate practice is informed by what we know from theory and literature about how children develop and learn. In particular, a review of that literature yields a number of well supported generalizations, or principles.

No linear listing of principles—including the one below—can do justice to the complexity of the phenomenon that is child development and learning. While the list is comprehensive, it certainly is not all-inclusive. Each principle describes an individually contributing factor; but just as all domains of development and learning are interrelated, so too do the principles interconnect. For example, the influence of cultural differences and individual

differences, each highlighted in a separate principle below, cuts across all the other principles. That is, the implication of any principle often differs as a function of cultural or individual givens.

A complete discussion of the knowledge base that informs developmentally appropriate practice is clearly beyond the scope of this document. Each of the principles rests on a very extensive research base that is only partially referenced here.[76]

All the limitations of such a list not withstanding, collectively the principles that follow form a solid basis for decision making—for decisions at all levels about how best to meet the needs of young children in general, and for decisions by teachers, programs, and families about the strengths and needs of individual children, with all their variations in prior experiences, abilities and talents, home language and English proficiency, personalities and temperaments, and community and cultural backgrounds.

1 All the domains of development and learning—physical, social and emotional, and cognitive—are important, and they are closely interrelated. Children's development and learning in one domain influence and are influenced by what takes place in other domains.

Children are thinking, moving, feeling, and interacting human beings. To teach them well involves considering and fostering their development and learning in all domains.[77] Because this full spectrum of development and learning is fundamental to children's lives and to their future participation as members of society, early care and education must address all the domains.

Further, changes in one domain often facilitate or limit development in other areas.[78] For example, when children begin to crawl or walk, they gain new possibilities for exploring the world, and their mobility affects both their cognitive development and sense of autonomy. Likewise, children's language development influences their ability to participate in social interaction with adults and other children; such interactions, in turn, support their further language development.[79] A growing body of work demonstrates the relationship between emotional and social factors and children's academic competence[80] and thus the importance of all these areas in educating young children. In brief, the knowledge base documents the importance of a comprehensive curriculum and the interrelatedness of the developmental domains in children's well-being and success.

2 Many aspects of children's learning and development follow well documented sequences, with later abilities, skills, and knowledge building on those already acquired.

Human development research suggests that relatively stable, predictable sequences of growth and change occur in children during the first nine years of life.[81] Predictable changes occur in all domains of development, although the ways that these changes are manifested and the meaning attached to them may vary widely in different cultural and linguistic contexts.[82] Knowledge of how children within a given age span typically develop and learn provides a general framework to guide teachers in preparing the learning environment, considering curriculum, designing learning experiences, and teaching and interacting with children.

Also important for educators to know are the sequences in which children gain specific concepts, skills, and abilities, building on prior development and learning. In mathematics, for example, children's learning to count serves as an important foundation for their acquiring an understanding of numerals.[83] Familiarity with known learning sequences should inform curriculum development and teaching practice.

3 Development and learning proceed at varying rates from child to child, as well as at uneven rates across different areas of a child's individual functioning.

Individual variation has at least two dimensions: the inevitable variability around the typical or normative course of development and the uniqueness of each child as an individual. Children's development follows individual patterns and timing; children also vary in temperament, personality, and aptitudes, as well as in what they learn in their family and within the social and cultural context or contexts that shape their experience.

All children have their own strengths, needs, and interests. Given the enormous variation among children of the same chronological age, a child's age is only a crude index of developmental abilities and interests. For children who have special learning needs or abilities, additional efforts and resources may be necessary to optimize their

development and learning. The same is true when children's prior experiences do not give them the knowledge and skills they need to thrive in a specific learning environment.

Given this normal range of variation, decisions about curriculum, teaching, and interactions with children should be as individualized as possible. Rigid expectations of group norms do not reflect what is known about real differences in development and learning. At the same time, having high expectations for all children is essential, as is using the strategies and providing the resources necessary to help them meet these expectations.

4 Development and learning result from a dynamic and continuous interaction of biological maturation and experience.

Development is the result of the interplay between the growing, changing child and the child's experiences in the social and physical worlds.[84] For example, a child's genetic makeup may predict healthy growth, but inadequate nutrition in the early years of life will keep this potential from being fulfilled. Conversely, the impact of an organic condition on a young child's learning and development can be minimized through systematic, individualized intervention. Likewise, a child's innate temperament—such as a predisposition to be either wary or outgoing—shapes and is shaped by how other children and adults interact with that child. In light of the power of biology and the effects of children's prior experiences, it is important for early childhood educators to maintain high expectations and employ all their knowledge, ingenuity, and persistence to find ways to help every child succeed.

5 Early experiences have profound effects, both cumulative and delayed, on a child's development and learning; and optimal periods exist for certain types of development and learning to occur.

Children's early experiences, whether positive or negative, are cumulative. For example, a child's social experiences with other children in the preschool years may help him develop social skills and confidence that enable him or her to make friends in subsequent years, and these experiences further enhance the child's social competence and academic achievement. Conversely, children who fail to develop minimal social skills and thus suffer neglect or rejection from peers are at risk for later outcomes such as school dropout, delinquency, and mental health problems.[85] Similarly, early stimulation promotes brain development and the forming of neural connections, which in turn enable further development and learning. But if the very young child does not get this stimulation, he is less able to benefit from subsequent learning opportunities, and a cumulative disadvantage is set in motion.

Intervention and support are more successful the earlier a problem is addressed. Prevention of reading difficulties, for example, is far less difficult and expensive than remediation.[86] In addition, the literature shows that some aspects of development occur most efficiently at certain points in the life span. The first three years of life, for example, appear to be an optimal period for oral language development.[87] Ensuring that children get the needed environmental inputs and supports for a particular kind of learning and development at its "prime time" is always the most reliable route to desired results.

6 Development proceeds toward greater complexity, self-regulation, and symbolic or representational capacities.

A pervasive characteristic of development is that children's functioning becomes increasingly complex—in language, social interaction, physical movement, problem solving, and virtually every other domain. Increased organization and memory capacity of the developing brain make it possible with age for children to combine simple routines into more complex strategies.[88] The younger the child, the more she or he tends to think concretely and in the here and now. Yet in some ways, young children's thinking can be quite abstract. For example, preschoolers know that adding always makes *more* and subtracting makes *less,* and they are able to grasp abstract ideas about counting objects such as the one-to-one principle.[89]

All young humans must negotiate the transition from total dependence on others at birth to competence and internal control, including learning to regulate their emotions, behaviors, and attention. For young infants, there are tasks such as learning to soothe themselves from arousal to a settled state. A few years later, self-regulation means developing the capacity to manage strong emotions and keep one's attention focused. Throughout the early years, adults play significant roles in helping children learn to self-regulate.

Caregivers are important in helping very young children to modulate their emotional arousal; for example, soothing babies and then helping them learn to soothe themselves.[90] In the preschool years, teachers can help children develop self-regulation by scaffolding high-level dramatic play,[91] helping children learn to express their emotions, and engaging children in planning and decision making.[92]

During the early years of life, children move from sensory or behavioral responses to symbolic or representational knowledge.[93] For example, young children are able to navigate their homes and other familiar settings by recall and sensory cues, but later they come to understand and can use abstractions such as *left* and *right* or read a map of the house. It is around age 2 that children begin to represent and reconstruct their experiences and knowledge.[94] For example, children may use one object to stand for another in play, such as a block for a phone or a spatula for a guitar.[95] Their ability to use various modes and media to convey their meaning increases in range and scope. By the preschool years, these modes may include oral language, gestures and body movement, visual arts (drawing, painting, sculpting), construction, dramatic play, and writing. Their efforts to represent their ideas and concepts in any of these modes enhance the knowledge itself.[96]

7 **Children develop best when they have secure, consistent relationships with responsive adults and opportunities for positive relationships with peers.**

From the earliest years of life, warm, nurturing relationships with responsive adults are necessary for many key areas of children's development, including empathy and cooperation, self-regulation and cultural socialization, language and communication, peer relationships, and identity formation.[97]

When children and caring adults have the opportunity to get to know each other well, they learn to predict each other's signals and behavior and establish attunement and trust.[98] The first and most important relationships are those a child forms with parents or other primary caregivers. Forming one or more such attachments sets the stage for other relationships, as children move into the wider world beyond their immediate family.[99] Young children benefit from opportunities to develop ongoing, trusting relationships with adults outside the family and with other children. Notably, positive teacher-child relationships promote children's learning and achievement, as well as social competence and emotional development.[100]

Nurturing relationships are vital in fostering high self-esteem and a strong sense of self-efficacy, capacity in resolving interpersonal conflicts cooperatively, and the sociability to connect with others and form friendships. Further, by providing positive models and the security and confidence to try new experiences and attempt new skills, such relationships support children's learning and the acquisition of numerous capabilities.[101]

8 **Development and learning occur in and are influenced by multiple social and cultural contexts.**

Understanding children's development requires viewing each child within the sociocultural context of that child's family, educational setting, and community, as well as within the broader society.[102] These various contexts are interrelated, and all powerfully influence the developing child. For example, even a child in a loving, supportive family within a strong, healthy community is affected by the biases of the larger society, such as racism or sexism, and may show some effects of its negative stereotyping and discrimination.

Here *culture* is intended to refer to the customary beliefs and patterns of behavior, both explicit and implicit, that are inculcated by the society—or by a social, religious, or ethnic group within the society—in its members. Even though culture is discussed often in the context of diversity and immigrant or minority groups, all of us are members of cultures and are powerfully influenced by them. Every culture structures and interprets children's behavior and development in its own way.[103] Early childhood teachers need to understand the influence of sociocultural contexts and family circumstances on learning, recognize children's developing competencies, and be familiar with the variety of ways that children may demonstrate their developmental achievements.[104] Most importantly, educators need to be sensitive to how their own cultural experience shapes their perspective and to realize that multiple perspectives, not just their own, must be considered in decisions about children's development and learning.

As children grow up, they need to learn to function well in the society and in the increasingly global economy and to move comfortably among

groups of people from backgrounds both similar and dissimilar to their own. Fortunately, children are capable of learning to function in more than one social or cultural context and to make behavioral or linguistic shifts as they move from one context to another, although this complex ability does not occur overnight and requires adult support. Acquiring a new language or the ability to operate in a new culture can and should be an additive process, rather than causing the displacement of the child's first language and culture.[105] For example, immigrant children are able to develop English proficiency without having to give up their home language, and it is important that they retain their fluency in the language of their family and community. Likewise, children who speak only English benefit from learning another language and can do so without sacrificing their English proficiency.[106]

9 **Always mentally active in seeking to understand the world around them, children learn in a variety of ways; a wide range of teaching strategies and interactions are effective in supporting all these kinds of learning.**

Several prominent theories and bodies of research view cognitive development from the constructivist, interactive perspective.[107] That is, young children construct their knowledge and understanding of the world in the course of their own experiences, as well as from teachers, family members, peers and older children, and from books and other media. They learn from the concrete (e.g., manipulatives); they also apparently are capable of and interested in abstract ideas, to a far greater degree than was previously believed.[108] Children take all this input and work out their own understandings and hypotheses about the world. They try these out through interactions with adults and other children, physical manipulation, play, and their own thought processes—observing what happens, reflecting on their findings, imagining possibilities, asking questions, and formulating answers. When children make knowledge their own in these ways, their understanding is deeper and they can better transfer and apply their learning in new contexts.[109]

Using multiple teaching strategies is important in meeting children's different learning needs. The *Eager to Learn: Educating Our Preschoolers* report concluded:

Good teachers acknowledge and encourage children's efforts, model and demonstrate, create challenges and support children in extending their capabilities, and provide specific directions or instruction. All of these teaching strategies can be used in the context of play and structured activities. Effective teachers also organize the classroom environment and plan ways to pursue educational goals for each child as opportunities arise in child-initiated activities and in activities planned and initiated by the teacher.[110]

Thus, children benefit when teachers have at their disposal a wide range of teaching strategies and from these teachers select the best strategy to use in a situation, depending on the learning goal, specific context, and needs of individual children at that moment, including children who may need much more support than others even in exploration and play.[111]

10 **Play is an important vehicle for developing self-regulation as well as for promoting language, cognition, and social competence.**

Children of all ages love to play, and it gives them opportunities to develop physical competence and enjoyment of the outdoors, understand and make sense of their world, interact with others, express and control emotions, develop their symbolic and problem-solving abilities, and practice emerging skills. Research shows the links between play and foundational capacities such as memory, self-regulation, oral language abilities, social skills, and success in school.[112]

Children engage in various kinds of play, such as physical play, object play, pretend or dramatic play, constructive play, and games with rules. Observed in all young animals, play apparently serves important physical, mental, emotional, and social functions for humans and other species, and each kind of play has its own benefits and characteristics. From infancy, children act on the world around them for the pleasure of seeing what happens; for example, repeatedly dropping a spoon on the floor or pulling the cat's tail. At around age 2, children begin to demonstrate symbolic use of objects—for instance, picking up a shell and pretending to drink as from a cup—at least when they have had opportunities to observe others engaging in such make-believe behavior.[113]

From such beginnings, children begin to engage in more mature forms of dramatic play, in which by the age of 3–5 they may act out specific

roles, interact with one another in their roles, and plan how the play will go. Such play is influential in developing self-regulation, as children are highly motivated to stick to the roles and rules of the play, and thus grow in the ability to inhibit their impulses, act in coordination with others, and make plans.[114] High-level dramatic play produces documented cognitive, social, and emotional benefits.[115] However, with children spending more time in adult-directed activities and media use, forms of child play characterized by imagination and rich social interactions seem to be declining.[116] Active scaffolding of imaginative play is needed in early childhood settings if children are to develop the sustained, mature dramatic play that contributes significantly to their self-regulation and other cognitive, linguistic, social, and emotional benefits. Adults can use proven methods to promote children's extended engagement in make-believe play as well as in games with rules and other kinds of high-level play.[117] Rather than detracting from academic learning, play appears to support the abilities that underlie such learning and thus to promote school success.[118]

11 **Development and learning advance when children are challenged to achieve at a level just beyond their current mastery, and also when they have many opportunities to practice newly acquired skills.**

Human beings, especially children, are motivated to understand or do what is just beyond their current understanding or mastery.[119] Effective teachers create a rich learning environment to activate that motivation, and they make use of strategies to promote children's undertaking and mastering of new and progressively more advanced challenges.[120]

In a task just beyond a child's independent reach, adults and more-competent peers contribute significantly to the child's development by providing the support or assistance that allows the child to succeed at that task. Once children make this stretch to a new level in a supportive context, they can go on to use the skill independently and in a variety of contexts, laying the foundation for the next challenge. Provision of such support, often called *scaffolding*,[121] is a key feature of effective teaching.[122]

At the same time, children need to be successful in new tasks a significant proportion of the time in order for their motivation and persistence to be maintained.[123] Confronted by repeated failure, most children will simply stop trying. Repeated opportunity to practice and consolidate new skills and concepts is also essential in order for children to reach the threshold of mastery at which they can go on to use this knowledge or skill and apply it in new situations. Young children engage in a great deal of practice during play and in other child-guided contexts.[124]

To set challenging, achievable goals for children and to provide the right amount and type of scaffolding require knowledge of child development and learning, including familiarity with the paths and sequences that children are known to follow in acquiring specific skills, concepts, and abilities. This general knowledge, along with what the teacher learns from close observation and probing of the individual child's thinking, is critical to matching curriculum and teaching experiences to that child's emerging competencies so as to be challenging but not frustrating.

12 **Children's experiences shape their motivation and approaches to learning, such as persistence, initiative, and flexibility; in turn, these dispositions and behaviors affect their learning and development.**

The National Education Goals Panel and its Goal One Technical Planning Group identified "approaches to learning" as one of five aspects of school readiness.[125] Focused on the *how* rather than the *what* of learning, approaches to learning involve both children's feelings about learning (including their interest, pleasure, and motivation to learn) and children's behavior when learning (including attention, persistence, flexibility, and self-regulation).[126]

Even in the early years, children differ in their approaches to learning. These differences may influence children's school readiness and school success. For example, children who start school more eager to learn tend to do better in reading and mathematics than do less motivated children.[127] Children with more positive learning behaviors, such as initiative, attention, and persistence, later develop stronger language skills.[128] Moreover, children with greater self-regulation and other "learning-related skills" in kindergarten are more skilled in reading and mathematics in later grades.[129]

Although temperament and other inherent differences may affect children's approaches to learn-

ing, their experiences in families and early education programs have a major influence. Programs can implement evidence-based strategies that will promote positive approaches to learning. These strategies include strengthening relationships with children; working with families; and selecting effective curriculum, assessments, and teaching methods.[130]

Guidelines for developmentally appropriate practice

Practice that promotes young children's optimal learning and development—what this statement terms *developmentally appropriate practice*—is grounded both in the research on child development and learning and in the knowledge base regarding educational effectiveness in early care and education.

But whether or not what actually happens in the classroom is, in practice, developmentally appropriate is the result of myriad decisions at all levels—by policy makers, administrators, teachers, and families about the care and education of young children. Effective early childhood professionals draw on all the principles of child development and learning outlined, as well as the knowledge base on effective practices, and they apply the information in their practice.

The following guidelines address decisions that early childhood professionals make in the five key (and interrelated) areas of practice: (1) creating a caring community of learners, (2) teaching to enhance development and learning, (3) planning curriculum to achieve important goals, (4) assessing children's development and learning, and (5) establishing reciprocal relationships with families.

1 Creating a caring community of learners

Because early childhood settings tend to be children's first communities outside the home, the character of these communities is very influential in development. How children expect to be treated and how they treat others is significantly shaped in the early childhood setting. In developmentally appropriate practice, practitioners create and foster a "community of learners" that supports *all* children to develop and learn. The role of the community is to provide a physical, emotional, and cognitive environment conducive to that development and learning. The foundation for the community is consistent, positive, caring relationships between the adults and children, among children,

among teachers, and between teachers and families. It is the responsibility of all members of the learning community to consider and contribute to one another's well-being and learning.

To create a caring community of learners, practitioners ensure that the following occur for children from birth through the primary grades.

A. Each member of the community is valued by the others. By observing and participating in the community, children learn about themselves and their world and also how to develop positive, constructive relationships with other people. Each child has unique strengths, interests, and perspectives to contribute. Children learn to respect and acknowledge differences of all kinds and to value each person.

B. Relationships are an important context through which children develop and learn. Children construct their understandings about the world around them through interactions with other members of the community (both adults and peers). Opportunities to play together, collaborate on investigations and projects, and talk with peers and adults enhance children's development and learning. Interacting in small groups provides a context for children to extend their thinking, build on one another's ideas, and cooperate to solve problems. (Also see guideline 5, "Establishing Reciprocal Relationships with Families.")

C. Each member of the community respects and is accountable to the others to behave in a way that is conducive to the learning and well-being of all.

1. Teachers help children develop responsibility and self-regulation. Recognizing that such abilities and behaviors develop with experience and time, teachers consider how to foster such development in their interactions

with each child and in their curriculum planning.

2. Teachers are responsible at all times for all children under their supervision, monitoring, anticipating, preventing, and redirecting behaviors not conducive to learning or disrespectful of the community, as well as teaching prosocial behaviors.

3. Teachers set clear and reasonable limits on children's behavior and apply those limits consistently. Teachers help children be accountable to themselves and to others for their behavior. In the case of preschool and older children, teachers engage children in developing their own community rules for behavior.

4. Teachers listen to and acknowledge children's feelings and frustrations, respond with respect in ways that children can understand, guide children to resolve conflicts, and model skills that help children to solve their own problems.

5. Teachers themselves demonstrate high levels of responsibility and self-regulation in their interactions with other adults (colleagues, family members) and with children.

D. Practitioners design and maintain the physical environment to protect the health and safety of the learning community members, specifically in support of young children's physiological needs for activity, sensory stimulation, fresh air, rest, and nourishment. The daily schedule provides a balance of rest and active movement. Outdoor experiences, including opportunities to interact with the natural world, are provided for children of all ages.

E. Practitioners ensure members of the community feel psychologically safe. The overall social and emotional climate is positive.

1. Interactions among community members (administrators, teachers, families, children), as well as the experiences provided by teachers, leave participants feeling secure, relaxed, and comfortable rather than disengaged, frightened, worried, or unduly stressed.

2. Teachers foster in children an enjoyment of and engagement in learning.

3. Teachers ensure that the environment is organized and the schedule follows an orderly routine that provides a stable structure within which development and learning can take place. While the environment's elements are dynamic and changing, overall it still is predictable and comprehensible from a child's point of view.

4. Children hear and see their home language and culture reflected in the daily interactions and activities of the classroom.

2 Teaching to enhance development and learning

From birth, a child's relationships and interactions with adults are critical determinants of development and learning. At the same time, children are active constructors of their own understanding of the world around them; as such, they benefit from initiating and regulating their own learning activities and from interacting with peers. Developmentally appropriate teaching practices provide an optimal balance of adult-guided and child-guided experiences. "*Adult-guided* experience proceeds primarily along the lines of the teacher's goals, but is also shaped by the children's active engagement; *child-guided* experience proceeds primarily along the lines of children's interests and actions, with strategic teacher support."[131] But whether a learning experience is adult- or child-guided, in developmentally appropriate practice it is the teacher who takes responsibility for stimulating, directing, and supporting children's development and learning by providing the experiences that each child needs.

The following describe teaching practices that are developmentally appropriate for young children from birth through the primary grades.

A. Teachers are responsible for fostering the caring learning community through their teaching.

B. Teachers make it a priority to know each child well, and also the people most significant in the child's life.

1. Teachers establish positive, personal

relationships with each child and with each child's family to better understand that child's individual needs, interests, and abilities and that family's goals, values, expectations, and childrearing practices. (Also see guideline 5, "Establishing Reciprocal Relationships with Families.") Teachers talk with each child and family (with a community translator, if necessary, for mutual understanding) and use what they learn to adapt their actions and planning.

2. Teachers continually gather information about children in a variety of ways and monitor each child's learning and development to make plans to help children progress. (Also see guideline 4, "Assessing Children's Development and Learning.")

3. Teachers are alert to signs of undue stress and traumatic events in each child's life and employ strategies to reduce stress and support the development of resilience.

C. Teachers take responsibility for knowing what the desired goals for the program are and how the program's curriculum is intended to achieve those goals. They carry out that curriculum through their teaching in ways that are geared to young children in general and these children in particular. Doing this includes following the predictable sequences in which children acquire specific concepts, skills, and abilities and by building on prior experiences and understandings. (Also see guideline 3, "Planning Curriculum to Achieve Important Goals.")

D. Teachers plan for learning experiences that effectively implement a comprehensive curriculum so that children attain key goals across the domains (physical, social, emotional, cognitive) and across the disciplines (language literacy, including English acquisition, mathematics, social studies, science, art, music, physical education, and health).

E. Teachers plan the environment, schedule, and daily activities to promote each child's learning and development.

1. Teachers arrange firsthand, meaningful experiences that are intellectually and

creatively stimulating, invite exploration and investigation, and engage children's active, sustained involvement. They do this by providing a rich variety of materials, challenges, and ideas that are worthy of children's attention.

2. Teachers present children with opportunities to make meaningful choices, especially in child-choice activity periods. They assist and guide children who are not yet able to enjoy and make good use of such periods.

3. Teachers organize the daily and weekly schedule to provide children with extended blocks of time in which to engage in sustained play, investigation, exploration, and interaction (with adults and peers).

4. Teachers provide experiences, materials, and interactions to enable children to engage in play that allows them to stretch their boundaries to the fullest in their imagination, language, interaction, and self-regulation as well as to practice their newly acquired skills.

F. Teachers possess an extensive repertoire of skills and strategies they are able to draw on, and they know how and when to choose among them, to effectively promote each child's learning and development at that moment. Those skills include the ability to adapt curriculum, activities, and materials to ensure full participation of *all* children. Those strategies include, but are not limited to, acknowledging, encouraging, giving specific feedback, modeling, demonstrating, adding challenge, giving cues or other assistance, providing information, and giving directions.

1. To help children develop initiative, teachers encourage them to choose and plan their own learning activities.

2. To stimulate children's thinking and extend their learning, teachers pose problems, ask questions, and make comments and suggestions.

3. To extend the range of children's interests and the scope of their thought, teachers present novel experiences and

introduce stimulating ideas, problems, experiences, or hypotheses.

4. To adjust the complexity and challenge of activities to suit children's level of skill and knowledge, teachers increase the challenge as children gain competence and understanding.

5. To strengthen children's sense of competence and confidence as learners, motivation to persist, and willingness to take risks, teachers provide experiences for children to be genuinely successful and to be challenged.

6. To enhance children's conceptual understanding, teachers use various strategies, including intensive interview and conversation, that encourage children to reflect on and "revisit" their experiences.

7. To encourage and foster children's learning and development, teachers avoid generic praise ("Good job!") and instead give specific feedback ("You got the same number when you counted the beans again!").

G. Teachers know how and when to *scaffold* children's learning—that is, providing just enough assistance to enable each child to perform at a skill level just beyond what the child can do on his or her own, then gradually reducing the support as the child begins to master the skill, and setting the stage for the next challenge.

1. Teachers recognize and respond to the reality that in any group, children's skills will vary and they will need different levels of support. Teachers also know that any one child's level of skill and need for support will vary over time.

2. Scaffolding can take a variety of forms; for example, giving the child a hint, adding a cue, modeling the skill, or adapting the materials and activities. It can be provided in a variety of contexts, not only in planned learning experiences but also in play, daily routines, and outdoor activities.

3. Teachers can provide the scaffolding (e.g., the teacher models the skill) or peers can (e.g., the child's learning buddy models); in either case, it is the teacher who recognizes and plans for each child's need for support and assistance.

H. Teachers know how and when to use the various learning formats/contexts most strategically.

1. Teachers understand that each major learning format or context (e.g., large group, small group, learning center, routine) has its own characteristics, functions, and value.

2. Teachers think carefully about which learning format is best for helping children achieve a desired goal, given the children's ages, development, abilities, temperaments, etc.

I. When children have missed some of the learning opportunities necessary for school success (most often children from low-income households), programs and teachers provide them with even more extended, enriched, and intensive learning experiences than are provided to their peers.

1. Teachers take care not to place these children under added pressure. Such pressure on children already starting out at a disadvantage can make school a frustrating and discouraging experience, rather than an opportunity to enjoy and succeed at learning.

2. To enable these children to make optimal progress, teachers are highly intentional in use of time, and they focus on key skills and abilities through highly engaging experiences.

3. Recognizing the self-regulatory, linguistic, cognitive, and social benefits that high-quality play affords, teachers do not reduce play opportunities that these children critically need. Instead, teachers scaffold and model aspects of rich, mature play.

J. Teachers make experiences in their classrooms accessible and responsive to *all* children and their needs—including children who are English language learners, have special needs or disabilities, live in poverty

or other challenging circumstances, or are from different cultures.

1. Teachers incorporate a wide variety of experiences, materials and equipment, and teaching strategies to accommodate the range of children's individual differences in development, skills and abilities, prior experiences, needs, and interests.

2. Teachers bring each child's home culture and language into the shared culture of the learning community so that the unique contributions of that home culture and language can be recognized and valued by the other community members, and the child's connection with family and home is supported.

3. Teachers include all children in all of the classroom activities and encourage children to be inclusive in their behaviors and interactions with peers.

4. Teachers are prepared to meet special needs of individual children, including children with disabilities and those who exhibit unusual interests and skills. Teachers use all the strategies identified here, consult with appropriate specialists and the child's family, and see that the child gets the adaptations and specialized services he or she needs to succeed in the early childhood setting.

3 Planning curriculum to achieve important goals

The curriculum consists of the knowledge, skills, abilities, and understandings children are to acquire and the plans for the learning experiences through which those gains will occur. Implementing a curriculum always yields outcomes of some kind—but *which* outcomes those are and *how* a program achieves them are critical. In developmentally appropriate practice, the curriculum helps young children achieve goals that are developmentally and educationally significant. The curriculum does this through learning experiences (including play, small group, large group, interest centers, and routines) that reflect what is known about young children in general and about these children in particular, as well as about the sequences in which children acquire specific

concepts, skills, and abilities, building on prior experiences.

Because children learn more in programs where there is a well planned and implemented curriculum, it is important for every school and early childhood program to have its curriculum in written form. Teachers use the curriculum and their knowledge of children's interests in planning relevant, engaging learning experiences; and they keep the curriculum in mind in their interactions with children throughout the day. In this way they ensure that children's learning experiences—in both adult-guided and child-guided contexts—are consistent with the program's goals for children and connected within an organized framework. At the same time, developmentally appropriate practice means teachers have flexibility—and the expertise to exercise that flexibility effectively—in how they design and carry out curricular experiences in their classrooms.[132]

The following describe curriculum planning that is developmentally appropriate for children from birth through the primary grades.

A. Desired goals that are important in young children's learning and development have been identified and clearly articulated.

1. Teachers consider what children should know, understand, and be able to do across the domains of physical, social, emotional, and cognitive development and across the disciplines, including language, literacy, mathematics, social studies, science, art, music, physical education, and health.

2. If state standards or other mandates are in place, teachers become thoroughly familiar with these; teachers add to these any goals to which the standards have given inadequate weight.

3. Whatever the source of the goals, teachers and administrators ensure that goals are clearly defined for, communicated to, and understood by all stakeholders, including families.

B. The program has a comprehensive, effective curriculum that targets the identified goals, including all those foundational for later learning and school success.

1. Whether or not teachers were participants in the decision about the curricu-

lum, they familiarize themselves with it and consider its comprehensiveness in addressing all important goals.

2. If the program is using published curriculum products, teachers make adaptations to meet the learning needs of the children they teach.

3. If practitioners develop the curriculum themselves, they make certain it targets the identified goals and they use strong, up-to-date resources from experts to ensure that curriculum content is robust and comprehensive.

C. Teachers use the curriculum framework in their planning to ensure there is ample attention to important learning goals and to enhance the coherence of the classroom experience for children.

1. Teachers are familiar with the understandings and skills key for that age group in each domain (physical, social, emotional, cognitive), including how learning and development in one domain impact the other domains.

2. In their planning and follow-through, teachers use the curriculum framework along with what they know (from their observation and other assessment) about the children's interests, progress, language proficiency, and learning needs. They carefully shape and adapt the experiences they provide children to enable each child to reach the goals outlined in the curriculum.

3. In determining the sequence and pace of learning experiences, teachers consider the developmental paths that children typically follow and the typical sequences in which skills and concepts develop. Teachers use these with an eye to moving all children forward in all areas, adapting when necessary for individual children. When children have missed some of the learning opportunities that promote school success, teachers must adapt the curriculum to help children advance more quickly.

D. Teachers make meaningful connections a priority in the learning experiences they provide children, to reflect that all learners, and certainly young children, learn best when the concepts, language, and skills they encounter are related to something they know and care about, and when the new learnings are themselves interconnected in meaningful, coherent ways.

1. Teachers plan curriculum experiences that integrate children's learning *within* and *across* the domains (physical, social, emotional, cognitive) and the disciplines (including language, literacy, mathematics, social studies, science, art, music, physical education, and health).

2. Teachers plan curriculum experiences to draw on children's own interests and introduce children to things likely to interest them, in recognition that developing and extending children's interests is particularly important during the preschool years, when children's ability to focus their attention is in its early stages.

3. Teachers plan curriculum experiences that follow logical sequences and that allow for depth and focus. That is, the experiences do not skim lightly over a great many content areas, but instead allow children to spend sustained time with a more select set.

E. Teachers collaborate with those teaching in the preceding and subsequent grade levels, sharing information about children and working to increase the continuity and coherence across ages/grades, while protecting the integrity and appropriateness of practices at each level.

F. In the care of infants and toddlers, practitioners plan curriculum (although they may not always call it that). They develop plans for the important routines and experiences that will promote children's learning and development and enable them to attain desired goals.

4 Assessing children's development and learning

Assessment of children's development and learning is essential for teachers and programs in order to plan, implement, and evaluate the effective-

ness of the classroom experiences they provide. Assessment also is a tool for monitoring children's progress toward a program's desired goals. In developmentally appropriate practice, the experiences and the assessments are linked (the experiences are developing what is being assessed, and vice versa); both are aligned with the program's desired outcomes or goals for children. Teachers cannot be intentional about helping children to progress unless they know where each child is with respect to learning goals.

Sound assessment of young children is challenging because they develop and learn in ways that are characteristically uneven and embedded within the specific cultural and linguistic contexts in which they live. For example, sound assessment takes into consideration such factors as a child's facility in English and stage of linguistic development in the home language. Assessment that is not reliable or valid, or that is used to label, track, or otherwise harm young children, is not developmentally appropriate practice.

The following describe sound assessment that is developmentally appropriate for children from birth through the primary grades.

A. Assessment of young children's progress and achievements is ongoing, strategic, and purposeful. The results of assessment are used to inform the planning and implementing of experiences, to communicate with the child's family, and to evaluate and improve teachers' and the program's effectiveness.

B. Assessment focuses on children's progress toward goals that are developmentally and educationally significant.

C. There is a system in place to collect, make sense of, and use the assessment information to guide what goes on in the classroom (formative assessment). Teachers use this information in planning curriculum and learning experiences and in moment-to-moment interactions with children—that is, teachers continually engage in assessment for the purpose of improving teaching and learning.

D. The methods of assessment are appropriate to the developmental status and experiences of young children, and they recognize individual variation in learners and allow children to demonstrate their competence

in different ways. Methods appropriate to the classroom assessment of young children, therefore, include results of teachers' observations of children, clinical interviews, collections of children's work samples, and their performance on authentic activities.

E. Assessment looks not only at what children can do independently but also at what they can do with assistance from other children or adults. Therefore, teachers assess children as they participate in groups and other situations that are providing scaffolding.

F. In addition to this assessment by teachers, input from families as well as children's own evaluations of their work are part of the program's overall assessment strategy.

G. Assessments are tailored to a specific purpose and used only for the purpose for which they have been demonstrated to produce reliable, valid information.

H. Decisions that have a major impact on children, such as enrollment or placement, are never made on the basis of results from a single developmental assessment or screening instrument/device but are based on multiple sources of relevant information, including that obtained from observations of and interactions with children by teachers and parents (and specialists, as needed).

I. When a screening or other assessment identifies children who may have special learning or developmental needs, there is appropriate follow-up, evaluation, and, if indicated, referral. Diagnosis or labeling is never the result of a brief screening or one-time assessment. Families should be involved as important sources of information.

5 Establishing reciprocal relationships with families

Developmentally appropriate practices derive from deep knowledge of child development principles and of the program's children in particular, as well as the context within which each of them is living. The younger the child, the more necessary it is for practitioners to acquire this particular knowledge through relationships with children's families.

Practice is not developmentally appropriate if the program limits "parent involvement" to scheduled events (valuable though these may be), or if the program/family relationship has a strong "parent education" orientation. Parents do not feel like partners in the relationship when staff members see themselves as having all the knowledge and insight about children and view parents as lacking such knowledge.

Such approaches do not adequately convey the complexity of the partnership between teachers and families that is a fundamental element of good practice. The following describe the kind of relationships that are developmentally appropriate for children (from birth through the primary grades), in which family members and practitioners work together as members of the learning community.

A. In reciprocal relationships between practitioners and families, there is mutual respect, cooperation, shared responsibility, and negotiation of conflicts toward achievement of shared goals. (Also see guideline 1, "Creating a Caring Community of Learners.")

B. Practitioners work in collaborative partnerships with families, establishing and maintaining regular, frequent two-way communication with them (with families who do not speak English, teachers should use the language of the home if they are able or try to enlist the help of bilingual volunteers).

C. Family members are welcome in the setting, and there are multiple opportunities for family participation. Families participate in program decisions about their children's care and education.

D. Teachers acknowledge a family's choices and goals for the child and respond with sensitivity and respect to those preferences and concerns, but without abdicating the responsibility that early childhood practitioners have to support children's learning and development through developmentally appropriate practices.

E. Teachers and the family share with each other their knowledge of the particular child and understanding of child development and learning as part of day-to-day communication and in planned conferences. Teachers support families in ways that maximally promote family decision-making capabilities and competence.

F. Practitioners involve families as a source of information about the child (before program entry and on an ongoing basis) and engage them in the planning for their child.

G. The program links families with a range of services, based on identified resources, priorities, and concerns.

Policy considerations

Teachers and administrators in early childhood education play a critical role in shaping the future of our citizenry and our democracy. Minute to minute, day to day, month to month, they provide the consistent, compassionate, respectful relationships that our children need to establish strong foundations of early learning. By attending to the multiple domains of development and the individual needs of those in their care, early childhood professionals who employ developmentally appropriate practices engage young children in rich out-of-home early learning experiences that prepare them for future learning and success in life.

Regardless of the resources available, early childhood professionals have an ethical responsibility to practice according to the standards of their profession. It is unrealistic, however, to expect that they can fully implement those standards and practices without public policies and funding that support a system of early childhood education that is grounded in providing high-quality developmentally appropriate experiences for all children.

The goal must be advancement in both realms: more early childhood professionals engaging in developmentally appropriate practices, and more policy makers establishing policies and committing public funds to support such practices.

Many elements of developmentally appropriate practice should be reflected in our federal, state, and local policies. Policy areas that are

particularly critical for developing a high-quality, well financed system of early childhood education, which includes the implementation of developmentally appropriate practice, must include at a minimum: early learning standards for children and related/aligned curricula and assessment; a comprehensive professional development and compensation system; a program quality rating and improvement system to improve program quality as well as to inform the families, the public, and policy makers about quality; comprehensive and coordinated services for children; attention to program evaluation; and commitment of additional public funds to support program affordability and quality in every setting.

NAEYC regularly provides information to inform advocates and policy makers in their efforts to establish sound policies in these areas.

In order for such information and recommendations to be up to date, NAEYC's policy-relevant summaries and information appear not in this position statement but in their own location on the Association's website at www.naeyc.org.

Notes

[1]NAEYC. 1986. Position statement on developmentally appropriate practice in programs for 4- and 5-year-olds. *Young Children* 41 (6): 20–29; Bredekamp, S., ed. 1987. *Developmentally appropriate practice in early childhood programs serving children from birth through age 8.* Expanded edition. Washington, DC: NAEYC; NAEYC. 1996. Developmentally appropriate practice in early childhood programs serving children from birth through age 8. A position statement of the National Association for the Education of Young Children. In *Developmentally appropriate practice in early childhood programs,* Rev. ed., eds. S. Bredekamp & C. Copple, 3–30. Washington, DC: Author.

[2]NAEYC & NAECS/SDE (National Association of Early Childhood Specialists in State Departments of Education). 2002. *Early learning standards: Creating the conditions for success.* Joint position statement. Online: www.naeyc.org/dap; NAEYC & NAECS/SDE (National Association of Early Childhood Specialists in State Departments of Education). 2003. *Early childhood curriculum, assessment, and program evaluation: Building an effective, accountable system in programs for children birth through age 8.* Joint position statement. Online: www.naeyc.org/dap; NAEYC. 2005. *Code of ethical conduct and statement of commitment.* Position statement. Online: www.naeyc.org/dap; NAEYC. 2005. *NAEYC early childhood program standards and accreditation criteria.* 11 vols. Washington, DC: Author.

Critical issues in the current context

[3]Children's Defense Fund. 2005. *The state of America's children, 2005.* Washington, DC: Author.

[4]Cochran, M. 2007. *Finding our way: The future of American early care and education.* Washington, DC: Zero to Three.

[5]Sandall, S., M.L. Hemmeter, B.J. Smith, & M.E. McLean, eds. 2005. *DEC recommended practices: A comprehensive guide for practical application in early intervention/early childhood special education.* Longmont, CO: Sopris West, and Missoula, MT: Division for Early Childhood, Council for Exceptional Children; Hemmeter, M.L., L. Fox, & S. Doubet. 2006. Together we can: A program-wide approach to addressing challenging behavior. In *Social emotional development,* eds. E. Horn & H. Jones, Young Exceptional Children Monograph Series, vol. 8. Missoula, MT: Division for Early Childhood.

[6]Gitomer, D.H. 2007. *Teacher quality in a changing policy landscape: Improvements in the teacher pool.* Princeton, NJ: Educational Testing Service. Online: www.ets.org/Media/Education_Topics/pdf/TQ_full_report.pdf.

[7]Whitebook, M., C. Howes, & D. Phillips. 1990. *The national child care staffing study: Who cares? Child care teachers and the quality of care in America.* Final report. Oakland, CA: Child Care Employee Project.

[8]Cochran, M. 2007. *Finding our way: The future of American early care and education.* Washington, DC: Zero to Three.

[9]Klein, L.G., & J. Knitzer. 2006. Effective preschool curricula and teaching strategies. *Pathways to Early School Success,* Issue Brief No. 2. New York: Columbia University, National Center for Children in Poverty; Brooks-Gunn, J., C.E. Rouse, & S. McLanahan. 2007. Racial and ethnic gaps in school readiness. In *School readiness and the transition to kindergarten in the era of accountability,* eds. R.C. Pianta, M.J. Cox, & K.L. Snow, 283–306. Baltimore: Paul H. Brookes.

[10]Heath, S.B. 1983. *Ways with words: Language, life, and work in communities and classrooms.* New York: Cambridge University Press; Vogt, L., C. Jordan, & R. Tharp. 1993. Explaining school failure, producing school success. In *Minority education: Anthropological perspectives,* eds. E. Jacob & C. Jordan, 53–65. Norwood, NJ: Ablex.

[11]Hart, B., & T.R. Risley. 1995. *Meaningful differences in the everyday experience of young American children.* Baltimore: Paul H. Brookes; Hart, B., & T.R. Risley. 1999. *The social world of children learning to talk.* Baltimore: Paul H. Brookes.

[12]Farkas, G., & K. Beron. 2004. The detailed age trajectory of oral vocabulary knowledge: Differences by class and race. *Social Science Research* 33: 464–97.

[13]Barbarin, O., D. Bryant, T. McCandies, M. Burchinal, D. Early, R. Clifford, & R. Pianta. 2006. Children enrolled in public pre–K: The relation of family life, neighborhood quality, and socioeconomic resources to early competence. *American Journal of Orthopsychiatry* 76: 265–76; Zill, N., & J. West. 2001. *Entering kindergarten: Findings from the condition of education, 2000.* Washington, DC: U.S. Department of Education, National Center for Education Statistics.

[14]Lee, V.E., & D.T. Burkam. 2002. *Inequality at the starting gate: Social background differences in achievement as children begin school.* New York: Economic Policy Institute.

[15]Aber, L., K. Burnley, D.K. Cohen, D.L. Featherman, D. Phillips, S. Raudenbush, & B. Rowan. 2006. *Beyond school reform: Improving the educational outcomes of low-income children.* Report to the Spencer Foundation. Ann Arbor, MI: University of Michigan, Center for Advancing Research and Solutions for Society; Klein, L.G., & J. Knitzer. 2006. Effective preschool curricula and teaching strategies. *Pathways to Early School Success,* Issue Brief No. 2. New York: Columbia University, National Center for Children in Poverty.

[16]See, e.g., Mullis, I.V.S., M.O. Martin, & P. Foy. 2009, in press. *TIMSS 2007 international report and technical report.* Chestnut Hill, MA: Lynch School of Education, Boston College, TIMSS & PIRLS International Study Center; NCES (National Center for Education Statistics). 2006. *Comparing mathematics content in the National Assessment of Educational Progress (NEAP), Trends in International Mathematics and Science Study (TIMSS), and Program for International Student Assessment (PISA) 2003 assessments: Technical report.* Washington, DC: U.S. Department of Education, National Center for Education Statistics, Institute of Education Sciences. Online: purl.access.gpo. gov/GPO/LPS70522.

[17]U.S. Dept. of Education, Office of Elementary and Secondary Education. 2007. Title I—Improving the academic achievement of the disadvantaged; Individuals with Disabilities Education Act (IDEA): Final rule. *Federal Register* 72 (67): 17747–81. Online: www.ed.gov/legislation/ FedRegister/finrule/2007-2/040907a.html.

[18]Johnson, J., A.M. Arumi, & A. Ott. 2006. *Reality Check 2006—Education insights: A Public Agenda initiative to build momentum for improving American schools.* New York: Public Agenda.

[19]The goals of NCLB—Goal 1: To strengthen the school's core academic program so that by 2013-2014 all students (in aggregate and for each subgroup) will demonstrate academic skills at the "proficient" level or above on the State's assessments and be engaged in high quality teaching and learning. Goal 2: To increase the number of students making successful transitions between schools and school levels. Goal 3: To increase the level of parental involvement in support of the learning process via communication between school and home. Goal 4: To align staff capacities, school processes, and professional development activities to implement effective methods and instructional practices that are supported by scientifically-based research. Goal 5: To recruit, staff, and retain highly qualified staff that will implement effective methods and instructional practices.

[20]NIEER (National Institute for Early Education Research). 2007. *The state of preschool 2007: State preschool yearbook.* New Brunswick, NJ: Rutgers University, Graduate School of Education. Online: nieer.org/yearbook/pdf/yearbook.pdf.

[21]U.S. Dept. of Health and Human Services, Administration on Children, Youth, and Families, & Head Start Bureau. 2003. *The Head Start path to positive child outcomes.* Washington, DC: Authors. Online: www.headstartinfo.org/pdf/hsoutcomespath28ppREV.pdf.

[22]Bowman, B.T., S. Donovan, & M.S. Burns. 2000. *Eager to learn: Educating our preschoolers.* Washington, DC: National Academies Press; Shonkoff, J.P., & D.A. Phillips, eds. 2000. *From neurons to neighborhoods: The science of early child development.* A report of the National Research Council. Washington, DC: National Academies Press.

[23]NAEYC & NAECS/SDE (National Association of Early Childhood Specialists in State Departments of Education). 2002. *Early learning standards: Creating the conditions for success.* Joint position statement. Online: www.naeyc.org/ dap; NAEYC & NAECS/SDE (National Association of Early Childhood Specialists in State Departments of Education). 2003. *Early childhood curriculum, assessment, and program evaluation: Building an effective, accountable system in programs for children birth through age 8.* Joint position statement. Online: www.naeyc.org/dap.

[24]Takanishi, R., & K. Kauerz. 2008. PK inclusion: Getting serious about a P–16 education system. *Phi Delta Kappan* 89 (7): 480–87.

[25]Pedulla, J.J. 2003. State-mandated testing: What do teachers think? *Educational Leadership* 61 (3): 42–46; Goldstein, L.S. 2007. Embracing multiplicity: Learning from two practitioners' pedagogical responses to the changing demands of kindergarten teaching in the United States. *Journal of Research in Childhood Education* 21 (4): 378–99; Goldstein, L.S. 2007b. Examining the unforgiving complexity of kindergarten teaching. *Early Childhood Research Quarterly* 22: 39–54.

[26]U.S. House of Representatives and Senate. 2007. *Bill H.R.1429.* "The Improving Head Start for School Readiness Act." (P.L. 110–34). Online: www.washingtonwatch.com/ bills/show/110_PL_110-134.html.

[27]Takanishi, R., & K. Kauerz. 2008. PK inclusion: Getting serious about a P–16 education system. *Phi Delta Kappan* 89 (7): 480–87.

[28]Graves, B. 2006. PK–3: What is it and how do we know it works? *Foundation for Child Development Policy Brief, Advancing PK–3* 4; Ritchie, S., K. Maxwell, & R.M. Clifford. 2007. FirstSchool: A new vision for education. In *School readiness and the transition to kindergarten in the era of accountability,* eds. R.C. Pianta, M.J. Cox, & K.L. Snow, 85–96. Baltimore: Paul H. Brookes; Takanishi, R., & K. Kauerz. 2008. PK inclusion: Getting serious about a P–16 education system. *Phi Delta Kappan* 89 (7): 480–87.

[29]NAEYC & NAECS/SDE (National Association of Early Childhood Specialists in State Departments of Education). 2003. *Early childhood curriculum, assessment, and program evaluation: Building an effective, accountable system in programs for children birth through age 8.* Joint position statement. Online: www.naeyc.org/dap.

[30]Neuman, S.B., K. Roskos, C. Vukelich, & D. Clements. 2003. *The state of state prekindergarten standards in 2003.* Report for the Center for the Improvement of Early Reading Achievement (CIERA). Ann Arbor, MI: University of Michigan.

[31]NAEYC. 2005. *Screening and assessment of young English-language learners.* Supplement to the NAEYC and NAECS/ SDE Joint Position Statement on Early Childhood Curriculum, Assessment, and Program Evaluation. Washington, DC: Author. Online: www.naeyc.org/dap.

Developmentally Appropriate Practice, 3d Edition

[32]NAEYC & NAECS/SDE (National Association of Early Childhood Specialists in State Departments of Education). 2002. *Early learning standards: Creating the conditions for success.* Joint position statement. Online: www.naeyc.org/dap.

[33]NCTM (National Council of Teachers of Mathematics). 2006. *Curriculum focal points for prekindergarten through grade 8 mathematics: A quest for coherence.* Reston, VA: Author.

[34]Wien, C.A. 2004. *Negotiating standards in the primary classroom: The teacher's dilemma.* New York: Teachers College Press.

[35]See, e.g., Kagan, S.L., & K. Kauerz. 2007. Reaching for the whole: Integration and alignment in early education policy. In *School readiness and the transition to kindergarten in the era of accountability,* eds. R.C. Pianta, M.J. Cox, & K.L. Snow, 11–30. Baltimore: Paul H. Brookes; Ritchie, S., K. Maxwell, & R.M. Clifford. 2007. FirstSchool: A new vision for education. In *School readiness and the transition to kindergarten in the era of accountability,* eds. R.C. Pianta, M.J. Cox, & K.L. Snow, 85–96. Baltimore: Paul H. Brookes.

[36]Goldstein, L.S. 2007a. Embracing multiplicity: Learning from two practitioners' pedagogical responses to the changing demands of kindergarten teaching in the United States. *Journal of Research in Childhood Education* 21 (4): 378–99; Goldstein, L.S. 2007b. Examining the unforgiving complexity of kindergarten teaching. *Early Childhood Research Quarterly* 22: 39–54.

[37]Barnett, W.S. 2004. Better teachers, better preschools: Student achievement linked to teacher qualifications. *Preschool Policy Matters* 2: 2–7. Online: nieer.org/docs/?DocID=62.

[38]NAEYC & NAECS/SDE (National Association of Early Childhood Specialists in State Departments of Education). 2003. *Early childhood curriculum, assessment, and program evaluation: Building an effective, accountable system in programs for children birth through age 8.* Joint position statement. Online: www.naeyc.org/dap.

[39]Darling-Hammond, L., & J. Bransford. 2005. *Preparing teachers for a changing world: What teachers should learn and be able to do.* San Francisco: Jossey-Bass.

Applying new knowledge to critical issues

[40]Klein, L.G., & J. Knitzer. 2006. Effective preschool curricula and teaching strategies. *Pathways to Early School Success,* Issue Brief No. 2. New York: Columbia University, National Center for Children in Poverty.

[41]U.S. Dept. of Health and Human Services, Administration on Children, Youth, and Families, & Head Start Bureau. 2003. *The Head Start path to positive child outcomes.* Washington, DC: Authors. Online: www.headstartinfo.org/pdf/hsoutcomespath28ppREV.pdf.

[42]NICHD (National Institute of Child Health and Human Development). 2003. The NICHD study of early child care: Contexts of development and developmental outcomes over the first seven years of life. In *Early child development in the 21st century,* eds. J. Brooks-Gunn, A.S. Fuligni, & L.J. Berlin, 181–201. New York: Teachers College Press.

[43]NICHD (National Institute of Child Health and Human Development). 2001. *Quality of child care and child care outcomes.* Paper presented at the biennial meeting of the Society for Research in Child Development. April 19–22,
Minneapolis, MN; Klein, L.G., & J. Knitzer. 2006. Effective preschool curricula and teaching strategies. *Pathways to Early School Success,* Issue Brief No. 2. New York: Columbia University, National Center for Children in Poverty; Schweinhart, L.J., J. Montie, & Z. Xiang, W.S. Barnett, C.R. Belfield, & M. Mores. 2005. *Lifetime effects: The High/Scope Perry preschool study through age 40.* Monographs of the High/Scope Educational Research Foundation, vol. 14. Ypsilanti, MI: High/Scope Press.

[44]Loeb, S., B. Fuller, S.L. Kagan, & B. Carrol. 2004. Child care in poor communities: Early learning effects of type, quality, and stability. *Child Development* 75 (1): 47–65.

[45]Hamre, B.K., & R.C. Pianta. 2001. Early teacher-child relationships and the trajectory of children's school outcomes through eighth grade. *Child Development* 72 (2): 625–38; Hamre, B.K., & R.C. Pianta. 2005. Can instructional and emotional support in the first grade classroom make a difference for children at risk of school failure? *Child Development* 76 (5): 949–67.

[46]Dickinson, D.K., & P.O. Tabors. 2001. *Beginning literacy with language: Young children learning at home and school.* Baltimore: Paul H. Brookes; NELP (National Early Literacy Panel). In press. *Developing early literacy: Report of the National Early Literacy Panel: A scientific synthesis of early literacy development and implications for intervention.* Washington, DC: National Institute for Literacy.

[47]Snow, C.E. 2007. *Is literacy enough? Pathways to academic success for adolescents.* Baltimore: Paul H. Brookes.

[48]Snow, C.E. 2005. From literacy to learning. *Harvard Education Letter* (July/August). Online: www.edletter.org/current/snow.shtml; Snow, C.E. 2007. *Is literacy enough? Pathways to academic success for adolescents.* Baltimore: Paul H. Brookes.

[49]Snow, C.E. 2005. From literacy to learning. *Harvard Education Letter* (July/August). Online: www.edletter.org/current/snow.shtml.

[50]Dickinson, D.K., & P.O. Tabors. 2001. *Beginning literacy with language: Young children learning at home and school.* Baltimore: Paul H. Brookes.

[51]National Early Literacy Panel. In press. *Developing early literacy: Report of the National Early Literacy Panel: A scientific synthesis of early literacy development and implications for intervention.* Washington, DC: National Institute for Literacy.

[52]See, e.g., IRA (International Reading Association) & NAEYC. 1998. *Learning to read and write: Developmentally appropriate practices for young children.* Joint position statement. Online: www.naeyc.org/dap; NAEYC & NAECS/SDE (National Association of Early Childhood Specialists in State Departments of Education). 2002. *Early learning standards: Creating the conditions for success.* Joint position statement. Online: www.naeyc.org/dap; Snow, C.E., M.S. Burns, & P. Griffin. 1998. *Preventing reading difficulties in young children.* Washington, DC: National Academies Press.

[53]NAEYC & NCTM (National Council of Teachers of Mathematics. 2004. *Early childhood mathematics: Promoting good beginnings.* Joint position statement. Online: www.naeyc.org/dap; Ginsburg, H.P., J.S. Lee, & J.S. Boyd. 2008. Mathematics education for young children: What it is and how to promote it. *Social Policy Report* 22 (1): 3–11, 14–22.

[54]Duncan, G.J., C.J. Dowsett, A. Claessens, K. Magnuson, A.C. Huston, P. Klebanov, L.S. Pagani, L. Feinstein, M. Engel, & J. Brooks-Gunn. 2007. School readiness and later achievement. *Developmental Psychology* 43 (6): 1428–46.

[55]Early, D.M., O. Barbarin, D. Bryant, M. Burchinal, F. Chang, R. Clifford, G. Crawford, et al. 2005. Pre-kindergarten in eleven states: NCEDL's multi-state study of pre-kindergarten and study of statewide early education programs (SWEEP): Preliminary descriptive report. New York: The Foundation for Child Development. Online: www.fcd-us. org/usr_doc/Prekindergartenin11States.pdf; Ginsburg, H.P., J.S. Lee, & J.S. Boyd. 2008. Mathematics education for young children: What it is and how to promote it. *Social Policy Report* 22 (1): 3–11, 14–22.

[56]Clements, D.H. 2004. Major themes and recommendations. In *Engaging young children in mathematics: Standards for early childhood mathematics education,* eds. D.H. Clements, J. Sarama, & A.M. DiBiase, 7–72. Mahwah, NJ: Lawrence Erlbaum; Ginsburg, H.P., J.S. Lee, & J.S. Boyd. 2008. Mathematics education for young children: What it is and how to promote it. *Social Policy Report* 22 (1): 3–11, 14–22.

[57]Roskos, K.A., J.F. Christie, & D.J. Richgels. 2003. The essentials of early literacy instruction. *Young Children* 58 (2): 52–60; Worth, K., & S. Grollman. 2003. *Worms, shadows and whirlpools: Science in the early childhood classroom.* Portsmouth, NH: Heinemann; Bennett-Armistead, V.S., N.K. Duke, & A.M. Moses. 2005. *Literacy and the youngest learner: Best practices for educators of children from birth to 5.* New York: Scholastic; Ginsburg, H.P., J.S. Lee, & J.S. Boyd. 2008. Mathematics education for young children: What it is and how to promote it. *Social Policy Report* 22 (1): 3–11, 14–22.

[58]See, e.g., Linares, L.O., N. Rosbruch, M.B. Stern, M.E. Edwards, G. Walker, H.B. Abikoff, & J.M.J Alvir. 2005. Developing cognitive-social-emotional competencies to enhance academic learning. *Psychology in the Schools* 42 (4): 405–17; Raver, C.C., P.W. Garner, & R. Smith-Donald. 2007. The roles of emotion regulation and emotion knowledge for children's academic readiness: Are the links causal? In *School readiness and the transition to kindergarten in the era of accountability,* eds. R.C. Pianta, M.J. Cox, & K.L. Snow, 121–48. Baltimore: Paul H. Brookes.

[59]McClelland, M.M., A.C. Acock, & F.J. Morrison. 2006. The impact of kindergarten learning-related skills on academic trajectories at the end of elementary school. *Early Childhood Research Quarterly* 21 (4): 471–90; McClelland, M., C. Cameron, C.M. Connor, C.L. Farris, A.M. Jewkes, & F.J. Morrison. 2007. Links between behavioral regulation and preschoolers' literacy, vocabulary, and math skills. *Developmental Psychology* 43 (4): 947–59; Snow, K.L. 2007. Integrative views of the domains of child function: Unifying school readiness. In *School readiness and the transition to kindergarten in the era of accountability,* eds. R.C. Pianta, M.J. Cox, & K.L. Snow, 197–214. Baltimore: Paul H. Brookes.

[60]See, e.g., Montessori, M. 1949. *The absorbent mind.* Madras: Theosophical Publishing House; Hymes, J.L. 1955/1995. *A child development point of view: A teacher's guide to action.* Rev. ed. West Greenwich, RI: Consortium Publishing; Bredekamp, S., ed. 1987. *Developmentally appropriate practice in early childhood programs serving children from birth through age 8.* Expanded edition. Washington, DC: NAEYC.

[61]DeLoache, J.S., & A.L. Brown. 1987. Differences in the memory-based searching of delayed and normally developing young children. *Intelligence* 11 (4): 277–89; Flavell, J.H. 1987. *Development of knowledge about the appearance-reality distinction.* Monographs of the Society for Research in Child Development, vol. 51, no. 1. Chicago: University of Chicago Press; Zimmerman, B.J., S. Bonner, & R. Kovach. 1996. *Developing self-regulated learners: Beyond achievement to self-efficacy.* Washington, DC: American Psychological Association; Ladd G.W., S.H. Birch, & E.S. Buhs. 1999. Children's social and scholastic lives in kindergarten: Related spheres of influence? *Child Development* 70 (6): 1373–400; McClelland, M.M., A.C. Acock, & F.J. Morrison. 2006. The impact of kindergarten learning-related skills on academic trajectories at the end of elementary school. *Early Childhood Research Quarterly* 21 (4): 471–90; Blair, C., H. Knipe, E. Cummings, D.P. Baker, D. Gamson, P. Eslinger, & S.L. Thorne. 2007. A developmental neuroscience approach to the study of school readiness. In *School readiness and the transition to kindergarten in the era of accountability,* eds. R.C. Pianta, M.J. Cox, & K.L. Snow, 149–74. Baltimore: Paul H. Brookes.

[62]Bodrova, E., & D.J. Leong. 2001. *The Tools of the Mind Project: A case study of implementing the Vygotskian approach in American early childhood and primary classrooms.* Geneva, Switzerland: International Bureau of Education, UNESCO; Bodrova, E., & D.J. Leong. 2003. Chopsticks and counting chips. *Young Children* 58 (3): 10–17; Diamond, A., W.S. Barnett, J. Thomas, & S. Munro. 2007. Preschool program improves cognitive control. *Science* 318 (5855): 1387–88.

[63]Rathbun, A., J. West, & E.G. Hausken. 2004. *From kindergarten through third grade: Children's beginning school experiences.* Washington, DC: National Center for Education Statistics.

[64]Bogard, K., & R. Takanishi. 2005. PK–3: An aligned and coordinated approach to education for children 3 to 8 years old. *Social Policy Report* 19 (3).

[65]See, e.g., Graves, B. 2006. PK–3: What is it and how do we know it works? *Foundation for Child Development Policy Brief, Advancing PK–3* 4; Sadowski, M. 2006. Core knowledge for PK–3 teaching: Ten components of effective instruction. *Foundation for Child Development Policy Brief, Advancing PK–3* 5; Ritchie, S., K. Maxwell, & R.M. Clifford. 2007. FirstSchool: A new vision for education. In *School readiness and the transition to kindergarten in the era of accountability,* eds. R.C. Pianta, M.J. Cox, & K.L. Snow, 85–96. Baltimore: Paul H. Brookes.

[66]Takanishi, R., & K.L. Bogard. 2007. Effective educational programs for young children: What we need to know. *Child Development Perspectives* 1: 40–45; Kauerz, K. Forthcoming. *P–3: What does it look like from a state policy perspective?* Denver, CO: Education Commission of the States.

[67]Katz, L.G., & S.C. Chard. 2000. *Engaging children's minds: The project approach.* 2d ed. Norwood, NJ: Ablex.

[68]AERA (American Education Research Association). 2003. Class size: Counting students can count. *Research Points: Essential Information for Education Policy* 1 (2). Online: www.aera.net/uploadedFiles/Journals_and_Publications/ Research_Points/RP_Fall03.pdf.

[69]See, e.g., Maeroff, G.I. 2006. *Building blocks: Making children successful in the early years of school.* New York: Palgrave Macmillan; Ritchie, S., K. Maxwell, & R.M. Clifford. 2007. FirstSchool: A new vision for education. In *School readiness and the transition to kindergarten in the era of accountability,* eds. R.C. Pianta, M.J. Cox, & K.L. Snow, 85–96. Baltimore: Paul H. Brookes.

[70]Takanishi, R., & K. Kauerz. 2008. PK inclusion: Getting serious about a P–16 education system. *Phi Delta Kappan* 89 (7): 480–87.

[71]Bowman, B.T., S. Donovan, & M.S. Burns. 2000. *Eager to learn: Educating our preschoolers.* Washington, DC: National Academies Press; Hamre, B.K., & R.C Pianta. 2007. Learning opportunities in preschool and early elementary classrooms. In *School readiness and the transition to kindergarten in the era of accountability,* eds. R.C. Pianta, M.J. Cox, & K.L. Snow, 49–83. Baltimore: Paul H. Brookes; Pianta, R.C. 2008. Neither art nor accident: A conversation with Robert Pianta. *Harvard Education Letter* (January/February). Online: www.edletter.org/insights/pianta.shtml.

[72]Hamre, B.K., & R.C Pianta. 2007. Learning opportunities in preschool and early elementary classrooms. In *School readiness and the transition to kindergarten in the era of accountability,* eds. R.C. Pianta, M.J. Cox, & K.L. Snow, 49–83. Baltimore: Paul H. Brookes.

[73]Horowitz, F.D., L. Darling-Hammond, J. Bransford., et al. 2005. Educating teachers for developmentally appropriate practice. In *Preparing teachers for a changing world: What teachers should learn and be able to do,* eds. L. Darling-Hammond & J. Bransford, 88–125. San Francisco: Jossey-Bass.

[74]Layzer, J.I., C.J. Layzer, B.D. Goodson, & C. Price. 2007. *Evaluation of child care subsidy strategies: Findings from Project Upgrade in Miami-Dade County.* Washington, DC: U.S. Department of Health and Human Services, Administration for Children and Families, Office of Planning, Research and Evaluation.

[75]Reeves, C., S. Emerick, & E. Hirsch. 2006. *Creating non-instructional time for elementary school teachers: Strategies from schools in North Carolina.* Hillsborough, NC: Center for Teaching Quality.

Principles of child development and learning that inform practice

[76]For fuller reviews, see, e.g., Snow, C.E., M.S. Burns, & P. Griffin. 1998. *Preventing reading difficulties in young children.* Washington, DC: National Academies Press; Bowman, B.T., S. Donovan, & M.S. Burns. 2000. *Eager to learn: Educating our preschoolers.* Washington, DC: National Academies Press; Bransford, J., A.L. Brown, & R.R. Cocking. 1999. *How people learn: Brain, mind, experience, and school.* Washington, DC: National Academies Press; Shonkoff, J.P., & D.A. Phillips, eds. 2000. *From neurons to neighborhoods: The science of early child development.* A report of the National Research Council. Washington, DC: National Academies Press; Kilpatrick, J., J. Swafford, & B. Findell, eds. 2001. *Adding it up: Helping children learn mathematics.* Washington, DC: National Academies Press; Renninger, K.A., & I.E. Sigel, eds. 2006. *Handbook of child psychology, Vol. 4: Child psychology in practice.* 6th ed. New York: John Wiley & Sons.

[77]Bransford, J., A.L. Brown, & R.R. Cocking. 1999. *How people learn: Brain, mind, experience, and school.* Washington, DC: National Academies Press; Shonkoff, J.P., & D.A. Phillips, eds. 2000. *From neurons to neighborhoods: The science of early child development.* A report of the National Research Council. Washington, DC: National Academy Press; ASCD (Association for Supervision and Curriculum Development). 2006. *The whole child in a fractured world.* Prepared by H. Hodgkinson. Alexandria, VA: Author. Online: www.ascd.org/ascd/pdf/fracturedworld.pdf.

[78]Shonkoff, J.P., & D.A. Phillips, eds. 2000. *From neurons to neighborhoods: The science of early child development.* A report of the National Research Council. Washington, DC: National Academies Press.

[79]Pellegrini, A.D., L. Galda, M. Bartini, & D. Charak. 1998. Oral language and literacy learning in context: The role of social relationships. *Merrill-Palmer Quarterly* 44 (1): 38–54; Dickinson, D.K., & P.O. Tabors. 2001. *Beginning literacy with language: Young children learning at home and school.* Baltimore: Paul H. Brookes.

[80]La Paro, K.M., & R.C. Pianta. 2000. Predicting children's competence in the early school years: A meta-analytic review. *Review of Educational Research* 70 (4): 443–84; Howes, C., & K. Sanders. 2006. Child care for young children. In *Handbook of research on the education of young children,* 2d ed., eds. B. Spodek & O.N. Saracho, 375–92. Mahwah, NJ: Lawrence Erlbaum; Raver, C.C., P.W. Garner, & R. Smith-Donald. 2007. The roles of emotion regulation and emotion knowledge for children's academic readiness: Are the links causal? In *School readiness and the transition to kindergarten in the era of accountability,* eds. R.C. Pianta, M.J. Cox, & K.L. Snow, 121–48. Baltimore: Paul H. Brookes; Snow, K.L. 2007. Integrative views of the domains of child function: Unifying school readiness. In *School readiness and the transition to kindergarten in the era of accountability,* eds. R.C. Pianta, M.J. Cox, & K.L. Snow, 197–214. Baltimore: Paul H. Brookes; Pianta, R.C., K.M. La Paro, & B.K. Hamre. 2008. *Classroom assessment scoring system (CLASS).* Baltimore: Paul H. Brookes.

[81]See, e.g., Erikson, E. 1963. *Childhood and society.* New York: Norton; Sameroff, A.J., & M.M. Haith. 1996. *The five to seven year shift: The age of reason and responsibility.* Chicago: University of Chicago Press; Bransford, J., A.L. Brown, & R.R. Cocking. 1999. *How people learn: Brain, mind, experience, and school.* Washington, DC: National Academies Press; Shonkoff, J.P., & D.A. Phillips, eds. 2000. *From neurons to neighborhoods: The science of early child development.* A report of the National Research Council. Washington, DC: National Academies Press.

[82]Lynch, E., & M. Hanson. 2004. *Developing cross-cultural competence: A guide for working with children and their families.* 3d ed. Baltimore: Paul H. Brookes.

[83]Wang, M.C., L.B. Resnick, & R.F. Boozer. 1970. *The sequence of development of some early mathematics behaviors.* Pittsburgh, PA: University of Pittsburgh, Learning Research and Development Center; Clements, D.H., J. Sarama, & A.M. DiBiase. 2004. *Engaging young children in mathematics: Standards for early childhood mathematics education.* Mahwah, NJ: Lawrence Erlbaum.

[84]Scarr, S., & K. McCartney. 1983. How people make their own environments: A theory of genotype—environment effects. *Child Development* 54 (2): 425–35; Plomin, R. 1994.

Genetics and experience: The interplay between nature and nurture. Thousand Oaks, CA: Sage Publications; Plomin, R. 1994b. Nature, nurture, and social development. *Social Development* 3: 37–53; Shonkoff, J.P., & D.A. Phillips, eds. 2000. *From neurons to neighborhoods: The science of early child development.* A report of the National Research Council. Washington, DC: National Academies Press.

[85]Asher, S., S. Hymel, & P. Renshaw. 1984. Loneliness in children. *Child Development* 55 (4): 1456–64; Parker, J.G., & S.R. Asher. 1987. Peer relations and later personal adjustment: Are low-accepted children at risk? *Psychology Bulletin* 102 (3): 357–89.

[86]Snow, C.E., M.S. Burns, & P. Griffin. 1998. *Preventing reading difficulties in young children.* Washington, DC: National Academies Press.

[87]Kuhl, P. 1994. Learning and representation in speech and language. *Current Opinion in Neurobiology* 4: 812–22.

[88]Nelson, C.A., & M. Luciana, eds. 2001. *Handbook of developmental cognitive neuroscience.* Cambridge, MA: MIT Press; Ornstein, P.A., C.A. Haden, & A.M. Hedrick. 2004. Learning to remember: Social-communicative exchanges and the development of children's memory skills. *Developmental Review* 24: 374–95.

[89]Seo, K.H., & H.P. Ginsburg. 2004. What is developmentally appropriate in early childhood mathematics education? Lessons from new research. In *Engaging young children in mathematics: Standards for early childhood mathematics education,* eds. D.H. Clements, J. Sarama, & A.M. DiBiase, 91–104. Hillsdale, NJ: Lawrence Erlbaum; Gelman, R., & C.R. Gallistel. 1986. *The child's understanding of number.* Cambridge, MA: Harvard University Press.

[90]Thompson, R.A. 1994. *Emotion regulation: A theme in search of a definition.* Monographs of the Society for Research in Child Development, vol. 59, nos. 2–3. Chicago: University of Chicago Press.

[91]Bodrova, E., & D.J. Leong. 2005. Self-regulation: A foundation for early learning. *Principal* 85 (1): 30–35; Diamond, A., W.S. Barnett, J. Thomas, & S. Munro. 2007. Preschool program improves cognitive control. *Science* 318 (5855): 1387–88.

[92]Kendall, S. 1992. *The development of autonomy in children: An examination of the Montessori educational model.* Doctoral dissertation. Minneapolis, MN: Walden University; Palfrey, J., M.B. Bronson, M. Erickson-Warfield, P. Hauser-Cram, & S.R. Sirin. 2002. *BEEPers come of age: The Brookline Early Education Project follow-up study.* Final Report to the Robert Wood Johnson Foundation. Chestnut Hill, MA: Boston College.

[93]Bruner, J.S. 1983. *Child's talk: Learning to use language.* New York: Norton.

[94]Piaget, J. 1952. *The origins of intelligence in children.* New York: International Universities Press; Piaget, J. 1962. *Play, dreams and imitation in childhood.* New York: Norton; Uzgiris, I.C., & J.M. Hunt. 1975. *Assessment in infancy: Ordinal scales of psychological development.* Urbana, IL: University of Illinois Press.

[95]Fein, G. 1981. Pretend play in childhood: An integrative review. *Child Development* 52 (4): 1095–118; Fenson, L., P.S. Dale, J.S. Reznick, E. Bates, D.J. Thal, & S.J. Pethick. 1994. *Variability in early communicative development.* Monographs of the Society for Research in Child

Development, vol. 59, no. 5. Chicago: University of Chicago Press.

[96]Copple, C., I.E. Sigel, & R. Saunders. 1984. *Educating the young thinker: Classroom strategies for cognitive growth.* Hillsdale, NJ: Lawrence Erlbaum; Edwards, C.P., L. Gandini, & G. Forman, eds. 1998. *The hundred languages of children: The Reggio Emilia approach—Advanced reflections.* 2d. ed. Greenwich, NJ: Ablex; Epstein, A.S. 2007. *The intentional teacher: Choosing the best strategies for young children's learning.* Washington, DC: NAEYC.

[97]See, e.g., Dunn, J. 1993. *Young children's close relationships: Beyond attachment.* Newbury Park, CA: Sage Publications; Denham, S.A. 1998. *Emotional development in young children.* New York: Guilford; Shonkoff, J.P., & D.A. Phillips, eds. 2000. *From neurons to neighborhoods: The science of early child development.* A report of the National Research Council. Washington, DC: National Academies Press.

[98]Fein, G., A. Gariboldi, & R. Boni. 1993. The adjustment of infants and toddlers to group care: The first 6 months. *Early Childhood Research Quarterly* 8: 1–14; Honig, A.S. 2002. *Secure relationships: Nurturing infant/toddler attachment in early care settings.* Washington, DC: NAEYC.

[99]Bowlby, J. 1969. *Attachment and loss, Vol. 1: Attachment.* New York: Basic; Stern, D. 1985. *The psychological world of the human infant.* New York: Basic; Garbarino, J., N. Dubrow, K. Kostelny, & C. Pardo. 1992. *Children in danger: Coping with the consequences of community violence.* San Francisco: Jossey-Bass; Bretherton, I., & K.A. Munholland. 1999. Internal working models in attachment relationships: A construct revisited. In *Handbook of attachment theory, research, and clinical applications,* eds. J. Cassidy & P.R. Shaver, 89–114. New York: Guilford.

[100]Pianta, R.C. 1999. *Enhancing relationships between children and teachers.* Washington, DC: American Psychological Association; Howes, C., & S. Ritchie. 2002. *A matter of trust: Connecting teachers and learners in the early childhood classroom.* New York: Teachers College Press.

[101]Shonkoff, J.P., & D.A. Phillips, eds. 2000. *From neurons to neighborhoods: The science of early child development.* A report of the National Research Council. Washington, DC: National Academies Press.

[102]Bronfenbrenner, U. 1979. *The ecology of human development: Experiments by nature and design.* Cambridge, MA: Harvard University Press; Bronfenbrenner, U. 1989. Ecological systems theory. In *Annals of child development, Vol. 6,* ed. R. Vasta, 187–251. Greenwich, CT: JAI Press; Bronfenbrenner, U. 1993. The ecology of cognitive development: Research models and fugitive findings. In *Development in context: Acting and thinking in specific environments,* eds. R.H. Wozniak & K.W. Fischer, 3–44. Hillsdale, NJ: Lawrence Erlbaum; Bronfenbrenner, U., & P.A. Morris. 2006. The bioecological model of human development. In *Handbook of child psychology, Vol. 1: Theoretical models of human development,* 6th ed., eds. R.M. Lerner & W. Damon, 793–828. Hoboken, NJ: John Wiley & Sons.

[103]Tobin, J., D. Wu, & D. Davidson. 1989. *Preschool in three cultures: Japan, China, and United States.* New Haven, CT: Yale University Press; Rogoff, B. 2003. *The cultural nature of human development.* Oxford: Oxford University Press.

[104]Bowman, B.T., & F. Stott. 1994. Understanding development in a cultural context: The challenge for teachers.

In *Diversity and developmentally appropriate practices: Challenges for early childhood education*, eds. B. Mallary & R. New, 119–34. New York: Teachers College Press.

[105]Gonzales-Mena, J. 2008. *Diversity in early care and education: Honoring differences*. 5th ed. Boston: McGraw-Hill; Tabors, P.O. 2008. *One child, two languages: A guide for early childhood educators of children learning English as a second language*. 2d ed. Baltimore: Paul H. Brookes.

[106]Hakuta, K., & E.E. Garcia. 1989. Bilingualism and education. *American Psychologist* 44 (2): 374–79; Krashen, S.D. 1992. *Fundamentals of language education*. Torrance, CA: Laredo Publishing.

[107]Dewey, J. 1916. *Democracy and education: An introduction to the philosophy of education*. New York: Macmillan; Piaget, J. 1952. *The origins of intelligence in children*. New York: International Universities Press; Vygotsky, L. 1978. *Mind in society: The development of higher psychological processes*. Cambridge, MA: Harvard University Press; Fosnot, C.T., ed. 1996. *Constructivism: Theory, perspectives, and practice*. New York: Teachers College Press; Malaguzzi, L. 1998. History, ideas, and basic philosophy. In *The hundred languages of children: The Reggio Emilia approach—Advanced reflections*, 2d ed., eds. C. Edwards, L. Gandini, & G. Forman, 49–97. Greenwich, NJ: Ablex.

[108]Gelman, R., & C.R. Gallistel. 1986. *The child's understanding of number*. Cambridge, MA: Harvard University Press; Seo, K.H., & H.P. Ginsburg. 2004. What is developmentally appropriate in early childhood mathematics education? Lessons from new research. In *Engaging young children in mathematics: Standards for early childhood mathematics education*, eds. D.H. Clements, J. Sarama, & A.M. DiBiase, 91–104. Hillsdale, NJ: Lawrence Erlbaum.

[109]Bransford, J., A.L. Brown, & R.R. Cocking. 1999. *How people learn: Brain, mind, experience, and school*. Washington, DC: National Academies Press.

[110]Bowman, B.T., S. Donovan, & M.S. Burns. 2000. *Eager to learn: Educating our preschoolers*. Washington, DC: National Academies Press. 8.

[111]Sandall, S., M.L. Hemmeter, B.J. Smith, & M.E. McLean, eds. 2005. *DEC recommended practices: A comprehensive guide for practical application in early intervention/early childhood special education*. Longmont, CO: Sopris West, and Missoula, MT: Division for Early Childhood, Council for Exceptional Children.

[112]Davidson, J.I.F. 1998. Language and play: Natural partners. In *Play from birth to twelve and beyond: Contexts, perspectives, and meanings*, eds. D.P. Fromberg & D. Bergen, 175–83. New York: Garland; Bronson, M.B. 2000. *Self-regulation in early childhood: Nature and nurture*. New York: Guilford; Elias, C., & L.E. Berk. 2002. Self-regulation in young children: Is there a role for sociodramatic play? *Early Childhood Research Quarterly* 17 (1): 216–38; Clawson, M. 2002. Play of language: Minority children in an early childhood setting. In *Play and culture studies, Vol. 4: Conceptual, social-cognitive, and contextual issues in the fields of play*, ed. J.L. Roopnarine, 93–110. Westport, CT: Ablex. Fantuzzo, J., & C. McWayne. 2002. The relationship between peer-play interactions in the family context and dimensions of school readiness for low-income preschool children. *Journal of Educational Psychology* 94 (1): 79–87; Duncan, R.M., & D. Tarulli. 2003. Play as the leading activity

of the preschool period: Insights from Vygotsky, Leont'ev, and Bakhtin. *Early Education and Development* 14: 271–92; Lindsey, E.W., & M.J. Colwell. 2003. Preschoolers' emotional competence: Links to pretend and physical play. *Child Study Journal* 33 (1): 39–52; Zigler, E.F., D.G. Singer, & S.J. Bishop-Josef, eds. 2004. *Children's play: The roots of reading*. Washington, DC: Zero to Three; Johnson, J.E., J.F. Christie, & F. Wardle. 2005. *Play, development, and early education*. Boston: Pearson; Diamond, A., W.S. Barnett, J. Thomas, & S. Munro. 2007. Preschool program improves cognitive control. *Science* 318 (5855): 1387–88; Hirsh-Pasek, K., R.M. Golinkoff, L.E. Berk, & D.G. Singer. 2009. *A mandate for playful learning in preschool: Presenting the evidence*. New York: Oxford University Press.

[113]Fein, G. 1981. Pretend play in childhood: An integrative review. *Child Development* 52 (4): 1095–118.

[114]Vygotsky, L. 1966/1977. Play and its role in the mental development of the child. In *Soviet developmental psychology*, ed. M. Cole, 76–99. Armonk, NY: M.E. Sharpe; Bronson, M.B. 2000. *Self-regulation in early childhood: Nature and nurture*. New York: Guilford; Elias, C., & L.E. Berk. 2002. Self-regulation in young children: Is there a role for sociodramatic play? *Early Childhood Research Quarterly* 17 (1): 216–38.

[115]Isenberg, J.P., & N. Quisenberry. 2002. Play: Essential for all children. A position paper of the Association for Childhood Education International. *Childhood Education* 79 (1): 33–39; Fromberg, D.P., & D. Bergen, eds. 2006. *Play from birth to twelve: Contexts, perspectives, and meanings*. 2d ed. New York: Routledge; Diamond, A., W.S. Barnett, J. Thomas, & S. Munro. 2007. Preschool program improves cognitive control. *Science* 318 (5855): 1387–88.

[116]Golinkoff, R.M., K. Hirsh-Pasek, & D.G. Singer. 2006. Why play = learning: A challenge for parents and educators. In *Play = learning: How play motivates and enhances children's cognitive and social-emotional growth*, eds. D. Singer, R.M. Golinkoff, & K. Hirsh-Pasek, 3–12. New York: Oxford University Press; Chudacoff, H.P. 2007. *Children at play: An American history*. New York: New York University Press.

[117]Smilansky, S., & L. Shefatya. 1990. *Facilitating play: A medium for promoting cognitive, socioemotional, and academic development in young children*. Gaithersburg, MD: Psychosocial & Educational Publications; DeVries, R., B. Zan, & C. Hildebrandt. 2002. Group games. In *Developing constructivist early childhood curriculum: Practical principles and activities*, eds. R. DeVries, B. Zan, C. Hildebrandt, R. Edmiaston, & C. Sales, 181–91. New York: Teachers College Press; Bodrova, E., & D.J. Leong. 2007. *Tools of the mind: The Vygotskian approach to early childhood education*. 2d ed. Upper Saddle River, NJ: Pearson/Merrill Prentice Hall.

[118]Bodrova, E., & D.J. Leong. 2001. *The Tools of the Mind Project: A case study of implementing the Vygotskian approach in American early childhood and primary classrooms*. Geneva, Switzerland: International Bureau of Education, UNESCO; Zigler, E.F., D.G. Singer, & S.J. Bishop-Josef, eds. 2004. *Children's play: The roots of reading*. Washington, DC: Zero to Three.

[119]White, S.H. 1965. Evidence for a hierarchical arrangement of learning processes. In *Advances in child development and behavior*, eds. L.P. Lipsitt & C.C. Spiker, 187–220. New York: Academic Press; Vygotsky, L. 1978. *Mind in soci-*

ety: *The development of higher psychological processes.* Cambridge, MA: Harvard University Press.

[120]Bodrova E., & D.J. Leong. 2006. Vygotskian perspectives on teaching and learning early literacy. In *Handbook of early literacy research, Vol. 2,* eds. D.K. Dickinson & S.B. Neuman, 243–56. New York: Guilford; Berk, L.E., & A. Winsler. 2009, in press. *Scaffolding children's learning: Vygotsky and early childhood education.* Rev. ed. Washington, DC: NAEYC.

[121]Wood, D., J. Bruner, & G. Ross. 1976. The role of tutoring in problem solving. *Journal of Child Psychology and Psychiatry and Allied Disciplines* 17: 89–100.

[122]Vygotsky, L. 1978. *Mind in society: The development of higher psychological processes.* Cambridge, MA: Harvard University Press; Bodrova E., & D.J. Leong. 2006. Vygotskian perspectives on teaching and learning early literacy. In *Handbook of early literacy research, Vol. 2,* eds. D.K. Dickinson & S.B. Neuman, 243–56. New York: Guilford; Berk, L.E., & A. Winsler. 2009, in press. *Scaffolding children's learning: Vygotsky and early childhood education.* Rev. ed. Washington, DC: NAEYC.

[123]Sanders, S.W. 2006. Physical education in kindergarten. In *K today: Teaching and learning in the kindergarten year,* ed. D.F. Gullo, 127–37. Washington, DC: NAEYC; Lary, R.T. 1990. Successful students. *Education Issues* 3 (2): 11–17; Brophy, J. 1992. Probing the subtleties of subject matter teaching. *Educational Leadership* 49 (7): 4–8.

[124]Garner, B.P., & D. Bergen. 2006. Play development from birth to age four. In *Play from birth to twelve: Contexts, perspectives, and meaning,* 2d ed., eds. D.P. Fromberg & D. Bergen, 3–12. New York: Routledge; Johnson, J.E. 2006. Play development from ages four to eight. In *Play from birth to twelve: Contexts, perspectives, and meaning,* 2d ed., eds. D.P. Fromberg & D. Bergen, 13–20. New York: Routledge.

[125]Kagan, S.L., E. Moore, & S. Bredekamp, eds. 1995. *Reconsidering children's early learning and development: Toward common views and vocabulary.* Report of the National Education Goals Panel, Goal 1 Technical Planning Group. ERIC, ED391576. Washington, DC: U.S. Government Printing Office; NEGP (National Education Goals Panel). 1997. *The National Education Goals report: Building a nation of learners.* Washington, DC: U.S. Government Printing Office.

[126]Hyson, M. 2008. *Enthusiastic and engaged learners: Approaches to learning in the early childhood classroom.* New York: Teachers College Press.

[127]NCES (National Center for Education Statistics). 2002. *Children's reading and mathematics achievement in kindergarten and first grade.* Washington, DC: Author. Online: nces.ed.gov/pubs2002/kindergarten/24.asp?nav=4.

[128]Fantuzzo, J., M.A. Perry, & P. McDermott. 2004. Preschool approaches to learning and their relationship to other relevant classroom competencies for low-income children. *School Psychology Quarterly* 19 (3): 212–30.

[129]McClelland, M.M., A.C. Acock, & F.J. Morrison. 2006. The impact of kindergarten learning-related skills on academic trajectories at the end of elementary school. *Early Childhood Research Quarterly* 21 (4): 471–90.

[130]Frank Porter Graham Child Development Center. 2001. *The quality and engagement study. Final report.* R.A. McWilliam, principal investigator. Chapel Hill, NC: Author; Stipek, D. 2002. *Motivation to learn: Integrating theory and practice.* 4th ed. Boston: Allyn & Bacon; Rimm-Kaufman, S.E., K.M. La Paro, J.T. Downer, & R.C. Pianta. 2005. The contribution of classroom setting and quality of instruction to children's behavior in kindergarten classrooms. *Elementary School Journal* 105 (4): 377–94; Hyson, M. 2008. *Enthusiastic and engaged learners: Approaches to learning in the early childhood classroom.* New York: Teachers College Press.

Guidelines for developmentally appropriate practice

[131]Epstein, A.S. 2007. *The intentional teacher: Choosing the best strategies for young children's learning.* Washington, DC: NAEYC. 3.

[132]For a more complete discussion of principles and indicators of appropriate curriculum and assessment, see NAEYC & NAECS/SDE (National Association of Early Childhood Specialists in State Departments of Education). 2003. *Early childhood curriculum, assessment, and program evaluation: Building an effective, accountable system in programs for children birth through age 8.* Joint position statement. Online: www.naeyc.org/dap.

To Be an Excellent Teacher

Carol Copple and Sue Bredekamp

Developmentally appropriate practice is at the core of being an excellent early childhood professional—that is the central premise of this book. Developmentally appropriate practice is grounded in the research on child development and learning and in the knowledge base regarding educational effectiveness. From this knowledge base, we know a great deal about how children develop and learn at various ages and what approaches and conditions tend to work best for them.

This knowledge is the starting place for teachers in the many decisions they make—the long-term ones as well as the minute-by-minute ones: how to organize the environment to help children do their best, how to plan curriculum that engages children and helps them reach important goals, how to adapt teaching strategies for the group and for individual children—the list goes on and on. But to the question "Is this decision developmentally appropriate?" the response always begins with two words: "It depends." That is, whether a given teaching practice or policy is developmentally appropriate depends: for which child or children? . . . for which families? . . . in what context? . . . for what purpose?

This chapter describes what excellent teachers decide to do in their classrooms to translate the developmentally appropriate practice framework, outlined in the position statement, into high-quality experiences for children, birth to age 8.

To be an excellent teacher means . . .
being intentional

Whenever you see a great classroom, one in which children are learning and thriving, you can be sure that the teachers (and the administrators who support them) are highly intentional. In everything that good teachers do—

creating the environment, considering the curriculum and tailoring it to the children as individuals, planning learning experiences, and interacting with children and families—they are purposeful and thoughtful. As they make myriad decisions, big and small, they keep in mind the outcomes they seek. Even in responding to unexpected opportunities—"teachable moments"—intentional teachers are guided by the outcomes the program is trying to help children reach and by their knowledge of child development and learning.

Having a clear sense of how all aspects of the program relate to and promote the desired goals contributes to an intentional teacher's effectiveness. Learning goals are usually identified for groups of children within a given age span. But teachers must determine where each child is in relation to a goal and adjust their teaching accordingly. For example, some children from poverty backgrounds are behind what is typical for other children in their age group in such areas as vocabulary, math and literacy learning, and self-regulation. For these children, excellent teachers, schools, and programs provide more extended, enriched, and intensive learning opportunities—such as more small-group activities and one-on-one interaction—to accelerate their learning and help them to catch up.

Similarly, in serving children with disabilities and other special needs, teachers' attention to individual variation is essential. In addition to age-appropriate goals, an individualized plan for such a child will identify individually appropriate goals, which teachers implement in conjunction with families and specialists. In many cases, the plan necessitates more systematic, intentional teaching for the child to function and learn well in an inclusive setting.

Having their objectives and plans in mind, intentional teachers are well prepared to tell others—parents, administrators, colleagues—about what they are doing. Not only do they know what to do, they also know *why* they are doing it and can describe their purposes.

Excellence in all areas of practice

Excellent teachers are intentional in *all* aspects of their role. The position statement identifies these areas as: creating a caring community of learners, teaching to enhance development and learning, planning curriculum to achieve important goals, assessing children's development and learning, and establishing reciprocal relationships with families.

The various facets of the teacher's role are blended into a whole, which is illustrated here as a five-pointed star. Each point of the star represents one vital part of what teachers and early childhood programs must do to promote children's learning and development and enable them to reach important goals. Clearly, these five facets are closely interrelated, and none can be left out or shortchanged without seriously weakening the whole.

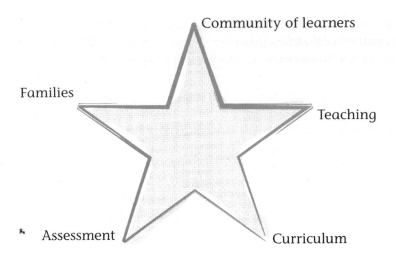

To be an excellent teacher means . . .
creating a caring community of learners

Children learn and develop best when they are part of a community of learners—a community in which all participants consider and contribute to one another's well-being and learning. To create such a classroom community, good teachers make a point of getting to know every child and family well. They make the effort to learn about each child's personality, abilities, interests, and ways of learning, and they work to build a strong sense of group identity among the children in the group.

Toward this end, teachers plan ways for children to work and play together collaboratively, and they work to bring each child's home culture and language into the shared culture of the class. They make a point of including children with special needs in all aspects of the program, so that not only do these children benefit but *all* the children in the group gain an understanding of how all people are similar and different. Inclusion of children with disabilities and other special needs means more than their simply being present in the classroom; it means, rather, they are active participants as part of the classroom community.

The excellent teacher makes it a priority to develop a warm, positive relationship with each child. This relationship is vital to young children's learning and development in all areas, and it makes effective, positive guidance possible. In the early childhood years, guidance should not be just something teachers do so they can get on with the curriculum. Instead, children's self-regulation and social and emotional competence are essential curricular goals in their own right. These capabilities do in fact help children to learn and succeed in school (McClelland, Acock, & Morrison 2006; Hyson 2008). Equally important, they have great intrinsic value for children's present and future lives.

Guidance is effective when teachers help children learn how to make better decisions the next time. Excellent early childhood teachers recognize children's conflicts and "misbehavior" as learning opportunities. Hence, they listen carefully to what children say, model problem solving, and give patient

reminders of rules (and reasons for them)—this, too, is effective guidance. A caring community of learners provides young children with a foundation that they will carry with them into their future lives in and out of school.

To be an excellent teacher means . . .
teaching to enhance development and learning

Good teachers continually use their knowledge and judgment to make intentional decisions about which materials, interactions, and learning experiences are likely to be most effective for the group and for each individual child in it. Many different teaching approaches and strategies have value in the early childhood classroom.

Excellent teachers use a wide range of teaching strategies

An effective teacher makes use of the strategy that fits a particular situation and the purpose or purposes she has in mind. She considers what the child or children already know and can do and the learning goals for the specific situation. Often she may try one strategy, see that it doesn't work, and then try something else. She has a variety of strategies at the ready and remains flexible and observant so that she can determine which to use. Here are some of the strategies excellent teachers have at their disposal:

- Teachers **acknowledge** what children do or say. They let children know that they have noticed by giving children positive attention, sometimes through comments, sometimes through just sitting nearby and observing (*"Thanks for your help, Kavi," "Brian, you found another way to show 5"*).

- Teachers **encourage** persistence and effort rather than just praising and evaluating what the child has done (*"You're thinking of lots of words to describe the dog in the story—let's keep going!"*).

- Teachers **give specific feedback** rather than general comments (*"The beanbag didn't get all the way to the hoop, James, so you might try throwing it harder"*).

- Teachers **model** attitudes, ways of approaching problems, and behavior toward others, showing children rather than just telling them (*"Hmm, that didn't work and I need to think about why," "I'm sorry, Ben, I missed part of what you said. Please tell me again"*).

- Teachers **demonstrate** when they show the correct way to do something. This usually applies to a procedure that needs to be done in a certain way (e.g., using a wire whisk, writing the letter P).

- Teachers **create or add challenge** so that a task goes a bit beyond what the children can already do. (For example, when the teacher removes several chips from a set, asks how many are left, and finds the children can count the remaining chips accurately, he may then add difficulty by *hiding* the remaining chips. Figuring out how many are left just from knowing the number that were removed is more challenging.) In other cases, teachers **reduce challenge** to meet children where they are (e.g., by simplifying the task).

- Teachers **ask questions** that provoke children's thinking (*"If you couldn't talk to your partner, how else could you let him know what to do?"*).

- Teachers **give assistance** (e.g., a cue or hint) to help children work on the edge of their current competence (*"Can you think of a word that rhymes with your name, Matt? How about* bat . . . Matt/bat? *What else rhymes with* Matt *and* bat?").

- Teachers **provide information**, directly giving children facts, verbal labels, and other information (*"This one that looks like a big mouse with a short tail is called a vole"*).

- Teachers **give directions** for children's action or behavior (*"Touch each block only once as you count them," "You want to move that icon over here? Okay, click on it and keep holding down, then drag the icon to wherever you want"*).

Some of these strategies involve less action and direction on the part of the adult and more on the part of the child; in others, the adult is more proactive or directive. Both kinds of strategies may be used in any context. The classroom example below illustrates how a teacher makes use of various strategies, first to extend children's play and then following up on their play interests to promote literacy learning.

Marica teaches 4-year-olds in a Head Start program. Early in the year, she observes that although the children like to play in the house area, they do little more than pile the dishes on the table, dump them in the sink, or open and close cupboards. Their play lacks focus and conversation, and it often breaks down into arguments. She wants to introduce other possibilities and help the children learn to play at a higher level.

One day when Ashley, Elizabeth, and Josue are in the house area, Marica joins their play. Choosing a theme that she knows these three children have experienced—birthdays—she enters the area and **models** the role of the birthday person. "Hi, I'm planning to have a party for my birthday. Can you help me?" When she **asks a question**, "What will we need for my party?" the children respond, "A cake!" "We'll need balloons!" "Presents!"

Marica brings the shopping cart over and the children seize on it, pushing it around the room and pretending to find various party items. Marica steps back while the children are immersed in playing that they are shopping. When this winds down, she asks, "Whom shall we invite to the party?" The children start shouting out names, and Marica says, "I can't remember all those names. We need to make a list." She **creates a challenge**—one she knows will vary for each individual child—by asking, "Who can write their name on the list?"

Paper for the list is found, and the children begin to take turns "writing" their name or the name of a friend. For Elizabeth, Marica **gives assistance** in the form of a name card the child can copy. For Ashley, she **demonstrates** how to make the first letter of her name. For Josue, who can write at least some letters of his name on his own, she **adds more challenge.** "What comes after your J?" she asks Josue. "What letter do you think your friend Dariska's name starts with?" As the children write, Marica **acknowledges** and **encourages** their efforts. "You made an N, like in your last name, Nuncio," she tells Josue. "I know you've been practicing writing that

letter every day." When she sees that two children are ready to go further with the spelling of their names, Marica **provides information,** telling them what the next letter in each name is and how it is made.

Although play is inherently an open-ended and child-guided activity, the teacher may directly provide information, create challenges, supply vocabulary, and otherwise enhance what children gain in the play setting. Likewise, in a planned small or large group, the teacher may ask questions and use other techniques to engage the children in problem solving or generating ideas.

All these strategies are also effective in teaching children with disabilities and other special needs. However, teachers may use more systematic instruction to help children acquire a skill or change an unacceptable behavior. For example, when working with children with challenging behaviors, an effective strategy is for teachers to identify the conditions that tend to propel the behavior and the consequences that usually follow. Then, teachers can anticipate and work to prevent problem behavior, as well as make sure that the negative behavior does not achieve its goal—as when hitting makes another child give up a toy. At the same time, teachers can "catch them doing something right," giving such children positive attention and encouragement for desired behaviors when they occur.

Excellent teachers scaffold children's learning

Developmentally appropriate goals are *both* challenging *and* achievable. The most effective learning experiences build on what children already know and can do, but also encourage them to stretch a reasonable amount toward a new level of achievement.

Of course, learners cannot spend all their time "on their tiptoes." They also need plenty of opportunity to practice the skills they have just begun acquiring. They need to feel solid mastery and a sense of being successful, of the goal having been achieved, rather than always feeling rushed on to the next challenge. Young children will often practice newly acquired or developing skills during their play, as when a toddler repeatedly fills and dumps a bucket of toys, or when a preschooler

© Ellen B. Senisi

continually counts every peg or every block in a tall tower. Once children have mastered a new skill or concept, they are ready for the next stretch.

As a child begins a new challenge, he may need some support from the teacher to enable him to manage it. A skilled teacher doesn't overdo the help. The aim is to provide the least amount of support that the child needs to do something he cannot quite do on his own. For example, if the goal is to walk a balance beam, the teacher might stand beside the child as he walks the beam, so that he can put his hand on the adult's arm as needed to keep from falling. If, instead, the teacher held the boy's hand throughout, whether he was unsteady or not, he would be less likely to learn to balance on his own.

As the child begins to acquire the new skill or understanding, the teacher gradually reduces her support. Soon the child who has been receiving assistance will be able to handle the skill or task independently. Because the teacher provides support only as long as it is needed, what she does is called *scaffolding*—like the platforms painters stand on to reach spots high up on a house they couldn't otherwise reach and then take away when the job is done. For example, for a child who is usually rejected by the other children, a teacher may at first directly coach her in how to successfully enter play ("*Try saying, 'I could be the customer in your grocery store'* "). If the child's overtures are successful, her new behavior is encouraged by the other children's responses, and the teacher can withdraw.

Excellent teachers use scaffolding to help children progress in all areas of learning and development throughout the day. And their scaffolding can take many forms. They might ask a question, point out a discrepancy, give a hint about an aspect of the problem or task that the child has missed, add a cue or support such as a picture or diagram, take the child's hand, or pair the child with a peer so that the two can be successful with their combined strengths.

Excellent teachers make purposeful use of various learning formats

Besides choosing from a repertoire of teaching strategies and scaffolding children's learning, effective teachers are also intentional in using different learning venues or formats for different purposes. In most early childhood settings (for children 3 years of age and older), at least four learning formats occur: large groups, small groups, play/learning centers, and daily routines.

Large groups (whole group, class meeting, or circle time). One function of whole-group time is sharing experiences—singing together, welcoming a new classmate, contributing ideas for naming the class hamster, and the like. Further, large-group time gives children opportunities to practice skills such as talking to a group, listening to their classmates, responding appropriately with questions or comments, working cooperatively, and using and processing new information. These skills and times are increasingly important in the primary grades, and whole-group time is a great venue for young children to begin learning them. To a greater extent than is the case in preschool, kindergarten and primary teachers are able to make effective use of large-group time to introduce a concept or skill and then have children take it further, apply the new knowledge, or practice a new skill individually and in small groups.

As for the recommended duration of large-group meetings, there is no hard-and-fast rule. The most important principle is to be alert to the children's cues and not keep going after they start to lose interest. If the children are getting restless, they usually are not benefiting from the large-group activity at hand. Changing to a movement activity or transitioning to small groups or centers will finish the large-group time on a high note.

Small groups. Working with three to six children in a group enables teachers to offer more focused experiences, perhaps introducing a new skill or concept, engaging children in solving a problem, or applying a concept already introduced. In a small-group setting, the teacher can give each child more attention and can provide support and challenges tailored to children's individual levels. He can give support, ask follow-up questions, and notice what every child is able to do and where each has difficulty. Giving children opportunities to engage in conversations with peers and solve problems collaboratively is another major benefit of the small-group experience. Small-group interactive book reading, for example, has been found to be very effective in promoting vocabulary learning among children from low-income families and children who are English language learners.

In preschool, small groups tend to take place during the part of the day devoted to learning centers. In a two-teacher classroom, some children might work in a small group with one of the adults while the other children are engaged in the centers, where the second adult monitors and supports their activities. In the primary grades, teachers might work with children in a small group while the others write in journals or read silently or in pairs.

Play/learning centers. In preschool and kindergarten (and to some extent, in first and second grade), part of the classroom is often divided into learning centers, or interest areas, that offer children a range of options for engagement. Teachers establish centers for blocks, dramatic play, art, and books. There are also places—sometimes set up as separate centers, sometimes not—where children can find math manipulatives and games, science materials (which may include a sand and/or water area), writing supplies, and a computer or two.

Vital to young children's learning and development is having significant periods of time in which they choose what they want to do and, together with other children, direct their own activities. Such times, which include outdoor play as well as "choice time" in the classroom interest areas, require a degree of teacher support and involvement to be of optimal value to children. Teachers' thoughtful planning of the materials and activities to support educational goals in each center is essential. And observing children during this time guides teachers in their on-the-spot interactions with children and in their subsequent planning. As children involve themselves in the various activities, the teacher talks with them, gives them information or feedback, and extends their thinking and engagement. Children largely direct their play along the lines of their ideas and interests, with teachers getting involved at times to provide support and interact with them.

Routines of the day. Many valuable learning opportunities occur in daily routines such as arrival and departure, cleanup, hand washing, meals and

© Rich Graessle

snacks, and transitions. For infants and toddlers, there are also diapering, feeding, napping, and dressing. In all these routines, the excellent teacher interacts with children, from imitating an infant's vocalizations while diapering her to chatting with children over lunch about what they did in the weekend snowfall. During a transition, the teacher may choose to sing a song with funny rhymes that promotes phonological awareness. And later she may ask the snack helper, "How many crackers will we need so that each person can have two?" When children apply and practice new skills during such routines, the skills become meaningful to them.

To be an excellent teacher means . . .
planning curriculum to achieve important goals

The curriculum consists of the knowledge and skills to be acquired in the educational program as well as the plans for experiences through which children's learning will take place. Research clearly demonstrates that children learn more in programs where there is a well planned and implemented curriculum (Schweinhart & Weikart 1997; Bowman, Donovan, & Burns 2000; Landry 2008). Thus, it is essential for every early childhood setting—be it a school, a center, or a family child care home—to have a high-quality curriculum in written form and for teachers and care providers to use it to guide their planning and imple-

mentation of learning experiences. And it is equally essential for them to adapt their plans and the actual learning experiences to help individual children make progress toward the curriculum's goals. To be effective, a curriculum must have goals that are clearly defined, shared, and understood by all stakeholders, including administrators, teachers, and families (NAEYC & NAECS/SDE 2003). Then the curriculum must be designed to address these goals in a unified, coherent way.

A central question informs the development of curriculum: What goals do we have for the children during the time that they are with us? In other words, what significant learning and development outcomes do we want to see children attain? A growing research base is helping to identify certain skills, abilities, knowledge, and approaches to learning that enable children to succeed in school and beyond. This knowledge base has informed the work of states, professional organizations, and other entities in creating standards for what children should know and be able to do. High-quality, developmentally appropriate standards are important guides in curriculum development and in teaching. In cases where standards are not developmentally appropriate and need to be substantially improved, it is important for teachers, parents, and administrators to work together to change them.

A curriculum is much more than a collection of activities. It provides the framework for developing a coherent set of learning experiences that enables children to reach the identified goals. Whether the curriculum is a published product or one written by teachers, it must be effective and comprehensive in addressing all the developmental domains and important content areas. Excellent teachers continually refer to the curriculum to give coherence to the classroom experiences they plan. Teachers must be familiar with the learning goals that comprise the curriculum and carefully shape its learning experiences to enable each child to gain those understandings, knowledge, and skills.

Sequence matters in curriculum. In many areas of development and learning, some concepts and skills logically come first and others build on them (e.g., the understanding of the alphabetic principle lays the foundation for reading). And in some instances, it appears that what a child most readily learns first and what comes later depend on brain organization and the sequence of brain development. For example, phonological awareness proceeds from the child noticing gross auditory differences (e.g., the separations between words and between syllables), to noticing distinctions that are more refined (e.g., individual phonemes) (Lonigan 2006). Knowledge of such progressions guides the excellent teacher in planning the sequence of experiences and materials—for the group and for individual children. Further, this knowledge enables the teacher to scaffold children in taking the logical next steps in their individual developmental progression.

Meaningful connections are another priority in the curriculum planning of good teachers. Young children learn best when the concepts, vocabulary, and skills they encounter are related to something they already know and care about and when the new learnings are themselves interconnected in meaningful, coherent ways. Children do not learn as readily when information and experiences are presented in isolated, unrelated chunks. Learning experiences

are integrated and meaningful when children work on projects and other studies in which they can see the connections between concepts and skills they encounter.

Well sequenced curriculum is important, especially as children enter the early grades and particularly in the areas of mathematics and literacy (which are sequential by nature). Each skill or concept should be introduced when prior learning has prepared children for it. And then instructional time to enable children to master the new skill or understand the concept must be adequate. Unfortunately, too often children's time is wasted as the same topics—fractions, let's say—are taught again and again, shallowly each time. Some children catch on the first time and then are bored when the topic recurs. Other children are frustrated because they haven't fully grasped the ideas that prepare the way for understanding fractions (or another topic) and because the time given to the topic is insufficient for them to reach real comprehension. Efforts are under way (e.g., in the work of the National Council of Mathematics [2006]) to address the prevalent problem of such "mile-wide, inch-deep" curriculum that makes it difficult for children to acquire true understanding of mathematical concepts.

For their part, excellent teachers make every effort—adapting the curriculum if necessary—to allow children to have sustained learning time for a given topic or skill. When learning is meaningful, integrated, and in-depth, it is more likely to be engaging. It is also more likely to stick.

© Ellen B. Senisi

To be an excellent teacher means . . .
assessing children's development and learning

If curriculum is the path children and their teachers take toward the desired goals, assessment is the process of looking at children's progress toward those goals. Thoughtful attention to assessment is essential to developmentally appropriate practice in order to

• monitor children's development and learning,

• guide planning and decision making,

• identify children who might benefit from special services or supports, and

• report and communicate with others, including families (McAfee, Leong, & Bodrova 2004).

Assessing children by observing and talking with them and closely considering their work is key for teachers in their efforts to get to know each child and his or her abilities and needs. Getting valid information about young children is made more challenging by several realities: They grow and change rapidly, their development is uneven, and they are easily distracted. One guideline is to never rely on a single assessment measure. Potentially useful sources of information are observation, examination of each child's work, talking with a child in a "clinical interview" format (an extended dialogue in which the adult seeks to discern the child's concepts or strategies), individually administered assessments, and talking with families. Information about children also should be gathered in different settings or contexts.

Finally, assessing children in developmentally appropriate ways requires attention to what is

• **appropriate for the child's age or developmental status**—anticipating and responding to the age/developmental characteristics of children that are likely to influence the validity of assessment methods;

• **individually appropriate**—including making choices and adaptations of assessment methods to get the best information about a particular child; and

• **culturally appropriate**—considering what will make sense to a child given his or her linguistic and cultural background (e.g., avoiding materials that will not be understood), as well as interpreting a child's behavior in light of the social and cultural contexts in which the child lives (e.g., not taking a limited verbal response to the test situation to mean she is deficient in language or intellect).

Assessment information is vital to guide teachers' planning. The excellent teacher uses her observations and other information gathered to inform her planning and teaching, giving careful consideration to the learning experiences needed by the group as a whole and by each individual child. By observing what children explore, what draws their interest, and what they say and do, the teacher determines how to adapt the environment, materials, or daily routines. The teacher can make an activity simpler or more complex according to what individual children are ready for. Then, her follow-up plans can include

giving children repeated experiences with an idea or skill to get a solid grasp of it. Effective planning also means considering where the child or group of children might go next.

To be an excellent teacher means . . .
establishing reciprocal relationships with families

Parents are the most important people in their child's life. They know their child well, and their preferences and choices matter. Excellent teachers work hard to develop reciprocal relationships with families, with communication and respect in both directions.

The effective teacher recognizes that families are an invaluable source of information about their child as an individual, and she understands that a family wants to know that their knowledge and insights are regarded as important. Besides, by drawing on each family's in-depth knowledge of their child, she also can learn about their home and community environment, including its cultural dimensions. This context is critical in making classroom decisions that are appropriate for each child, as well as in fostering positive relationships with the parents themselves.

For their part, early childhood professionals have a lot to share with families. They have valuable knowledge of and experience with children in general. And teachers can give parents the particulars about what their own child said and did that day: what he is exploring, learning, and achieving in the class. Teacher-parent communication is important in achieving a degree of consistency in the ways that the significant adults in the child's life guide and relate to that child. And young children feel more secure when they see that the adults who care about them share trust and respect.

When it comes to making decisions about a child, sharing that decision making with families is important. Teachers and families are a partnership, working for the best interests of the child. Good teachers take intentional steps to build such partnerships, including

- making family members feel welcome in the classroom and inviting their participation in the program;

- working to create a relationship that allows for open dialogue;

- maintaining frequent, positive, two-way communication (planned conferences and messages sent home are important, as is day-to-day communication with families); and

- acknowledging parents' choices and goals for their child and responding with sensitivity and respect to their preferences and concerns.

In our diverse society, teachers need to be tuned into the cultural dimension in their relationships with families (see the box "Bridging Cultural Differences" on the next page). Excellent teachers know that listening well and keeping an open mind about different perspectives are vital where cultural differences exist and essential with *all* the families they serve.

Bridging Cultural Differences

Sometimes a family expresses a strong preference or acts in a way that you feel conflicts with what's best for the child and consistent with developmentally appropriate practice. When this happens, you should take the opportunity to find out more about the other person's perspective. The preliminary conversation may bring to light some cultural differences, and you may feel out of your depth. But also know that the family may feel lost or confused by the differences in how *you* view children. What you need to keep in mind when you encounter cultural differences is this: When a family behavior or preference seems to be at odds with developmentally appropriate practice, do not jump to negative judgments.

Here's a true story that illustrates the point:

> Jamal's father and mother insisted that he not go outside to play. The teacher, Ms. Harrison, wanted to insist right back that *all* the children, including Jamal, were going outside to play. But when she engaged the parents in a dialogue about their reasons, she found out that their concern was Jamal getting sand in his hair, which they found unacceptable. Together the family and teachers reached a solution: All the children would be required to wear shower caps during sand play, just as they wore smocks for painting and water play.

Culture is deeply rooted and highly complex, and teachers cannot have a detailed understanding of every culture they encounter through the children and families they serve. More importantly, teachers cannot know how different cultures and expectations will interact, or what form the cultural norms take for each individual or family.

Hitting a cultural bump means you first need to learn more about the family and their culture. You can do this by observing the family members interacting with their children. You can listen to their expectations for their child's behavior and interaction with adults and peers and try to come to an understanding of the family's beliefs about children and childrearing. Then, take some time to comment (with no judgment implied) on what you see, and talk to the family about your

concept of child development as well as the teaching and care practices used in the program.

Families will want to know that what their children will learn in the early childhood program is in harmony with their values. Aiming for harmony between program and home can come about through *culturally responsive* practices. Cultural responsiveness can be compared to music, where notes that are harmonious aren't the exact same notes, but they do go together. The point is to avoid driving a wedge between children and their families by continuing with practices that aren't mutually agreeable.

To create harmony even in the face of differing practices, it is important to move away from viewing contrasting practices as right or wrong, instead thinking of them simply as different. This change in perspective doesn't mean that "anything goes." Nor does the change mean that you should abandon your commitment to good practice. Remember, just because it's *cultural* doesn't always mean it's good for children. First, you must first seek to understand the family's perspective and the identity issues involved, and then you can better judge what's actually harmful or beneficial for the particular child. Obviously, even while being open to accepting cultural differences as valid and right, you must consider the nonnegotiable legal and ethical boundaries involved in caring for children.

So when your professional knowledge about what children need is in contrast with the practice of a particular family or individual, the solution lies in *communicating about the differences.* Together everyone involved can figure out what to do about those differences, as Jamal's family and teacher did with their shower cap solution. Professional knowledge is valuable, but there is always room to expand on it. The goal, unless a family sees it differently, is to keep children safe, trusting, developing, growing, *and* connected to their culture *while also* learning how to operate in the world outside it.

Janet Gonzalez-Mena *is an early childhood consultant who writes frequently on issues of culture in early care and education*

Seeing the bigger picture

The primary purpose of this chapter was to answer seemingly simple questions: What is developmentally appropriate practice? What does it look like in the classroom? On one level the answers, too, are simple: It is practice that promotes young children's optimal learning and development. . . . It is what excellent teachers do in the classroom. But on another level, the answers are highly complex, as this chapter has tried to make clear: Enacting the concept of developmentally appropriate practice in a classroom is complex because the answer to "How do I know if a given practice is developmentally appropriate?" always begins with "It depends."

Given that complexity, it is maybe no wonder that despite NAEYC's decades-long advocacy of such practice, what is and is not developmentally appropriate is still subject to misinterpretation, misconceptions, and misrepresentation. For example, some of the most persistent myths are

- "direct instruction is always inappropriate";

- "developmentally appropriate practice is maturationist" (i.e., teachers are encouraged to simply wait for children's development to unfold rather than actively promoting it); and

- "developmentally appropriate practice is soft" (i.e., teachers are urged to put off introduction of robust subject content until later grades).

To challenge these and other myths—and also to communicate more clearly among ourselves and with others—the early childhood field needs to widen the lens through which we view practice, as well as become more precise in how we describe best practice.

The metaphor of a lens here is useful in two ways. First, a camera lens has the capacity to narrow as well as widen the view we see. It can be turned on one individual or expanded to include a whole group. For example, consider how different the picture looks when we focus on a child only as an individual, as opposed to widening the lens to include the child's peers or family members. Second, a lens can be brought into sharper focus for greater clarification and precision, as the following example illustrates.

Consider the critically important role of *play* in young children's development. Sometimes early childhood advocates make the sweeping assertion that "children learn through play." There is truth in the statement, but it needs qualification. There are many different kinds of play—constructive play, pretend play, games, rough-and-tumble play—offering different potential benefits for children. For instance, mature dramatic play (e.g., developing a play scenario and staying within its constraints) contributes significantly to children's self-regulation, while simply manipulating play objects in the dramatic play area (e.g., putting a dish in the play oven, taking it out) does not promote self-regulation skills.

And evidence suggests that higher-level play does not automatically unfold on its own (Hirsh-Pasek et al. 2009). Teachers have essential roles in ensuring that play meets its potential for children. Thus, to effectively use play to promote children's development and learning, we must sharpen the lens through which we view play. And as we advocate for play and other practices

we think serve children best, it is particularly vital that we be clear in our own thinking and precise in our communication with parents, administrators, and policy makers.

Returning to the lens metaphor, there's another way that adjusting our lens to view a wider frame helps us think about practice in more useful ways. It is what the previous edition of this book characterized as *both/and* thinking. While polarized ways of thinking ("The best way must be *either* this *or* that") are prevalent in debates about education, a more productive route is to recognize that developmentally appropriate practice often means using a mix of approaches or modifying one approach depending on the situation.

For example, the question "Do children learn best when the teacher dictates the course of the activity or when children do?" sets up a false choice. Evidence indicates that *both* child-guided *and* teacher-guided experiences play important roles in children's learning and development (Epstein 2007).

Finally, here are a few very important *both/ands* to keep in mind.

Excellent teachers know . . .
it's *both* what you teach *and* how you teach

The early childhood field has paid a great deal of attention to pedagogy—the *how* of teaching and learning—and has identified characteristics of effectiveness that have held up over time, such as meaningful, active learning and individualizing our teaching methods to the learner. Certainly the importance of worthwhile content has been noted (e.g., Katz & Chard 2000); but on the whole, content (the *what* of learning) has been given less emphasis in early education than have the processes of teaching and learning. Research and student achievement data (especially for the primary grades and beyond), along with common sense, indicate that what we teach and how we teach it both matter in educating young children.

Sometimes research does not yet provide clear answers about the best teaching methods and the most important learning goals at a given age or grade level. But when such answers exist, early childhood teachers need this knowledge and the professional development and support to enable them to understand and use it in their classrooms.

Excellent teachers know . . .
it's *both* teacher-guided *and* child-guided experiences

There are forms of teacher-directed experiences that are not appropriate for children in preschool, kindergarten, and the primary grades. Heavy use of seatwork or lecturing with little or no time for children's interaction, exploration and investigation, play, and choice are not effective teaching strategies for active young children. However, that doesn't mean that all teacher-planned experiences are inappropriate. Such experiences, both large- and small-group, can be valuable occasions for giving children information and instruction. For example, they may be the most efficient and effective way to introduce children to skills and

Both/And Thinking in Early Childhood Practice

One of the most well received and oft-quoted sections of NAEYC's 1996 position statement on developmentally appropriate practice was its challenge to the field to move from *either/or* to *both/and* thinking. The call was in response to a recurring tendency in the American discourse on education: the polarizing into *either/or* choices on many questions that were more fruitfully seen as *both/ands*.

Some of that polarizing continues today. For example, regardless of the subject area, heated debates continue about whether children benefit more from *either* direct instruction *or* child-guided activity. In reality, each approach works best for different kinds of learning, and elements of both can be combined effectively. In studying science, for example, the teacher in one kindergarten classroom may give a 20-minute lecture, while in another classroom children might be given materials and left to explore entirely on their own—neither approach is likely to be effective by itself. A more effective course would be to draw on *both* approaches, with children conducting hands-on experiments guided by teachers who provide clear explanations of concepts and introduce scientific language.

In the process of updating the position statement, it became evident that many in the early childhood field have moved toward valuing the *both/and* way of thinking. However, a new worry arises: that sometimes *both/and* thinking may be applied quite superficially as just a "pinch of this and a dash of that." Most questions about what is and is not developmentally appropriate practice require more nuanced and evidence-based responses.

The following statements are offered as a few examples of the many ways that early childhood practice draws on *both/and* thinking and conveys some of the complexity and interrelationship among the principles that guide our practice.

- Teachers *both* need to have high expectations for all children's learning *and* need to recognize that some children require additional assistance and resources to meet those expectations.

- Children *both* construct their own understanding of concepts *and* benefit from instruction by more competent peers and adults.

- Children benefit *both* from engaging in self-initiated, spontaneous play *and* from teacher-planned and -structured activities, projects, and experiences.

- Children benefit from *both* opportunities to see connections across disciplines through integration of curriculum *and* opportunities to engage in focused, in-depth study in a content area.

- Children benefit *both* from predictable structure and orderly routine in the learning environment *and* from the teacher's flexibility and responsiveness to children's emerging ideas, needs, and interests.

- Children benefit *both* from opportunities to make meaningful choices *and* from having a clear understanding of the boundaries within which choices are permissible.

- Children benefit *both* from situations that challenge them to work at the edge of their developing capacities *and* from ample opportunities to practice newly acquired skills.

- Children benefit *both* from opportunities to collaborate with peers and acquire a sense of being part of a community *and* from being treated as individuals with their own strengths, interests, and needs.

- Children need to develop *both* a positive sense of their own self-identity *and* respect for other people whose perspectives and experiences may be different from their own.

- Children *both* have enormous capacities to learn and almost boundless curiosity about the world *and* have recognized, age-related limits on their cognitive and linguistic capacities.

- Children who are English language learners *both* need to acquire proficiency in English *and* need to maintain and further develop their home language.

- Teachers must commit themselves *both* to closing the achievement gap that exists between children of various socioeconomic, cultural, and linguistic groups *and* to viewing every child as capable of achieving.

knowledge that they cannot construct on their own, such as introducing new vocabulary words (*"This shape is called a* rhombus. *Can you describe it for me?"*). Nor do all child-guided experiences promote children's development.

Whether in child-guided experience or in teacher-guided instruction, the most significant educational experiences are those that deeply engage children's minds. There are classrooms in which children are free to choose and play, but that offer them little sustained involvement in activities and play situations. Others hum with children's interest and involvement in their activities. Likewise, children can be highly engaged in a well-planned and lively adult-guided experience. Or they may be bored, frustrated, or overwhelmed in an inappropriate one.

Excellent teachers know . . .
it's *both* joy *and* learning

Joy and learning are not only both important—they go hand in hand. From infancy, children explore visually, manipulate objects, and experience what Piaget called "pleasure at being a cause" (1962, 91). They love to make things happen. When a baby kicks an object accidentally and hears a noise, she kicks her legs again to try to repeat the effect. Is this pleasure or learning? It's both.

Brain experts testify to the close link of learning and delight:

> A wonderful cycle of learning is driven by the pleasure in play. A child is curious; she explores and discovers. The discovery brings pleasure; the pleasure leads to repetition and practice. Practice brings mastery; mastery brings the pleasure and confidence to once again act on curiosity. All learning—emotional, social, motor and cognitive—is accelerated and facilitated by repetition fueled by the pleasure of play. (Perry, Hogan, & Marlin 2000, xx)

Children love to find out more about their world, seek and master new challenges, and gain in competence (Hyson 2008). Teachers are always more effective when they tap into this natural love of learning rather than dividing work and enjoyment. As some early childhood educators like to put it, children love nothing better than "hard fun."

■   ■   ■

This chapter has focused on the kinds of decisions that excellent teachers make that add up to developmentally appropriate practice. Good decisions are never made in a vacuum—some choices are better than others. An excellent teacher's decisions are informed first by what the early childhood field knows about how best to promote children's development and learning. The chapters that follow each focus on one of four age groups—The Infant and Toddler Years, The Preschool Years, The Kindergarten Year, and The Primary Grades. They describe in a broad way what children's development and learning are like in each period, along with some major implications of those developmental considerations for practice.

the
infant
& toddler
years

Developmentally Appropriate Practice in
the Infant and Toddler Years—Ages 0–3

Development in the First Three Years of Life

ZERO TO THREE

Scientists all over the world are studying how very young babies listen to language; understand number concepts; learn from their changing perspectives as they roll over, sit, and stand; and always . . . always how they count on trusted adults to help them gain new awareness of themselves, others, and the world.

We are learning why relationships are so important to development. We are learning about individual differences such as temperament and developmental challenges, the influence of a family's and a community's cultural beliefs, and the impact of early experiences on the brain. Because so many babies are in nonparental care, we are also studying both the positive effects and the challenges of providing group care for infants and toddlers.

Group care may provide unique opportunities to support relationships and learning. Infants and toddlers develop expectations about people and about themselves on the basis of how parents and others treat them. It is exceedingly important that in these first relationships, babies experience sensitive, affectionate care. When infants learn that adults meet their needs predictably and consistently, trust and emotional security develop. At the same time, infants and toddlers develop self-confidence as the adults around them help them master challenges in the world.

- Young infants (birth to 9 months) seek *security*.

- Mobile infants (8 to 18 months) eagerly engage in *exploration*.

- Toddlers (16 to 36 months) continue to form their *identity*.

Like NAEYC, the organization ZERO TO THREE® is a source of information, resources, and new ideas for those who work with and care about young children and their families. And like NAEYC, it has made developmentally appropriate practice a special focus of its work.

ZERO TO THREE publishes its own guide to good practice, directed specifically at the infant-toddler caregiver and program director. The second edition of *Caring for Infants & Toddlers in Groups: Developmentally Appropriate Practice,* from which this chapter is excerpted, "describes the current understanding of early development and explores the elements of quality group care that support strong relationships and positive learning experiences" (vii). *Caring: DAP-II* also reflects the major concepts articulated in NAEYC's own position statement on developmentally appropriate practice.

2000 M Street NW, Suite 200
Washington, DC 20036-3307
www.zerotothree.org

Security, exploration, and identity formation are all important developmental factors in relationships and learning throughout the first three years of life. However, each dominates a different period. Security is the prime motivation for the young infant. Responsive adults help young infants to feel comfortable and to be focused as they develop a sense of trust in the adult's ability to understand them, keep them safe and secure, and make predictability possible.

Mobile infants rely on this foundation of security as they feel secure to move and explore. The quality of their experience as explorers becomes incorporated into their sense of who they are. They may begin to think of themselves as "someone who can make things happen and can learn about how my world works." As they venture out, they will check back with the adult to make sure they are safe. They also count on the adult to provide rich opportunities for them to investigate the world.

Although toddlers are naturally still very involved in exploration, this period of development is dominated by the work of forming an identity. As a toddler comes to understand his own experience and becomes aware of the experiences of others being separate from his, he is solidifying his sense of self.

Throughout the first three years of life, each child's development needs to be understood within the context of her relationships. Sensitive parents and teachers respond to all of the ways that infants and toddlers communicate their feelings, interests, and distress. They also change their actual responses as infants and toddlers grow. Providing security for a 6-month-old who is still establishing her sense of trust in the adult is a different challenge, for example, than providing security for a 12-month-old who is consumed with the urge to explore but needs to feel secure in order to venture into new territory. Nonetheless, the need to read the child's signals and to respond to what the child needs remains the same.

This chapter on development uses the central motivation of each period as an organizing principle as we describe the child's emerging capabilities, how infant care teachers can support development in a group setting, and how families and infant care teachers can create an alliance to support the child and each other.

Young infants (birth to 9 months)

Young infants need security most of all. They thrive on the warmth and caring that come from close relationships. Having someone special who responds quickly to their cues helps babies build a base of security that will support their exploration, learning, and identity formation.

The child

Babies are individuals with individual caregiving needs. Even newborns differ from one another in their biological rhythms and the way they use their senses (sight, hearing, touch, smell, and taste) to learn about the world around them. By the time they enter child care, most babies will have established distinct sensory preferences and activity patterns.

Babies enter the world ready for relationships. Very young infants show a particular interest in the people around them. They like to look and listen; they follow the father's voice as well as the mother's. Babies recognize and show interest in the sounds of their family's language, already heard for months in the womb. They look intently at the light and dark contours of the human face, and they can discriminate between an accurate drawing of a human face and one in which the main features are out of place. They can match the emotional tone of language with the expression on a person's face. Babies have many ways to participate in relationships.

By the time they are 3 months old (a time when many infants are first placed in group care settings), they are masters at attracting and holding the attention of familiar, responsive people. They can smile, laugh, cuddle, coo, reach

out, and hold tight. They engage with their parents and infant care teachers in back-and-forth exchanges of gazes, grimaces, and grins. Adults learn how to understand these messages over time.

Babies delight in hearing language. They smile and gurgle when talked to and develop different types of cries to express different needs. Long before they speak in words, infants coo, babble, and then make sounds that imitate the tones and rhythms of adult talk—particularly those of their families and home culture. Before they understand even simple word combinations, they read gestures, facial expressions, and tone of voice and participate in the turn taking of conversation. An infant just a few months old will engage as a conversational partner: She coos, her infant care teacher coos back, and the infant coos in reply. If one partner turns away or becomes distracted, the other partner calls her back with a gesture or sound. Some particularly social babies even "converse" with each other!

Toward the end of the early infancy period, babies enjoy learning simple back-and-forth games that are traditional in their culture or the cultures of their infant care teachers. Peekaboo, pat-a-cake, "I roll the ball to baby," and hand-clapping games such as *Debajo de un botón* are just a few of the games that many infants learn.

Babies learn through movement. As they move their arms, legs, and other body parts and encounter the world through touching and being touched, babies become more aware of how their bodies move and feel. They soon discover that they can change what they see, hear, or feel through their own actions—how delightful to kick, see the mobile move, and be able to do it again!

Babies learn best when they are alert and calm. They can become deeply engrossed in practicing a newly discovered skill, such as putting their hands together to grasp an object or batting at a mobile circling over their crib. Through the repetition of actions, they develop their gross and fine motor skills and physical strength. They explore objects, people, and

On Monday morning, Janeen greets Davis and his father at the door. "Hi, Davis! Hi, Michael!" "Aiii! Aiii!" says 6-month-old Davis, waving his arms. "Wooeee! What a hello! Look at those hands! Good to see you, little guy." Michael and Janeen talk about Davis's weekend and his morning, pausing from time to time to let Davis babble happily in response to their conversation. "Davis, you have so much to say!" says Janeen. Davis moves his arms and legs and turns his body back and forth so he can look at both Janeen and his father. "Let's go play. Where should we play?" Janeen holds her arms out, and Davis's father places a kiss on his cheek as he confidently hands Davis over to Janeen.

As Davis's father and his teacher talk about his weekend, they look at Davis and engage his attention. He happily joins in their conversation, gesturing his greeting, turning from face to face to watch as well as listen to the language, and babbling away when they pause to give him a turn to "talk." His transition from his father to his teacher is a smooth one because both adults are tuned in to his needs and understand his communications.

things by kicking, reaching, grasping, pulling, and letting go. Babies enjoy looking at family pictures and at board books with pictures of other babies.

In a group setting, young infants like to watch other babies and older children, and they light up when a friend smiles and coos at them. Many young babies enjoy being "part of the action," at least for short periods. At the same time, they can be overwhelmed by too much social stimulation, and their excitement can turn quickly to tears. They depend upon adults to respond to their signs of interest, overstimulation, fatigue, or boredom and to help them keep their excitement or distress within bounds.

Babies use their senses and emerging physical skills to learn about the people and objects around them. They touch different textures and put things in their mouths. Babies learn to anticipate how familiar adults will respond to them, a skill that will evolve much later into an ability to "read" people and anticipate how to behave in

new situations. Ideally, young infants are learning that their needs are understood and will be met. They are learning that new skills and new experiences most often bring pleasure, that determined efforts can lead to success, and that those they love will share their joy at each new accomplishment. These early experiences build a child's confidence, affecting her approach to learning far into the future.

The infant care teacher

The infant care teacher's responsive interactions help infants believe the world is safe, interesting, and orderly—a place where infants are understood and their actions bring pleasure to themselves and others. Like dancers, the infant care teacher and infant synchronize their interactions, each responding to and influencing the other. The challenge is doing this with three, four, or five infants at once.

Infant care teachers need layers of supportive adult relationships themselves in order to be ready for these fleeting but highly meaningful moments of responsiveness they provide. Within a program, fellow teachers or assistants often share casual moments of friendship and helpfulness. They may help each other manage the stresses of the day and share the joyful moments. Families, by sharing information or demonstrating appreciation, may support the infant care teacher's sense of the worthiness of her work. Directors and supervisors should provide a supportive, reflective environment that offers a range of opportunities for staff to understand and manage the many feelings elicited by working with infants and toddlers. The chance to discuss the children in their care with fellow teachers and supervisors can deepen an infant care teacher's understanding of each child and of herself and can promote creative, responsive, and individualized planning.

The infant care teacher's task is to learn each baby's individual eating and sleeping rhythms, how he approaches new objects and people, and how he prefers to be held for feeding, sleeping, or comforting. While the adult learns to predict what the infant needs and

how he will respond to different kinds of experiences, the baby is learning what to expect from his infant care teacher. The infant's feelings of safety, security, and confidence grow with his sense that the people and the world around him are predictable and offer interesting experiences.

The infant care teacher must be comfortable with this intimate physical care and the vulnerability and dependency of the first months. The young infant's day revolves around caregiving routines: diapering, dressing, eating, and sleeping. These routines offer important opportunities for one-on-one interaction involving talking, laughing, rocking, singing, and touching. Over time, the baby will learn to participate and even "help" during routines (e.g., by holding on to a bottle or lifting his arms or legs). The infant care teacher devotes this time to each baby while remaining aware of the other children in the room—not an easy task.

To help make this task easier, each area where routines take place should be carefully planned so that the infant care teacher's time in preparation and sanitation procedures, such as getting needed supplies and careful hand washing, can be handled efficiently, leaving more time for interaction with the baby. During diapering, for example, pictures and objects at the infant's eye level capture his interest, while clean, safe, and warm surfaces help him feel comfortable and secure. A mirror over the changing table or a few easy-to-sanitize toys kept nearby can invite play and prompt further conversation while the infant care teacher attends to the baby's needs. When routines are pleasurable, infants learn that their needs and their bodies are important.

Both during and between routines, young infants need many opportunities to sample a variety of sensory and motor experiences. Before they can creep or crawl, babies depend on adults to carry them to places where there is an interesting object or activity. They need to spend some time being carried and cuddled, and some time on the floor or another firm surface where they can move freely. "Tummy time" preferably occurs near other babies with whom

© Marilyn Nolt

they can share smiles and touches. A trusted adult stays nearby to place toys within reach or just beyond and to encourage their efforts and explorations.

A well organized environment offers babies a comfortable mix of familiar and new experiences that each infant can engage at his own pace and in his own way without becoming overwhelmed. Intriguing objects rest on low shelves or hang where they can be watched, batted, kicked, or safely tugged. However, most important to the baby is having the trusted infant care teacher close at hand.

The infant care teacher–family alliance

For families and infants, entering child care is a transition that, among other things, means building new relationships. By the time an infant enters group care, parents have learned a great deal about their baby. The baby has also learned a great deal. She has learned to expect a certain pattern of response from her immediate family—a pattern that reflects the values, culture, and childrearing beliefs of the family and community. For example, the family may believe

that infants should never be away from an adult and that adults must respond immediately to the smallest sign of distress. The infant will expect this pattern from her primary infant care teacher in the group care setting. The infant care teacher, however, may believe that waiting a few moments helps the child to become more independent over time. It will take time for the baby to adjust to differences in adults' responses, touch, tone of voice, and the sights, sounds, and smells of a new environment.

To build solid relationships at the beginning of an infant's child care experience, infant care teachers need to observe and learn from the experiences, knowledge, culture, and childrearing beliefs of family members. The partnership grows when infant care teachers value the family as the primary source of information about the child and as the constant in the baby's life, and when the family values the knowledge and personal characteristics of the infant care teacher. The parent–infant care teacher relationship becomes one of mutual support and learning about how best to care for the baby—an alliance is created.

Establishing and maintaining the alliance between parent and infant care teacher requires ongoing communication. The infant care teacher sets aside time to communicate with parents through written notes, photographs, telephone calls, casual conversations, and scheduled meetings. This way, the family and infant care teacher can share information about the baby's health, sleeping, eating, and elimination patterns, as well as her interests and accomplishments. The infant care teacher uses his observational skills to learn more about the individual baby's needs, interests, preferences, and particular ways of responding to people and things. The knowledgeable infant care teacher can anticipate new developmental challenges and help the parents adjust to the changes in behavior and moods that often accompany a baby's intense effort to master a new skill.

Families and infant care teachers may have different perspectives on what a baby needs or the best way to meet his needs. The skilled infant care teacher listens and watches for such differences and approaches these as opportunities to learn more about the family and their community. Acknowledging and giving equal validity to different perspectives provides an opportunity to build the alliance, thus creating an environment for the baby that reflects his home experience.

Good communication skills help the infant care teacher learn from the baby's family how his behaviors and reactions reflect his individual style, physical needs, and home experience. These skills, which take time and training to develop, also help the infant care teacher discuss openly with the family any differences and hopefully arrive at a mutually satisfying solution. This form of dialogue becomes easier

Catori's pediatrician had suggested trying a strict daily eating and sleeping schedule because the 7-month-old was not gaining weight adequately and was not settling into any kind of daily schedule. Maddie, the family child care provider, adopted the pediatrician's suggested routine at the parents' request. As she got to know Catori, though, she felt that Catori needed more flexibility. Maddie told Catori's parents how she was having a difficult time getting Catori to sleep, that Catori was cranky and hungry a half hour before her scheduled feeding time, and that she got angry when Maddie tried to insist that Catori finish her bottle. Soon, though, Maddie felt she was failing Catori and was sometimes ignoring the two toddlers she also cared for. She decided to have a serious discussion with Catori's parents about the possibilities of giving up the fixed schedule.

Sitting in her living room, Maddie described to Catori's parents what she observed and asked whether either parent was seeing similar behavior at home. They said that despite the doctor's recommendations, they also saw early signs of hunger or fatigue and that Catori seemed much happier when they responded right away. The parents were torn about disregarding the doctor's ideas but thought Maddie's observations made sense. They liked Maddie's ideas about ways to catch Catori's early signs so that she could learn to follow her own body signals. Catori's parents agreed to discuss these concerns with the pediatrician.

After her conversation with Catori's parents, Maddie was relieved because such negotiations do not always go well. There are many reasons parents might want a particular routine: it has worked well for them so far; it is what they know from their own upbringing; it may be valued in their culture; they may have read something that suggested this approach as best for their baby; or, as in Catori's case, a health professional may have suggested the schedule. Catori's parents came from a community in which medical professionals, or other healers, were highly respected authorities.

Maddie's good communication skills, careful observation, knowledge of child development, and respectful approach helped her and Catori's family trust their own shared and developing understanding of Catori's emerging needs. By carefully observing and responding to her signals, Catori's parents stayed focused on her individual needs. Focusing on her behaviors helped both parents and teacher avoid slipping into a confrontation about who knows what is best for the child—a kind of competition the experienced provider knows is never productive.

as the family–infant care teacher relationship grows stronger.

For parents, leaving their young infant in the care of someone else is difficult. Parents have varied reactions to this experience and express their feelings in a variety of ways. Many parents are able to negotiate this phase and form an open, caring relationship with their child's infant care teacher. Some parents are clearly sad and need more emotional support and reassurance. Others steel themselves by acting aloof; they may even appear uncaring. Others may become competitive with the infant care teacher. Becoming sensitive to differences in how parents express their feelings requires time and training.

Infants and toddlers evoke strong feelings in adults—both family members and infant care teachers. Recognizing, accepting, and working to overcome conflicting feelings are just some of the major challenges of sharing care effectively. For infant care teachers, the availability of a supportive supervisor and opportunities to reflect on the emotional aspects of this work can be very helpful. Coworkers can remind each other about their unique role in developing close and caring relationships with the babies while always trying to support the infant-parent relationship. Infant care teachers can help parents, in turn, by taking every opportunity to point out to parents their baby's need and love for them. This will help parents feel comfortable leaving their baby in the child care setting while staying emotionally close, certain that they are still the most important people in their baby's life.

Young infants thrive on responsive caregiving, an engaging environment, and unhurried time to experience the simple joys of being with others. Knowledge of early development and skill in observation help both parents and infant

Adalia (4 months) had been a fussy baby. Her parents and infant care teacher had learned to respond quickly to the first signals of discomfort because her cries became unbearably loud within seconds. One day her father came into the center grinning. He reported with pride that when he awoke to Adalia's first morning call for a bottle, he had rushed to the crib, saying, "*Calladito bebé.* I know you're hungry. Papa's coming." Rather than the usual red-faced, screaming baby, he found Adalia with her thumb in her mouth, intently watching her kicking feet. At least for a moment, Adalia had learned to soothe and entertain herself. In their excitement, the infant care teacher and parent marveled at Adalia's new ability. Adalia did not know what she had done that was so exciting, but she enjoyed their enthusiasm!

This parent and infant care teacher clearly have a good relationship. One of the many rewards of this relationship is their shared enthusiasm for Adalia's accomplishments. Another is that through sharing their observations and thoughts, parents and infant care teachers can learn from each other. When one discovers a caregiving strategy that works, the other can try it too. This creates continuity and reinforces the baby's ability to anticipate effective adult responses to her needs.

Very young infants are frequently fussy as their central nervous system, digestive system, and other systems develop. Depending on how adults respond, infants learn very different lessons about themselves and their world. Responsive, consistent care helped Adalia trust that those who loved her would relieve her distress. When physically capable as well as emotionally and cognitively ready, she could begin to soothe her own physical discomfort, trusting that the sound of a familiar voice meant that relief was on its way.

Adalia's first successful attempt at self-soothing reflects multiple domains of learning. Physically, Adalia is using her thumb to satisfy the urge to suck and her kicking to distract her from her hunger. Cognitively, she can now associate the adult's voice with relief. Socially, she has taken an important step toward regulating or managing her reactions and will receive the rewards of happier and more relaxed caregiving. Emotionally, she has taken a giant step toward establishing trust and building a strong, secure attachment, while also gaining a new sense of her own competence. When the infant care teacher understands such normal developmental challenges and achievements in the first nine months of an infant's life, she can offer encouragement, insight, and support to both infants and family members.

care teachers be more responsive to babies, whose needs, moods, and interests can vary from moment to moment. The alliance between parent and infant care teacher has many benefits for the adults; but most important, it helps them provide better and more responsive care for the baby.

Mobile infants (8 to 18 months)

As infants become mobile, exploration takes center stage. Like little scientists, they investigate everything they can get their hands—or mouths—on. "What will happen," they seem to ask repeatedly, "if I push this button or pull on this blanket or poke my friend Mikey?" A trusted infant care teacher becomes a secure base from which mobile infants can explore, checking back for reassurance and encouragement. Mobile infants develop feelings of confidence and competence as their infant care teachers share their pleasure in new discoveries and accomplishments. It is important for infant care teachers to remember that at this stage infants practice exploration but still need the security that trusted adults provide.

The child

Mobile infants thrive on exploration and interaction. Mobility opens new worlds for infants. They can now move to what or whom they want by scooting, using their hands and bouncing forward, commando-crawling with stomach on the ground, one-legged stand-crawling, crawling on all fours, walking with assistance, and finally, toddling. They develop their large muscles as they creep, crawl, cruise, walk holding on to furniture or push toys, climb up onto couches and ramps, and descend stairs. Freedom to move about safely in an interesting, inviting environment is vital for these busy infants.

Mobile infants are fascinated by the daily activities of the other children and adults around them. Most likely they are found "in the fray" where they can observe what is going on and participate in their own way. They imitate

actions they have seen, holding a comb to a doll's head, pretending to drink from a cup, and mimicking facial expressions of sadness or anger. The mental images mobile infants create of how things work and of sequences of peer and adult behaviors will become part of their rich repertoire of toddler play themes.

Mobile infants find their peers very interesting. Sometimes they smile and babble at each other socially. Other times they treat each other more like objects, experimenting to see what happens when they poke, prod, or crawl over them. They may choose a favorite friend to follow or imitate.

With mobile infants' new physical, cognitive, social, and emotional abilities come new discoveries and fears. They can look for a person who is momentarily out of sight, enjoy a game of peekaboo, and learn to wave bye-bye as they gain an understanding that people and objects exist even when they are out of sight. Although babies respond with differing degrees of intensity on the basis of both their individual temperaments and their experiences, almost all infants show some wariness of strangers during this period. A clown face, a firefighter in uniform, or a mask can be terrifying, especially if a trusted adult is not right there to provide comfort and reassurance.

Mobile infants express strong emotional ties to the adults they love, and they are acutely aware of their vulnerability when their loved ones are gone. A cherished object (a "lovey")—such as a blanket, a piece of their parent's clothing, or a stuffed toy—can be very helpful as mobile infants navigate this very complicated and important emotional voyage toward independence.

Although new fears and anxieties are distressing to mobile infants and the adults who love them, these powerful feelings reflect new depths of understanding. Over these months, mobile infants are gradually developing an understanding that other people have their own experiences, feelings, and desires.

As they play, these young explorers can be totally absorbed. Opening and shutting, filling and dumping, and picking up and dropping are

© Tyler Hamlet

endlessly fascinating activities that challenge infants' mobility and dexterity as well as their ideas about objects and what they can do. They discover, test, and confirm that objects can be out of sight (inside a box or in a cabinet) and then found; that objects can be all together, separated into pieces, and then put together again; and that adults can be resources for reaching what has been dropped.

As they play and use their new physical skills, mobile infants learn the rudimentary rules of cause and effect. They learn to push buttons—on toys or a TV remote—and make interesting things happen. These infants use and manipulate tools (e.g., using a cup to scoop water). They also begin to group and compare objects and may enjoy a simple stacking or nesting toy. They demonstrate a basic understanding of quantities of *more* and *less.* They work intently at simple problems, like fitting a lid on a pan or picking up a slippery ice cube or a strand of spaghetti.

Using language helps mobile infants stay connected with their infant care teachers

over small distances. As these infants build their vocabularies, they listen to the sing-song rhythms, elevated pitch, and exaggerated emphasis on important words and sounds that most adults naturally use when talking with them. Reciprocal conversations take place with adults, as infants use babbles, squeaks, and grunts. They begin to string together the familiar sounds of the languages in their environment into "expressive jargon" or "gibberish" that sounds a lot like sentences even though it does not contain meaningful words. The infants soon learn to respond to their name and to recognize the names of objects and people. They also learn to use simple gestures such as pointing, reaching up, pushing away, bouncing, and shaking their heads to signal their desires. Some will say their first words before their first birthdays; others will respond to words but be slower to use them.

Infant care teachers can encourage this interest in language by cuddling with one or two infants and reading simple board books to them several times each day. Pointing at pic-

tures, naming people or objects, and making the sounds of animals in the pictures are good introductions to literacy and the importance of books.

Mobile infants love to play and interact with the caring adults in their lives and can use their new language and motor skills to participate in baby games that are traditional in their culture(s). These games may include versions of peekaboo, hand-clapping rhymes, bouncing games, and games that involve pointing or gesturing. As they learn these routines, babies will come to anticipate the fun parts and will laugh and gesture at the appropriate times.

The mobile infant is both practicing independence and using new ways to stay connected to those he loves and trusts to protect him as he moves about on his own. Eye contact, vocalizing, and gesturing take on added importance as tools for maintaining that connection, although physical contact continues to be essential. A strong, loving relationship with a trusted adult gives the mobile infant the secure base from which he can explore his world.

The infant care teacher

Mobile infants' new language, physical, and cognitive abilities may have a profound effect on relationships between them and their primary infant care teachers. Some infant care teachers miss the closeness of the young infant who depended so much on the teacher for meeting basic needs such as food and comfort. An infant care teacher may reflect with her supervisor about how changes in the infant are affecting her. One infant care teacher mourned for one young infant she had loved. When he neared his first birthday, she felt as though he was testing her every time he gleefully emptied a container of toys or toddled in the other direction when she called to him. The support of an understanding supervisor can be helpful in seeing such behavior from a developmental perspective.

The infant care teacher has a vital role in language development. Mobile infants are beginning to understand words. With an increased

Pierre looks tenderly at 8-month-old Yves, a little boy with Down syndrome, as he holds him in his lap and feeds him his bottle. After a few eager sucks, Yves takes the bottle in his hands, drinks for a bit, then pulls it out of his mouth, looks at Pierre, and smiles. "What a big boy!" he says in his home language. "I'll sing you a song while you drink your milk." Yves watches him and sucks contentedly as Pierre softly sings "Sur le Pont D'Avignon."

Pierre is proud of Yves's ability to hold up his own bottle and feed himself. He knows, though, that Yves loves taking his bottle in Pierre's lap and still needs the security of his comforting arms and soothing voice. He also knows that propping a bottle for a baby or handing it to Yves to hold himself can contribute to gastrointestinal discomfort (from swallowing air and not being burped), tooth decay (when a child falls asleep with a bottle in his mouth or carries it around and takes frequent sucks), and even middle ear infections (when fluid pools at the back of the throat and gets into the Eustachian tubes).

understanding of language, a new era of relatedness emerges. The earliest words children are exposed to often reflect the social environment, and these are usually the names of important adults, objects, and activities in their daily lives. Understanding of words is facilitated when infant care teachers slow down their speech and enunciate words clearly. Repeating names of people, objects, and actions; "narrating" what the infant is doing or seeing; giving the infant words for feelings; and using words from the infant's primary language are among the many ways that adults help babies learn new words.

An attentive infant care teacher can often interpret a child's actions and babbling and translate them into words. A teacher may say, "You want the truck" when she sees a child reach toward the shelf with the trucks and say "tuk." This reinforces the infant's sense that she can communicate her needs and wishes to others. The joy in her eyes when her communication is understood, or when she hears the teacher use words spoken at home, reveals her

Joanie (10 months) was in motion. She used a large yellow truck to pull herself up to a standing position, dropped to her knees, and crawled and scooted about the room. Then she crawled up the two-step platform and sat for a moment to survey the room. With her eyes, she called to Gina, her primary infant care teacher. Gina was with two other children, but Gina and Joanie smiled at each other. Gina called across the room, "You're so busy, Joanie! You go, girl!" Joanie rolled onto her tummy and slid down the carpeted steps, where she sat and, again, looked over toward Gina.

When Gina picked up Malik, Joanie crawled across the floor and pulled herself up holding Gina's knee, pouting. Gina stroked her hair, knelt down, and put her free arm around Joanie, saying, "Hey girl, you want me to pick you up? I'm holding Malik, right now. How about we come watch you climb some more?" Joanie followed Gina's eyes to the steps and then crawled back to the platform. She looked back to be sure Gina had followed and called, "Ji! Ji! Ji!" in an excited voice.

This baby and her teacher have many ways of communicating. Eye contact is mutual and regular. Adult and child are in tune and check in regularly. A gesture of the arms, a sound, or a pout lets Gina know what Joanie needs. Gina responds with gestures (by putting her arm around Joanie to soothe her) and also puts Joanie's facial expressions into words. Joanie may not understand all of Gina's words, but she is beginning to understand many of them. She also knows from Gina's tone of voice and facial expressions that she can have her teacher's attention even when she has to share it with another baby.

This brief interaction reinforces Joanie's sense of herself as someone who is able to communicate, get what she needs, and control her intense feelings. It also lets her know that she is someone whose achievements are valued by an adult she loves and trusts.

excitement and eagerness to become competent in using language.

The care teacher has a special role in supporting infants who are dual-language learners. A mobile infant whose family speaks a different language than her teacher will feel supported in using her home language if her teacher learns some words of affection and songs from her family and gets simple picture books with captions in the family's language. The message to the infant and her family is that their home language and culture are acknowledged and respected.

Infant care teachers sensitively support the mobile infant's peer interactions. Mobile infants tend to be very curious about other children and will grab at another's hair or pull his clothes with the same interest they show in sharing a picture book or crawling up a ramp side by side. Over time, an older infant may develop special affection for a same-aged playmate or older child and imitate her behavior, hand her a toy or a bite of food, or want to be near her. Because infants are not yet experienced in interacting with each other, they often require assistance from their infant care teachers so they do not unintentionally hurt each other.

Infant care teachers who regularly observe and document an infant's emerging interests and abilities can create inviting challenges that help mobile infants as they construct an understanding of the world. Mirrors, board books, sand and water, unusual textures, locks and latches, balls, push carts, doors, tubes, ramps, busy boards, and containers of all shapes and sizes are among the many things that fascinate mobile infants.

Infants with sensory or motor impairments or delays can be helped by infant care teachers who give them lots of opportunities to explore and experiment with objects and discover the results. Consultation with families or early interventionists may provide ideas for physical positioning or adapting toys and materials. Infant care teachers maintain the same emphasis on developing close relationships and supporting attachment and competence with infants with disabilities as with all infants.

Because mobile infants can be so easily overstimulated, sensitive adults will ensure that a good balance is maintained in the levels of intensity of play—from active to quiet to sleep. The infant care teacher sets up a developmen-

tally appropriate environment that supports the infant's new mobility, but also provides protected areas for quieter play. Structures (e.g., low platforms, tunnels) invite the infant to pull herself up, take steps, climb up steps or risers, and crawl into partially enclosed spaces to gain new perspectives on the world. Spaces can be organized to invite specific types of activities. For example, a small nook, softly lit with cushions and books in pockets hung on the wall, says to the baby, "This is a place for quiet activities, books are special, and I am protected while I read."

Ensuring health and safety requires extra precautionary measures. Infant care teachers must check the environment regularly for potential dangers. Unlocked cabinets containing cleaning materials, uncovered electrical outlets, pot handles within the infant's reach, small objects, pieces of balloons, splinters, a purse left open, medications left out, and toys that are drooled on and shared are but a few of the long list of potential threats to an infant's health or safety. Infants who are just learning to toddle need room to roam or to push a toy without running over not-yet-mobile infants. Infant care teachers need to rapidly adapt to the changing needs of individual babies and the group as a whole.

The infant care teacher–family alliance

The mobile infant, his family members, and his infant care teacher are entering a stage of development that is laced with complicated feelings about separation and attachment. There is much excitement and many challenges. At one moment, the baby is consumed with his own movement, crawling, scooting, or toddling off with abandon. In the next, he is fighting to keep the adult close and crying if left for a moment. Each partner in this triangle of relationships may experience different feelings at different times, each having his or her own complicated feelings about separation and attachment. Working together, parents, teachers, and supervisors can keep their focus on what is most

important for the infant. They can identify and experiment with ways to maintain his sense of security in the child care setting, daily reinforcing his understanding that his family will be back, that they still love him, and that his infant care teacher will care for and protect him while separated from his family.

Many families place their infants in group care around the time they become mobile, often at a time when stranger wariness is at its height. At this time, the infant care teacher–family alliance becomes critical. An infant who sees that his mother or father trusts a new infant care teacher will relax in her presence and, with time, become secure enough to leave his parent with less distress. The relationships among adults constantly influence the child's experience with the adults.

Open and frequent communication is needed to assure continuity between the family and infant care teacher. Parents will want to know not just about the baby's eating and sleeping patterns but also about her development and discoveries. The baby's milestones—first words, first steps, or first drink from a cup—are exciting to both parents and infant care teachers. Often a sensitive teacher will resist the temptation to tell a child's family about a really big accomplishment until the parents have the opportunity to see it for themselves. Instead, the teacher might cue the parents to watch for the big moment: "She's almost walking. I think she might take some steps this week!"

Because parents are highly sensitive to how a care teacher may feel about their baby, it is useful to genuinely and explicitly comment at times on how good-natured, lovable, serious, giggly, alert, or fun their baby is. It is reassuring to parents to hear how it is for the care teacher to be with their baby.

Negotiations with families must be guided by the infant care teacher's commitment to reaching a mutual understanding. A mutual understanding of the baby's use of the word *no* is a good example. While mobile infants might be encouraged by the infant care teacher to use *no* as a tool for self-defense and a statement of

As a young infant, Maya had moved easily through morning and evening transitions in her family child care, and a warm relationship had developed between Marina, Maya's mother, her partner Kristin, and Shanita, the family child care provider. At 16 months, however, Maya clung to Shanita one evening, unwilling to let her mother or Kristin hold her. The next evening, as Marina and Kristin arrived while Maya was playing, they were greeted with her tears.

Shanita spoke to them about Maya's tears. "You know, this can feel terrible to parents, but it happens all of the time with children. Now she understands that you are still out there somewhere when you go. Her tears may be telling you she is confused and mad that you left her. This is really normal. Or she may be telling you that she wants some time to make the transition from child care to home and wants you to spend some time with her playing in her space before you go home." Marina and Kristin thought about this. Kristin said, "I guess this is a part of separations we just didn't see." Marina sat on the floor with Maya, looked intently into her eyes, and said in a soft voice, "Hey baby, let's play." Maya, with bright eyes, repeated, "Mama play? Mama play?"

Shanita, knowing how different infants work through the strong emotions associated with managing different relationships and dealing with separations from loved ones, responds empathically by telling her parents that what is happening is normal and does not mean that the baby now prefers her provider to her parents. By doing so, she avoids the development of jealousy that might undermine her relationship with Marina or Kristin. Shanita offers several ways to understand Maya's behavior and some strategies they can use to work through the transition together. Shanita is using her knowledge and skills to help both parents and baby negotiate what will be one of many emotionally charged moments in parenting.

independence, many families do not believe that it is appropriate to allow a young child to say no. In some cultures, such statements of independence, especially when directed toward an adult, are viewed as highly inappropriate. Cultural beliefs and rules about infants' self-feeding, being "loud," and moving without restraint also vary.

The infant care teacher who anticipates that cultural and childrearing beliefs will differ among families is prepared for open communication in an equitable and nonjudgmental way. If their beliefs conflict, a care teacher and family can try to find a mutually acceptable approach by talking over a range of strategies. The skilled infant care teacher appreciates that being a competent professional requires the ability to listen carefully, explore parents' perspectives fully, and to work toward compromise and agreement. Some of these differences can be very difficult to resolve. Whatever feelings are aroused in caring for a young child, it is critical for there to be a strong alliance between the infant care teacher and parents so that they can support and share insights with each other.

Toddlers (16 to 36 months)

Toddlers are primarily concerned with developing an understanding of who they are. Beginning at around 18 months, identity becomes the dominant theme for them. Developing this sense of self has a lot to do with their desire and drive for independence and control. Whether toddlers are still teetering with a wide-based gait, confidently getting around on two legs, or standing only with assistance, they are busy "standing up for themselves." They use their rapidly developing communication skills to indicate their desires and refuse what they do not want at the moment. As their social awareness expands, they pick up cultural messages about who they are and how they should be. Their most frequent statements are likely to include "No," "Mine," "Why," and "Me do it."

Of course, the sense of security that began to develop in the earliest months and the desire to explore (with increasing purposefulness) continue. Toddler care teachers can help toddlers find appropriate ways to assert themselves by supporting their individuality, giving them choices whenever possible, and introducing social guidelines. Toddlers work very hard

to understand social rules and get things right. The toddler care teacher fosters cooperation and facilitates the toddler's development of a strong sense of self. A well designed environment offers toddlers many chances to be in control as they participate in group play, fantasy play, and independent activities.

The child

Young toddlers are busy exploring the world from their new, upright vantage point. At the same time they are, quite literally, gaining a new sense of themselves as either a "big boy" or a "big girl." They do the things they see the important people in their lives do, or at least they try. Reassured by the presence of a loved family member or toddler care teacher, they busily explore and construct an understanding of the world.

Once toddlers master walking, their motor skills grow by leaps and bounds. They learn to jump, tiptoe, march, throw and kick a ball, and make a riding toy go by pushing with their feet or perhaps even by pedaling. Toddlers love to tear paper, pull all of the toys off of a shelf at once, tromp through every puddle they can find, carry as much as they can hold from one place to another, and make lots of noise. Excited by their new motor abilities, they plunge ahead full speed before figuring out how to stop.

Toddlers are especially intrigued with the daily activities they see adults engage in and watch intently as grown-ups go about daily tasks of cooking, cleaning, building, and fixing. These experiences provide fuel for "stories" that toddlers tell over and over in their play, both with and without words. Instead of just pushing a truck, for example, they may drive it to a spot, fill it with sand, and then drive it to a new location to dump the sand. They might also use miniature figures to replay a frightening event, such as being barked at by a big dog or getting a "boo-boo."

Toddlers are fascinated by words. They constantly ask "Wha's dat?" and repeat words and phrases they hear. They enjoy following simple instructions, and, as they learn to talk, even give instructions to themselves. For example, a toddler may tell herself "No, no, no" or "Hot" as she tries to contain her exuberance. Toddlers can also use words to express strong feelings and to evoke what is not present. A child may repeat a phrase such as "Daddy come back" in a ritualistic way to comfort herself when feeling the sadness of separation, to reassure herself that the separation is not permanent.

Toddlers love to hear stories about themselves and the people and things they love. They also love books—especially sturdy ones they can easily manipulate, with clear pictures and lots of things to do—textures to feel, holes to peek through or poke fingers into, sounds to make, and actions to imitate. Illustrations of familiar objects and activities (or photo albums of favorite people) and simple, poetic text in their home language invite toddlers to join in the

---

Kirsty, a 22-month-old who was just beginning to put words together, lived in a rural area. One winter day a fox trotted past the living room window. Kirsty's father pointed excitedly as it ran out of sight, then showed Kirsty the tracks in the snow. "See fox," said Kirsty the next morning. "Yes," replied her father, "we saw a fox." "Feet," said Kirsty. Her father elaborated. "Its feet made tracks in the snow," and Kirsty repeated "snow." Over the next several days, Kirsty told the fox story dozens of times, helped by her mother and father and then by her clued-in toddler care teacher. Kirsty's few contributions—"See fox," "feet," and "snow"—were soon supplemented with "run," "fast," "tracks," "tail," and "red" as the story grew more elaborate.

Kirsty is as excited as her parents and toddler care teacher by her new ability to use words to share a memory. Her father's delight encourages Kirsty to tell the story over and over again. Over time, her father scaffolds Kirsty's learning by adding just a bit more. Because Kirsty's parents and toddler care teacher talk frequently about the skills that Kirsty is working on and the new interests she is showing, Kirsty's mother and then her toddler care teacher are able to pick up with Kirsty where she and her father left off.

telling of the story. They do this in many ways: by repeating words and phrases, imitating the sounds of animals and machines, naming or pointing out pictures and details upon request, asking questions, and turning the pages. Many classic stories for toddlers involve searching for a mother, running away and coming back, being lost and found again, or doing something bad and being forgiven. These themes resonate with the toddler's ongoing struggles to balance his desires for independence and closeness, for being "big" and being a "baby."

As toddlers' verbal skills expand, so does their ability to use objects, to put together a series of actions in play, and to remember events for later reenactment. Adults are especially valued play partners because they can keep the story going as they respond to the child's lead by adding missing words or by suggesting next steps or new elements. An adult can support a toddler's need to repeat the same story over and over again, encourage her to do more of the storytelling each time, and help her to extend or elaborate on her story. Peers are also highly valued play partners as they heighten the emotional tone of play, take different roles, or share ideas for solving problems.

Through their experimentation with objects, language, and social interactions, toddlers enter a new phase of cognitive growth. They love to divide objects into categories by shape, size, color, or type. What toddlers are learning through play, observation, and exploration is truly amazing. They might call anything with four legs and a tail a "doggie" or remember which blocks go with the shape puzzle. They might line up rubber animals according to their height, find all of the cows, or even pair a big animal with a little one and call them "mommy and baby." They are developing increasingly sophisticated mental representations of the real world and mastering them through using them in play.

Toddlers' social awareness is far more complex than that of infants. They actively seek out their friends and especially enjoy imitating each other's behavior and engaging in group activities such as a simple game of follow the leader. Toddlers will work together to carry a large object, dig a hole in the sandbox, or make a bed for a doll. As their language and social skills become more sophisticated, they may begin to take on simple pretend play roles like doctor and patient or parent and child. They choose friends who share their interests and will play with them. Over time, in pairs or small groups, toddler friends develop their own rituals, favorite games, and deepening affections and attachments.

Even very young toddlers are capable of empathy and touching kindness in their own ways. Their interactions with children and adults may at times seem very sophisticated, for example, when they imitate a gentle adult and comfort a hurt friend or tenderly pat a baby. At other times, fatigue, anxiety, or other distress overwhelms them, and they burst into tears or full-blown tantrums.

As they increasingly tune in to the social world, toddlers become particularly interested in their bodies and those of others. They begin to learn what it means to be a boy or a girl—both physically, when they notice differences in their body parts, and socially, especially as they

All of the children in Lei-Ann's family child care home are busy "writing letters." It started when Rosa was sick one day, and Nadia wanted to send her a get well card. Nadia, at 5, knew that a proper letter required a stamp and had to be put in a mailbox, so Lei-Ann gave her an envelope and a stamp and helped her write Rosa's address. Then the whole group took a walk to the mailbox. Noticing that her toddlers were fascinated with the idea that a letter could disappear into a box and end up at someone's house, Lei-Ann made up some address labels and return address stickers so the children could send each other mail—both within the group by putting them in a special box and, for really special messages, through the U.S. Postal Service.

Toddlers benefit from opportunities to imitate reading and writing in their pretend play. They can participate in these grown-up activities by scribbling "notes," making pictures and books, dictating words and seeing how they appear in print, and "reading" their messages.

© Marilyn Nolt

notice the differences in gender roles within their culture. Some of this awareness develops as learning to use the toilet becomes an important issue during the third year of life, especially as children see peers giving up diapers. Toilet learning should begin when the child shows signs of interest and readiness. Adults need to follow the child's lead as she shows a desire for privacy when having a bowel movement in a diaper, expresses discomfort in a filled diaper, and shows interest in toileting.

Toddlers' exploration of the social world often involves conflict. The most basic conflict centers on "what is mine" and "what is yours." Toddlers react impulsively, but their feelings of empathy blossom as they negotiate these conflicts and see that other people have feelings too. They are beginning to understand that other people's thoughts and feelings may differ from their own (e.g., "I want to pull this lamp down, but Mama doesn't want me to"). Sometimes they try to do things they are told not to, just to see the other person's reactions. Toddlers can easily fall into despair at not getting what they want or when they sense the

displeasure of a beloved adult; just as easily, they can react with true generosity and warmth. Through such experiences, toddlers build a sense of themselves as social beings: competent, cooperative, and emotionally connected.

The toddler care teacher

The toddler care teacher wears many hats. She is likely to be teacher, comforter, referee, diaper changer, playmate, and storyteller—all in the course of a day. Remaining emotionally available in so many roles to several toddlers at once is challenging. Coteachers, parents, and supervisors each become members of the nesting of adult relationships that support the infant or toddler care teacher to remain present and positive with the children. The toddlers, in turn, observe these adult relationships and learn how to build strong, positive relationships with other people.

Part of the care teacher's role in supporting the child's growing identity includes showing him how positively he is seen in her eyes and helping him understand how he affects others.

She recognizes that while striving to be independent and self-reliant, toddlers count on the understanding and watchfulness of the adults who love them. Whether setting limits for safety or joining in exploring a puddle, the responsive toddler care teacher gives the consistent message to each toddler that "you are loveable and capable."

Even with consistent routines, conflicts are inevitable as toddlers learn the rules of their culture in ways that keep their dignity intact. Simple explanations help toddlers understand and accept necessary warnings and limits: "That will break," "Hold my hand so you don't fall," or "It hurts your friend when you pull his hair." Toddlers need consistent limits by adults who can be counted on and who mean what they say. Clear rules and limits enable toddlers to learn to make good decisions.

Adults who know a toddler well can help her cope with frustrations and disappointments. These trusted adults can recognize her signs of stress and may prevent her from losing control. At the same time, they can help the child learn to manage her impulses by giving her strategies such as "Touch gently" or "Use your words." They also know when a toddler is acting out deep emotions and give her the space—and support—to work them through.

One of the great benefits of group care is the ongoing presence of peers, because this provides the invaluable opportunity for children to learn social rules and to get along with others—a critical life skill. The toddler care teacher helps the child understand how he is seen by others and consider how his actions affect others. As the child becomes aware of other people's thoughts and feelings, the care teacher helps him begin to understand how the experiences of others may also affect his feelings. On a practical level, the care teacher must be prepared to prevent injuries and handle conflicts as toddlers learn to defend themselves, share, and cooperate with others. He gives them opportunities to help others and takes advantage of unplanned encounters that allow the toddler to show his competence.

Skilled toddler care teachers offer toddlers many opportunities to do things for themselves, both as individuals and as members of the group. They equip the setting with materials that facilitate self-help skills, such as small pitchers and serving utensils or easy-to-put-on smocks. They give toddlers opportunities to help with tasks such as setting the table and cleaning up. Participating in these activities increases the toddler's sense of himself as a competent person with valuable contributions to make. Sensitive teachers make themselves available without intruding and offer hints and suggestions that provide just enough help for

Donna held Haniya, a toddler with cerebral palsy, so that Haniya could hold her hands under the faucet. Jonathan came in from the adjoining play area to wash his hands before snack. Donna said to Jonathan, "Please turn on the faucet for Haniya." Jonathan did. Haniya glanced at him and gave a faint smile. She stuck her hands under the faucet of running water, seeming to enjoy the warm feeling on her hands. Jonathan stuck his hands under the water also and they splashed the water together. Haniya's smile filled her face and they laughed. Jonathan pushed the soap dispenser for Haniya and then for himself. Donna helped both children wash between their fingers then gave Haniya a paper towel to give Jonathan, who took it gently from her saying, "Tank you, Haniya."

This care teacher knows how to extend this moment of intimacy and cooperation between these two toddlers, letting each use his or her skills to help the other. She only intervenes to be sure that each child learns proper hand washing. Thus, good habits of personal hygiene, essential for reducing the spread of infection in child care settings, are taught within the context of interaction and cooperation. The bathroom is also set up to offer such opportunities. It allows both children to reach the sink, soap, and paper towels on their own. Teaching proper personal hygiene is critical as toddlers are increasingly capable of doing things by themselves and especially when learning to use the toilet. What could be better than the magic of one toddler helping another and showing off new competence at proper hand washing?

the toddler to feel successful. In this case, the teacher is primarily observing and supporting the child's intentions. This may seem disorganized to parents in some cultural communities. At the same time, teachers recognize that the value families place on developing self-help skills varies from culture to culture, especially around meal times. Some parents may be concerned about spills or wasted food or feel that feeding and dressing children are important ways in which adults show their love and care. It would be helpful to discuss parents' feelings and ideas about self-direction and how the toddler care teacher is helping the children.

Toddler care teachers do a lot of talking and asking. They also do a lot of listening. As they talk with toddlers individually and in small groups, teachers often wonder with children: "What do you think this book is about?" "What will happen when we mix these colors?" "How can we help our friend who is crying?" Recognizing that 2-year-olds are beginning to develop ideas about how things work, their teachers provide lots of opportunities to explore interesting phenomena, make predictions, and talk about what happened. Toddlers who hear and practice lots of rich and varied language develop extensive vocabularies. They learn to "use their words" to play with their friends, control their own behavior, ask interesting questions, and solve problems. Skilled toddler care teachers talk with toddlers about the past and the future as well as the present. They expand upon children's ideas, not only by phrasing them in complete sentences but also by introducing new words and concepts and asking questions that make children think. A skilled toddler care teacher is also aware that when a dual-language learner's attention is on trying to understand the mainstream language, he may be "silent" for a period of time and it does not necessarily mean he has a language delay. She would recognize and acknowledge his attempts at communicating through nonverbal gestures or facial expressions.

A skillful care teacher shares books with toddlers both individually and in small groups and both spontaneously and at predictable times within the daily routine. She might read a special story to a toddler who needs calming or comforting, help a child share a book from home with a small group of friends, or introduce a book that recognizes a child's special interest. She might also have regular "story times" early in the day and just before nap, when children who are interested can listen to a story together. It is important to note that toddlers are not "required" to join the circle or stay for the whole story; other quiet activities can also be available that will spark their curiosity or help them make the transition from lunch or playtime to nap.

Balancing the needs of individuals with those of the group presents daily challenges because some toddlers may still have individual patterns of eating, sleeping, active play, and need for quiet engagement with a favorite adult or an intriguing activity. At the same time, they are drawn to each other and can enjoy simple small-group activities that provide opportunities for imitation, parallel play, or group participation. A consistent but flexible routine gives toddlers a sense of security and creates opportunities for a variety of stimulating group activities, while still accommodating individual needs. The toddler care teacher may need to help toddlers with special needs to stay close to other children and participate in their play.

A predictable routine allows toddler care teachers to plan a mix of play opportunities that balance physical activities such as running, climbing, and dancing with quieter, focused activities that involve rich conversation. Toddler care teachers frequently join children in their pretend play, following a child's lead and helping her to tell her story. They balance new toys, books, songs, and activities with old favorites, giving children time to consolidate new skills and vocabulary, while also fueling their curiosity. Children's emerging interests—expressed in questions, worries, play themes, favored activities, and requests—shape a "curriculum" as the teacher plans from her observation and documentation of the children's activities.

During a walk in the park, Richie (32 months) picked up a large branch that had fallen from a tree. As Amy began her customary speech about leaving sticks on the ground because they might poke someone, Richie explained that the stick was his cello. He ran his hand across the branch singing "De-dah," tapping his toes, and moving his head to the beat. "Okay," Amy said, "we'll take the cello back with us." Richie's father, a musician, had recently moved out of the house, and Richie was struggling with how thoroughly everything in his life seemed to change. Amy wondered if music might be a connection with his father. When the group got back to the center, Richie, sitting on a milk crate and using a wooden spoon for a bow, gave the group a concert with his cello. It was the beginning of a ritual. Every afternoon after nap, children would help get the cello out from under the red sofa, and there would be a concert as Richie recreated a connection with his father.

In a few critical minutes during an ordinary outing, this sensitive toddler care teacher draws on many areas of knowledge, skill, and experience. As Richie picks up a stick, Amy's practiced vigilance about children's safety and health lead her to intervene quickly. But as Richie explains (his experience with Amy must have taught him that she will listen), Amy slows down. Her general knowledge of toddler development helps her to appreciate Richie's emerging capacities to express himself through language and dramatic play. Her awareness of Richie's specific situation helps her to grasp the emotional meaning of the "cello" for Richie and to find a way to support this young child's courageous effort to maintain a connection with his father. Amy adapts rapidly. She agrees to carry the stick, while simultaneously protecting the group's safety, the group's respect for safety rules, Richie's dignity, and her individual relationship based on trust with Richie. Once back at the center, Amy creates an opportunity for Richie to use his creativity not only to master his own pain but also to contribute to the shared life of the group.

In conversations with Richie's mother and father, Amy will listen for opportunities to tell them about the cello concerts and then listen carefully for clues to help her support the whole family during their difficult transition. She may share books and pictures of musical instruments with Richie and his classmates, as well as read them stories in which characters stay emotionally connected while they are physically apart. She knows that Richie's sharing of favorite books with her and with his father and mother can help the child maintain strong connections with all of the people he loves.

Unfortunately, many infants and toddlers experience the trauma of fighting in the family, divorce, chronic illness, death of a family member, or violence in the community. Their ability to overcome the hurt and fear depends, in large measure, on whether they are secure in relationships with a few caring adults who understand what they have experienced. Teachers try to provide these children with extra attention, tolerance, and appreciation for their feelings and help them to manage them. The care teacher's greatest assets in dealing with such situations are her responsiveness to the child and her commitment to being a resource and support to the family.

The toddler care teacher–family alliance

Caring for toddlers can be challenging for adults. The toddler's bouts of frustration can be emotionally draining, while the pure joy of discovery is heartwarming. It is difficult at times to understand that as he pushes away and hurls himself into action, the toddler is still very much in need of his special adults and the secure base they offer.

A healthy toddler's inner world is filled with conflicting feelings: independence and dependence, pride and shame, confidence and doubt, fear and omnipotence, and hostility and intense love. These feelings challenge parents' and toddler care teachers' resourcefulness and knowledge, as they work together to provide toddlers with emotional security. "What is this child trying to tell us with his behavior?" is a question that parents and toddler care teachers share and can help each other answer. When care teachers and families keep each other informed of the toddler's emerging interests and the significant events in her life, they can help the toddler put her knowledge, feelings, and questions into words that, in turn, help parents and teachers better support her.

A child's sense of identity is rooted in his family and community. Each toddler brings a world of family-based learning into a group care situation. His words, patterns of movement, preferences for foods and music, play themes, and ways of asking questions and expressing emotions reflect his home experiences. When toddlers see that care teachers and families are comfortable with each other, they observe communication and respect for both home and group care. Parents and teachers with a good relationship can help each other better understand the toddler as they share their experiences, insights, and encouragement. They also share their pleasure in just who this child is, his special ways of being and doing. This provides a sturdy, positive background if concerns arise about the child's development in a particular area or in the persistence of troubling behaviors. The parents and teachers have a relationship to draw on if they need to seek additional consultation or early intervention assessment and work together to follow up on any recommendations.

Communication between families and toddler care teachers builds mutual understanding and creates continuity between home and child care. It is particularly essential when there are cultural or language differences. If the child's primary toddler care teacher does not speak his home language, there are strategies available to meet the challenge. For example, bilingual, bicultural members of the family's community can be recruited to help the toddler care teacher learn at least a few important words, interpret during family–toddler care teacher conferences, and explain important program policies. There are many ways to show respect and help the family feel welcome in the child care setting.

Toddlers whose home language is different from that used in the group care environment need to hear their own language spoken and see it written. These opportunities help them build on their home language while learning English. In valuing the child's home language, his teachers reinforce his pride in family and community as well as his feelings of competence in mastering the challenges of a culturally and linguistically different environment.

The issues of identity, interdependence, and control that are paramount for toddlers can hold different meaning and value for different cultures and families. Some families encourage early independence in feeding and dressing, whereas others see these caretaking activities as essential ways that adults show love throughout the early childhood years. Some families are comfortable with messy play and are amused when their toddlers cover themselves with dirt or food as they try to do things themselves. Others are uncomfortable with and work hard to limit these behaviors. Some families have firm ideas about gender roles and do not want their boys playing with dolls or their girls playing with trucks. Others are worried when they see their children fall into stereotypical gender patterns, and they deliberately encourage a wider range of activities. In some families, toys belong to individual children who can choose whether and when to share. In others, toys and other objects belong to everyone and sharing is expected. Talking these issues through with parents when they arise, both in one-on-one conferences and in parent group meetings, can assure that deeply held beliefs are respected, differences accommodated, and necessary compromises made so that all children feel at home in the group.

In some areas there are no compromises. Some parents believe that toddlers should work out conflicts for themselves, and that it is all right for a toddler to hit back.

In a group setting, it is never right, nor is it ever acceptable, to hit, shake, or shame a child, or to encourage or permit one child to hurt another—even in self-defense. This does not mean, however, that toddler care teachers should always intervene in children's quarrels. Often children will solve the problem themselves when they are not competing for a grown-up's attention. The toddler care teacher who knows the children well is alert to signs of stress and frustration and can help them "use

Haida, an 18-month-old from Iran, was starting child care in the United States. For the first week, Haida's grandmother accompanied her to the child care program to help ease the transition. As long as her grandmother was there, Haida seemed to be making a good adjustment, although she seemed a bit wary of Jennifer, her new teacher.

Haida's other teacher, Paul, had been out sick and came back to work on the first day that Haida arrived without her grandmother. He found Haida sitting in Jennifer's lap crying. Paul had prepared for the arrival of this new child and learned a few words of Farsi. "*Salaan*," he greeted Haida. "*Halet chatore?*" Haida did not need words in any language to answer that she was fine. She reached her arms up to Paul, accepted his big hug, and stayed near him for the rest of the day. Paul became Haida's primary toddler care teacher; Haida's instant and ongoing affection for Paul soon helped her feel comfortable with Jennifer, as well.

Although Paul did not share Haida's culture or language, just the fact that he knew a few familiar words was enough to help Haida feel safe in a very stressful situation. Ideally, child care programs for infants and toddlers would include teachers who speak their home languages and are intimately familiar with their cultures. A toddler who is not speaking in sentences yet will still prefer the words she hears at home. Although she may learn a new language rapidly in a child care setting, her home language will continue to be a vital part of her identity. When a child's primary toddler care teacher does not speak her home language, even a few words can help—especially if they are words of friendly greeting, endearment, or the names of the toddler's favorite things.

their words" and devise a solution before a conflict escalates. She also finds time to teach cooperation skills as she engages in pretend play, explores, and wonders with children about how other children or characters in books might feel. The toddler care teacher prepares her children for new experiences with other children. As they read favorite books together, she takes the opportunity to talk with them about the feelings, choices, and actions of the characters.

For families who are struggling with poverty, low literacy levels, family disruptions or violence, or adjustment to a new community and culture—and for every family dealing with the everyday challenges of parenting a toddler—the community that forms around a shared child care setting can be a vital support. Potluck suppers, special celebrations, parents' nights out, and family reading parties help build a community that enjoys their young children together and supports them as they grow.

When families and teachers work together, each family's expertise can enrich the group experience. Families can be invaluable resources for each other, sharing information, trading parenting ideas, and helping each other in times of need. Family friendships formed during toddler play dates and child care events often last a lifetime; teachers can play an important role in making and supporting these links.

Good relationships among the adults who love and care for toddlers help them deal with their inevitable emotional ups and downs. The adults can share strategies for helping the toddler manage or avoid tantrums, prepare for new situations, take on a challenge such as toilet learning, and practice safe behavior. Toddlers need continuity between the expectations of their families and those of their care teachers. However, children can cope with different approaches as long as the adults work together to make the differences clear and show support of each other.

When parents and care teachers inform each other about the issues that arise in the group care setting and at home, they can share techniques for helping children express their feelings and practice positive ways to handle challenging social situations. Parents and care teachers who have built a good relationship can help each other better understand and help the toddler as they share their experiences and insights and offer each other encouragement.

Developmentally Appropriate Practice in
the Infant and Toddler Years—Ages 0–3

Examples to Consider

The framework of developmentally appropriate practice derives from what the early childhood field knows from research and experience about how children develop and learn. Major points from this knowledge base are highlighted in the position statement and summarized in chapter 2. As the authors of that overview chapter's many vignettes well know, no learning tool clarifies understanding better than examples. The chart below presents many more examples of infant/toddler practices to consider.

The chart addresses developmentally appropriate practice in six areas particularly important to infant/toddler care: relationships between caregiver and child, environment, exploration and play, routines, reciprocal relationships with families, and policies. The set of examples offered here is not exhaustive, and the goal is not to describe best practice comprehensively. We have tried to capture major aspects of practice that one sees in excellent early childhood programs and, by contrast, in those programs that in some respects have not achieved a high level of quality. Neither is the aim to issue a prescriptive formula to be rigidly followed. Instead, the examples are meant to encourage readers to reflect on their practice. Establishing a habit of thoughtful reflection is essential in caring for young children because of their varying family backgrounds, preferences, and needs.

In the chart's left column, under the heading "Developmentally Appropriate," are examples of practices consistent with available research and that most in the field agree promote young children's optimal learning and development. The examples in the "In Contrast" column are intended to aid reflection by helping readers see clearly the kinds of things that well-intentioned adults might do but that are not likely to serve children well. Many of the "In Contrast" examples are very prevalent in early childhood settings. A few of those practices are dangerous or would cause children lasting damage. Others are unlikely to harm children significantly but also are less likely to promote their optimal development. Sometimes context affects whether a practice should be used or adapted.

Where they appear, the comments sections expand on the practice examples presented in the chart cells above them. Many of the comments speak

of cultural factors to consider when determining what practices to use. The cultural dimension, important for any age group, is particularly significant with infants and toddlers. In their first three years of life, children are learning who they are and where they belong. Thus, the experiences that infants and toddlers have with their caregivers in the care setting need to be in harmony with what their family wants them to learn. Achieving harmony between program and home comes about through care that is respectful and responsive to each family's cultural preferences for their child, negotiated within the best practices framework.

Finally, most of the examples are phrased as descriptions of what caregivers do or fail to do. For the "In Contrast" examples, however, that wording is not meant to imply that deficient or questionable care is necessarily caregivers' fault. Most infant and toddler caregivers are working hard and doing their best—but often constrained by very challenging circumstances, including limited training, inadequate staff:child ratios, low compensation, high staff turnover, and meager resources. The hope of this chapter is to help them in their efforts.

Infants

Developmentally appropriate	In contrast

Relationship between Caregiver and Child

Primary caregiving, continuity of care

There is sufficient continuity of care to ensure that every infant and parent can form a positive relationship with one or two primary caregivers.	■ Infants are shifted from group to group or cared for by whichever adult is available at the moment.
The infant's primary caregiver comes to know the child and family well, and so is able to respond to that child's individual temperament, needs, and cues and develop a mutually satisfying pattern of communication with the child and family.	■ Caregivers are not familiar with the preferences and cues of individual infants because they do not have the same children in their care consistently. ■ Caregivers do not see relating to families as part of their job; they may even view forming warm relationships with parents as unprofessional.
Infants and their parents are greeted warmly each morning by each child's primary caregiver, who is available to each infant upon arrival and helps the child become a part of the caregiver's small group of children as needed. A peaceful transition time for parent and child is a part of the daily routine.	■ Caregivers receive children hurriedly and without individual attention. Babies are promptly placed in a crib or infant seat with little or no caregiver interaction. ■ Caregivers receive children warmly but neglect to give any attention to the family member who brought the baby.

Developmentally appropriate	In contrast

Relationship between Caregiver and Child (cont.)

Primary caregiving, continuity of care (cont.)

Comments on primary caregiving and continuity of care:

—*Primary caregiving* means that each child is cared for by only the same one or two adults, allowing the adult to come to know the child very well and the child to form a strong emotional bond (*attachment*) with that adult. *Continuity of care* means a child stays with the same primary caregiver in the same peer group over many months (and from year to year, if possible). If caregivers change frequently, infants either never attach or must continually deal with separation and readjustment, which can make both infants and parents feel insecure.

—Some cultures prefer *group attachment,* where children come to see themselves as part of a group of people. In this arrangement, the infant may have multiple caregivers, but there is stability in these relationships.

—Responsive and consistent infant care depends not only on individual caregivers but also on the program in the form of policies that make it a priority (see **Policies** below).

Interactions

Caregivers spend most of the day holding or touching infants, in one-on-one interactions that are warm and caring. Caregivers stroke and pat infants and talk in a pleasant, calm voice, making frequent eye contact.	▧ Caregivers leave infants for long periods in cribs, playpens, or seats. They follow "no-touch policies," ignoring the importance of touch to children's healthy development. ▧ Caregivers interact with infants harshly or impersonally, or they ignore infants' cues that they do not want to be held or touched. Or they give more attention and warmth to certain children (e.g., in family care, favoring their own child).
Caregivers learn and watch for each infant's cues, so they are able to judge when the baby needs to eat, is uncomfortable, or would like to be held. Every infant gets responsive care.	▧ Caregivers give attention and care according to their own schedule or preferences rather than children's.
Caregivers respond consistently to infants' needs for food and comfort in ways that are *caring* and *specific* to each child. Over time infants develop trust in these adults who care for them, from which they generalize that the world is a secure place for them to explore and that they themselves are loveable and worthy.	▧ Caregivers are unpredictable in their responses, don't respond at all, or respond in ways that are not caring or specific to the child.
Caregivers know that infants are curious about each other and are just beginning to build social skills. Because touching is a natural urge, caregivers allow interested infants to explore each other, while making sure that they treat each other gently.	▧ Caregivers do not allow infants to touch each other, even gently. ▧ Caregivers push infants to play together when they have no interest in doing so. If one child is very rough with another, adults take no action to protect the child who is being hurt.

Developmentally appropriate	In contrast

Relationship between Caregiver and Child (cont.)

Interactions (cont.)

Caregivers respect infants' individual abilities and respond positively as each baby develops new abilities (i.e., they give children no more assistance than they need). Experiencing caregivers' pleasure in their achievements, infants feel competent and enjoy mastering new skills.

■ Infants are pushed to develop skills even though they demonstrate that they are not yet ready.

■ Caregivers do things for children that they could do for themselves or that they could do with some assistance.

Comments on interactions:

—There is much evidence that one-on-one interactions keep child and adult close both physically (e.g., touching, gazing) and emotionally (Honig 2002). At the same time, these kinds of interactions may not be valued in all cultures. For example, some cultures establish intimacy through eye contact, but others don't.

—Cultures that value verbal language closely attend to and encourage infants' beginning vocalizations. But in cultures where infants are in constant physical contact with a family member, interactions occur through body language, not words.

—To allow two infants to safely interact physically, caregivers often put them on the floor together. This can make families uncomfortable if they are from a culture where infants are carried constantly by a caregiver and so are rarely on the floor or close enough to play together.

—Wanting babies to feel good about themselves and their individual accomplishments can be regarded negatively as personal pride by cultures that value humility.

Respect for infants as people

Caregivers often talk to the infant about what is going on (e.g., "I am putting your sweater on now so we can go outside"), especially to an older infant who can understand somewhat. Caregivers treat each baby like the person he or she is—that is, caregivers respect the child not just as "becoming" but as already "being" someone who has preferences, moods, and thoughts.

■ Caregivers move the infant about without explaining why, sometimes abruptly or at the adult's convenience. They act as if children are a bother or are cute, doll-like objects rather than people.

Caregivers have healthy, accepting attitudes about children's bodies and their bodily functions.

■ Caregivers talk or act in a way that implies to infants that they are not to touch their bodies and that bodily functions are disgusting.

Caregivers adjust to each infant's individual feeding and sleeping schedules. They respect each infant's food preferences and eating style.

■ Caregivers follow schedules that are rigid and based on their needs rather than children's.

Comments on respect for infants as people:

—Treating babies as objects to be manipulated and not respecting or talking to them about what is happening to them can undermine their sense of security and control. And when they don't understand and aren't involved in the action, they are less inclined to cooperate.

—Each infant is an individual with likes and dislikes. To start learning each infant's preferred foods and eating style, caregivers can ask the family.

Developmentally appropriate	In contrast

Relationship between Caregiver and Child (cont.)

Communication

Recognizing that infants communicate through crying and body movements, caregivers respond to cries or calls of distress in ways that are calm, tender, and respectful.	■ Caregivers treat a crying child as a nuisance. Crying is ignored or responded to erratically at the convenience of the adult.
Caregivers observe and listen and respond to sounds the infant makes. Caregivers imitate children's vocalizations and appreciate the sounds as the beginnings of communication.	■ Caregivers are brusque and inattentive, ignoring the child's vocalizations. ■ Caregivers attend to the child's vocalizations, but they do not wait for the infants to finish before beginning to talk (i.e., adults don't wait their turn in the "conversation").
Caregivers frequently talk with, sing to, and read to infants. Even before babies understand speech, language is a vital, lively part of the communication that adults have with children; it is important in infants' language development, as well.	■ Caregivers use language indiscriminately, either too much or too little, and they use a very limited range of words in their conversations with infants.

Comments on communication:
—When crying babies get a response from their caregiver and their needs are met reasonably soon, the amount of crying diminishes. In cultures where a baby is continually carried by a caregiver, infants tend to cry less, because they communicate their needs in a different way.

Environment

Sensory environment

The play areas offer children a variety of touch experiences (e.g., soft and hard areas, different levels).	■ There is no carpeting and no contrast between soft areas and harder ones. The play areas are sterile, designed for easy cleaning, but lack different textures or levels.
The visual environment has a good balance of things that are interesting to look at from the baby's perspective. It is uncluttered and aesthetically pleasing.	■ Walls are cluttered with posters and other items. The visually overwhelming environment creates a confusing blur for babies, makes it hard for them to focus on any one thing, and may even make them irritable. ■ Surroundings are sterile and bland.

Developmentally appropriate	In contrast

Environment (cont.)

Sensory environment (cont.)

Caregivers have arranged and decorated the space from the perspective of babies lying on their backs.	■ No visual displays are in an infant's line of sight. Or the display makes babies uncomfortable (e.g., a bright overhead light) or overstimulated (e.g., books with bright colors along crib walls), but it can't be escaped. ■ Caregivers provide visual elements (e.g., mobile over a crib) with the aim of entertaining the baby as a substitute for appropriate social interaction with other babies and adults.
The environment is a mix of quiet and sounds. To judge what is just the right amount of sound, caregivers look for cues in babies' reactions. Caregivers play music and other recordings that infants enjoy.	■ Caregivers play music that they prefer, often loudly and constantly. Babies find the sound environment overstimulating or distracting (e.g., infants have difficulty focusing on speech sounds and hearing their own vocalizations).

Comments on sensory environment:

—Hard floors give babies the feedback and resistance they need to experience gravity and learn motor and sensory skills. Soft is nice, but when the whole environment is soft, infants have a harder time moving (e.g., rolling over, crawling).

—Although their vision is not as good as that of adults, infants have considerable visual abilities even at birth, and these improve substantially over the first few months of life. By 4 or 5 months of age, infants typically recognize familiar faces and easily distinguish shades of light and dark.

—Although a relatively quiet environment is ideal for most infants, those who come from homes filled with people, noise, and activity get used to what would be distressing to another child.

Play spaces

Play areas are comfortable: They have surfaces that are both soft (e.g., carpeting) and hard (e.g., vinyl flooring). Comfortable furniture for adults is available for caregivers/parents and infants to relax in together.	■ There is no area where an adult can sit comfortably with an infant.
Areas are the right size for the age of the babies and the number in the group: Young infants have small and cozy areas, so they can feel secure. Older infants enjoy periods of both quiet play by themselves and play with other babies. They have ample space to move freely (e.g., roll over). Once they are mobile, they have space to roll or crawl toward interesting objects.	■ Spaces are too large and open, so infants feel insecure. ■ Spaces are cramped and/or unsafe for children who are learning how to move their bodies.

Developmentally Appropriate Practice, 3d Edition

Developmentally appropriate	In contrast

Environment (cont.)

Play spaces (cont.)

Open areas (indoor and outdoor) for mobile infants encourage them to test gross motor skills and coordination with balls, push and pull toys, wagons, and other big play equipment. There also are safe, right-sized climbing structures, ramps, and steps.

■ Caregivers allow balls and other moving toys outdoors only.

■ There are no structures for crawling up/down or under/through. Or structures are safe only for toddlers or older children.

Caregivers put infants in cribs mainly to sleep, not to play. During play periods, they place babies on firm surfaces where they can move freely and safely.

Caregivers move nonmobile infants periodically throughout the day to give them different perspectives and a reasonable variety in what children are able to look at and explore.

■ Babies are confined to cribs, infant seats, or playpens for long periods (e.g., for caregivers' convenience or "to keep infants safe").

■ Children are able to move around and explore, but caregivers don't separate nonmobile babies from mobile ones. Or they don't stay nearby to protect children from getting hurt.

Comments on play spaces:

—It's important that caregivers as well as children feel comfortable. Long days in a setting that doesn't support the adults' physical comfort will add to their fatigue and stress, which is bad for children.

—Being outdoors, rather than being inside all the time, contributes to children's health and well-being as well as giving them a larger variety of sensory experiences. Even in colder climates, infants benefit from being outside every day.

Exploration and Play

Playful interactions

Caregivers value infants' exploration and play. They observe what each child is doing or focusing on, comment verbally on the play, and provide a safe environment for it. This quiet support encourages children's active engagement.

■ Infants are interrupted; toys are dangled, put into their hands, or whisked away. Caregivers impose their own ideas on the play without regard to the child's interests, or they even play with toys themselves while the child merely watches.

Caregivers play with babies in ways that are sensitive to each child's interests and tolerance for physical movements, loud sounds, or other changes to the child's surroundings.

■ Attempting to be playful, caregivers frighten, tease, or upset children with their unpredictable behaviors.

Developmentally appropriate	In contrast

Exploration and Play (cont.)

Playful interactions (cont.)

Appropriate games, such as peekaboo, are played with interested infants, the adult being careful not to intrude on how the infant wants to play or interrupt the infant's concentration.

- ▪ Games and activities are imposed on infants regardless of their interest.
- ▪ Caregivers are rarely playful with babies.

Caregivers often hold infants on their laps to enjoy a book together. Much of this book time is shared page turning, commenting on pictures, and conversation around the content of the book.

- ▪ Caregivers pressure babies to engage with books, expecting them to sit still and stay focused the way older children would.

Comments on playful interactions:

—A pattern of adult interruptions of infants' exploration and play contributes to short attention spans, so caregivers need to be sensitive to the baby's engagement and avoid breaking in.

—In some cultures, playing with babies is not encouraged. Babies spend their time in adult settings (e.g., carried in a sling during chores, brought into the family workplace). Playing may be something babies do on their own, not with adults. Caregivers may need to help adults from those cultures understand the benefits of play-oriented infant care.

—Some adults were not brought up around books; some are functionally illiterate. Rather than having a book culture in their homes, such families sometimes have an oral or storytelling tradition, which caregivers can encourage parents to share with their children and perhaps with the group as a whole. Caregivers can also lend books to families and encourage them to look at these with children and point out and talk about things on the pages.

Objects to manipulate and explore

Caregivers appreciate that very young babies play first with their own bodies as they explore what their major muscles can do, change positions, feel sensations, and eventually discover their own hands and feet.

- ▪ Caregivers restrain babies (e.g., in infant seats, swings, restrictive clothing) or keep them in cribs to restrict their movements and exploration.

Caregivers provide play objects made of materials and scaled to a size that lets infants grasp, chew, and manipulate them (e.g., clutch balls, teethers, soft and washable dolls or play animals).

- ▪ Caregivers provide toys too large to handle or so small that infants could choke on or swallow them. They hang toys above the nonmobile infant, making them available only to look at or perhaps bat at, but not to manipulate, mouth, or fully explore.

Developmentally appropriate	In contrast

Exploration and Play (cont.)

Objects to manipulate and explore (cont.)

Caregivers provide a variety of safe household items that infants can use as play materials (e.g., measuring cups, wooden spoons, unbreakable bowls).

■ Household items, which help make the care setting more homelike, are not provided.

Books made of sturdy cardboard (board books) are placed where babies can easily reach them. The books show everyday objects and activities; the people depicted are diverse (e.g., in age, abilities, ethnicity, culture, family configuration).

■ Books are not provided (because "babies can't read" or "they'll just get ruined").

■ The books available are made of paper that tears easily. Books do not show images of things familiar or interesting to children.

Once babies can reach and grasp, caregivers provide play objects carefully chosen to be responsive to the child's actions and perhaps allowing different types of manipulation (e.g., turning, squeezing, inserting).

■ Caregivers provide toys that are battery powered or windup, so the baby just watches. Toys lack variety in texture, size, and shape. Caregivers put toys into the infant's hand before the grasp reflex weakens, so the child can't let go of them.

Any play objects that make noise are made so the infant can see and understand where the noise comes from.

■ Rattles and other noise-making and busy-box toys have hidden mechanisms, so any explorations don't help the baby understand how the object works.

Comments on objects to manipulate and explore:
—Babies get an early sense of power when they discover what they can do with their bodies. Accidental at first, then growing more purposeful as babies develop, experiencing their own movement teaches babies they can make things happen. Practice and repetition of self-chosen movements support self-regulation.

—In some cultures, play objects are less important, especially if infants are in body contact most or all of the time with their caregivers. Sensory experiences (i.e., sights, sounds), rather than objects, are what such infants "play" with. Families from such cultures may stress their baby developing observation skills more than manipulation skills.

Organization and access to materials

Play materials are well organized and made accessible to children. For example, caregivers organize objects for different activities on different shelves (e.g., fill-and-empty materials are on a shelf separate from three-piece puzzles or moving/pushing toys).

■ Caregivers give no thought to organization. They are unaware that how they arrange toys and materials can affect how children interact with the items.

| Developmentally appropriate | In contrast |

Exploration and Play (cont.)

Organization and access to materials (cont.)

Play materials are stored on open shelves at children's eye level and within their reach. Caregivers space individual items so infants can make deliberate choices. Infants with special needs who are developmentally ready and able to manipulate objects (but may be challenged in mobility skills) have access to play objects.

■ Toys are dumped in a box and come out in a jumble. Caregivers don't understand that choosing from a jumble isn't the same to a child as being able to look at an orderly selection and make a careful choice.

■ Toys are kept out of children's reach. Caregivers make the child ask for a desired toy, or they make the selection for the child.

Comments on organization and access to materials:
—Some cultures emphasize human relationships above manipulating objects; in such families, adults may remove a toy or other object if it is distracting the infant from focusing on a person or people. And, while many cultural groups in the United States (and other Western countries) stress independence, families from a culture that places greater value on *inter*dependence, who want their children to have very close, enduring connections with the family, may resist their child becoming more self-sufficient as an infant.

Routines

Caregivers are attentive to infants during caregiving routines such as eating, sleeping, diapering, changing clothes, and the like. The caregiver explains what is happening and involves the infant in the routine.

■ Routines are accomplished quickly and mechanically, without involving the infant. Little or no warm interaction takes place during routines.

Comments on routines:
—During routines, caregivers need to understand and follow good practice for health, safety, nutrition, etc. For more specific information, please reference the NAEYC Health and Safety accreditation criteria: "Physical Environment" and "Health."

Eating

Infants feeding from a bottle are always held, their bodies at an angle. The primary caregiver or other familiar adult always feeds the infant.

■ Young infants are strapped into infant seats to be fed. Who holds the bottle is random, not the primary caregiver or even necessarily the same caregiver each time.

■ Babies are put into their infant seats or cribs and their bottles are propped up (e.g., on a pillow) while caregivers do other things.

Developmentally appropriate	In contrast

Routines (cont.)

Eating (cont.)

Until infants can get into a sitting position on their own, they are placed in secure chairs such as highchairs (but only at mealtimes) or held by their primary caregiver or other familiar adult while being fed.	■ Babies are fed in highchairs, as a group, and not necessarily by the primary caregiver or even a familiar adult. ■ Highchairs are used to contain babies at other times during the day, too.
Caregivers use mealtimes as occasions for fostering children's independence and self-help mastery (e.g., letting mobile infants who can get into chairs by themselves). At the same time, caregivers try to accommodate a family's cultural preferences, which in some cases may include continuing to feed older infants.	■ Caregivers feed all children in the same way regardless of family preference.
Older infants eat in small groups at low tables. Their caregiver sits nearby to provide assistance as needed.	■ There are no small tables and chairs/stools to invite mobile infants to use their fine and gross motor control at meal times. ■ Large groups of children are fed in sequence or left to their own devices.
Caregivers allow children to feed themselves (including using utensils and cups), even when their efforts are messy. Finger foods are provided to increase children's likelihood of success.	■ Caregivers insist on feeding infants because it's more convenient or efficient (e.g., "she takes too long," "he always makes a mess"). ■ Caregivers expect infants to handle utensils or finger food neatly when children don't have those fine motor skills yet.
Small servings of healthy foods are offered, and each child selects how much to eat and when to stop. Mealtime is treated as a sociable, happy time.	■ Caregivers are not responsive to children's cues as to what foods they prefer and when they've had enough. Conversation between adults and children is limited. ■ Food is used to pacify or reward, or it is withheld as punishment.

Comments on eating:
—Eating meets a basic physical need; it also is a rich sensory and emotional experience.
—There are many different cultural perspectives on what, when, and how infants should eat. For example, talking while eating is not a universal practice, nor is eating with the fingers. In some cultures, spoon feeding children after they are capable of feeding themselves is regarded as a way of cementing a close bond between infant and adult.

Developmentally appropriate	In contrast

Routines (cont.)

Sleeping

The infant sleeping area is separate from active play and eating areas. Babies sleep in cribs reserved for them. Family members bring comforting objects from home to personalize their baby's crib.

■ Cribs line the walls in the play area. Cribs are all alike, and a baby is put into whichever crib is available. Infants do not have their own supplies, and there is nothing personal to help the baby feel that "this is my place."

The lighting is dim, but every infant is still visible. The sleeping area is quiet, perhaps with soft music while babies are falling asleep.

■ Bright lights and the sounds of playing babies or loud music disturb babies trying to sleep.

Each infant is put down by the primary caregiver or another familiar adult.

■ Different caregivers put babies down each time.

Comments on sleeping:
—That infants feel "at home" as much as possible is important in all caregiving activities, but especially for sleeping. For example, a baby whose large family lives in a small apartment where there is always activity and noise may have problems going to sleep in dim light, separate and apart from the activity of others.

Diapering

Infants are usually diapered by the child's primary caregiver or another familiar adult. Treated as a personal, one on-one interaction—where the caregiver seeks the baby's attention and cooperation—diapering builds a sense of teamwork, and their relationship grows as a result.

■ One person diapers all babies, not necessarily the primary caregiver or an adult familiar to every child.

Diapering supplies and extra clothes for each child are within easy reach of the changing table. The caregiver has the needed time and tools to make diapering an efficient and pleasant experience for adult and child.

■ Because the diapering area is not well designed or organized, diapering takes a long time and can be uncomfortable and annoying to caregiver and infant alike.

■ In the rush to get diapers changed, the adult may forget or skip essential health and safety steps or handle the infant brusquely.

Developmentally appropriate	In contrast

Reciprocal Relationships with Families

Developmentally appropriate	In contrast
Caregivers communicate daily with parents in a warm, honest, and respectful way to build mutual understanding and trust, which help in resolving any issues that may arise.	■ Caregivers communicate with parents only rarely or only when there are problems or conflicts.
Caregivers help parents feel good about their babies (e.g., by sharing some of the positive and interesting things that happened that day).	■ Caregivers don't share the experiences they have with the child each day, causing parents to feel isolated from this part of their child's life. Or caregivers share plenty but focus on their negative experiences with the child instead of the positive.
Caregivers listen carefully to what parents say; they seek to understand parents' goals, priorities, and preferences for their children.	■ Rather than listening and trying to understand (the key to culturally responsive care particularly and family-responsive care more generally), caregivers do all or most of the talking. Caregivers may view their own cultural or other perspective as the only right one.
Caregivers support parents as being their child's most important relationship and as being ultimately responsible for the child's well-being and care (e.g., caregivers keep records of diaperings to share with parents). Caregivers focus on parents' expertise, attachment to their infants, and children's strong connections to their parents.	■ Caregivers set themselves up as experts, criticize parents' skills, or try to compete for babies' affection.
Caregivers and families collaborate in making decisions about how best to support children's development or handle issues if they do arise. Caregivers and parents figure out together how to solve problems and see beyond differences to common concerns.	■ Caregivers avoid difficult issues or make decisions unilaterally rather than problem solving with parents. ■ Caregivers see parents as the "problem" rather than part of the solution.
Caregivers are respectful of parents' cultural and family preferences. Using a team approach, caregivers try to accommodate those preferences, if it can be done in a developmentally appropriate way, and, if it cannot, try to help parents understand why (e.g., parents want caregivers to leave the baby alone to cry himself out whenever he cries).	■ Caregivers ignore or disparage parents' goals or preferences for their children. Caregivers may see their opinions as superior or view preferences other than their own as being odd or wrong rather than just different. ■ Caregivers capitulate to parent demands (e.g., spanking) or preferences, even when these are at odds with developmentally appropriate practice.

Developmentally appropriate	In contrast

Reciprocal Relationships with Families (cont.)

Caregivers always make parents feel welcome (e.g., warmly receive and support nursing mothers who are able to come in for breastfeeding).	■ Caregivers communicate a competitive or patronizing attitude to parents, or they make parents feel like they are in the way.
Pictures of infants and their family members are hung on walls where infants can see them.	■ Caregivers try not to remind infants of their families because they hope to avoid any displays of separation anxiety. ■ Decorations are at adult eye level and do not include family photos.

Comments on reciprocal relationships with families:

—Helping parents feel good about their child's positive qualities leads to family support for those qualities. Most parents want to feel good about their child, but in some cultures they may not want to hear that their child feels good about him or herself. In cultures that value humility over self-pride, adults may want to downplay a child's positive qualities, fearing the child will get conceited.

—Sometimes family preferences can be accommodated; other times caregivers see the parents' request as one they cannot go along with. Then a conversation between caregivers and family about their different perspectives is called for.

—Seeing images of family members reminds infants of their loved ones and helps them feel that they belong to their family and their family is connected to the program. If seeing the images upsets infants, coping with feelings is one of the early lessons they can learn in programs where the caregivers are willing to help them with separation.

Policies

Health and safety

Caregivers follow health and safety procedures, including proper hand washing methods and universal precautions to limit the spread of infectious disease. There are clearly written sanitation procedures specific to each task or routine to help staff remember to follow procedures completely and consistently.	■ Policies and procedures to ensure a sanitary facility have not been clearly thought through and are not written down. Consequently, adults forget hand washing or other essential steps in diapering, cleaning cribs and play areas, handling food, and cleaning food-preparation areas. Caregivers are not consistent in maintaining sanitary conditions and procedures.

Developmentally appropriate	In contrast

Policies (cont.)

Health and safety (cont.)

The space has been constructed and set up with health and safety in mind (e.g., walls are painted with lead-free, easy-to-clean paint; carpeting and flooring are easy to clean; diapering and food-preparation areas are separate; storage for disinfectants, gloves, and plastic bags is clearly labeled).

■ The space is not organized to foster health and safety (e.g., supplies, even disinfectants, do not have a designated space out of the reach of infants, so caregivers tend to leave them on the diapering counter).

■ The environment is clean and safe but has a sterile, institutional feel.

Infants are placed on their backs for sleeping unless otherwise directed by a doctor.

■ Caregivers place children to sleep in any position that seems to make children happy or to quiet them down quickest.

Comments on health and safety:
—Caregivers need training, support, and reminders to understand and consistently follow proper health and safety procedures (e.g., to diaper hygienically). For more specific information, please reference the NAEYC Health and Safety accreditation criteria: "Physical Environment" and "Health."

Staffing

Program hires caregivers who enjoy working with infants in particular and who have had training specifically related to infant development and caregiving. Caregivers are open to ongoing training and support in order to deepen their understanding and skills in caring for this age group.

■ Program hires caregivers who view working with infants as a custodial chore or who have little or no training specific to infant development and caregiving.

Caregivers cope well with stress, and they model in their interactions with others (e.g., co-workers, family members, directors) the style and tone they want children to develop.

■ Caregivers don't cope well under stress; they become tearful, aggressive, or overwrought. Or caregivers are cold and aloof and never show any emotion.

Program limits group size and the adult:child ratio to allow caregivers one-on-one interactions with and intimate knowledge of individual babies.

■ Groups are too large and staff:child ratio too high to permit individual attention and constant supervision.

In its staffing patterns, the program is committed to primary caregiving.

■ Staffing patterns require infants to relate to more than two adults during the caregiving day.

Developmentally appropriate	In contrast

Policies (cont.)

Staffing (cont.)

In its staffing patterns, the program ensures continuity of care. Child and caregiver are able to maintain their relationship, and each child's ongoing relationship with the other children in the group is supported.

■ Staffing patterns shift caregivers around from infant to infant or group to group. This may even be intentional (e.g., so "children don't get too attached").

■ Child groupings change constantly (e.g., daily to suit the schedule preferences of staff, or periodically as infants are "graduated" to the next room and new caregivers).

■ High staff turnover (e.g., due to inadequate compensation, poor working conditions) results in low continuity and frequent disruption of infants' budding attachments to caregivers.

Comments on staffing:
—No one automatically has the knowledge of how to care for infants in groups, and not all adults have the interest in or disposition for infant care. When hiring and assigning staff, directors should consider individuals' strengths and preferences to determine the age group(s) with which each person fits best. Ability to work with other adults, attitudes toward diversity, and willingness to communicate about differences should also be considered. For more specific information, please reference the NAEYC Health and Safety accreditation criteria: "Teachers."

Toddlers

Relationship between Caregiver and Child

Primary caregiving, continuity of care

There is sufficient continuity of care to ensure that every toddler and parent can form a positive relationship with one or two primary caregivers.

■ Toddlers are shifted from group to group or cared for by whichever adult is available at the moment.

The toddler's primary caregiver comes to know the child and family well and so is able to respond to that child's individual temperament, needs, and cues and develop a mutually satisfying pattern of communication with the child and family.

■ Caregivers are not familiar with the preferences and cues of individual toddlers because they do not have the same children in their care consistently.

■ Caregivers do not see relating to families as part of their job; they may even view forming warm relationships with parents as unprofessional.

Developmentally Appropriate Practice, 3d Edition

Developmentally appropriate	In contrast

Relationship between Caregiver and Child (cont.)

Primary caregiving, continuity of care (cont.)

Toddlers and their parents are greeted warmly by name by that child's primary caregiver when they arrive. Caregivers help to create smooth transitions by being available to the toddler who needs help with separating from parents and assisting each toddler in settling into the group by showing what has been set up and interacting with the child as needed.

■ Caregivers receive children hurriedly and without individual attention. Toddlers are expected to begin the day with free play and little adult interaction.

■ Caregivers receive toddlers warmly but neglect to give any attention to the family member who brought the child.

Comments on primary caregiving and continuity of care:

—*Primary caregiving* means that each child is cared for by only the same one or two adults, allowing the caregiver to come to know the child very well and the child to form a strong emotional bond (*attachment*) to that caregiver. *Continuity of care* means a child stays with the same primary caregiver in the same peer group over many months (and from year to year if possible). If caregivers change frequently, toddlers either never attach or must continually deal with separation and readjustment, which can make both toddlers and parents feel insecure.

—Some cultures prefer *group attachment,* where children come to see themselves as part of a group of people. In this arrangement, the toddler may have multiple caregivers, but there is stability in these relationships.

—Responsive and consistent toddler care depends not only on individual caregivers but also on the program in the form of policies that make it a priority (see **Policies** below).

Interactions

Caregivers spend most of the day in one-on-one interactions with toddlers. The tone of the interactions is warm and caring; caregivers use pleasant, calm voices as well as simple language and nonverbal cues.

■ Caregivers leave some toddlers alone for long periods and give their energy and attention to other children (e.g., in family care, favoring their own child). Or caregivers focus their attention elsewhere altogether and don't interact much with children.

■ Caregivers interact with toddlers in a harsh or impersonal manner.

Caregivers learn each toddler's cues and respond consistently in ways that are *caring* and *specific* to each child, which lets the child explore, knowing he can trust the adults to be there for help or comfort as needed.

■ Caregivers give attention and care according to their own schedule or preferences rather than children's.

■ Caregivers are unpredictable in their responses, don't respond at all, or respond in ways that are not caring or specific to the child.

Developmentally appropriate	In contrast

Relationship between Caregiver and Child (cont.)

Interactions (cont.)

Developmentally appropriate	In contrast
Caregivers frequently read to toddlers—to one child individually or to groups of two or three—always in close physical contact. Caregivers sing with toddlers, do finger plays, and act out simple stories or folktales, with children participating actively.	■ Caregivers impose "group time" on toddlers, expecting a large group to listen or watch an activity without children having opportunities to participate or to interact with caregivers individually.
Caregivers comfort toddlers and let them know they are valued through warm responsive touches, such as pats on the back and hugs and holding toddlers in their laps. Caregivers are sensitive to whether a child welcomes the touches.	■ Caregivers follow "no-touch policies," ignoring the importance of touch to children's healthy development. ■ Caregivers ignore children's cues that they do not want to be held or touched.
Caregivers create an emotionally and physically inclusive classroom. They give every toddler warm, responsive care. They make sure that spatial organization, materials, and activities are planned such that all children can participate actively (e.g., a child with a physical disability eats at the table with other children).	■ Caregivers do not include children with special needs in all activities (e.g., a child who requires adaptive equipment or special procedures eats or plays apart from peers).
To satisfy toddlers' natural curiosity, caregivers give simple, brief, accurate responses when children stare at or ask questions about a person with a disability or other difference.	■ Caregivers disregard children's curiosity about a person's disability or adaptive equipment. ■ Caregivers criticize a child for noticing or asking questions about differences. ■ Caregivers make comments or offer explanations that show their own discomfort or disparage others with disabilities.

Comments about interactions:

—There is much evidence that one-on-one interactions keep child and adult close physically and emotionally (Honig 2002). Touch is a mode of communication that is particularly important in the early years. Some toddlers shy away from touches, and caregivers need to be sensitive to individual differences. Where and how a person may be touched also is highly cultural; in some cultures being touched on the head is considered demeaning or even dangerous.

—In some cultures, children—even toddlers—are expected to learn by observing rather than by participating (e.g., sitting for a long time in a large group). Toddlers generally are or like to be physically active, however. In the early childhood setting, they should be allowed to move around and participate in play and active learning throughout most of the day.

—Caregivers must make the effort to integrate children with special needs as fully as possible. After giving curious toddlers a simple explanation of the disability or difference, the adult might say a bit about the child's interests and abilities ("Susan likes to draw and finger-paint. Here's a picture she made this morning").

Developmentally Appropriate Practice, 3d Edition

| Developmentally appropriate | In contrast |

Relationship between Caregiver and Child (cont.)

Respect for toddlers as people

Caregivers have appropriate expectations for toddlers. When a child is trying to do something (e.g., putting on her boots), the caregiver watches to see what the toddler can manage on her own and provides support as needed.

■ Caregivers are impatient with toddlers who are learning new skills. Because it is faster, the adult does tasks for toddlers that they could have done themselves.

■ Caregivers foster overdependence; children are overprotected and made to feel inadequate.

■ Caregivers often allow toddlers to become frustrated, to the extent that children become very upset or give up on tasks they cannot do or problems they can't solve alone.

Caregivers have healthy, accepting attitudes about children's bodies and their bodily functions.

■ Caregivers talk or act in a way that makes toddlers feel ashamed of their bodies and think bodily functions are disgusting.

Caregivers respect each child's developing preferences for familiar objects, foods, and people. They permit toddlers to keep their own favorite objects, and they let children choose (from a limited set of options) what they prefer to eat or wear.

■ Caregivers prohibit toddlers from bringing a favored object (e.g., a blanket or toy) from home. Or they arbitrarily take the object away or expect a toddler to share it with other children.

■ Children are not given choices, and having/expressing preferences is not encouraged. Children are all expected to do the same thing.

Caregivers respect toddlers' interest in objects—to carry objects around with them, collect objects, move them from one place to another, and to roam around or sit and parallel play with toys and other objects.

■ Caregivers restrict objects to certain locations ("Books must stay in the reading corner"); they do not tolerate children's hoarding, collecting, or carrying objects about.

Comments on respect for toddlers as people:

—Toddlers are developing confidence in their abilities, which leads to increased self-esteem. Some cultures downplay self-pride and teach humility instead, and families may raise issues relating to this difference with caregivers.

—When a family's culture gives greater priority to *inter*dependence than to independence, caregivers may view some parent behaviors as being overprotective or creating an overly dependent child when the actual goal is mutual dependence. At times, these parents may emphasize teaching the child to graciously receive help when he is trying to do something on his own.

—Toddlers' awareness of themselves as individuals who have preferences and personal possessions is growing; allowing them to practice making choices is good for their self-concept. Children at this age begin developing a notion of having "favorites," which their caregivers should recognize and respect. Children find comfort in familiar objects and also enjoy figuring out which objects belong to categories or groups.

Developmentally appropriate	In contrast

Relationship between Caregiver and Child (cont.)

Communication

An adult initiating a conversation with a toddler gives the child ample time to respond. Caregivers also listen attentively for children's verbal initiations and respond to these.	■ Caregivers talk *at* toddlers and do not wait for a response. ■ Adult voices dominate. Or caregivers do not speak to children because they think they are too young to converse.
Caregivers label or name objects, describe events, and reflect feelings ("You're angry that Yvette took the block?") to help children learn new words. Caregivers simplify their language for toddlers who are just beginning to talk. Then as children acquire their own words, caregivers expand on the toddler's language (Child: "Mark sock." Adult: "Oh, that's Mark's missing sock, and you found it").	■ Caregivers do not try to build toddlers' understanding of the world around them through interacting with them. They assume toddlers are too young for any level of verbal communication. ■ Caregivers either talk "baby talk" or use language that is too complex for toddlers to understand.
Caregivers ask the family what sounds, words, and nonverbal cues their toddler uses to better understand what the child means when she uses beginning speech or a home language that is not understood by the caregivers.	■ Caregivers do not talk with parents about the toddler's speech, communication patterns, or home language. They cannot understand what the toddler is trying to convey, which frustrates the child in her efforts to communicate. ■ Caregivers tell parents to speak English to their children even if the parents lack facility in the English language.
Caregivers learn what each child's cries mean (e.g., fear, frustration, sleepiness, pain) and when to wait (e.g., to see if the child solves his own problem) or take action. They respond promptly to toddlers' cries or other signs of distress.	■ Crying is ignored or responded to erratically or at the caregiver's convenience.

Comments on communication:

—Talking *with* toddlers instead of *at* them greatly facilitates their language development and expands their vocabulary, which in turn eventually will help them learn to read. Language use can vary greatly from culture to culture. For example, in some cultures, children are never asked questions to which the adult already knows the answer. So a child from such a family may think it strange behavior and not respond if the caregiver holds up a book and asks, "What is this?"

—It's very important to learn from parents how their toddlers express themselves at home. Understanding the context behind what the toddler is trying to convey, which parents can often provide, facilitates communication and builds relationships. When the toddler's home language is different from the program's, every effort should be made to support the child's continued language development in both. Speaking one's family language is a part of identity formation and connection with the home culture.

—Although words will eventually replace it, crying is a form of toddler communication, so caregivers should seek to understand what a child is crying about, rather than just trying to make it stop or ignoring it.

Developmentally appropriate	In contrast

Relationship between Caregiver and Child (cont.)

Positive guidance

In their interactions with others, caregivers model how they want children to behave. To help a toddler resolve differences, caregivers use words to express what is happening and what the toddler might be feeling ("You want to play with that car? Shantel is playing with it now; let's see if we can find another car on the shelf").

■ Caregivers themselves show aggression, shout, or exhibit a lack of coping behaviors under stress.

■ Caregivers' attempts to punish or control an aggressive toddler escalate the hostility. They do not model for toddlers the words to say to resolve a conflict.

Caregivers patiently redirect toddlers to help guide them toward controlling their own impulses and behavior.

■ Caregivers do not anticipate behaviors that are likely to occur and so do not prevent children from getting hurt or hurting others.

■ Caregivers ignore disputes and other problematic behaviors, leading to a chaotic atmosphere.

■ Caregivers punish infractions harshly, frightening and humiliating children.

Caregivers recognize that toddlers constantly test limits and express opposition ("No!") as part of developing a healthy sense of self as an autonomous individual.

■ Caregivers punish children for asserting themselves or for saying no.

Caregivers try to limit telling children no only to situations that relate to their immediate safety or emotional well-being. Adults give positively worded directions or choices ("Bang on the drum or the floor"), not just restrictions ("Don't bang on the table").

■ Caregivers are constantly telling toddlers no without giving an alternative. Or they become involved in power struggles over issues that do not relate to the child's safety or well-being.

Comments on positive guidance:

—Understanding how toddler behaviors relate to their stage of development helps caregivers to respond in positive ways without taking children's negativity personally or getting upset and angry. Staying out of power struggles is particularly important.

—Observation is an important skill for caregivers to develop so they are able to anticipate toddlers' actions and prevent dangerous or aggressive situations. Toddlers need to know that the adult will provide control when they lack it.

—Adults' responses to a toddler's behavior play a role in forming that child's sense of self. Because the value placed on a character trait such as cooperation or independence can vary by culture, caregivers and families may disagree about which behaviors are acceptable in their children. For example, if parents value obedience, they are less likely to want the caregiver to tolerate their toddler's testing limits and expressing opposition.

Developmentally appropriate	In contrast

Environment

Sensory environment

Carpeting and flooring materials are selected to provide a soft background so that toddlers' eyes are drawn to the materials and activity choices.

■ Walls are cluttered. Or walls are sterile and bland.

■ Carpet and rugs are a confusion of distracting colors and patterns.

Toddlers' artwork and other creative projects are hung at a level just above their reach but low enough to be seen clearly. Caregivers display pictures of the children and their families or place them in albums for children to look at when they wish.

■ Toddlers' art is not displayed, or it is hung too high for them to see.

■ There is no indication of family involvement (e.g., no familiar objects from home).

Toddlers are surrounded by sensory objects for their play activities (e.g., banging objects, mounding sand, kneading dough). To a reasonable extent, they also can enjoy sensory play during routines such as hand washing (e.g., squirting the soap).

■ Children are denied the natural enjoyment of sensory play and exploring their environment during activities because "it's too noisy" or "messy" or "dirty." As a result, they play during cleanup or with their food whenever they can, often disrupting routines or requiring guidance.

Comments on sensory environment:

—When children with special needs are part of the program, caregivers need to make appropriate accommodations: For example, visually impaired children may need more contrast than usual (e.g., dark objects placed on a white tray) in order to focus on something. It also is vital that the arrangement of the environment remain much the same, so such children can find their way around. Constantly rearranging furniture and materials makes it very hard for a toddler with a visual impairment to concentrate on learning.

—Photos of home or family help toddlers deal with separation and feel that they belong to their family and the family is connected to the program. Not all cultures are comfortable with displays of home photographs, however; such a family may prefer to have an object from the home available for their child to see during the day.

—Toddlers learn about the world through exploration, which adults should encourage. As toddlers develop the ability to understand limits, caregivers can offer a larger variety of sensory materials.

Play and learning areas

Floor coverings are appropriate for the activities that occur there (e.g., easy-to-clean, shock-absorbent tiles for open areas where toddlers push and pull toys around and for art, eating, and water or sand play areas; low-pile, easy-to-clean carpeting or nonslip area rugs for quiet play areas).

■ Floors are covered with thick-pile carpeting that requires constant cleaning or is left dirty. Or the floor covering is hard and cold.

Developmentally Appropriate Practice, 3d Edition

Developmentally appropriate	In contrast

Environment (cont.)

Play and learning areas (cont.)

Caregivers organize the space into interest or activity areas, including areas for concentrated small-group play, solitary play, dramatic play, and construction.	■ The space is not separated into interest areas, which makes it more difficult for children to get engaged in an activity.
Activity areas are separated by low partitions, shelves, or sitting benches, creating clear traffic patterns and making it less likely that running toddlers will inadvertently bump into and thus disturb peers engaged in concentrated play.	■ Space is open, with no clear traffic pattern from one interest area to another. Running toddlers bump into those who are engaged in concentrated play.
The environment contains private spaces, with room for one or two children. The spaces are situated to be easily supervised by adults.	■ The environment provides no private spaces. Or spaces are too private because they are out of view of adults.
Indoor areas are open and safe; space is set up to allow active, large muscle play.	■ Toddlers' indoor space is cramped and unsafe for children who are just learning how to move their bodies and need to run more than walk.
Toddlers' outdoor play space is separate from that of older children. Outdoor play equipment includes small-scale climbing equipment that lets toddlers go around and in and out, as well as solitary play equipment that requires supervision, such as swings and low slides. The equipment is sized so toddlers don't need to be lifted onto it or helped to get down.	■ Toddlers share outdoor space and equipment with larger, older children. Equipment is not designed for younger children; it is too large or difficult for toddlers to maneuver around in.

Comments on play and learning areas:

—How children behave in their environment depends to some extent on how the space is organized and the messages the room arrangement conveys. When there is a clear path from one interest area to another, the message is "Come see what else there is to do."

—Keeping program goals in mind is important when considering location of the various learning and caregiving areas. For example, placing the art area and the eating area close to a sink invites toddlers (with adult encouragement) to learn to use the sink on their own before and after these activities.

—Toddlers who spend long hours in group care need to be able to occasionally get away by themselves or perhaps with one other child. The value of spaces to provide privacy will be understood by parents who value independence. In some cultures, however, children are always part of the adult environment, and adults may be puzzled by spaces set up specifically for children.

Developmentally appropriate	In contrast

Exploration and Play

Play development

Caregivers do everything they can to support toddlers' play so that children stay interested in an object or activity for increasing periods of time. For example, they don't interrupt when children are engaged, whether as individuals or as a group.

■ Because caregivers do not understand the importance of supporting children's play, they control or intrude on the play.

Caregivers respect toddlers' solitary and parallel play. When a toy is a favorite with children, adults provide a number of them to allow several toddlers to play with the toy at once.

■ Because caregivers do not understand the value of solitary and parallel play, they strive to get children to play together.

■ Adults expect toddlers to share. Popular toys are not provided in duplicate and are fought over constantly, while other toys are seldom used.

Caregivers play with toddlers, especially when they can help children to see expanded play possibilities. For example, some children may need adult help to play imaginatively, and caregivers can model for them (e.g., playing "tea party").

■ Caregivers never play with toddlers because the adults feel self-conscious or awkward.

Caregivers allow toddlers the freedom to explore their movements by testing what their bodies are capable of doing.

■ Caregivers spend time attempting to control toddlers' movements.

Caregivers understand that toddlers learn about the world through exploration and give them daily opportunities for exploratory activity at children's developmental level.

■ Caregivers do not offer exploratory play, or they limit it when it naturally occurs. They do not offer older, capable toddlers paint, sand, playdough, or clay because these materials are messy and require supervision.

Comments on play development:

—Some cultures do not view play as a tool for learning and development, and families from these cultures may not understand or appreciate the value of play. Caregivers must make clear why play is developmentally appropriate and important for toddlers.

—Toddlers need plenty of room to move. Encouraging their freedom of movement allows toddlers to learn about themselves, their world, and their own abilities and limitations; such learning helps them to avoid mishaps.

Developmentally Appropriate Practice, 3d Edition

Developmentally appropriate	In contrast

Exploration and Play (cont.)

Objects to manipulate and explore

Toddlers are given appropriate art materials, such as large crayons, watercolor markers, and large pieces of paper. Caregivers offer nontoxic materials but avoid using food for art; toddlers are developing self-regulatory skills and must learn to distinguish between food and objects that are not to be eaten.	■ Because toddlers are likely to put things in their mouths, adults give them edible, often tasty finger paints or playdough.
Caregivers allow toddlers to explore and manipulate art materials and do not expect them to produce a finished art product.	■ Toddlers are "helped" by teachers to produce a product, copy the adult-made model, follow directions, or color a coloring book or sheets with adult drawings outlined.
Cups, paint cans, and other containers are small so that toddlers can easily manage them and cleanup is easy.	■ Toddlers must start and end art projects at the same time so that caregivers can get them ready and clean them up as a group.
A child-size sink with a good supply of paper towels is located near areas designated for messy activities so toddlers learn that cleaning up and washing their hands follow any messy activity.	■ Caregivers restrict messy activities. ■ Toddlers are not taught individual responsibility in cleaning up.
Sturdy picture books are provided. People of different ages, racial and cultural groups, family types, occupations, and abilities/disabilities are depicted.	■ Books are not available because they get might be torn or soiled. ■ Books do not contain objects familiar or interesting to children.

Comments on objects to manipulate and explore:

—Art gives toddlers opportunities to explore what various materials can do. They are just discovering what it feels like to put marks on paper or to play with paint or clay, and only later do they begin to pay attention to the result. Exploration is not about "making something" but rather about creating and observing some kind of effect. Not all toddlers like messy activities, however, and they shouldn't be pressured if they are reluctant. Most will eventually join in when they see their peers enjoying the activity.

—While excellent for older toddlers' explorations, paint, sand, playdough, and clay tend to be too advanced for young toddlers (16–18 months). If such materials were made available to young toddlers, caregivers would have to restrict and supervise play very closely to keep children safe.

—In some families, books are not part of either children's or adults' lives. If these families are carrying on oral instead of literary traditions, caregivers acknowledge and honor them by inviting storytelling into the program.

Developmentally appropriate	In contrast

Exploration and Play (cont.)

Organization and access to materials

Play materials are well organized. For example, caregivers organize objects for different activities on different shelves (e.g., fill-and-empty materials are on a shelf separate from three-piece puzzles or moving/pushing toys).

■ Caregivers give no thought to organization. They are unaware that how they arrange toys and materials can affect how children interact with the items.

Play materials are stored on open shelves at children's eye level and within their reach. For example, smocks are on low hooks so toddlers can reach them.

Toddlers with special needs who are developmentally ready and able to manipulate objects (but may be challenged in mobility skills) have access to play objects.

■ Toys are dumped in a box at the end of each day and come out in a jumble, making children dig through to choose something to play with.

■ Materials are inaccessible. Or they are too unwieldy for children to access on their own.

Caregivers space individual items so toddlers can make deliberate choices.

■ Caregivers don't understand that choosing from a jumble isn't the same to a toddler as being able to look at an orderly selection and make a careful choice.

■ Toys are kept out of children's reach. Caregivers make the toddler ask for the toy he wants, or they make the selection for him.

Comments on organization and access to materials:

—Some cultures emphasize human relationships above manipulating objects; such a family may want caregivers to remove a toy or other object if it is distracting the toddler from focusing on a person or people.

—Many cultures stress independence, but families from a culture that places greater value on *inter*dependence (e.g., who want their child to have very close, enduring connections with the family) may resist letting the child make choices or access materials on her own.

Scheduling

Caregivers adapt schedules and activities to meet individual children's needs within the group setting. Time schedules are flexible and smooth, dictated more by children's needs than by adults'. There is a relatively predictable sequence to the day.

■ Activities are dictated by rigid adherence to time schedules.

■ Lack of a time schedule makes the toddlers' day unpredictable.

Developmentally appropriate	In contrast

Scheduling (cont.)

Recognizing toddlers' need to repeat tasks until they master the steps and skills involved, caregivers allow each child to go at his or her own pace. Adults have time to assist a child with special needs because the rest of the children know what is expected and are engaged.

■ Caregivers lose patience with toddlers' desire for repetition.

■ Toddlers must either do things in groups according to the caregiver's plan or follow adult demands that they spend a certain amount of time on an activity.

■ Caregivers have little time for a child with special needs.

Caregivers plan walks around the neighborhood or to a park and special trips so that toddlers see many outdoor environments and experience natural settings.

■ Toddlers rarely go outside because it takes so much time for adults to get organized. Or caregivers consider toddlers too young to appreciate "field trips."

Comments on scheduling:

—Toddlers are cognitively ready to learn sequences of events, and they feel more secure when they know what will happen next in their day.

—When caregivers let children set the direction and pace of an activity, toddlers can learn on their own and practice what they are learning. It is important for adults to resist hurrying toddlers when they are engaged; their engagement frees adults up to give time to every child, including any with special needs.

—Being outside every day is important for toddlers' physical, mental, and emotional health. Fresh air is important, as is exercise, for the children's growing and developing body and brain.

Routines

The diapering/toileting, sleeping, and eating areas are separate, both for sanitation and to ensure quiet, restful areas.

■ Areas are combined and thus very noisy, distracting, and unhealthy.

Caregivers recognize that routine tasks of living, such as eating, toileting, and dressing, are important opportunities to help children learn about their world, acquire skills, and regulate their own behavior.

■ Caregivers perform for toddlers routine tasks that the children could do for themselves.

Comments on routines:

—Positive responses to children's attempts to do for themselves encourage them to continue trying. When consistently given opportunities to practice, children learn to use utensils, toilet independently, and dress themselves. Not all cultures value independence, so such families may initially think their toddlers are being neglected when caregivers don't spoon feed or dress them.

—Communication with parents about daily routines and needs should be ongoing. For example, if caregivers learn that a child didn't get enough breakfast or refused to eat anything, they can offer the child an early snack.

—During routines, caregivers need to understand and follow good practice for health, safety, nutrition, etc.

—For more specific information, please reference the NAEYC Health and Safety accreditation criteria: "Physical Environment" and "Health."

Developmentally appropriate	In contrast

Routines (cont.)

Eating

Toddlers are provided snacks more frequently and in smaller portions than are older children (e.g., two morning snacks rather than preschoolers' usual single snack). Liquids are provided frequently. Children's and families' food preferences are respected.	▇ Hungry children are allowed to become fussy and cranky, waiting for food that is served on a rigid schedule. ▇ Caregivers use food for rewards or withhold it as punishment.
Caregivers supply utensils that toddlers can use easily for meals and snacks, such as bowls, spoons, and graduated versions of bottles and cups.	▇ Children feel incompetent or frustrated because the eating utensils are too difficult for them to manage. ▇ Children are expected to do things for themselves but are reprimanded for spills or accidents.
Toddlers eat in small groups at low tables. Their caregiver sits nearby to provide assistance as needed.	▇ Toddlers are fed in large groups in sequence or left to manage on their own.

Napping

Toddlers can nap in the play area as long as their cots are well separated from each other and the space is cleared of play objects (e.g., stored on shelves). Caregivers plan where each toddler's cot will go according to the child's ease or difficulty in resting, distractibility, need for quiet, or length of normal nap.	▇ Caregivers place cots too close together. No thought is given to planning for each toddler's sleeping needs.
Each toddler has his or her own labeled cot and bedding. Retrieving their own blankets or special stuffed toys is a part of children's nap routine.	▇ Cots and sheets are used interchangeably by all children. ▇ Bringing special items from home is discouraged because children "only lose them" or "just fight over them."
Caregivers establish a transition into naptime with a predictable sequence of events and a change in the environment. It begins with a quiet activity, such as reading a story. Once the cots are in place, toddlers get their stuffed toys or blankets and go to their cots. Lights are turned down, and soft music or a story tape plays for toddlers who are awake.	▇ There is no transition to naptime; once toddlers are lying down, caregivers just turn off the lights, expecting children to be quiet immediately. ▇ Naptime is chaotic. Some toddlers sleep; others are disruptive, wandering about the room.

Developmentally appropriate	In contrast

Routines (cont.)

Napping (cont.)

Comments on napping:

—Naptime can be difficult no matter how prepared the caregiver is. Some children may be overtired and some not tired enough. Toddlers who are feeling insecure may have a hard time relaxing enough to go to sleep.

—Some toddlers have trouble ignoring the other children. Caregivers' understanding of individual differences is key: To relax, some toddlers need visual privacy (they can't see the others), some need auditory privacy (can't hear them), and some toddlers need both, which is not easy to arrange, but creative caregivers find ways.

—In some families, toddlers never sleep alone, so they may find naptime in the program difficult. For toddlers who normally sleep in cribs, the freedom of a cot can invite them to get up and move about.

Diapering and toileting

Developmentally appropriate	In contrast
Caregivers work cooperatively with families in encouraging children to learn to use the toilet. When toddlers reach an age when they feel confident and unafraid to sit on a toilet seat, caregivers take them to use the toilet regularly in response to each child's biological needs, help them as needed, provide manageable clothing, and positively reinforce them.	■ Caregivers do not discuss toilet learning with families, but they impose it on children for the adults' convenience, whether children are ready or not. ■ Caregivers make children sit on the toilet for undue lengths of time. ■ Children are punished or shamed for toileting accidents.
Toddlers who are not ready to use the toilet or who have had an accident are usually diapered by the child's primary caregiver or another familiar adult. Treated as personal, one-on-one interaction, diapering builds the caregiver-toddler relationship and a sense of teamwork.	■ All toddlers are diapered by the same person, not necessarily the child's primary caregiver or a familiar adult. ■ Diapering is performed brusquely.

Comments on diapering and toileting:

—The developmental perspective on toileting focuses on individual readiness and takes a positive approach. Caregivers let the child and family take the lead on toileting, rather than following a rigid set of guidelines. Positive toileting grows naturally out of a caregiver's (and the parents') relationship with the child during diapering—if the adults treated the child as part of the team during diapering as an infant, as a toddler, the child will continue to see his or her role as cooperating with them in learning to use the toilet.

—Toddler-size toilets, which don't require children to use a stepstool, are ideal. The toilet should be in a well-lit, inviting, relatively private space. Families from cultures that start toilet training in infancy may be surprised by programs that take a more flexible and gradual approach; caregivers working with such families may be surprised that year-old babies and very young toddlers are already out of diapers.

Developmentally appropriate	In contrast

Routines (cont.)

Dressing

Toddlers' attempts to dress themselves and put on shoes are supported and positively encouraged.

■ Caregivers discourage toddlers from putting on or taking off items of clothing by themselves because "they take so long."

■ Because caregivers fail to encourage toddler-friendly clothes (e.g., no tiny buttons or laces), children struggle in learning how to dress themselves, and adults spend a lot of time helping them.

Comments on dressing:
—Toddlers can more feasibly learn to dress themselves when their clothes do not require a lot of fine motor precision (e.g., shoes with Velcro, pants with an elastic waist).

Reciprocal Relationships with Families

Caregivers work in partnership with parents, communicating daily to build mutual understanding and trust and to ensure each toddler's well-being and optimal development.

■ Caregivers do not seek to communicate with parents.

Caregivers respect parents as being their child's most important relationship and as having ultimate responsibility for the child's well-being and care. They focus on parents' expertise and attachment to their toddlers.

■ Caregivers set themselves up as "the experts" and cause parents to feel inadequate and peripheral to the care of their child.

Caregivers listen carefully to what parents say about their child; seek to understand parents' goals, priorities, and preferences; and show respect for cultural and family differences. They solicit and incorporate parents' knowledge in making decisions about how best to support the toddler's development or to handle problems or differences of opinion as they arise.

■ Caregivers ignore parents' concerns, or they capitulate to parent demands or preferences, even when these are at odds with developmentally appropriate practice.

■ Caregivers blame parents when children have difficulty. Or they demand that parents punish children at home for something that happened in the program.

Caregivers help parents feel good about their toddlers and their parenting (e.g., by sharing some of the positive and interesting things that happened that day).

■ Caregivers mention only problems to parents.

Developmentally Appropriate Practice, 3d Edition

Developmentally appropriate	In contrast

Reciprocal Relationships with Families (cont.)

Caregivers always make parents feel welcome in the toddler program setting.

■ Caregivers communicate a competitive or patronizing attitude to parents.

■ Caregivers make parents feel in the way.

Comments on reciprocal relationships with families:

—When parents (and other family members) and caregivers take a team approach, they are able to figure out together how to solve problems and support children. Caregivers who see themselves as partners with families go out of their way to build relationships, even though there may be time constraints that make this difficult. In a team approach, caregivers spend less time trying to convince parents of anything and more time trying to understand their point of view as well as share developmentally appropriate practices with them.

—Helping parents feel good about their child's positive qualities leads to family support for those qualities. Most parents want to feel good about their child, but in some cultures, they may not want to hear that their child feels pride in herself. Such a family may instead choose to downplay a child's positive qualities and promote humility.

Policies

Health and safety

Caregivers follow health and safety procedures, including proper hand washing methods and universal precautions to limit the spread of infectious diseases. There are clearly written sanitation procedures specific to each task or routine to help staff remember to follow procedures completely and consistently.

■ Policies and procedures to ensure a sanitary facility have not been clearly thought through and are not written down. Consequently, adults forget hand washing or other essential steps in toileting, handling food, and eating utensils.

■ Caregivers are not consistent in maintaining sanitary conditions and procedures.

The space has been constructed and set up with health and safety in mind (e.g., walls are painted with lead-free, easy-to-clean paint; carpeting and other floor coverings are easy to clean; a first-aid kit is kept stocked and easily accessible).

■ The space is not organized to foster toddlers' health and safety.

■ The space is clean and safe but has a sterile, institutional feel.

Comments on health and safety:

—Caregivers need training, support, and reminders to understand and consistently follow proper health and safety procedures (e.g., not letting toddlers share cups or spoons).

—For more specific information, please reference the NAEYC Health and Safety accreditation criteria: "Physical Environment" and "Health."

—See also *Healthy Young Children: A Manual for Programs, 4th ed.* (Aronson & Spahr 2002); *Model Child Care Health Policies, 4th ed.* (Aronson 2002); and the American Academy of Pediatrics website at www.aap.org.

Developmentally appropriate	In contrast

Policies (cont.)

Staffing

Program makes every effort to hire caregivers who have training in child development/early education specific to the toddler age group. Caregivers are open to ongoing training and support in order to increase and improve their knowledge and skills. They know how to work with toddlers in groups and individually. Staff are competent in first-aid.

▓ Program hires caregivers who have no training in child development/early education. Or their training and experience are limited to working with older children.

▓ Caregivers view toddlers as immature preschoolers rather than appreciating their unique stage of development.

▓ Caregivers are unaware of what signals to look for that might indicate developmental delays or a need for evaluation.

Program hires caregivers who enjoy working with toddlers, respond warmly to their communications and needs, and demonstrate considerable patience in supporting children as they become increasingly competent and independent.

▓ Program hires caregivers who view work with toddlers as a custodial chore.

▓ Caregivers expect little of toddlers. Or they push children to achieve and are impatient with their struggles.

▓ Caregivers take toddlers' limit testing ("No!") personally and continually get into power struggles over trivial matters.

Program limits group size and the adult:child ratio to minimize the number of adults that toddlers must relate to each day.

▓ Both group size and staff:child ratio are too large to permit individual attention and constant supervision. Staffing patterns require toddlers to relate to multiple different adults during the caregiving day.

Program ensures continuity over time for each toddler's relationship with one or two primary caregivers. Child and caregiver are able to form and maintain their relationship, and each child's ongoing relationship with the other children in the group is supported.

▓ Staffing patterns shift caregivers around often, from toddler to toddler or group to group.

▓ Child groupings change constantly (e.g., children "graduate" to the next room and staff).

▓ Each adult cares for so many children or is responsible for only one or two aspects of care (e.g., dressing), so caregivers don't spend enough time with each toddler.

▓ High staff turnover results in low continuity of care and frequent disruption of toddlers' budding, satisfying attachments to caregivers.

Developmentally appropriate	In contrast

Policies (cont.)

Staffing (cont.)

Comments on staffing:

—Staff training and support are very important. Toddlerhood is a developmental stage different from either infancy or preschool age.

—Toddlers require relationship-based care and education; group size and adult:child ratio should be limited to allow for the intimate, interpersonal atmosphere and high level of supervision that toddlers require. With a small number of consistent adults to relate to, toddlers can feel safe and secure, which contributes to their learning and development. Conversely, toddlers tend to avoid attachment if caregivers come and go.

—For more specific information, please reference the NAEYC Health and Safety accreditation criteria: "Teaching" and "Teachers."

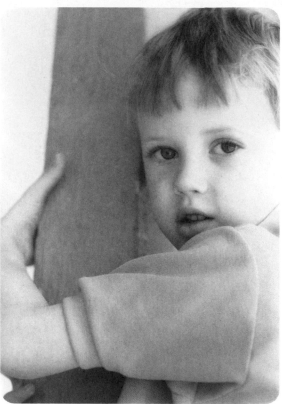

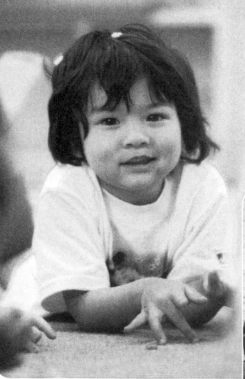

the
preschool
years

4

Developmentally Appropriate Practice in
the Preschool Years—Ages 3–5

An Overview

Heather Biggar Tomlinson and Marilou Hyson

In ever-increasing numbers, children in this age group are involved in out-of-home programs, including child care centers, family child care homes, and public or private full- and half-day prekindergartens. In fact, more than half of 3- and 4-year-olds in the United States are enrolled in some type of preschool program (NCES 2008), with public schools serving more than 20 percent of 4-year-olds (Pre-K Now 2008a).

We refer to children ages 3 to 5 as preschoolers, even though the label has lost its former meaning as "the years before school attendance." Now the preschool year or years before kindergarten are recognized as a vitally important period of learning and development in their own right, not merely as a time for growth in anticipation of the "real learning" that will begin in school. It is well established that important development and learning occur during these early years in all areas of human functioning—physical, social and emotional, cognitive (including perception, reasoning, memory, and other aspects of academic and intellectual development), and language.

It is also well established that optimal development and learning during these years is most likely to occur when children establish positive and caring relationships with adults and other children; receive carefully planned, intentional adult guidance and assistance; and explore interesting environments with many things to do and learn. These conditions can and do occur for many young children at home with their parents. But those children who attend out-of-home early childhood programs spend many hours of their day away from their families.

Early childhood teachers, in collaboration with families, are responsible for ensuring that the program promotes the development and enhances the learning of each individual child served; in other words, professionals must ensure that the program is developmentally appropriate.

Ensuring this requires that teachers have a great deal of knowledge, skill, and training. Children entering preschool vary significantly in what they know

and can do. Some have had rich learning experiences at home, in a program, or both prior to entering preschool; some have not had the kinds of stimulating or supportive environments that contribute to optimal development and learning. Because there is such a range in the types and quality of learning experiences—not to mention individual differences in children's temperament and interests—children enter preschool with different developmental strengths.

One child might love to look at picture books and know lots of letters already, but, having had little exposure to other children, he finds it difficult to share materials, cooperate in group projects, and enter play situations. Another child coming into the same program might have three siblings and find it easy to initiate play and share toys with new classmates. She also has wonderful capacities with real-world activities such as cooking because of her experiences at home, but she has almost no knowledge of the enchanting world of books.

While every child has areas of strength and weakness, unfortunately some children living in difficult situations tend to struggle in several areas. On average, 4-year-olds living in poverty are about 18 months behind what is typical for others in their age group. This translates into achievement and school readiness gaps between children from poor families versus middle-class families in math, language, and other academic areas—gaps that are seen in preschool and that persist into elementary school and beyond (Snow 2005; Klibanoff et al. 2006). These gaps are cause for concern for every community because an alarming 43 percent of preschool age children across the country come from low-income families. In other words, 3.5 million 3- and 4-year-olds and 1.7 million 5-year-olds—and their families and teachers—are affected (Douglas-Hall & Chau 2008).

Children living in poverty are often vulnerable in a multitude of ways, one of which is that they are more likely than other children to live with a disability. Sixteen percent of low-income families have a child with a disability, a rate nearly 50 percent higher than

that for higher-income families (Lee, Sills, & Oh 2002). Of course, disabilities and delays affect all families, regardless of income; about five percent of preschoolers across the country are known to have some kind of special need (U.S. Dept. of Education 2001). Early childhood teachers welcome these and all children into their classrooms, understanding the richness that inclusion brings in terms of diversity and interdependence.

In addition, the demographics in early childhood programs reflect the country's ever-greater cultural diversity. Teachers must be adept at integrating cultural knowledge into their teaching. This integration requires reaching out to parents and involving and empowering every family. Doing so enriches communication about their child. And it both strengthens the bond between teachers and families and builds stronger connections between teachers and children—enhancing benefits and learning experiences for children well into their future schooling (Espinosa 2007).

Considerable growth and change occur in children during the preschool years in all areas of development. To function most effectively, preschool teachers need to know about the goals, sequences, and trajectories of development in all those areas—to avoid using a scaled-down version of curriculum intended for older children and to understand the importance of communicating with kindergarten and other teachers and aligning the curriculum accordingly.

Three-year-olds are no longer toddlers, but they behave like toddlers at times, and they are not steady in their gains. Children's social skills are still uncertain, they are still working on how to regulate and appropriately express strong emotions, and they are not yet able to communicate their ideas and feelings in skilled, complex ways. They believe in fairies and monsters and have trouble with logical sequences that seem basic to adults—hence adults' tendency to underestimate their actual abilities. Yet at other times, their language ability, motor skills, reasoning abilities, and other behaviors make them seem older than they are.

The challenge for the preschool teacher is to maintain appropriate expectations, providing each child with the right mix of challenge, support, sensitivity, and stimulation that promotes development and learning—all of which can only happen within the context of a close, nurturing teacher-child relationship (Burchinal et al. 2008).

Fortunately, the challenges of working with preschoolers are balanced out by the joys. Preschoolers revel in their increasing coordination, using their bodies exuberantly. They thrive in environments that encourage them to experiment with new materials, roles, and ideas through various projects and especially through play; they have great interest in feelings and are better able to express and label their emotions and identify others' emotions; they make some important gains in cognition, allowing them the pleasure of representing their world in pretend play, symbols, objects, drawings, and words; and, given a rich language environment, they show astonishing gains in language skills.

In general, preschoolers are an enchanting, enthusiastic, curious, and inherently playful and imaginative bunch, providing the adults who work with them entry to a world of great charm and delight.

Physical development

Preschoolers are extremely physical creatures—constantly moving, running, and jumping. They react joyfully to opportunities for dancing, creative movement, physical dramatic play, and being outdoors where they can move without

© Jean-Claude LeJeune

constraint. "They should spend at least a quarter of their school day in physical activity. This is an age when much learning is transmitted through the large muscles, when learning goes from the hand to the head, not the other way around" (Wood 2007, 49). In preschool, paper-and-pencil activities are far less useful teaching tools, on the whole, than hands-on activities such as dramatizing fairy tales, squeezing clay into animal shapes, hanging from a jungle gym, building block castles, or getting messy with paint.

The development of basic movement skills that takes place between ages 2 and 7 is the "fundamental" movement phase (Gabbard 2007). Coordination improves with each year: The movements of most 2- and 3-year-olds are generally still fairly immature and uncoordinated; 4- and 5-year-olds have greater control but are not yet fluid in their movements; fluidity begins to be evident by age 6 or 7 (Sanders 2006). Overall, most children around age 4 might be viewed as a bit clumsy, and spills and collisions are not uncommon (Wood 2007). Children experience different degrees of difficulty with various motor tasks, and gender differences are observable as well. Preschool age girls tend to be more advanced than boys in fine motor and gross motor skills requiring precision, such as hopping and skipping; boys generally hold an edge in physical skills that require force and power, such as running and jumping (Berk 2008).

The connection between physical activity and healthy lifestyles is more important than ever with the rise of childhood obesity and its long-term negative health effects. Today there are about three times (14 percent) as many overweight children between ages 2 to 5 as there were in the 1960s (Land 2008). Research studies (Kuczmarski et al. 2002; AHA 2008) confirm that regular physical activity helps children by:

- building and maintaining healthy bones, muscles, and joints;

- controlling weight;

- building lean muscle and reducing fat;

- preventing or delaying development of high blood pressure;

- reducing feelings of depression and anxiety; and

- increasing capacity for learning (Sanders 2002).

Physical well-being emerges not only from appropriate levels of physical activity but also from access to good health care, adequate shelter and hygiene, good sleeping habits, and a nutritious diet. Preschoolers (and other children) need frequent opportunities to eat and drink throughout the day to stay energized, avoid headaches and fatigue, maintain focus, and enjoy their surroundings.

Physical growth and maturation

The amount and rate of growth in children between the ages of 3 and 5 vary. Some children grow as much as six inches over this three-year period while others grow only a few inches; but all children develop a less toddler-like trunk and become less top-heavy. Growth in this period takes place mostly in the trunk and legs. The physical growth rate is steadier overall but still slower than during the first three years of life. On average, children gain five to six pounds and two to three inches per year from ages 3 to 6. However, the amount of growth varies greatly among individuals and also among children of different groups. All 20 baby teeth have emerged by around age 3. Simply put, the preschooler is physically not an infant anymore. These processes of growth and maturation promote many new abilities in all areas of development.

Preschoolers' image of their body often lags behind their increasing size. Learning how to monitor their bodies in space is a challenge, and frequent mishaps arise from children's lack of awareness of just how much they have grown (as when a child does not believe that a favorite shirt no longer fits) and from their lack of motor skill planning (as when a child picks the more difficult way to get somewhere).

Sensation and perception

Perceptual development is largely dependent on the development of the brain and central nervous system—the exact timing of which varies—but for the most part, the senses of sight, touch, smell, taste, and hearing are well developed by the preschool period. In fact, preschool children's sense of taste is actually *more* acute than that of adults; they have additional taste buds in the cheeks and throat (which partially accounts for their reputation as "picky eaters") (Harris 1986). In spite of their physical capacities for excellent sensation and perception, their processing of the incoming information is less than complete; children have yet to develop some of the cognitive strategies and language refinements needed to interpret and communicate the sensory data.

Children around age 3 improve in their ability to perceive patterns and discriminate various forms. Gradually children begin to recognize and then repeat and design visual patterns. Throughout preschool, children show increasing interest in producing designs and patterns in art, puzzles, constructions, and letters and words. However, children are farsighted and have trouble switching focus between close and distant targets; they are still developing their coordination of binocular vision (the ability of

© Shari Schmidt

the eyes to work together), which necessitates the use of large print. Also, children this age do not have great depth perception, which means they tend to run into things and each other (Pica 2004). Children may make letter reversals (e.g., confusing the letters q and p or d and b), but this is not a perceptual problem. Rather, it is a natural confusion based on previous experience; unlike symbols such as letters, objects in the physical world have the same function and name regardless of their directional orientation (e.g., a block is still a block whether facing left or right).

Like their other senses, young children's sense of hearing is well developed by preschool age. They can listen intently to stories and pay attention to conversations that interest them. They begin to recognize rhyming words and play with the sounds of language. These activities require auditory recognition and processing of sounds. At age 4 or 5, children perceive when two words sound the same or begin with the same sound (i.e., phonemic awareness) (Wasik 2001). Preschool children who appear unable to do these types of activities (e.g., listen to stories, rhyming) may have a hearing problem. Chronic middle ear infections during infancy or toddlerhood can impair hearing.

Gross motor development

Physical growth during this age lowers the child's center of gravity, making more steady and surefooted movements possible. Gross motor development includes increased functional use of limbs for activities such as jumping, running, and climbing. Most preschoolers, unless they have experienced some developmental difficulty or delay, are able to perform basic gross motor skills such as running.

In general, younger preschoolers (ages 3 and 4) are just beginning to work on skills such as balancing, jumping, and hopping and are challenged by an obstacle course or the like; older preschoolers will find these tasks easier. Because the nervous system is still immature overall, the preschooler's reaction time is generally much slower than that of a 6- or 7-year-old.

As in other domains, children move through a sequence of refining their gross motor skills. This sequence is a product of physical maturation, instruction, and opportunity to practice newly discovered skills. Variation in motor development is due to a combination of genetic and environmental factors, including motivation, experience, and adult support. Differences among racial groups in motor development have been documented; for instance, norms of motor development among African American children exceed those of Caucasian children in walking, running, and jumping (Berk 2009).

During preschool, any specific motor difficulties will become more apparent to parents and teachers, who may need to involve specialists (e.g., early childhood special educators, physical therapists, occupational therapists) in assessing and planning appropriate intervention and support for children's physical development.

The rise of youth sports programs for children as young as age 3 is misleading and based in developmental misunderstanding; preschoolers are not physically ready to handle the skills needed for specific sports, nor are they emotionally or cognitively equipped for the rules and pressures of competition. Instead, teachers should encourage children to enjoy movement for its own sake; even though preschoolers appear a bit uncoordinated or kinesthetically unaware at times, they have fun using and exploring their body's capacity for movement (Sanders 2002).

Fine motor development

Given opportunities to practice, preschoolers do make gains in their fine motor skills, but they do not attain any kind of sophisticated manual dexterity. Writing, drawing, and cutting with precision are activities that can be difficult for many preschoolers, who are still developing comfort and agility with fine motor work. They may experience failure and frustration if they often are expected to perform tasks requiring precise control of the hand muscles, careful

perceptual judgment involving eye-hand coordination, and refined movements requiring steadiness and patience.

Handedness is fairly well established around age 4, although the wrist contains some cartilage that will not harden into bone until about age 6, placing some constraint on fine motor capacity (Berk 2008). As a result, most preschoolers cannot make fully circular wrist motions, such as those needed for cursive writing (neither do they have the wrist strength to propel themselves on overhead horizontal bars).

They make progress through opportunities for open-ended activities that develop their hand muscles and fine motor skills, such as exploring drawing and painting, working with playdough and clay, or constructing with Duplos or Legos. Such activities—along with plenty of time and encouragement—engage children and prepare them for the demands of handwriting and other skills developed later. Children at this age can also learn to use their hands and fingers by watching others.

Promoting physical development in preschool

Becoming more adept, coordinated, and skillful involves an interplay between children's emerging physical capacities, resulting from growth and maturation, and the skills that develop from adult instruction (physical education) and opportunities to practice specific new skills (recess, free play). While children may develop many of their physical capabilities through play, they also need planned movement activities, explicit instruction (both verbal and modeled), and structured physical skill development opportunities to guide them in becoming physically active and healthy for a lifetime (NASPE 2002; Sanders 2002).

The National Association for Sport and Physical Education (2002) recommends that preschoolers accumulate daily at least 60 minutes of structured physical activity (e.g., in short bouts of 15 minutes each) and between 60 minutes and several hours of unstructured physical activity. They should not be sedentary for more than 60 minutes at any time (except for sleep, of course). As preschool teachers know, requiring too much sitting is at odds with young children's characteristic mode of learning through activity—through moving, exploring, and acting on objects.

Early childhood educators plan for active play indoors and outdoors, are sensitive to the needs of children at different ages, and pay attention to the individual capabilities and interests of children as they run, jump, climb, balance, throw, catch, and explore their fine motor skills. In addition, teachers make sure to move beyond group games (such as Duck Duck Goose) in their curriculum planning and include activities to develop children's basic movement skills through a variety of physical learning tasks. Preschoolers need to experience an array of objects and events in their daily environment that they can explore and learn about with their senses. Throughout the preschool years, children benefit from materials, experiences, and teaching strategies that help them learn the distinctive features of objects, graphical symbols, and other stimuli.

Daily activities should include many opportunities for young children to develop competence and confidence in their gross motor skills. For example, as part of the daily routine, children carry objects, take nature walks, exercise and move to music, and engage in role-playing actions and short dramas. Play equipment should include a diverse array of things, such as cup stilts, a small trampoline, steps, a balance beam, hoops for jumping, jump ropes, bean bag toss, scooter boards, a puppet show, ring toss, a parachute, floor puzzles, hollow blocks, large Legos, and strollers for dramatic play. Large floor areas (carpeted and not) are needed inside for movement and other activities, such as throwing and jumping.

The outdoors is an ideal environment for promoting gross motor development, but its use must be planned and supervised. Equipment is needed, such as a small net and beach balls for playing volleyball, foam bats and balls, tric or scooter boards. Teachers can plan ou

activities that include parachute games, hoop activities, ball games, an obstacle course, group games (e.g., Fruit Basket), and an exercise station with a balance beam, ladder, climbing pole, and tires.

Teachers can employ a wide variety of teaching strategies to facilitate children's gross motor development, combining the themes of locomotor, stability, and manipulative skills with the concepts of space awareness, effort, and relationship with other people and the environment:

> What's important in a developmentally appropriate movement program for young children is for the young child to develop physical skills plus an awareness of how movement concepts relate to those skills. Limiting children's movement experiences simply to throwing or kicking a ball (manipulative skills), for example, without introducing the concepts of kicking *hard*, throwing *high*, or kicking *under*, fails to provide the knowledge base young children need to become movement proficient. (Sanders 2002, 38)

Because preschoolers are engaging in many gross motor activities for the first time and children's perceptual judgments are still immature, a significant amount of direct adult supervision is necessary. The physical environment should have pieces of equipment that vary in skill level according to the degree of balance and coordination required. Under climbing structures, six to twelve inches of appropriate cushioning material is necessary to protect children from

Developmentally Appropriate Practice, 3d Edition

falls, a major cause of childhood injury (see AAP & APHA 1992; Kendrick, Kaufmann, & Messenger 1995). Planned outdoor activities should challenge children to use a range of motor skills, as obstacle courses do, but allow for and be adapted to a wide range of difference among children due to maturational rates; motivation level; experience, practice, and adult coaching; nutrition; and identified or potential disabilities and exceptional abilities.

Fine motor development progresses slowly during the preschool years but can be fostered by providing ample opportunities, appropriate tools, and adult support—as can be seen in settings where children's experiences and the cultural expectations are highly conducive to fine motor skill development (Reggio Emilia Department of Early Education 1987; Tobin, Wu, & Davidson 1989). Pushing children too early into fine motor tasks is likely to be both unsuccessful and frustrating for children and may leave them feeling incompetent and stressed. Acknowledging what children can do and supporting their efforts to try new activities result in fewer discouraged young learners. By kindergarten, children are able to engage in fine motor activities more readily and for longer periods of time.

Preschoolers should have access to many kinds of materials and objects to help them develop and practice fine motor skills, such as small objects to sort and count; pegboards and beads to string; clothing and things that zip, button, and tie for dress-up play; dolls and accessories; drawing and writing materials; scissors, paint, and clay; and opportunities to practice functional skills, such as pouring milk, setting the table, eating, and dressing.

When children seem interested and persistent in writing their name and forming letters, adults should offer assistance, both formal and informal. Inviting 3- and 4-year-olds to explore writing their names and accepting children's attempts at approximations of letters recognize their growing skills (IRA & NAEYC 1998). Daily writing activities, such as a sign-in sheet, and exposure to the many purposes of writing help build their understanding of the power of the written word, while respecting their as yet undeveloped fine motor control for precise letter formation.

Assessment of children's physical progress occurs best through planned observation of an appropriate task. Watching a group of children running is not very helpful in identifying the more able or less able children in this age range. Teachers get a fuller picture of children's individual levels of gross motor skill by watching each child go through an obstacle course that includes a balance beam and something to jump into, out of, and over (such as hoops and tunnels). When children are identified with a disability, the usual activities may require adaptation.

For example, children unable to use their hands are able to draw and construct to practice fine motor skills if provided assistive technologies such as modified keyboards, switches, pointing devices, and graphics programs (Behrmann & Lahm 1994). It is also important to provide preschoolers who have developmental disabilities with ways to be active and mobile. Again, adaptations of equipment or the environment may be necessary, such as making playgrounds and equipment wheelchair accessible or using signs and symbols to help a child with hearing loss participate in music or movement.

Two statements from the National Association for Sport and Physical Education help define developmentally appropriate physical activity programs for all children: *Appropriate Practices in Movement Programs for Young Children* (NASPE 2000) and *Active Start: A Statement of Physical Activity Guidelines for Children Birth to Five Years* (NASPE 2002).

Social and emotional development

Parents and teachers are delighted but sometimes frustrated by preschool age children's social and emotional characteristics. From ages 3 to 5, young children make great advances in their relationships with others, their self-understanding, and their ability to understand

and regulate their emotions. The path is bumpy, however; all preschoolers continue to struggle with social and emotional issues. Carlos avoids playing with others; sociable Lisa sometimes hits her playmates when they don't go along with her ideas; Kirsten can't calm down after an exciting morning.

To support this developmental process, relationships with caring adults within a quality early childhood environment are critical. This support is important for all children but especially for those whose social and emotional development may be at risk because of disabilities or because of difficult circumstances in their family or community environments.

Positive social and emotional development in the preschool years will provide an essential foundation for cognitive and academic competence, not only in preschool but also in later years (McClelland, Morrison, & Holmes 2000; Blair 2002; Raver 2002; Zins et al. 2004). More than ever, early childhood educators recognize that these aspects of development must be given the same level of focused attention and planning as is given to children's literacy development or their understanding of mathematical concepts.

The preschool years are now seen as the key period for establishing positive attitudes and behaviors about learning. These attitudes and behaviors are closely related to social and emotional development but affect virtually all aspects of children's development and learning. In 1997 the National Education Goals Panel identified "approaches to learning" as one of its five components of school readiness. Many states now include this approaches to learning domain as its own category in their early learning guidelines.

Approaches to learning include children's *enthusiasm* for learning (i.e., interest, pleasure, and motivation to learn) and their *engagement* in learning (i.e., ability to focus attention, persist, be flexible, and regulate thoughts, feelings, and behavior) (Hyson 2008). Children who are enthusiastic about and engaged in learning are likely to be more successful learners, not only in preschool but in later years, as well (Fantuzzo, Perry, & McDermott 2004; McClelland, Acock, & Morrison 2006).

Children may be born with a basic temperament, but they are not born with positive or negative approaches to learning. Their experiences at home and in early childhood programs can either support or undermine this enthusiasm and engagement.

Social development

During the preschool years, children truly come into their own as social beings. "My friend" is a phrase used proudly by a 3-year-old, even if the child does not yet have a full understanding of the concept of friendship. In preschool, children also become better able to sustain close relationships with adults other than their parents—most important, their teachers (Howes & Ritchie 2002).

Out of the many aspects of preschoolers' social development, four are sketched out in this section: (1) children's social interactions, relationships with teachers and peers, and friendships; (2) development of prosocial behavior; (3) aggression and other challenging behaviors; and (4) sense of self in relation to others.

Social interactions, relationships with teachers and peers, and friendships. Most preschoolers live in a wider social world than they did before age 3. Even those who have been in child care since infancy are now much more aware of and connected to other children and adults beyond their immediate family. Preschoolers often have close relationships with their teachers, developing attachments that are similar but not identical to those they have with their parents (Howes & Ritchie 2002). Such relationships can be rich and valuable. Preschoolers who have positive relationships with their teachers are likely to be more interested and engaged in school, and they are more likely to be socially competent in later years (Howes 2000; Morrison 2007).

Peers also take on more importance during the years from 3 to 5. Most children interact much more with other children than when they were toddlers, and they interact in more complex ways (Rubin, Bukowski, & Parker 2006). Although many continue to play alone or in parallel to classmates (Rubin & Coplan 1998), preschoolers become increasingly able to enter and remain involved in mature sociodramatic play—that is, able to agree about the topic of the play ("*You be the driver and I'll be the lady going to the store, okay?*"), to take on more complex roles, and to sustain the play with other children for longer periods of time (Bodrova & Leong 2007). Extensive involvement in sociodramatic play not only builds preschoolers' social skills but also is associated with better language and literacy skills, self-regulation, and later school achievement (Rubin, Bukowski, & Parker 2006).

Preschool children generally value their friendships. At this age, most children have friends, though not necessarily a best friend. Friendship skills are important: Children who have an easier time making friends are likely to be more self-regulated and to have a better understanding of others' thoughts and feelings. All is not smooth in preschool friendships, however; children have more conflicts with friends than with other children, in part because friends spend more time together. Still, preschoolers are likely to solve conflicts with their friends in nonaggressive ways, and they cooperate more with their friends than with children who are not their friends (Fabes et al. 1996; Rubin, Bukowski, & Parker 2006).

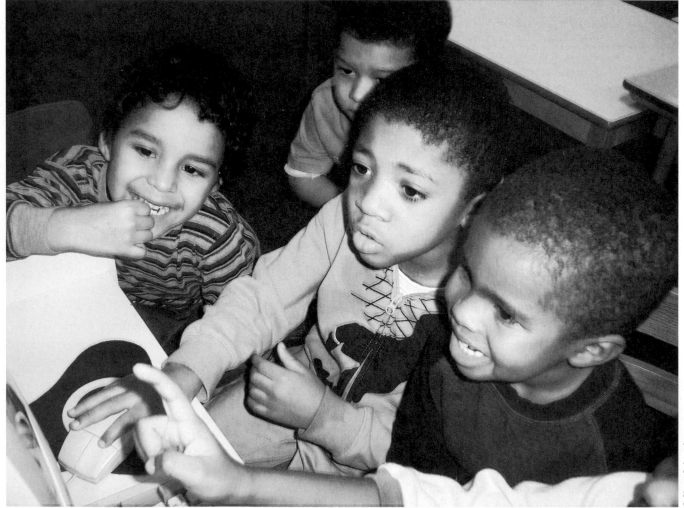

© Shari Schmidt

During the preschool years, children's language development and their growing social understanding also allow them to have conversations with their peers, chatting about events of interest and adjusting their talk to make themselves better understood (Rubin, Bukowski, & Parker 2006).

Development of prosocial behavior. When children act prosocially, they voluntarily assist others out of concern for others' well-being—behavior that has been called "caring, sharing, and helping" (Mussen & Eisenberg-Berg 1977). Between ages 3 and 6, children begin to show more frequent prosocial behaviors (Eisenberg, Fabes, & Spinrad 2006). Seeing a classmate starting to cry when her father leaves, 3-year-old Leslie may give her friend a hug; by age 5, Leslie may use comforting words or suggest a game she knows her friend usually enjoys.

There are many reasons for this increase in prosocial behaviors. Among them, children's cognitive development allows them to better understand others' feelings, and preschoolers have had many more experiences that contribute to their social understanding. Plus, adults usually expect more helpful behavior from children after age 3.

But it's also the case that some preschool children are more prosocial than others, and such differences are likely to carry over into later years. Those preschool children who are more self-regulated seem better able to focus on others' distress, making plans and taking action to help when needed. Children who have warm, secure relationships with their parents, and when parents help the children notice others' distress and support their children's helping behavior ("*Look, I think Ron is a little worried about coming in. Can you find something for him to play with?*"), are likely to continue to be helpful (Eisenberg, Fabes, & Spinrad 2006). And children who are in high-quality early childhood programs, and who have secure attachments to their preschool teachers (Howes, Matheson, & Hamilton 1994), are more likely to be prosocial and considerate of other children.

Aggression and other challenging behaviors. Compared with their behavior as toddlers, children over the age of 3 are less likely to have tantrums or other outbursts when they are frustrated, and they are less likely to hit or fight with other children. Conflicts over possessions continue to trigger aggressive behavior, along with differences of opinion between children.

In the preschool years, relational aggression (e.g., being mean or excluding another child) becomes another way of expressing aggressive feelings (Crick, Casas, & Mosher 1997). Children may use their improved cognitive and language skills as tools to intentionally hurt others' feelings ("*You can't come to my birthday party,*" "*Your hair is ugly*"). This relational bullying, as well as physical bullying, may be seen toward the end of the preschool years (Hanish et al. 2004), having potentially negative effects on both the bully and the bullied child.

Many things influence whether preschoolers are likely to use aggression and other challenging behaviors. Young children who have so-called difficult temperaments are more likely to react aggressively (Rothbart & Bates 2006), as are children who tend to be impulsive, irritable, and easily distracted. Without intervention, their aggressive responses are likely to continue into later childhood and adolescence, often leading to more serious antisocial difficulties (Tremblay et al. 1994). Additionally, some preschoolers have great difficulty processing information about situations involving other children's motives. For example, some children interpret social situations in overly negative ways. They are more likely to attribute hostile intentions to other children's actions ("*Zach tripped me!*") instead of assuming otherwise (Crick & Dodge 1994).

Sense of self in relation to others. Long before they reach preschool, children recognize themselves and have become self-aware. Children ages 3 to 5 are gaining a more fully developed sense of who they are, although this sense is still quite concrete. When asked, "Who are you?" 3-year-old Gus says, "I have two fish," "I'm really strong," and "I have black hair." Older preschoolers are beginning to add psychological descriptors: Five-year-old Denise says, "I'm

nice to my friends" (Harter 1999). Preschoolers' views of the self are usually all-or-nothing; at this age, children find it difficult to think that they could have opposing characteristics or feelings (e.g., being sometimes nice and sometimes mean).

These self-descriptions develop into a sense of self-esteem, which is the child's own internal evaluation or judgment about her or his worth and competence. Preschoolers typically evaluate themselves differently in different areas: Five-year-old Robert might report that he is really good at soccer but not good at counting, for example. It is only in later years of childhood that children develop a more general sense of being competent and worthwhile overall—or incompetent and not worthwhile.

Children get these beliefs about themselves primarily from noticing how others see them—adults as well as other children. In preschool and beyond, children who feel supported and accepted by adults, and who have secure attachments to adults, are likely to have higher self-esteem (Verscheuren, Marcoen, & Schoefs 1996; Harter 1999). In contrast, a young child who has been maltreated may tend to develop a sense of himself as a person who is not lovable and is incompetent (Harter 2006).

Culture also influences young children's developing sense of self, as many cultures emphasize collective or group worth rather than worth based on individual accomplishment (Rogoff 2003).

Another aspect of preschoolers' emerging sense of self is their feeling about the reasons for their success or failure at various tasks, such as completing a challenging puzzle. In general, children of this age are optimistic about their chances of success and believe that success will come if they keep trying. For this reason, it used to be thought that preschool children paid little attention to failure. However, more recent research shows that some preschool children already react negatively to the possibility of failure. Whereas Emily persists with her art project even when the pieces don't stick together well, Laura avoids even trying

the project, and Ben gives up at the first sign of difficulty (Dweck 2002). As with many other aspects of children's social and emotional (and cognitive) development, the kind of feedback preschoolers receive from adults has a strong influence on these kinds of beliefs and behavior (Hyson 2008).

Emotional development

Over the past 15 years, much greater attention has been given to preschoolers' emotional development. Many researchers believe that preschoolers' positive and negative emotions serve important functions, motivating every aspect of their development and learning (e.g., Campos et al. 1994; Denham 1998; Saarni 1999). Feelings of interest, pleasure, and curiosity encourage children to explore their world and motivate them to solve problems. Similarly, strong feelings of sadness, fear, or anger may cause children to avoid certain kinds of learning situations or relationships.

From ages 3 to 5, children gain much greater understanding of these and other emotions. Their ability to talk about emotions increases, and they become better able to regulate their expressions of emotion and develop a clearer sense of right and wrong. Finally, all children encounter stressful events, but during the preschool years, adult support helps them learn new coping strategies and build resilience.

In this section, of three aspects of preschoolers' emotional development are sketched out: (1) development of emotional competence; (2) development of conscience; and (3) stress, coping, and resilience.

Development of emotional competence. Emotions are present and important from infancy onward. But compared with younger children, preschoolers are able to express more complex "social" emotions such as pride, guilt, and shame and to do so with a broader repertoire of facial expressions, gestures, words, and symbols (e.g., think of a 4-year-old's crayon drawing of someone who is "mad"). Most children now are able to describe or label feelings

© Ellen B. Senisi

("*I'm a little scared of that dog*"), identify others' emotions, consider why others may feel that way, and express their anger or distress in more acceptable ways (Denham 1998; Hyson 2004; Saarni et al. 2006).

These abilities build an important foundation for children's school readiness and school success. Young children who cannot manage or regulate negative emotions or who have great difficulty understanding and responding to others' feelings do not do as well in school as children more emotionally competent (Raver 2002), and they are likely to be less socially competent and generally less well-adjusted.

Children's temperaments and their cultural context certainly influence how they express their feelings (Kitayama & Markus 1994; Rothbart & Bates 2006). But as with other aspects of development, what happens in children's families has a major influence. Different families have different ways of expressing feelings, and these influence their children's expressive styles (Halberstadt & Eaton 2002). Warm parents who help children understand and deal with their emotions have more emotionally competent children. In contrast, harsh or rejecting parenting and the experience of frequent conflict and angry adult outbursts undermine

Developmentally Appropriate Practice, 3d Edition

children's development in this area (Saarni et al. 2006). Early childhood teachers also play an important part in affecting preschoolers' emotional competence. For example, preschoolers who had close relationships with their teachers continued to have close teacher-child relationships even five years later (Howes 2000).

Development of conscience. One of the most important advances in children's development is their gradual internalization of values and expectations for behavior. The preschool years are a crucial time for children to develop qualities such as consideration for others, conscience, and a sense of right and wrong (Thompson 2006; Kochanska & Aksan 2007).

Even young preschoolers show "moral emotions" such as guilt and shame. They also become more able to refrain from doing something that is against the rules (e.g., taking a cookie from a plate) when no one is watching. By the end of the preschool years, most children have an inner sense of right and wrong. These developments make a difference in later years: Children who do not acquire this fledgling conscience in preschool are more likely to have later behavioral problems and to be less helpful than other children (Thompson 2006).

Preschoolers' relationships with others help children become more aware of others' feelings and become more concerned about them (Grusec 2006; Thompson, Meyer, & McGinley 2006). Children whose parents are more warm and nurturing and also use gentle rather than harsh discipline are likely to internalize those values. Children of parents who rely less on power (immediate obedience) and more on reasoning and reminders about the rules are more likely to understand right and wrong, internalizing those values that their families and society consider important (Kochanska & Aksan 2007).

Stress, coping, and resilience. For children as well as adults, stress arises when we feel that a situation is more than we are able to manage. When stressed, we respond with our feelings (becoming anxious or angry), our bodies (pro-

ducing more of the "stress hormone" cortisol), and our behavior (fighting or fleeing from the stressful situation) (Gunnar 2000).

Some of the sources of stress in early childhood are real—parents' divorce, hospitalization, entering a new child care program. But distress and fear may also arise from children's difficulty in separating the pretend from reality—there could *really* be a monster under the bed.

Not all stress is harmful; without some stress, children would not develop self-regulation and coping skills. However, without supportive adult relationships, young children can become overwhelmed by extreme stress, and long-term developmental difficulties can result (National Scientific Council on the Developing Child 2005).

The preschool years see much growth in children's coping capacities. Children are learning to regulate their emotions and to use many constructive ways of managing stressful situations. Again, adults are the key: When adults consistently react sensitively and responsively and when they have a secure relationship with children, children are less likely to be overwhelmed by stress (National Scientific Council on the Developing Child 2005).

There has been much discussion of the concept of "resilience" in children (Haggerty et al. 1996; Masten & Coatsworth 1998; Masten 2001). Among children who experience the same levels of intense stress (e.g., having a parent with serious mental illness, living in extreme poverty), some children seem to "bounce back," developing well despite the stress (Werner & Smith 2001). Although temperament and other inborn characteristics may contribute, other factors can help build children's resilience. Again, one of the most important is the presence of a supportive, accepting adult. Other factors are a positive sense of self-worth, the ability to think of alternative solutions to problems, and good communication skills (Haggerty et al. 1996). These qualities and many others can be nurtured in the preschool years.

Promoting social and emotional development in preschool

Research and experience indicate that preschoolers' social and emotional development is too important to leave to chance. Teachers who intentionally promote positive social and emotional development are making a significant investment in children's overall development and learning. Good teaching can influence whether preschoolers enter kindergarten as confident, happy members of a community of learners—able to work and play cooperatively, regulate emotions, and cope with stress—or enter lacking these competencies so essential to later success.

The most important contribution teachers can make to children's social and emotional competence is to establish a personal, nurturing, responsive relationship with every child. Essential for children at all ages, in the preschool years such relationships create a secure base for children to develop positive approaches to learning, create positive relationships with other children, and become more emotionally competent.

Many practical strategies are available (see, e.g., Howes & Ritchie 2002; Hyson 2004; 2008). Every day, teachers build these relationships by getting to know and respect children as individuals and as members of their cultural groups. They are thus better able to meet children's need to be sincerely known and understood and to involve children in activities that are relevant to their developmental and individual characteristics. Very concretely, teachers can help children know them as individuals ("*I am looking forward to planting my garden this weekend*"); and they can learn more about children and their families ("*Maybe you can make a picture of what you did at your grandpa's apartment last night*").

Teachers build positive relationships through individualized, culturally competent communication. Even a few minutes with one child, listening with care or sincerely asking about things the child is interested in, can be an investment valuable to teachers, children, and their families.

Another overarching priority for teachers is to promote children's positive approaches to learning. Once more, relationships are at the core: Teachers support positive approaches to learning when they build positive relationships with children, allowing them to explore and learn from a secure base (Ridley, McWilliam, & Oates 2000).

The curriculum, classroom environments, and teaching methods create enthusiasm and engagement when they involve children in meaningful activities and include substantial time for child-focused learning. Teachers also promote positive approaches to learning when they rely on small-group activities, which appear more likely to engage children (Rimm-Kaufman et al. 2005), and when they help children focus on "learning goals" rather than just on how well they perform in comparison with others.

Teachers can also help families see how they can support their preschooler's motivation and engagement in learning—not by external rewards but by affirming their child's efforts and modeling their own curiosity and persistence as continuous learners. Communication with families about children's approaches to learning should be built on respectful relationships within a "family-centered" program (Keyser 2006), and newsletters, bulletin boards, family meetings, and home visits can all contribute to this goal.

Promoting social development. Beyond these powerful general strategies, there are more specific things teachers can do to support positive social development in preschool. A "caring community of learners" does not just happen; it is intentionally created, beginning the first day of preschool (or even before, with notes and photos sent home, home visits, and other connections). Preschoolers look to their teachers as models, and teachers can use the kind of caring, respectful language they would like children to adopt ("*Thank you all so much for helping to clean up outdoors. Let's sit down and look at what we did together!*"). In small- and large-group discussions, teachers can draw

all children into the group, helping each communicate ideas in her or his own way. Shared rituals ("*Every Friday we add a page to our class book*") can also be ways of affirming a sense of community. Class projects, class meetings, "big jobs" for children to do together—all of these and more contribute to that important sense of "we" (Whitin 2001; Diffily & Sassman 2002; Jones 2005).

Preschoolers cannot become socially competent without many extended times to interact with one another. This requires teachers to plan the preschool day so that there are blocks of time available for children to play and work together. Rather than such times being a reward for those who complete seatwork, these times should be considered absolutely essential developmental investments. Such periods can include time for pretend (sociodramatic) play (Bodrova & Leong 2007), as well as time

for projects or other small-group activities (Edwards, Gandini, & Forman 1998; Helm & Katz 2001).

Given the challenges preschoolers still have in sustaining social relationships and working through conflicts, it is not enough for teachers just to schedule "social time" and let it run its course. In this as in other areas of the program, teacher involvement in and scaffolding of children's social interactions are essential. For example, teachers may help children plan what they will play, what roles they and their friends might take, and how to sustain and extend the play (Bodrova & Leong 2007). Teachers may need to help younger, more inhibited, or less skilled preschoolers enter other children's play ("*I wonder if you could be the rabbit that comes to the barn. Maybe you could bring some food for the other animals. What do you think?*"). In these interactions, teachers can also help children

© Ellen B. Senisi

understand and interpret other children's intentions, helping prevent "hostile attributions." For example, a teacher might explain, "You know, I think Adrienne was trying to get you to sit with her for lunch. I don't think she was trying to hurt you; she was trying to have you come over to her table when she pulled at your shirt."

As conflicts occur, teachers can support children's development of strategies to resolve conflicts—not by taking over, but by modeling and discussing ideas about how to work things out in a positive way. Social problem-solving skills can be intentionally taught, both embedded in everyday activities and in evidence-based programs such as the PATHS curriculum (Kusche & Greenberg, in press) or The Incredible Years (Webster-Stratton, Reid, & Hammond 2001). These and similar programs help teachers promote positive social behavior, reduce challenging behavior, and support children's self-regulation in the preschool years.

Children's prosocial behavior can be encouraged when teachers themselves serve as models of how to help others and how to show care and concern. Teachers can also make a point of calling attention to another child's distress or needs ("*Oh, it looks like Titus might need some help with that block tower. I wonder if you could give him a hand with that?*").

Effectively preventing and (when that isn't successful) addressing preschoolers' aggression, bullying, and other challenging behaviors, while simultaneously strengthening children's social and emotional competence, must be a high priority. The Center for the Social and Emotional Foundations of Early Learning (CSEFEL) (2008) offers many practical resources. These include "universal" interventions (everyday approaches for all children in a group) as well as "targeted" interventions for those children who have more serious difficulties.

All preschool children—those who do and do not exhibit challenging behaviors—need their teachers' help to develop a positive sense of self. The task may be especially difficult when a child has already developed a reputa-

tion among peers as being "mean." Teachers can help children recognize and value their own unique characteristics and competencies, as well as those of their classmates. In highlighting these qualities, teachers must also be aware that some families and cultures emphasize competence as a member of a group rather than focusing on individual accomplishment.

Promoting emotional development. Once more, this begins with relationships. Like caring parents, teachers of preschool children can provide an essential foundation of emotional security by creating a nurturing, predictable, and responsive relationship with each child.

The same kinds of program environments and curricula that support positive approaches to learning or social competence also promote emotional competence. Such curricula and environments emphasize predictability, acceptance, and responsiveness. Emotion-centered teachers (Hyson 2004) intentionally engage children in emotional communication, using their voices, facial expressions, and gestures. Smiling, looking into children's eyes, and using affectionate touch are likely to contribute to children's emotional security, as long as these behaviors are within a child's family and cultural norms.

Teachers also build emotional competence when they help children find words for feelings and when they help them find ways not only to understand feelings but also to express them in appropriate ways—talking, drawing, pretending. Teachers can also use the resources provided by emotions-based curricula and social skills training programs, if these curricula have been well validated with similar children (Webster-Stratton, Reid, & Hammond 2001; Kusche & Greenberg, in press).

Conscience development is another dimension of emotional development in which teachers can have a significant impact. Although families are the most important influence on children's conscience development, teachers can help by talking with children about feelings, values, behavior, and their consequences. Every day opportunities arise to do this: Is it fair, for example, for one child to be able to leave the

circle if others aren't allowed to? Why should we be concerned when classmates are rejected? Is it right to make fun of another child, or to tell a child she cannot play?

Rather than reacting to children's violations of rules with harsh discipline, teachers can reason together with children and help them think about the consequences of behavior. Class meetings, impromptu discussions, well selected children's books, and a classroom environment that reflects respect and justice will help all children move forward in this developmental area. It is also important that teachers remember that children are individuals, whose temperaments and levels of understanding will influence how they may respond to efforts at guidance and discipline. Teachers may need to change their approach to avoid confrontations with highly reactive or stressed children, gently guiding them with suggestions and reasoning.

When promoting preschoolers' ability to manage and cope with stress, teachers' first responsibility is to protect children from the kind of stress that can cause long-term damage. Some situations can require teachers to seek outside assistance or file reports of suspected maltreatment. But teachers also need to help children build coping skills and resilience in the face of a range of stressful events. Yet again, one of the best ways to help children cope is to give them the benefit of a close, nurturing relationship. Especially when children do not have such relationships at home, teacher-child relationships can help "buffer" the negative effects of stress.

Other things teachers can provide will help preschoolers develop a repertoire of coping skills and behaviors. For example, they might give a fearful child a chance to draw or write about her fears. Other coping strategies can include dramatic play, getting information from books or from teachers, talking about the stressful event, seeking comfort from an adult, learning ways to calm down, and learning to "reframe" (think differently about) a stressful situation. Preschoolers are unlikely to simply arrive at these strategies on their own; adults' support is essential.

A final note. The preceding examples of how teachers might promote preschoolers' social and emotional development illustrate how closely various aspects of children's development are connected. These same strategies are also likely to support children's cognitive development and later academic success, offering more evidence that the "whole child" emphasis in early childhood education is both sensible and essential.

Cognitive development

Some important cognitive changes occur during preschool, particularly in terms of mental representation. Whereas infants and toddlers have only a limited ability to form representations of their world (images, concepts) and hold them in memory, children in preschool possess more of that extraordinary ability. When asked about past or future events, preschoolers (unlike toddlers) are able to think about what happened weeks ago or anticipate what has not yet happened. They can create fanciful scenes (e.g., in which one child is a pilot and the other runs the control tower), coordinating roles and story lines, and by 4 and 5 years old, they do so with an awareness that they are acting out an imaginary idea (Sobel 2006). They become more efficient thinkers as they start to organize their thoughts into categories, and they show more sophisticated use of symbols through their use of pretend objects in play and drawings for learning and communicating.

In spite of their many advances, preschoolers can be illogical, egocentric, and one-dimensional in their thinking. Piaget referred to these years as a "*pre*operational" stage of development, emphasizing that children ages 2 to 7 are less capable in their thinking compared with older children. More recent research indicates that preschoolers have greater cognitive abilities than has been sometimes assumed, at least when children are in familiar situations and tasks are clearly explained to them.

Preschool children can appear to know or understand more—or less—than they actually

© Ellen B. Senisi

do. At times they seem mature and relatively advanced in their thinking, and then later seem limited and inflexible. As preschoolers move from and between simpler to more complex thinking skills, it is helpful to remember that they are not merely functioning less effectively than older children or adults; their narrow focus on a limited amount of information at any given time is actually useful while they are learning so many things so rapidly (Bjorklund 2007). That is, because they are just on the cusp of grasping a variety of concepts, words, and skills at a new level, they learn best when they can attend to just one thing at a time (e.g., putting all the yellow crayons and chalk in one bin and purple crayons and chalk in another—cementing awareness of color) rather than attending

to multiple things (e.g., yellow versus purple, crayons versus chalk, and broken versus whole, which is too many concepts to achieve success).

Below are brief descriptions of some influences on cognitive development, as well as characteristics of children's thought, that a preschool teacher might expect to see.

Influences of social interaction and play

As teachers are well aware, all learning for young children is interdependent: Cognitive development in the preschool years has important implications for children's social and language development, and social and language development play an essential role in stimulat-

ing cognitive growth. Children construct their understanding of a concept in the course of interaction with others (Vygotsky 1978; Berk & Winsler 1995).

In developing ideas about what "school" means, for example, children use what they hear people say about school, glimpses of buildings identified by others as schools, and stories about school that they have had read to them. Their initial ideas may be challenged, confirmed, elaborated on, or altered by subsequent interactions with peers, older children, or adults. And as Vygotsky demonstrated, much of children's understanding first occurs in communication with other people, then appears in "private speech" (thinking aloud), and eventually is internalized as thought. As children's memory, language, and other aspects of cognition improve and change, their relationships with others are affected.

Make-believe or pretend play, with guidance and support from adults, blossoms in the preschool years and allows children to make a number of cognitive gains as they try out new ideas and skills. Advances in children's play skills not only serve as indicators of preschoolers' advancing cognitive skills but also are crucial in fostering further cognitive development.

Other types of play, such as drawing or doing puzzles, are important too. But there is something special about social pretend play for preschoolers. When they engage in mature sociodramatic play (pretend play that involves communication with other children), children's interactions last longer than they do in other situations, children show high levels of involvement, large numbers of children are drawn in, and children show more cooperation (Creasey, Jarvis, & Berk 1998)—all of which have important benefits for children's cognitive (and other types of) development.

Toddlers, too, engage in pretend play, but by the time children reach preschool age, they usually show more sophisticated play, especially when they have had parents' and teachers' support and such play opportunities (Bodrova & Leong 2007).

They show their growing sophistication in a number of ways. They are more flexible and begin to substitute various objects for items needed in the play; leaves might become lettuce, and rocks, onions in the pretend soup being made. They move away from self-centered play to involve others; for example, instead of just pretending to drink from a cup, as a toddler might do, preschoolers might have a pretend party that involves welcoming a friend into their pretend home, passing out pretend cups, pouring and stirring pretend tea, and offering pretend cookies. Such a series of many steps and combinations of actions and interactions tends to be too complex for toddlers (McCune 1993; Striano, Tomasello, & Rochat 2001; Kavanaugh 2006).

That is, by age 4 or 5, children often collaborate with a peer or peers to create a scene with various roles and story lines—say, a birthday party that includes a birthday boy, parents and friends, and a couple of different situations, perhaps opening gifts, a jealous sibling who gets in trouble, and time for candles and cake.

Piaget (1951) believed that pretend play strengthens newly acquired abilities to mentally picture different situations and allows children to take control of experiences in which they have little or no control in real life, such as going to the doctor's office or getting lost at the store. Vygotsky (1978) saw dramatic play, with its system of roles and rules (i.e., who does what and what is allowed in the play scenario) as uniquely supportive of self-regulation. Children's eagerness to stay in the play situation motivates them to attend to and operate within its structure, conforming to what is required by the other players and by the play scenario.

Indeed, research bears out the beliefs of these two prominent theorists and further extends our understanding of the benefits of play. A study of children from around the world, from Indonesia to Italy to Ireland (and the United States), showed that when preschool experiences at age 4 included lots of child-initiated, free-choice activities supported by a variety of equipment and materials—the kinds

of environments that support play—these children had better cognitive (and language) performance at age 7 than their peers (Montie, Xiang, & Schweinhart 2006).

Other research shows that pretend play strengthens cognitive capacities, including sustained attention, memory, logical reasoning, language and literacy skills, imagination, creativity, understanding of emotions, and the ability to reflect on one's own thinking, inhibit impulses, control one's behavior, and take another person's perspective (Kavanaugh & Engel 1998; Bergen & Mauer 2000; Elias & Berk 2002; Lindsey & Colwell 2003; Ruff & Capozzoli 2003; Berk 2006b).

Executive functioning

During the preschool years, the brain's cerebral cortex and the functions that ultimately regulate children's attention and memory are not fully developed, which accounts for some of the limitations in their capacity to reason and solve problems. They also haven't had as much experience as older children in being taught what to pay attention to or how to remember things, opportunity to practice self-regulation skills through sociodramatic play, and other environmentally supportive experiences. During the preschool years, as children have more instruction and opportunity to practice information-processing skills related to attention and memory, their skills improve.

Attention. Attention is crucial to our thinking because it decides what information will influence the task at hand. The ability to focus attention and concentrate enhances academic learning, including language acquisition and problem solving, as well as social skills and cooperation (Landry et al. 2000; Bono & Stifter 2003; Murphy et al. 2007). As teachers know, preschoolers may have trouble focusing on details, spend only a short time on most tasks, and tend to be more distractible than older children, especially when required to listen passively or work on a prescribed task (Lin, Hsiao, & Chen 1999; Goldberg, Maurer, & Lewis 2001). But attention does become more sustained and

under the child's control over the course of the preschool years.

For example, young preschoolers usually are not able to apply an attention strategy, whereas older preschoolers can use simple strategies. In one study, when doing a task in which the best strategy was to open only those doors with certain pictures on them (some doors pictured a type of house and other doors pictured a type of animal), 3- and 4-year-olds simply opened all the doors. But by age 5, children began to apply a selective strategy of opening only those doors with the relevant pictures on them—at least most of the time (Wood-Ramsey & Miller 1988).

Memory. As attention improves, so does memory and, more specifically, children's use of memory strategies. Memory strategies are deliberate mental activities that allow us to hold information first in working memory and then to transfer it to long-term memory. Preschoolers begin to use memory strategies, but these take so much effort and concentration that they are not very useful at first. As with other skills, memory strategies improve as preschoolers have opportunity and guidance to practice them (Berk 2009).

Younger children do not make effective use of memory strategies such as rehearsing a list or grouping items into meaningful categories (Bjorklund et al. 1994). Even when adults try to teach strategies for improving memory, younger children do not automatically or accurately apply the strategies in situations requiring memory.

But they do make memory-related gains in preschool. "Scripts" are schemas for routine events, such as going to the grocery store or eating lunch. As part of learning about their culture, children form script categories when items play the same role in a script (e.g., *peanut butter*, *bologna*, and *cheese* could be in the script category *lunch foods*). Three-year-olds are no more likely to group words by script than by general category; that is, they are equally likely to pair any foods together (e.g., *broccoli* and *donut*) as they are to pair lunch foods together (*bologna*

and *cheese*). Four-year-olds, on the other hand, are more likely to categorize words by a familiar script category (*lunch foods*) than by the broader general category (*foods*) (Nguyen & Murphy 2003). When words are highly associated, as they are in scripts, children do better on memory tasks (Krackow & Gordon 1998). (It is not until age 7 or so that children begin to use more abstract hierarchical taxonomies of categorization.)

In other words, preschoolers are more likely to understand and remember relationships, concepts, and strategies that they acquire through firsthand, meaningful experience. When 4- and 5-year-olds were either told to play with some toys or told to simply remember them, they later remembered better the toys they had played with, because they spontaneously organized them mentally into meaningful groups based on their play activities, say, putting a shoe on a doll's foot or narrating their play ("*Fly away in this helicopter, doggie*") (Newman 1990).

When they do begin grouping items for memory, children naturally organize items by their everyday associations, such as *hat:head* and *carrot:rabbit*. Preschoolers who cannot recall multiple steps in a set of repeated directions can, however, relate specific, even sequential, events from highly salient experiences (e.g., a trip on an airplane, a visit to a theme park) from as long as a year before.

Mental representation. Mental representations are internal depictions of information that

© Natalie Klein Cavanagh

our minds can manipulate—images or mental pictures of people or objects; concepts, which are categories by which the mind groups similar objects; and words, which are labels for these images and concepts now understood. Mental representation allows us to become more efficient thinkers and organize our experiences into meaningful, manageable, and memorable units (Berk 2009).

Children in the preschool years make exceptional advances in their ability to use mental representation. Around age 3, children begin to understand that an object can serve both as an object in its own right and as a symbol of something else; for example, a bowl can be a bowl, or it can be a hat or a bed for a baby mouse (DeLoache 2006). This development reveals an extraordinary increase in children's ability to mentally or symbolically represent concrete objects, action, and events.

As their understanding of the connections between symbols and the real world becomes stronger, they realize that each symbol in their world corresponds to a specific state of affairs in everyday life and that a symbol does not have to have a strong resemblance to what it represents. For example, a stick picture of Ms. Hei and Puggles represents the teacher walking her dog, even though the drawn creatures and the real creatures look very little alike. This opens up many new avenues to knowledge and communication and prompts new abilities in various areas. Pretend play and drawing efforts are both excellent examples of how preschoolers advance in their ability to use mental representation, and symbolic thought in particular (Berk 2009).

Toddlers, given a crayon and paper, will scribble happily in imitation of others. When, at around age 3, children realize that pictures serve as symbols, they begin to draw as an artistic expression (Golomb 2004)—perhaps not in any greatly recognizable form in the beginning. But to themselves at least, the drawing depicts a recognizable shape, and that is what matters. For example, a child might draw a bunch of random squiggles and then ask the teacher to label the picture "Worms wrestling."

Children reach a major milestone around age 3 or 4 when they use lines as symbols for the boundaries of an object, usually a person. Four-year-olds might also draw more detailed features, such as eyes, a nose, and a smile. By age 5, preschoolers might be drawing more realistic and complex pictures with more conventional aspects—but even theirs have perceptual distortions because children are just beginning to represent depth (Braine et al. 1993; Toomela 2002). Just as their understanding of a bowl as a hat reveals dual representation, so their use of drawing shows that marks on a page hold meaning.

This increasing ability to use mental representation allows children to think ahead a bit before taking action, and their activities take on a more purposeful, goal-directed character (Friedman, Scholnick, & Cocking 1987). Preschoolers can begin to separate their thoughts from their actions. They will not focus on the process of their thinking per se, but they begin to realize that what they think can be different from what they actually do.

For example, whereas toddlers continually repeat the same "mistake" and figure things out by doing something over and over, preschoolers can anticipate the consequences of their physical actions. For example, a child is more likely to anticipate a negative response from her teacher if she pulls her classmate's hair. She will not be able to control her impulse every time. But with the teacher's support in thinking of alternative ways to getting what she wants (e.g., using her words, waiting her turn, sharing a toy) and with practice using empathy and self-regulation skills (e.g., through pretend play), she will do better each time.

Logic and characteristics of thought. Piaget believed children in the preschool years were illogical in many ways because they have a largely egocentric perspective (difficulty taking others' perspective), an inability to grasp the notion of conservation (that certain physical characteristics of objects remain the same even when their outward appearance changes),

and a belief that inanimate objects have human thoughts, feelings, and wishes (Piaget 1930).

Although preschoolers do show these qualities and are certainly more limited than older children in their ability to reason, they are more advanced than Piaget assumed and than many adults might perceive. Children ages 3 to 5 do better on cognitive tasks than they did for Piaget—when the tasks occur with familiar elements and focus on one thing at a time (Berk 2009).

Reasoning. The ability to reason stems in part from our ability to take another's perspective. Preschoolers' thinking still tends to be egocentric; that is, they tend to take into account only their own point of view and have difficulty understanding how the world looks to other people. Instead, they assume that other people see and experience things the same way they do. For example, a child might share his graham cracker and peanut butter with his teacher when the teacher is sad, in the belief that she will be comforted by the same thing that comforts him. Three-year-olds who are shown that a candy box now holds pencils assume that others would likewise know it holds pencils—just like they do (Gopnik & Astington 1988).

But by age 4, children do have an awareness, albeit limited, of others' vantage points. For example, they will change the tone or level of their conversation when speaking with a toddler (Gelman & Shatz 1978; Newcombe & Huttenlocher 1992).

Even though research shows that preschoolers' capacities are at times underestimated, they do have limitations in their reasoning skills that affect learning. They have a limited understanding of ideas such as *time*, *space*, or *age*, for instance, and don't use these abstract concepts to help themselves reason unless the ideas are made real and relevant to their current lives.

That preschoolers are very concrete thinkers who focus on the tangible, observable aspects of objects is also apparent in their use of language. For example, a child may use the word *fuzzy* in relation to a peach skin or a blanket but have difficulty applying it to something abstract, as in "fuzzy thinking." And they typically reason from the particular to the particular ("*My dog is friendly, so this dog is friendly*"), a natural result of their budding classification skills.

But in general, they show some ability to reason logically when tasks are simple, consistent with what they already know, and made relevant to their everyday lives (Ruffman 1999; Berk 2009).

Concept acquisition and classification. One of the main developmental goals of young children is to make sense of their world and organize it into meaningful and manageable categories or schemas. Preschoolers are answering for themselves two basic questions: What kinds of things are there in the world, and how do they relate to one another? (Siegler, DeLoache, & Eisenberg 2006).

Children form basic categories first and gradually both expand to broader categories and narrow to more specific elements of the basic category. For example, they first recognize that a group of things with four legs that people sit on are called chairs; then they perceive the broader set (furniture) and more specific subsets (rocking chairs and La-Z-Boys—which is a more impressive classification than it sounds to adults, since La-Z-Boys are neither lazy nor boys).

Typically, preschoolers describe objects by their appearance and actions ("*the big, mean dog*"). They also organize information into categories based on attributes that define an object or an idea (e.g., four legs and you sit on it, four wheels and you ride in it), even if the members of this category look quite different (Mandler 2004). They may initially miss subtle differences in appearance that differentiate objects based on function (e.g., coin slot on a ceramic pig) but even toddlers perceive subtle defining features if adults explain them (Banigan & Mervis 1988). Preschoolers can also categorize by trait. For example, if told that two birds are sociable and one bird is shy, they know the two sociable birds (rather than the two that look alike) will

prefer the same types of activities (Heyman & Gelman 2000).

In fact, preschoolers tend to conceptualize best when they understand why things are the way they are, or what matters in a comparison. For example, when told that wugs (imaginary animals) have claws, spikes, and horns because they like to fight, whereas gillies have wings because they do not like to fight and they fly away from wugs, 4- and 5-year-olds remember the physical features better than if they were not told why the creatures have their respective features (Krascum & Andrews 1998).

In part because the why matters in preschoolers' ability to conceptualize and remember, they are hungry for more and more explanations—explaining their seemingly end-less stream of questions: "Why do cows moo?" "What do clouds feel like?" "Do the worms like to take walks?" The answers help preschool children learn how to think about the world and put things in categories (Siegler, DeLoache, & Eisenberg 2006).

As children broaden their knowledge of things in the world and how those things go together, they more effortlessly categorize according to any number of attributes: length, color, weight, function, texture, and so forth. But young preschoolers have trouble focusing on more than one thing at a time and sticking with one feature (e.g., the color red) in sorting objects into a class (Brooks et al. 2003). Secondary attributes (e.g., size) tend to distract them from using one dimension consistently

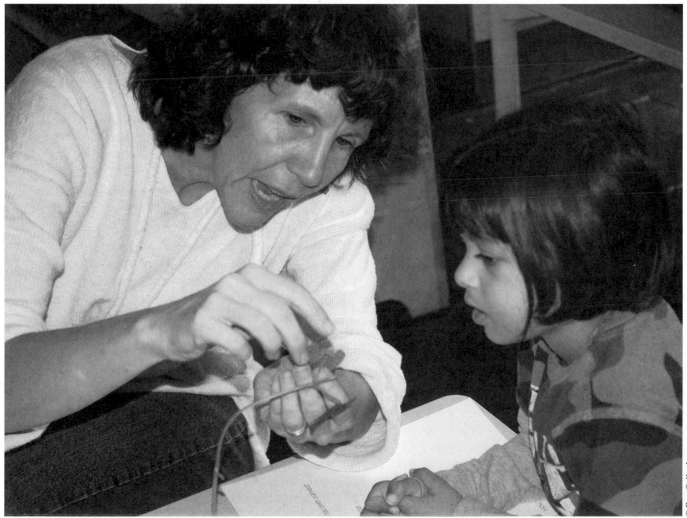

© Peg Callaghan

throughout the task. By age 4 or 5, however, children can sort and classify by more than one attribute of an object (e.g., color and size).

Because children are just beginning to understand part/whole and hierarchical relationships, they may have difficulty grasping that an object can be in more than one class (*"It's not a fruit—it's an apple!"*) or recognizing that with six girls and four boys there are more children than girls, for example.

These types of classification skills have obvious links to curriculum areas. For example, from ages 3 to 5, children show increasing interest in mathematical and scientific concepts such as *number* and *quantity*; they start counting, measuring, comparing, and doing more complex matching activities. They start noticing and copying simple repeating patterns (e.g., long-short-long-short), and as they start organizing groups according to color or size, they start comparing them to see which has more objects.

Magical thinking. Young children's reasoning is influenced by their tendency toward magical thinking and animism—that is, giving lifelike qualities to inanimate objects. They may mistakenly think, for instance, that certain vehicles such as trains or airplanes can be living creatures because they move—not surprising as the objects are sometimes depicted with lifelike features, such as headlights that look like eyes and appear to move on their own (Gelman & Opfer 2002). Or children might think a vacuum cleaner is a monster, or a thunderstorm means that God is angry.

Although individual differences in temperament play a big role in how fearful a child is, this tendency toward animism characterizes preschool cognition as a whole and accounts for many typical fears among this age group. They often believe also in the enchanted powers of fairies and goblins and such and believe that magic accounts for things they can't explain (Rosengren & Hickling 2000).

Even young preschoolers are savvy enough, however, to think that an action such as walking through a wall (which violates basic physical laws) would require magic, whereas taking a bath with one's shoes on (which merely breaks social convention) does not (Browne & Woolley 2004). Starting around age 4 or 5, children's magical beliefs begin to ebb as they realize magicians use tricks rather than magic or that Santa Claus is actually Uncle Kevin (Subbotsky 2004).

How quickly they give up their magical beliefs depends in part on culture, information from adults and older children, and religion. Regardless of how early it begins, the process of replacing magical thinking with more logical reasoning is gradual. Preschoolers will still be scared by scary stories and nightmares and monsters in the closet—and still believe in Santa for at least a few more years.

Promoting cognitive development in preschool

During the years from age 3 through age 5, children gradually develop their mental representation capacities, reasoning skills, classification abilities, attention, memory, and other cognitive capacities. These processes will take several years to be well developed, in part because the preschool child's brain has yet to mature in some important ways, and in part because they have had little experience using the new skills and strategies learned, so each task requires enormous mental effort. The skills become more automatic and effortless only with practice—and plenty of support.

That support comes in the form of cues, questions, modeling, and other assistance from adults and other children. For example, as a child struggles with a puzzle piece, instead of directly showing him how to place the piece, the teacher might say, "What color is it? Where do you see that color on the puzzle?" or "Try turning it around another way." These types of questions and suggestions help children stretch to achieve that next level of understanding or performance. Say, with the teacher's prompt, the child finds where the puzzle piece fits. The teacher will continue this way, gradually reducing the amount of help as the child's skills

improve, until eventually the child can succeed on his own. This kind of support, where the teacher (or a more competent peer) helps only just enough and until the child succeeds, is called scaffolding.

Of the many things that skilled teachers do to foster children's learning and intellectual development, one of the most important is ensuring guidance and ample time for sustained play. They realize its powerful benefits for cognitive development, including attention and memory gains and increased self-regulation (Bodrova & Leong 2005a). To develop these skills, preschoolers particularly need to engage in sociodramatic play that is intentional, imaginative, and extended. Children negotiate with each other to take on different roles in the pretend scene, first discussing and then acting out a scenario, and using various props in different ways.

"Although 4-year-old children are capable of this kind of complex play, many preschool and even kindergarten age children still play at the toddler level, repeating the same sequence of actions within a very limited repertoire of play themes and roles," write Bodrova and Leong (2005a, 4). Teachers need to help by giving children ideas for various scenes and roles; providing time, space, and play props and dress-up clothes; helping them implement some "rules" at first; and then backing away and letting children play with their peers alone so they internalize the skills needed to sustain play and develop cognitive (and other) skills.

Teachers take other active roles in promoting children's thinking and their acquisition of concepts and skills. These roles range from asking a well timed question that provokes further reflection or investigation to showing children how to use a new tool or procedure. Early childhood educators have evolved approaches that are very successful in promoting children's engagement in challenging, meaningful problems and enterprises; for instance, by encouraging children to plan and review their work and to represent what they know verbally, pictorially, and through other modes and media (Copple, Sigel, & Saunders 1984; Forman 1994;

Edwards, Gandini, & Forman 1998).

Preschoolers spontaneously pay attention to distinctive events and things, such as loud noises and brightly colored objects. Helping them to attend consciously to a specific aspect of something requires gentle scaffolding rather than generic demands to "Pay attention!" or "Listen!" which are not informative in honing children's attention. Preschoolers do not have the insight to know what specifically to pay attention to. A specific request or targeted question ("*Which two are alike?*") provides just enough structuring of the task to bring it within children's reach.

Attention advances most for children this age when they have opportunities to pursue their interests and try out new ideas and skills, especially through dramatic play (Bodrova & Leong 2007).

Research on cognitive development in preschool age children (e.g., Seifert 1993; Case & Okamoto 1996) leads to an important conclusion: Young children have age-related limits in their cognitive capacities, but they also have enormous capacities to learn and often underestimated capacities to think, reason, remember, and problem solve.

To demonstrate how teachers can promote cognitive skills in specific content and curriculum areas, examples using mathematics and science follow. Examples from other curriculum areas can be found in chapter 5.

An example: Teaching mathematics. To be effective, preschool mathematics curriculum and instruction need to be engaging to children, consistent with their developmental level, and focused on the important concepts and processes on which subsequent math learning will build. Teachers also help children connect various mathematics topics to one another. This helps strengthen their grasp of concepts in each area as well as their beliefs about mathematics as a coherent *system*. Most good mathematics activities also develop language and vocabulary. For example, teachers can ask children wearing something red to get their coats *first*, those wearing blue to go *second*, and so on (Sarama &

Clements 2006). Linking mathematics to other learning domains, such as literacy, strengthens both domains.

To promote math skills, teachers can:

- create learning environments to ensure that children "bump into interesting mathematics at every turn" (Greenes 1999, 46);

- investigate with children, observing what they do and say;

- answer children's questions and pose interesting questions and ideas for them to think about; and

- introduce the language of mathematics into everyday situations, and serve as examples by modeling math communication and investigation.

Children need to learn math concepts and relationships to become mathematical think-ers. Equally important, they need to learn basic but powerful things about problem solving and reasoning. For instance, children need to recognize that there are many different ways to solve a problem.

As children encounter mathematical challenges in the classroom or at home, teachers encourage them not only to tackle the problem but also to share their thinking with others. To promote children's mathematical thinking and learning, one of the most important things teachers can do is simply to talk with them about problems, patterns, and mathematical connections using mathematical language (e.g., *more than*, *less than*, *tallest*, *five*) and listening to what they say. Such dialogue helps children think about what they are doing and makes their own thoughts clearer. In addition, it improves children's math vocabulary, introduc-

---

Math for Preschool "Curriculum Focal Points"

Number and Operations: Developing an understanding of whole numbers, including concepts of correspondence, counting, cardinality, and comparison.

Children develop an understanding of the meanings of whole numbers and recognize the number of objects in small groups without counting and by counting—the first and most basic mathematical algorithm. They understand that number words refer to quantity. They use one-to-one correspondence to solve problems by matching sets and comparing number amounts and in counting objects to 10 and beyond. They understand that the last word that they state in counting tells "how many," they count to determine number amounts and compare quantities (using language such as "more than" and "less than"), and they order sets by the number of objects in them.

Geometry: Identifying shapes and describing spatial relationships.

Children develop spatial reasoning by working from two perspectives on space as they examine the shapes of objects and inspect their relative positions. They find shapes in their environments and describe them in their own words. They build pictures and designs by combining two- and three dimensional shapes, and they solve such problems as deciding which piece will fit into a space in a puzzle. They discuss the relative positions of objects with vocabulary such as "above," "below," and "next to."

Measurement: Identifying measurable attributes and comparing objects by using these attributes.

Children identify objects as "the same" or "different," and then "more" or "less," on the basis of attributes that they can measure. They identify measurable attributes such as length and weight and solve problems by making direct comparisons of objects on the basis of those attributes.

Source: Reprinted with permission from *Curriculum Focal Points for Prekindergarten through Grade 8 Mathematics: A Quest for Coherence,* copyright © 2006 by the National Council of Teachers of Mathematics. All rights reserved. The *Curriculum Focal Points* document may be viewed in its entirety at www.nctm.org/focalpoints.

---

ing them to words and phrases useful in mathematical reasoning and problem solving.

In short, such interactions with children help to "mathematize" the experiences and informal knowledge. As Sarama and Clements (2006) note, "In all activities, especially teacher-directed activities, teachers need to help children connect their informal knowledge to their budding explicit knowledge of mathematics" (86).

Young children solve lots of problems that arise in their everyday lives, but they do so intuitively, often impulsively, and tend to rely on habit or trial and error. On entering school, children will encounter a greater range of problems, including many that require careful thinking and systematic investigation. The skills and cognitive structures needed to solve problems in this deliberate, logical way are not well developed in preschoolers. However, teachers can work to enhance children's problem-solving dispositions and abilities by creating a learning environment in which children feel free to take risks and search for solutions to problems.

Children become more conscious of their own reasoning and problem-solving strategies when teachers comment on what they are doing or ask about how and why they are doing it. For example, "Andre divided the playdough so that each person has the same amount. How did you do that, Andre?" and "If you mix the yellow and the blue, what will happen?"

In high-quality learning environments, children become increasingly persistent, flexible, and proficient problem solvers—and they learn to *enjoy* solving problems.

An example: Teaching science. Scientist Karen Worth and education researcher Sharon Grollman have been studying and developing science education materials for young children for more than two decades. According to them,

> High-quality science programs for children ages 3 to 5 are based on an understanding of how children learn, what they are capable of learning, and appropriate science content. In such programs, science is an integral part of the classroom, supporting and supported by the overall goals for young children. In the hands of a skilled teacher, a good science program emerges from a carefully designed environment, clear goals, and children's interests, questions, and play. Science is not confined to a science table or focused on learning facts. Nor is it found in projects that focus on a narrow topic that does not involve direct experience, such as a study of bears or penguins. (2003, 3)

With that introduction, their book *Worms, Shadows, and Whirlpools* goes on (as excerpted here from pages 3–7) to define and illustrate the characteristics of a high-quality program:

• ***Builds on children's prior experiences, backgrounds, and early theories.*** All children come to school with experiences and the ideas and theories they have constructed to make sense of their surroundings. A good science program provides children with opportunities to share their ideas in multiple ways through both actions and words. Rather than being designed to correct early ideas, teach information, or provide explanations, new experiences provide children with opportunities to broaden their thinking and build new understandings.

• ***Draws on children's curiosity and encourages children to pursue their own questions and develop their own ideas.*** In an environment with carefully chosen materials and many opportunities to explore and ponder, children will raise many questions both in words and in actions. Teachers should encourage children to actively pursue such questions as "How do I get water in the tube?" or "What will happen if I make this ramp steeper?" Other questions that cannot be explored through close observation and simple experimentation, such as "How do worms have babies?" can be answered using books or other resources. In good science programs, questioning, trying things out, and taking risks are expected and valued. There is a balance between children's pursuit of their own interests and ideas and the pursuit of questions and ideas generated by other children or the teacher.

• ***Engages children in in-depth exploration of a topic over time in a carefully prepared environment.*** Time is a critical compo-

nent of a good early childhood science program. When children explore a few topics—water flow, tower construction, snails and worms—repeatedly in many different ways, they have the opportunity to think, analyze, and reflect on their work. Thus, they are able to organize what they know into deeper and more powerful theories or ideas. Such in-depth science studies last for weeks, if not months. One-week projects or 20-minute choice times simply cannot provide sufficient time for children to explore deeply.

Carefully selected materials are fundamental, creating many possibilities for children's explorations of science concepts and the development of the skills and processes of scientific inquiry. For each area of study, children need materials that they can use in multiple ways and that lead to interesting challenges and events. For example, during an exploration of water flow, children can use materials such as tubes, connectors, cups, funnels, and basters to create many ways for water to move. They also need tools such as magnifiers, measuring devices, and clipboards for observation, measurement, and the gathering and recording of data.

• *Encourages children to reflect on, represent, and document their experiences and share and discuss their ideas with others.* Direct experience with materials is critical but is not enough. Children also need to reflect on their work. They need to analyze their experiences, think about ideas such as patterns and relationships, try out new theories, and communicate with others. These processes allow children to think in new ways about what they did, how they did it, and what is significant to them.

Good science programs encourage children to document and represent their work in multiple ways—through drawings, dramatization, 3-D models, and dictation. Their teachers document as well, using photographs, video, drawings, and words. They use the documentation with children to help them reflect on their work. For example, a teacher might use children's drawings to help children describe and think about the role of different parts of plants they have observed.

Good programs also encourage ongoing discussion among children, between teacher and child, and in structured small- and large-group discussions. Such science talks are key, helping children to clarify their thinking with words and use evidence to support their developing theories, while learning from the perspectives of others.

• *Is embedded in children's daily work and play and is integrated with other domains.* A good science program is skillfully integrated into the total life of the classroom. Science may be the focus for a major project, such as living things or building structures. Science work may result from answering questions or exploring interests that emerge as children are cooking, looking at a book, painting, or talking about something from home. Children's play also can lead them to pursue science ideas. Sailing boats at the water table can lead to exploration of what sinks and what floats. Building a cave for the classroom bear can serve as an impetus for exploring the challenges of making strong buildings and roofs that span significant distances.

Science explorations are also integrally related to other domains. Many early mathematical ideas (e.g., *number*, *pattern*, and *shape*) are part of science, as are skills of counting and early measurement. Children sort their leaves by shape and compare the length of their worms and the height of their block towers. Scientific inquiry, mathematical problem solving, and technological design all take place as children build an environment for a worm, make shadow puppets, or create drums that have different sounds.

• *Provides access to science experiences for all children.* In a good science program, teachers are aware of each child's strengths, interests, needs, and challenges. They provide many entry points into a topic and use many strategies to engage children in science explorations. For example, tabletop blocks allow the child in a wheelchair to experience the challenge of building a structure that is tall and strong. Capitalizing on a child's fascination with knights and kings can encourage him to build castles

with strong fortresses. Many teachers have found that the active and challenging nature of scientific exploration often engages children who have trouble with classroom expectations. And, because science is the exploration of real things and events, children who are learning English can become fully engaged, while demonstrating what they know and can do.

Language and literacy development

In the preschool years, children's language and communication skills grow by leaps and bounds. These advances have significant implications across domains of development and learning, with language integral to emotional, social, and cognitive development. Moreover, language is critical for learning across the curriculum. For example, children need to learn the language of math as the foundation for understanding mathematics concepts in later years (Klibanoff et al. 2006). Similarly, language development is necessary for later reading comprehension and success in other subject areas such as science and social studies. Children's early literacy experiences, in turn, enrich their language learning.

Oral language and communication

The role of language development in children's emotional development is significant. Children who have the language needed to identify, understand, and respond to their own and other's emotions tolerate frustration and other strong emotions more easily and have more positive relationships with others (Denham & Weissberg 2004). A vocabulary for expressing emotions—the ability to name a feeling, such as angry, sad, disappointed, or frustrated—makes it possible for children to better understand and manage their emotions and express them to others (Schultz et al. 2001).

In social interaction, too, language has a clear role in the preschool years. As preschoolers gain sufficient language skill, they are able to state their feelings, desires, and ideas and respond to those of others. Socially competent children generally listen attentively to what others say and in their responses are able to mesh their behavior and verbalizations with what their play partners have said (Mize 1995). Verbal skills can help children enter an ongoing play group. For example, a child might use an opening such as "Can I work on this side of the building?" Well liked children also tend to give tactful rejections to their peer's requests and demands (Hazen, Black, & Feming-Johnson 1984); for example, "Sorry, I can't play right now because I already started this game, but we can play later, okay?"

Language is closely linked to cognition, as well. It provides tools for mental representation and for what Vygotsky (1978) termed "verbal mediation"—the ability to attach labels to objects and processes, which is important in concept development, generalization, and thought. Increasing capacity to use language in thought is a key development of the preschool period and enables children to solve new problems rather than rely solely on trial and error. Children with disabilities affecting their speech production may need assistive technology (and, for some, American Sign Language) to communicate, but they do acquire language and, just like other children, use it in thinking and solving problems.

Another indication that children use language as a mediator in thought is their private speech—the child's tendency to think out loud or control her own behavior by literally talking to herself (*"Slowly, slowly, don't spill it!"*). Vygotsky (1978) demonstrated the role this form of speech plays in children's problem solving and their coping with stressful or frustrating situations. He also observed the developmental changes that occur in how private speech is used. Younger children use it to announce the completion of an activity (*"There, I did it"*). With age, children begin to make use of private speech as they work on a task. Still more mature is children's use of private speech to plan in advance what they will do or how they

will proceed. Gradually private speech becomes internalized; children use it silently to think ahead, control, and reflect on their actions and behaviors.

The speed with which young children learn to understand and use language without being taught directly is one of nature's marvels and provides strong evidence of a biological basis for language acquisition (Chomsky 1968; Kuhl 2000). The people around a child serve as language models, and this is critically important in influencing the quantity and complexity of children's growing communication ability. But it is also children's desire to construct meaning and to communicate, along with their neurological readiness, that propels the rapid language development of the preschool years.

In observing and talking with preschool children, one is aware of the great variation in their language development, the range of differ-ences in vocabulary, sentence length, conversation, oral presentation, nonverbal behaviors, syntactical complexity, and ways of organizing thought.

Acquisition of language and communicative competence (the ability to use the full array of language skills for expression and interpretation) is strongly shaped by children's experiences and environment. And dramatic differences in children's early language experience are well documented. On average, children growing up in low-income households have significantly more limited experience with language than do middle-class children (Hart & Risley 1995; 1999; NICHD 2006). Children from low-income families hear far fewer words and are engaged in fewer extended conversations. Not surprisingly, substantial disparities exist in children's vocabulary knowledge by age 3 (Farkas & Beron 2004).

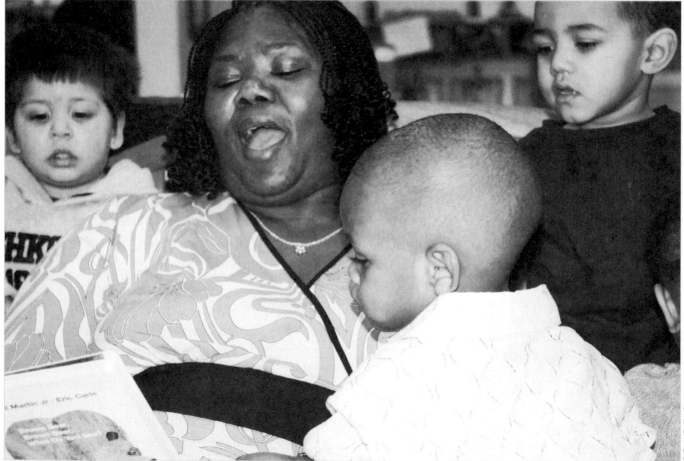

© Peg Callaghan

Cultural differences in language use exist as well. A primary function of language is to communicate with family and community members, so it is not surprising that cultural and social differences exist in children's acquisition and use of language (Hale-Benson 1986; Horton-Ikard 2006). For example, in some cultural groups, children are expected to learn more from observing adults than by talking with them, so children's language initiations are less likely to be encouraged or reinforced (Gonzalez-Mena 2008). Another example is found in Brice-Heath's classic study (1983) of two North Carolina communities, in which she found that teachers asked certain kinds of questions that the children were not accustomed to being asked by adults.

While many children grow up learning only one language, many learn two or more. The preschool years are an excellent time to acquire fluency in a second language. During this time, children are primed to learn their first language, and if introduced to a second language they can learn to speak it without an accent, as native speakers would. Not only are the preschool years a prime time for learning a new language, but cognitive benefits also appear to result from becoming bilingual or multilingual. Greater neural activity and denser tissue are found in the areas of the brain related to memory, attention, and language for children who learn more than one language, and these indicators are associated with long-term positive cognitive outcomes for children (Bialystok 2001; Mechelli et al. 2004; Kovelman, Baker, & Petitto 2006).

Among English language learners, common patterns in second-language acquisition occur. As in learning a first language, second language learners tend to acquire receptive language skills (understanding) much more quickly than they do speaking skills. In addition, many preschoolers learning a second language exhibit a silent period, in which they may virtually stop speaking in the classroom in order to focus intently on listening to the new language. The duration of the silent period varies depending on factors such as children's personality and temperament (e.g., whether they tend to be shy or risk takers). While the phenomenon occurs across the age spectrum, the silent period generally lasts longer among preschool age children than it does among older children (Tabors 2008).

Promoting language and literacy development

If well supported by adults, vocabulary, language, and an interest in print materials develop rapidly during the preschool years. Teachers can do many things to enrich and extend children's inherent interest in language, whether through attentive listening and good, extended conversation; reading books aloud and discussing them; or providing literacy materials, such as books and writing materials, in the classroom. To reach every child where she or he is, teachers need to bear in mind that while some children come from language-abundant households, others do not. In a stimulating classroom, every child will make important language gains in these years.

Promoting oral language and vocabulary knowledge. All children, and especially those who have ground to make up in vocabulary and other aspects of language, benefit significantly from sustained conversation, with adults and other children, particularly peers whose language skills are more advanced than their own. In such conversation, teachers need to give children their full attention, follow children's conversational lead, and add responses and comments that enrich the conversation and draw the children out. Offering expansions of children's sentences is helpful; for example, the child looking at a picture book might point and say, "A white bear!" and the adult responds, "Yes, there's a white mama bear with her baby—her little cub." This expansion enhances the meaning and adds additional linguistic information that assists the young language learner.

Conversations should include discussion of events, experiences, or people that are beyond the here and now—events from the past, the future, or the imagination (Dickinson & Tabors 2001). Such interaction requires children and

adults to use more explanations, descriptions, narratives, and pretend talk.

Knowledgeable teachers also recognize the value of expanding children's vocabulary in the course of studying topics of interest. For example, when children study transportation, they learn words such as *vehicle*, *enormous*, *haul*, and *propeller*. Projects and other in-depth studies in which children investigate new topics and ideas are excellent for sparking conversation and play and encouraging children to use language in generating ideas, evaluating solutions, planning, problem solving, and predicting outcomes.

In addition, teachers need to intentionally introduce new words that children might not encounter in everyday conversation. They should briefly describe each word in everyday language, use synonyms, and encourage children to use the word in applicable contexts. For example, the teacher might say, "When there is an emergency, we call 911. An emergency is when something dangerous happens—a fire or a car accident or when someone gets very sick. People need assistance right away. The situation is urgent. Let's put '911' next to the phone in your play house area to call in an emergency."

© Shari Schmidt

Most preschoolers are still making errors in their speech—or at least what adults perceive as errors—such as when a child says "mouses" or "I goed." In fact, such verbalizations show that the child has learned a rule or pattern in language structure—adding the -s to make the plural of *mouse* and -ed to form the past tense of *go*—overgeneralizing the pattern to instances in which English has irregular forms (*mice* and *went*). Teachers do not need to explicitly correct children's speech errors but should simply continue to use conventional English themselves. Given good modeling, the overgeneralizations and other preschool errors are typically self-corrected at a later stage.

Besides extended teacher-child conversation, another context with rich potential for language learning is play. Children use language to plan and negotiate in play, and they are highly motivated to communicate effectively in these situations. In the case of dramatic play, children also use language in enacting their roles. To optimize the value of play, teachers observe children and decide when and how to help them take the play to a higher level by, say, planning a play scenario or sustaining the play for longer. Higher-level play allows for more complex language interaction to take place as children plan scenarios, talk about the rules of the situation, negotiate roles, coordinate the use of props, and so forth (Bodrova & Leong 2003).

Of course, teachers also promote preschoolers' language growth by reading aloud high-quality books with rich vocabulary. As well as reading to the whole group, teachers should make opportunities to read to children in small groups. The small group, usually with three to six children, is especially conducive to conversation and especially effective in promoting vocabulary development in children from low-income families (Dickinson 2001b). Teachers can talk with the children about the story, invite them to retell or act it out, and encourage their comments (though, to the extent possible, teachers should do these things with the whole group, as well).

To be effective, the preschool program needs to fit with where children are developmentally, culturally, and linguistically. Teachers thus need to learn as much as they can about the children, their families, and the various cultural and language communities that they come from. Connecting with families is critical, so that teachers and parents can learn from each other how best to serve the children's needs. Teachers should always be looking for ways to bring the community (or communities) into the classroom and to connect children's experiences outside the program with the learning experiences that take place during the preschool day.

To this point, the discussion has focused on the critically important goal of helping children acquire proficiency in English, which is the home language of the majority of children in the United States. However, many programs today serve children whose first language is not English. For these children, the goal of acquiring English proficiency is essential, but support should also be provided for developing and maintaining the home language while the child acquires English (Espinosa 2008; Tabors 2008).

Well implemented bilingual preschool programs are most effective in reducing the achievement gap between English language learners and English speakers (Espinosa 2008), and these gains have long-term implications. When children between the ages of 3 and 8 receive systematic learning opportunities in their home language along with support for learning English, they often outperform their peers from English-only programs on measures of academic achievement during the middle and high school years (Campos 1995; Gutierrez-Clellan 1999; Restrepo & Kruth 2003).

For some preschool programs, incorporating all the languages spoken in the classroom may seem daunting. Relatively few of the nation's teachers at any grade level are fluent in more than one language. Moreover, preschool programs often include children and families from many different languages, not just two.

While it is important that programs increase the number of staff from the language and culture groups of the families served, bilingual fluency is not a prerequisite for creating a learning environment that respects and supports each child in use of the home language as well as in learning English. Toward this end, teachers should encourage parents to read to, speak to, and teach their children in the home language. Family members and others in the community can serve as resources for teachers in learning and sharing with all the children the rhymes, songs, and vocabulary of a given language.

Promoting the development of languages other than English enriches the learning for *all* children and adults in the classroom community (Barnett et al. 2007; Espinosa 2007).

Promoting early literacy interest and skills. Besides oral language development, a number of other elements are essential to an effective literacy program. A fundamental goal is making literacy experiences meaningful, interesting, and satisfying for children. In a literacy-rich environment, preschoolers enjoy looking at books and being read to, and they see that reading and writing help people do many useful and interesting things. The classroom should have a good selection of books, including storybooks and information books that reflect the full range of cultures among the children, and teachers should share the books with children in various ways. Reading aloud to children—individually, in small groups, and as a whole group—and enhancing this experience by reading expressively and actively engaging children (e.g., asking them to predict what happens next) is vital in fostering their enjoyment of books and interest in becoming readers.

Another strong predictor of reading success is phonological awareness (Whitehurst 1999); that is, noticing the sounds of spoken language—beginning speech sounds and rhythms, rhyme and other sound similarities, and, at the highest level, syllables and phonemes (the smallest units of speech that make a difference in communication). Most children do not automatically acquire phonemic awareness, but they gain this awareness when preschool teachers purposefully support it and provide the degree of assistance needed by each child.

Teachers can engage children in a range of activities that promote awareness of the sounds of language. With the teacher taking the lead, children can play rhyming games, sing songs and chant rhymes, do finger plays, and clap out the syllables of their names. When teachers read aloud books that play with language and rhymes (e.g., Dr. Seuss books) and include consistent language patterns such as alliteration and rhyme (e.g., *Brown Bear, Brown Bear*), children enjoy them greatly and gain in phonological awareness. Involving children in supplying their own rhymes, alliterations, and other variations further enhances their phonological awareness.

In acquainting children with written language, teachers should introduce them to concepts and skills such as understanding that print performs a variety of functions, recognizing print in the environment, distinguishing separate words, and realizing that English print is read left to right and top to bottom. Preschoolers benefit from environmental print when it is used in purposeful, functional ways—such as lists, sign-in charts, and labels indicating where various materials go—and when children increasingly have experiences in using print for such purposes.

Besides environmental print, the literacy-rich classroom includes a well stocked library corner and writing center, displays of children's writing, and theme-related literacy props (e.g., menus, order pads, signs) in play areas. Seeing print used for such purposes and increasingly making use of it in various ways are important components of preschool literacy learning.

At the most fundamental level, the ability to read and write depends on mastering the alphabetic principle—that there is a systematic relationship between letters and sounds, and that all spoken sounds and words can be represented by a limited set of symbols called letters. In the preschool years, teachers intro-

duce the alphabet to children in many contexts. For example, the teacher may incorporate letter knowledge into transitions ("*Everyone whose name starts with B may get their coats on*").

Teachers provide help when a child is striving to identify or form letters. Other strategies include placing alphabet charts and letters where children can refer to them, using alphabet books that illustrate letter sounds with pictures of objects, and inviting children to say what letter a word starts with or to say another word that starts with the same letter. In all such practices, teachers keep alphabet learning fun and meaningful.

Engaging children in early writing also helps them learn about print and the letters and words they eventually will read and spell (Burns, Griffin, & Snow 1999). Equally important, children have the experience of expressing themselves in the written mode and begin to think of themselves as writers. As young children experiment with writing, teachers have many opportunities to convey basic information about print. Children's earliest writing attempts are scribbles. Then they produce letter-like forms and eventually recognizable letters and developmental spellings—the child's initial attempts to associate sounds with letters (e.g., writing "bk" for *bike*). Preschool teachers should recognize developmental spelling as a valuable way for children to explore and learn sound/letter relationships. Observing children's

efforts helps teachers to monitor and scaffold children's understanding of the relationships.

In preschool, children's proper written formation of letters should not be a priority; such an emphasis would be likely to make early writing less meaningful and more frustrating to young children. In the developmentally appropriate preschool, writing experiences are focused on the use of print for functional reasons. Teachers introduce text forms that have differing purposes and are written differently; for example, a list versus a letter to a friend. Another activity that helps the child become a writer is dictating a story to a teacher, seeing the teacher write these words, and then hearing them read back.

Finally, a solid base of knowledge and conceptual development is essential for becoming a skilled reader. To expand children's content and vocabulary knowledge, teachers provide interesting objects, information books and storybooks, and encounters with the broader world (e.g., field trips and virtual field trips, which are now possible through technology). Meaningful projects and investigations enable children to expand and use their knowledge, as well as gain researching skills by looking up information in books, asking knowledgeable adults, or using the Internet. Teachers focus children's attention by asking questions that encourage children to observe carefully, make comparisons, or review their past experiences.

Developmentally Appropriate Practice in the Preschool Years—Ages 3–5
Examples to Consider

The framework of developmentally appropriate practice derives from what the early childhood field knows through research and experience about how children develop and learn. Major points from this knowledge base are highlighted in the position statement and summarized in chapter 4. As no learning tool clarifies understanding better than examples, the chart below presents many more examples of practices to consider.

The chart addresses developmentally appropriate practice in five areas important to the teacher's role: creating a caring community of learners, teaching to enhance development and learning, planning curriculum to achieve important goals, assessing children's development and learning, and establishing reciprocal relationships with families. The set of examples offered here is not exhaustive, and the goal is not to describe best practice comprehensively. We have tried to capture major aspects of practice that one sees in excellent early childhood programs and, by contrast, in those programs that in some respects have not achieved a high level of quality. Neither is the aim to issue a prescriptive formula to be rigidly followed. Instead, the examples are meant to encourage readers to reflect on their practice. Establishing a habit of thoughtful reflection is essential in working with young children because of their varying family backgrounds, preferences, and needs.

In the chart's left column, under the heading "Developmentally Appropriate," are examples of practices consistent with available research and that most in the field agree promote young children's optimal learning and development. The examples in the "In Contrast" column are intended to aid reflection by helping readers see clearly the kinds of things that well-intentioned adults might do but that are not likely to serve children well. Many of the "In Contrast" examples are very prevalent in early childhood settings. A few of those practices are dangerous or would cause children lasting damage. Others are unlikely to harm children significantly but also are less likely to promote their optimal development. Sometimes context affects whether a practice should be used or adapted.

Where they appear, the comments sections expand on the practice examples presented in the chart cells above them. Some of the comments speak to

cultural factors to consider when determining what practices to use. Other comments elaborate on a practice that is briefly described in a column, and some indicate the research finding on which a practice is based.

Finally, most of the examples are phrased as descriptions of what teachers do or fail to do. For the "In Contrast" examples, however, that wording is not meant to imply that deficient or questionable practices are necessarily teachers' fault. Most teachers are working hard and doing their best—but often constrained by very challenging circumstances, including limited training, inadequate staff:child ratios, low compensation, high staff turnover, meager resources, or administrative constraints. The hope of this chapter is to help them in their efforts.

Developmentally appropriate	In contrast

Creating a Caring Community of Learners

Fostering positive relationships

Developmentally appropriate	In contrast
Teachers are warm, caring, and responsive. They make it a priority to know every child and family well and build a relationship with each of them.	■ Large class sizes or the shifting of children from class to class makes it more challenging for teachers to know families and children well. ■ Teachers are businesslike and focused on keeping classroom control, but they do not make an effort to know children as individuals. ■ Staff know and pay attention to some children, typically those who stand out or present special challenges. Others get lost in the shuffle, and quiet children (including those with limited English) are likely to be given less attention.
Teachers help children learn how to establish positive, constructive relationships with others. They support children's forming of friendships and provide opportunities for children to play and work together.	■ When children lacking social skills are isolated or rejected by peers, teachers fail to help and support them in developing positive relationships with others. ■ Teachers treat children's conflicts and other undesired behaviors as problems to be handled directively rather than seeing them as learning opportunities for the children.
Teachers actively seek to ensure that all children, including children with special needs, are included in the social relationships, play, and learning experiences of the classroom.	■ When children do not readily find a place in the group, teachers do not take active measures to facilitate their full inclusion, so they tend to remain socially isolated. They are also likely to be marginalized in learning activities that involve group participation.

Developmentally appropriate	In contrast

Creating a Caring Community of Learners (cont.)

Fostering positive relationships (cont.)

Comments on fostering positive relationships:
—In NAEYC's set of Early Childhood Program Standards that together provide a definition of quality—and which are referenced in its program accreditation criteria—the very first standard is *relationships* (NAEYC 2005a). This prominent position reflects the belief that positive relationships are essential for learning and development, development of personal responsibility, and the capacity for self-regulation and constructive interactions with others, all of which relate to classroom functioning. Children who see themselves as cared about and connected are more likely to feel secure, thrive physically, get along with others, learn well, and feel like part of a community.

Building classroom community

Developmentally appropriate	In contrast
Teachers strive to create a sense of the group as a cohesive community. They often refer to "our class," "we," and "all of us together," and they engage children in cooperative experiences as well as experiences that demonstrate that each member of the group is valued (such as involving the children in making a "We miss you!" card for a sick classmate). Teachers recognize community-building opportunities in various parts of the day, such as mealtimes, cleanup, and whole-group times. During these activities, they engage children in talking about shared experiences, singing, and discussing problems or plans (such as planning an event for parents).	▓ Teachers fail to emphasize the importance of respecting every person and do not consistently take action when hurtful behaviors or remarks occur. They make little effort to build a sense of the group as a community and engage in actions that diminish the children's sense of community (e.g., setting up games in which sides are chosen or allowing children to engage in chronic tattling, scapegoating, or teasing). ▓ Priority is not given to continuity of children's participation in a consistent group. For administrative reasons (e.g., to keep staff hours within required limits or to maintain mandated staff:child ratios), children are shifted into different groupings across the course of a day or week.
Teachers provide many opportunities for children to play and work together, both in groups they form themselves and in small teacher-created groups. When a child asks for teacher assistance, the teacher sometimes makes a point of referring the child to a peer to provide the needed help or information.	▓ Children spend most of the day in whole-group time, doing workbooks, or in noninteractive small groups. They have few opportunities to work and play together. ▓ Teachers always solve problems for children and give any help they request. They do not encourage children to work through problems together and help one another.

Developmentally appropriate	In contrast

Creating a Caring Community of Learners (cont.)

Building classroom community (cont.)

Teachers create a classroom that reflects the diversity of the community and society and involves every child's home culture and language in the shared culture of the group. By showing that each child's family, culture, and language are valued, teachers promote children's positive self-identity and help them to respect and appreciate similarities and differences among people. Teachers include parents in selection of multicultural materials, photographs, books, play items, songs, and stories to ensure that these are authentic and that there are no offensive stereotypes presented to the children.

■ Cultural, linguistic, and other differences among children are ignored. Some children and/or families do not see their race, language, or culture reflected in the setting or experiences—in photographs, books, play items, songs, stories, and the like—so they do not feel like part of the group. No attempt is made to have someone who speaks each child's home language visit the classroom, or caregivers do not try to learn some words of each language represented.

■ Teachers draw attention to differences among children, including cultural and linguistic differences, to such an extent that some children are made to feel that they do not fit in.

Comments on building classroom community:
—It is important for the classroom environment, materials, and activities to reflect all the children's backgrounds without stereotyping them. Otherwise some children will not have a sense of belonging. In addition, an environment inclusive of multiple cultures gives all the children increased awareness and appreciation of differing cultures and helps them recognize that they can enjoy and work with others from many backgrounds.

Teaching to Enhance Development and Learning

Environment and schedule

Teachers ensure that the environment is safe, healthy, and conducive to children's exploration and independence, and they provide attentive supervision. Within safe boundaries, teachers support children's exploration and learning of new skills (e.g., cutting with a knife, climbing an outdoor climbing structure). Although teachers let children do for themselves what they can do safely, they recognize that some cultures stress interdependence over independence, and thus teachers work with parents to determine a mutually acceptable strategy.

■ Teachers are unfamiliar with the program safety rules and procedures. Or they are inattentive or careless about supervising children and monitoring the safety of all parts of the indoor and outdoor environments.

■ To save time or trouble, teachers do things for children that children could do themselves. Due to program policy or teacher preference, adults avoid certain learning activities they see as possibly unsafe (e.g., field trips, playground climbing, cooking) instead of working out safe ways for children to engage in them.

Developmentally appropriate	In contrast

Teaching to Enhance Development and Learning (cont.)

Environment and schedule (cont.)

Teachers create a learning environment that fosters children's initiative, active exploration of materials, and sustained engagement with other children, adults, and activities. In choosing materials and equipment, teachers consider children's developmental levels, interests, and established social/cultural contexts (e.g., providing items and experiences familiar in their homes).

■ The environment is disorderly, with little structure or predictability. Consequently, children's behavior is frantic or disengaged. The noise level is stressful for children and adults, making it hard to focus or have a conversation.

■ The way teachers arrange the environment severely limits children's interaction with peers and their opportunities to pursue engaging learning experiences. For example, children generally have to ask teachers for materials rather than finding materials readily accessible.

■ The environment, materials, and experiences reflect only a single culture or in other respects provide too little variety, interest, or choice for children (e.g., all puzzles are at one level of difficulty).

Teachers organize the daily schedule to allow for periods of alternating active and quiet time, adequate nutrition, and naptime (for younger children in full-day programs).

■ Teachers overschedule activities, so children become overtired and overstimulated from too much activity without respite. Very frequent transitions waste time and leave children restless and distracted rather than engaged.

Teachers allocate extended time periods in learning centers (at least 60 minutes) so that children are able to get deeply involved in an activity and sustain dramatic play, construction, and other activities at a complex level. Children have ample time and opportunity to investigate what sparks their curiosity.

■ Routines such as toileting or frequent transitions of activity take up excessive time in the day or interrupt children's engagement and focus, preventing them from gaining maximum benefit from sustained dramatic play, construction, investigations, or other such activities.

■ The time block allotted to play and other child-guided experiences is too brief (e.g., 15–20 minutes) for the activity to reach a complex level. Scheduled only at the beginning or end of the day, during arrival/pickup, some children miss it entirely.

Comments on environment and schedule:
—According to a large multistate study of state-funded prekindergarten programs, preschool children typically spend more than a third of their time in transitions and routines (e.g., standing in line, cleaning up, washing hands, eating) rather than in play and other learning experiences. Unfortunately, the researchers also found that teachers don't conduct such transitions and routines in ways that engage children in conversations with adults or otherwise promote children's learning and development (Early et al. 2005).

Developmentally appropriate	In contrast

Teaching to Enhance Development and Learning (cont.)

Teaching methods

To engage children actively in a variety of learning experiences, teachers create interest areas and furnish these with materials based on program goals and knowledge of children's varying interests and abilities. Materials include blocks, books, writing materials, math-related games and manipulatives, dramatic play props, equipment for physical movement, art and modeling materials, sand and water, and tools for science investigations.

■ Learning materials are primarily workbooks, worksheets, flash cards, and other materials that do not engage children's interest, promote their self-regulation, or involve them in problem solving and other higher-order thinking skills.

■ The same materials are available day after day. Children have few new choices and little variety in materials and activities.

■ Teachers choose materials and activities only to be fun and entertaining to children (or appealing to parents) rather than to foster children's abilities, attitudes, or knowledge.

Teachers use a number of formats, including large and small groups, choice time (in interest areas), and routines. For any learning goal, teachers choose the format that seems best suited to that specific purpose.

■ Teachers overuse one or two learning formats in the course of the day and make little or no use of others. For example, teachers give children very little time in interest areas or fail to use the small-group format when it would be the most effective approach.

■ Groups tend to be didactic, with little use of children's ideas and contributions by teachers.

To help children acquire new skills and understandings, teachers employ a range of strategies, choosing from and combining them to suit the goal, the child, and the situation. In addition to providing information, teachers may choose strategies such as asking questions, offering cues or suggestions, adding complexity or challenge to tasks, and providing opportunity and support for children to collaborate with peers.

■ Teachers view their role as just setting up the environment and keeping an eye on things, and thus they miss many opportunities to promote children's learning. Outside of talking to the whole group, teachers' interactions with children typically do not go beyond giving directions, responding to requests for help, mediating disputes, and the like.

■ Teachers make excessive use of direct instruction methods (e.g., giving directions, presenting information), which are useful for some purposes but not effective as the predominant strategy in teaching young children.

Teachers promote children's learning and development by scaffolding; that is, they provide assistance and/or add supports to enable each child to master a challenge just beyond his current level. The teacher gradually reduces this support as the child is able to proceed independently.

■ Teachers typically provide too much or too little scaffolding. They may fail to check to see where children are at the outset, and/or they may fail to vary the support they give based on the child's needs.

| Developmentally appropriate | In contrast |

Teaching to Enhance Development and Learning (cont.)

Teaching methods (cont.)

Teachers recognize the importance of both child-guided and adult-guided learning experiences. In supporting children's deep engagement in play and other child-guided activities, teachers find opportunities to enhance children's thinking and learning.

■ Teachers rarely plan adult-guided learning experiences. They rarely take action, even when children's behaviors are aimless or disruptive. When children are engaged in play and interest areas, teachers assume a largely passive role, contributing little or nothing to children's play and learning.

■ Teachers do not recognize how important it is for children to guide some of their own activities, such as play, and they frequently interrupt and undermine children's immersion in or managing of their own activities.

Teachers frequently engage children in planning or in reflecting on their experiences, discussing a past experience, and working to represent it (e.g., drawing, writing and dictating, making pictographs). Such opportunities help the teacher learn what children are thinking and enable children to deepen and refine their own concepts and understanding.

■ Feeling pressured to cover the curriculum and believing that returning to the same topic or experience is a waste of time, teachers present a topic or experience only once and fail to provide opportunities for revisiting and reexamining experiences, which would make fuller, more refined understanding possible.

■ Teachers typically look for one right answer when asking a question, and children often feel on the spot. Not realizing how much thought preschoolers are capable of, teachers do not take children's ideas seriously, nor do they encourage children's efforts to share ideas through various modes of communication and representation.

Teachers provide many opportunities for children to learn to collaborate with others and work through ideas and solutions, as well as develop social skills such as cooperating, helping, negotiating, and talking with other people to solve problems.

■ Children have few opportunities for meaningful social interaction with other children.

■ Though teachers may recognize the social dimension of children's interactions, they do not see teamwork as integral to children's cognitive development and learning. Thus, teachers rarely make use of children's interactions and relationships in addressing learning goals.

Developmentally appropriate	In contrast

Teaching to Enhance Development and Learning (cont.)

Teaching methods (cont.)

Comments on teaching methods:

—Children learn best when they are deeply engaged. Both when they themselves primarily shape the activity (as in play) and when adults thoughtfully plan and guide the activity (such as a large-group read aloud or small-group science project), the key element is the level of children's interest and engagement. Research supports the effectiveness of various teaching strategies and formats for different purposes (e.g., high-level dramatic play promotes self-regulation, while small-group book reading has been found to promote vocabulary development).

—For a discussion of the purposes behind each classroom format (small group, large group, etc.), see the position statement and chapter 1.

—For more on teaching strategies, see chapter 1.

Communication and language use

Developmentally appropriate	In contrast
Teachers talk often and warmly with every child—getting to know children, building positive relationships with them, and gathering information about them.	■ Teachers' speech is mostly one-way, much more often *telling* children things than conversing with or listening to them. ■ Teachers usually speak to children as a group. For the most part, teachers address individual children only to admonish or discipline them.
When talking with children, teachers take into account children's capabilities as listeners, recognizing that preschoolers' skills of recall and focused attention are still developing. Teachers communicate information in small units, tie new information to what children already know, check for understanding, and invite questions or comments to engage their interest.	■ Teachers talk at length or read aloud for long periods; they expect attentiveness during these times, but children often become restless or tune out. ■ Teachers put a high priority on children being silent unless addressed; they ignore or correct children for talking or for not waiting to be called on. ■ Teachers talk down to children or answer for children who are sometimes slow to respond (e.g., English language learners).
When children are talking, teachers take into account preschoolers' capabilities as speakers, giving children time to express themselves and responding attentively to their speech. Teachers share with children the role of setting the topic and purpose of talk.	■ Adult agendas dominate classroom conversations. Children's talk often is viewed as interruptions of the adults' talk or work. ■ Teachers don't respect children as speakers (e.g., asking questions without really meaning children to answer). ■ Teachers talk for children instead of waiting for them to respond to a question or comment and thus encouraging a two-way conversation.

Developmentally Appropriate Practice, 3d Edition

Developmentally appropriate	In contrast

Teaching to Enhance Development and Learning (cont.)

Communication and language use (cont.)

Teachers encourage children's efforts to communicate. They make it a priority to involve English language learners in meaningful interactions at whatever level children are able. Teachers allow children time to think about how they want to respond to a question or comment (*wait time*).	■ Teachers are so focused on the shortcomings of preschoolers' language skills that they neglect or miss the message children are attempting to communicate. ■ Teachers insist on children's speaking only in English or only with proper grammar, correcting them every time they diverge from standard English usage.
Teachers engage individual children and groups in real conversations about their experiences, projects, and current events. They encourage children to describe their work products or ideas, and teachers express interest in hearing children's opinions, observations, and feelings.	■ Teachers interrupt children and dominate conversations instead of taking conversational turns. ■ Teachers don't talk in-depth with children, often underestimating children's complexity of thought because they can't yet communicate it fully.
Teachers use wide-ranging vocabulary in their talk to and with preschoolers, including many words that are unfamiliar to children. When teachers use words unfamiliar to a child, they give sufficient information for the child to grasp the meaning. With an English language learner, teachers provide nonverbal cues to enable the child to learn what the new words mean (e.g., using gestures, pointing to objects or pictured items).	■ Teachers talk down to children in both content and oversimplified speech, using relatively limited vocabulary in their conversational exchanges. ■ Teachers use a fairly rich vocabulary, but when they use words unfamiliar to children, teachers do not give sufficient information for children to grasp the meaning.
Teachers talk with all children, making it a priority to talk often with children who are learning English and those with delayed language development or limited vocabulary.	■ Teachers don't make extra effort to talk to children who are shy or hesitant, have communication difficulties, or are in the process of learning English. ■ Teachers pay so much attention to English language learners (and draw their peers' attention to them, as well) that those children feel unusual or outside the community of learners.

Comments on communication and language use:

—By their interest in and responsiveness to what children say, teachers help initiate children to the back-and-forth sharing of conversation, and they enhance the complexity of children's language and the extent of their vocabulary.

—Drawing special attention to English language learners may be problematic for children from cultural groups in which getting singled out for attention, even positive attention, is not desirable.

Developmentally appropriate	In contrast

Teaching to Enhance Development and Learning (cont.)

Motivation and positive approaches to learning

Recognizing children's natural curiosity and desire to make sense of their world and gain new skills, teachers consistently plan learning experiences that children find highly interesting, engaging, and comfortable.

■ Most classroom experiences either are uninteresting and unchallenging or are so difficult and frustrating that they diminish children's intrinsic motivation to learn.

■ Seeking to motivate children, teachers rely heavily on external rewards (stickers, privileges, etc.) or chastise children for their mistakes or shortcomings.

Teachers use verbal encouragement in ways that are genuine and related to what the child is doing. They acknowledge the child's effort and work with specific, objective comments such as, "You really put a lot of detail in your drawing," and "I see you drew your older sister bigger than your brother."

■ Teachers make such frequent use of nonspecific praise ("What a pretty picture!" or "Good boy") that it becomes meaningless either to provide useful feedback or to motivate the child. Children may also become focused on pleasing the teacher rather than on the learning experience itself.

■ Teachers' feedback consists mostly of negative comments and correction of errors.

Comments on motivation and positive approaches to learning:
—There are some cases where using rewards for a limited time may help children (e.g., with certain special needs or challenging behaviors). Aquiring some basic self-help or social skills then becomes self-rewarding and leads to greater acceptance by peers, enabling children with special needs to participate more successfully in a group situation.

Guidance

Teachers model and encourage calm, patient behavior and facilitate children's development of self-regulation by supporting them in thinking ahead, planning their activities, and thinking about and using strategies to solve social problems. Teachers' support and scaffolding move children toward more mature levels of dramatic play, which promotes their self-regulation. Rather than focusing solely on reducing the challenging behavior, adults direct their efforts to teaching the child social, communication, and emotional regulation skills.

■ Teachers are uncontrolled in their own behavior (e.g., showing irritation, stress, and impulsive responses) with children and/or with other adults.

■ Not knowing what children of this age are capable of, teachers do not involve children in thinking through how to solve problems and learning to control their own behavior.

■ The classroom is so chaotic that children flit from one activity to another, simply reacting in the moment rather than being planful or reflective. Or the classroom is highly teacher-directed so that children become too adult-regulated.

Developmentally appropriate	In contrast

Teaching to Enhance Development and Learning (cont.)

Guidance (cont.)

Teachers set clear limits regarding unacceptable behaviors and enforce these limits with explanations in a climate of mutual respect and caring. They attend to children consistently, not principally when they are engaging in problematic behaviors. Teachers involve children, particularly older preschoolers, in considering rules of group behavior and responsibility.

■ Teachers do not set clear limits and do not hold children accountable to standards of acceptable behavior. Teachers do not help children learn or participate in setting classroom rules so that they can incorporate the rules as their own.

■ Teachers use guidance strategies that control children rather than promote their self-regulation, conflict resolution skills, and social problem solving. When problems arise between children, teachers quickly step in to solve the problems themselves.

When a child consistently displays challenging behaviors, teachers identify events, activities, interactions, and other contextual factors that occur with the challenging behavior and may provoke it. Then, to help the child progress toward more acceptable behavior, teachers (in collaboration with families) make modifications in the activities and environment and ensure that the child receives adult and peer support.

■ Teachers spend a great deal of time punishing unacceptable behavior, refereeing disagreements, and repeatedly putting the same children in time-out or disciplining them in other ways unrelated to their actions.

■ The director and/or staff encourage families of children with challenging behaviors to leave the program. Children with special needs or behavioral problems are isolated or rebuked for failure to meet group expectations rather than being provided with learning experiences that are at a reasonable level of difficulty.

Comments on guidance:

—Becoming self-regulated is one of the most significant developmental tasks of the preschool years. Chapter 4 discusses the benefits of self-regulation and how teachers can promote it.

—When a child regularly engages in challenging behavior, teachers need to communicate with the family to discuss what is going on with the child and what each adult can do to try to help. If challenging behaviors are persistent and serious, teachers, the family, and in some instances other professionals need to work as a team to develop and implement an individualized plan that supports the child's inclusion and success.

Developmentally appropriate	In contrast

Planning Curriculum to Achieve Important Goals

Curriculum essentials

Comprehensive scope; important goals

The curriculum addresses key goals in all areas of development (physical, social, emotional, cognitive) and in the domains of physical education and health, language and literacy, mathematics, science, social studies, and creative arts.	■ Curriculum goals are narrowly focused on a few learning domains (e.g., literacy and math or social and emotional development) without recognition that all areas of a child's development and learning are interrelated and important.
In each area, the curriculum is consistent with high-quality, achievable, and challenging early learning standards and recommendations of the relevant professional organizations.	■ Curriculum content lacks intellectual integrity and is trivial and unworthy of children's attention.
The curriculum is designed to help children explore and acquire the key concepts (the "big ideas") and tools of inquiry of each discipline in ways that are effective for preschool children (e.g., science experiences include opportunities in which children explore and directly observe changes and phenomena).	■ The curriculum is developed by extending kindergarten expectations downward, rather than by reflecting what preschool children are capable of—thus, expectations may be too high, too low, or otherwise not a good fit for the children.

Coherence and integration

Teachers are knowledgeable about the sequence and pace that development and learning typically follow as children build understanding and skill in each content area. For example, teachers' knowledge of the progression involved in learning to count enables them to introduce children to the concepts and skills in a coherent way and to scaffold children's progress from each idea and ability to the next.	■ Because the standards on which the curriculum is based include too many topics or learning objectives, learning experiences touch on topics only superficially, and children are unable to gain real understanding of any single topic.
	■ Teachers fail to recognize the sequence of learning in the discipline areas or how it applies to children in this age range. For example, teachers expect children to perform the task of addition before they understand one-to-one correspondence and other fundamentals of number.

Developmentally appropriate	In contrast

Planning Curriculum to Achieve Important Goals (cont.)

Coherence and integration (cont.)

Teachers integrate ideas and content from multiple domains and disciplines through themes, projects, play opportunities, and other learning experiences so that children are able to develop an understanding of concepts and make connections across content areas. For example, in discussing a certain kind of pattern in math, teachers draw children's attention to the same pattern in songs.

■ Children's learning is seen as occurring in separate content areas, and times are set aside to teach each subject without integration. Teachers fail to connect curriculum topics in ways that are meaningful to children. As a result, learning is often fragmented, and children are less likely to generalize ideas and apply them across content areas.

■ Teachers use a "holiday curriculum" or build units on other themes with only surface appeal (e.g., teddy bears), rather than using a curriculum based on characteristics of children's development and learning, the content and skills (including thinking skills) they need to acquire, and what they find deeply engaging.

Effective implementation

The curriculum, which is in written form, provides teachers with a useful and flexible framework for planning learning experiences and materials and for seeing how those experiences can fit together to accomplish the program's stated goals.

■ If there is a prescribed curriculum (published or adopted by a district or school), teachers do not have the flexibility or the capability to make adaptations in the curriculum to optimize its interest and effectiveness with the particular children in the group.

Teachers actually refer to and use the curriculum framework as they plan what they will do with children, so classroom experiences are coherent. Teachers plan and implement experiences that help children achieve important developmental and learning goals.

■ Teachers do not consider the curriculum framework in their planning (e.g., the "curriculum" is a book on a shelf). Children's learning experiences do not follow a logical sequence. Goals of the program are unclear or unknown.

In planning and implementing learning experiences, teachers draw on their knowledge of the content, awareness of what is likely to interest children of that age, and understanding of the cultural and social contexts of children's lives.

■ Teachers rigidly follow a prescribed curriculum plan without attention to individual children's interests and needs or the specific and changing context (e.g., studying snow with children in January, regardless of where the program is located or the local weather conditions). Teachers use previously planned topics without attention to circumstances or events (e.g., an egg in the incubator beginning to hatch, first snowfall in November).

Developmentally appropriate	In contrast

Planning Curriculum to Achieve Important Goals (cont.)

Effective implementation (cont.)

Teachers plan curriculum that is responsive and respectful to the specific context of children's experiences. Culturally diverse and nonsexist activities and materials are provided to help individual children develop positive self-identity, to relate new concepts to their own life experiences, and to enrich the lives of all children with respectful acceptance and appreciation of differences and similarities. For example, books and pictures include people of different races, ages, and abilities and of both genders in various roles.

■ Children's cultural and linguistic backgrounds and other individual differences are ignored or treated as deficits to be overcome.

■ Multicultural curriculum reflects a "tourist approach" in which the artifacts, food, or other particulars of different cultures are presented without meaningful connections to the children's own experiences. Teachers point out a culture's traditions in ways that convey these are exotic or deviations from the "normal" majority culture (and thus the children of this culture feel like outsiders).

Teachers assess each child's progress toward the program's stated curricular goals, and they reflect on their practice by monitoring the effectiveness of their teaching. They make changes to their teaching practice (environment, schedule, methods, etc.) as necessary to improve effectiveness for the group and for individual children.

■ Teachers do not regularly make use of assessment information to inform curriculum decisions.

Teachers connect curriculum topics with children's interests and with what children already know and can do. Young children learn best when the concepts, vocabulary, and skills they encounter are related to things they know and care about and when the new learnings are interconnected in meaningful ways.

■ Meaningful, connected learning is not a priority in the curriculum planning. No attempt is made to discover and build on children's prior knowledge, especially for children from diverse cultural and linguistic backgrounds whose competencies may not be immediately apparent.

Comments on effective implementation:

—Curriculum should be linked to and guided by early learning standards and the standards recommended by professional groups in the various disciplines when these standards are of high quality and are achievable and challenging for preschoolers (NAEYC & NAECS/SDE 2002; 2003). A consideration in adopting a subject-specific curriculum (e.g., in math or literacy) is its consistency with high-quality standards of relevant professional organization(s) such as NCTM (2000) or IRA/NCTE (1996).

Developmentally appropriate	In contrast

Planning Curriculum to Achieve Important Goals (cont.)

Physical development

Health and fitness

Teachers acquaint children with healthy habits in eating, exercise, and hygiene and introduce basic concepts of body functioning and physical health.

- The program serves foods with low nutrition value and with high sugar or fat content.
- Children spend too much time sitting and do not get adequate exercise.
- Teachers do not communicate with families about factors such as items of clothing that hamper children's participation (e.g., dress shoes a child can't run in).

Comments on health and fitness:
—The child and adolescent obesity crisis in the U.S. has serious implications for the health of the young as well as medical and human costs to the nation. Now more than ever, children need to begin early in developing the elements of a healthy, active lifestyle.

Gross motor development

Children spend little time sitting; they are able to move around freely throughout much of the day. Teachers make sure that children have plenty of opportunities to use large muscles in balancing, running, jumping, climbing, and other vigorous movements, both in their play and in planned movement activities. Children play outdoors every day except when weather is extremely inclement.

- Children's opportunity for gross motor activity is either very limited (e.g., a total of 15 minutes or less in a half-day program; 30 minutes or less over a full day) or irregular (e.g., only when the weather is very nice and children are taken outside).

Adults teach children the pleasure and importance of physical activity, as well as body and spatial awareness and key movement skills (e.g., catching, jumping, balancing). Equal encouragement is given to boys and girls.

- Teachers or other qualified adults are uninvolved during children's time outdoors (or in a large indoor space), except to provide basic supervision. Adults make little effort to involve less-active children and those lagging in physical skills or coordination or to help them develop the skills and confidence to engage in gross motor activities.
- Physical activity areas have very limited equipment, so children lack variety of choices and/or must often wait quite a while to get a turn.

Developmentally appropriate	In contrast

Planning Curriculum to Achieve Important Goals (cont.)

Gross motor development (cont.)

Comments on gross motor development:

—Physical activity and outdoor play too often are not recognized as integral to the curriculum; minimal time is designated for them because programs see them as taking away from instructional time. Even when children do get daily opportunity to "let off steam" through energetic activity, however, they may not master the fundamental physical skills they need to progress toward more advanced abilities unless adults support children's acquisition of skills, concepts, or confidence. Without fundamental skills, many children opt out of physical activities, thus becoming even less fit, less skilled, less comfortable with physical effort and challenge, and often less accepted by peers. Such children are at greater risk for childhood obesity and other health risks of insufficient exercise.

Fine motor development

Teachers provide opportunities throughout the day for children to develop fine motor skills through working with suitable materials (e.g., puzzles, playdough, drawing and writing implements, beads, paper and scissors, blocks, buttons and zippers on clothing). As needed, teachers help children acquire such skills through scaffolding their efforts.

■ Teachers give children fine motor tasks that are too difficult or hold them to an unrealistically high standard in executing tasks; for example, expecting them to write letters with precision when they lack the necessary fine motor control.

■ The tools and fine motor experiences that teachers provide have insufficient variety to allow children at many different levels to progress in eye-hand coordination and motor control. For example, there are only fat markers for the children to use.

Teachers provide opportunities and support for children to develop and practice fine motor self-help skills, such as dressing, toileting, serving and feeding themselves, brushing teeth, washing hands, and picking up toys. Adults are patient when there are occasional spills, accidents, and unfinished jobs.

■ To save time and mess, adults often perform routine tasks for children.

■ Adults display irritation or they shame children when spills or other accidents happen.

Comments on fine motor development:

—Teachers and parents sometimes push preschoolers in the technical skills of handwriting (e.g., forming letters with precision, writing consistently "on the lines") before the children have sufficient fine motor development for such exactness. At this age, the focus should be not on children's handwriting but on their emergent writing—that is, their learning to express themselves; to use writing for various purposes; and to become familiar with letters and words, print conventions, and other aspects of written language (as outlined in **Language and Literacy**).

—Dressing and eating independently build fine motor skills; however, some families may think their children are becoming independent too soon if teachers encourage self-sufficiency. Teachers will need to discuss the issue with parents to reach a decision all can live with.

Developmentally appropriate	In contrast

Planning Curriculum to Achieve Important Goals (cont.)

Language and literacy

Listening, speaking, and understanding

Teachers engage in conversations with both individual children and small groups. Whenever possible these are sustained conversations (with multiple conversational turns, complex ideas, rich vocabulary) and include *decontextualized language* (talk about events beyond the here and now) concerning what's past or future or imaginary ("What do you think we will see at the firehouse?").	■ Most of teachers' speech to children consists of brief comments or directions ("It's cleanup time" "Don't run!") rather than dialogue. ■ Teachers mostly ask children questions that call for brief or simple responses. ■ Conversations are limited to the current context ("Are you finished?").
Teachers create regular opportunities for children to actively listen to and converse with others during play and while working together in small groups on projects or to solve problems. They model the skills of speaking and listening in their interactions with children and with other adults. Teachers also provide frequent opportunities for children to talk with each other, so children also get modeling from their more skilled peers.	■ Adult agendas dominate classroom talk; most talk is *by* adults *at* children. Teachers provide few opportunities and little support for language interaction between children and for improving their language skills. ■ When talking with children, teachers don't speak clearly or listen attentively. They chastise children ("You're not listening") but are not good listeners themselves. They interrupt and dominate conversations instead of taking conversational turns.
Teachers teach children *how* to listen—by teaching and scaffolding it, just like any other language skill.	■ Teachers think that "listening" means that children behave well ("He doesn't listen"), and they do not help children with listening skills.
Teachers attend to the particular language needs of English language learners and children who are behind in vocabulary and other aspects of language learning. They engage the child more frequently in sustained conversations and make extra efforts to help them comprehend.	■ Teachers talk mostly with verbally skilled children, neglecting the children who most need language or communication help—children who are shy or hesitant, have communication difficulties, or are learning English. ■ When teachers talk to a child who is behind in language learning, they don't show the patience and attentiveness that the child requires to become successful as a conversational partner.

Developmentally appropriate	In contrast

Planning Curriculum to Achieve Important Goals (cont.)

Listening, speaking, and understanding (cont.)

Teachers support English language learners in their home language (e.g., by gathering books and tapes/CDs in each child's language and involving family members and others who speak the language in the program), as well as promoting their learning of English.

■ Teachers provide no support for children in maintaining and developing their home language.

■ A policy (sometimes imposed from above) specifies that children and teachers use only English in the classroom.

Teachers provide a wide range of vocabulary in their own speech and through reading to children. When using a word that children may not know, teachers give a synonym, explain briefly, or use nonverbal cues (e.g., imitating the object or action, pointing to the object or illustration). Teachers are especially attentive to helping English language learners grasp word meaning.

■ When using words unfamiliar to some or all of the children, teachers fail to give information to enable children to grasp the meaning. With English language learners, teachers do not provide the nonverbal cues that would allow children to learn what new words mean.

■ Teachers use limited vocabulary in their exchanges with children.

Teachers help children use communication and language as tools for thinking and learning. For example, during group time teachers provide ways for every child to talk (e.g., talk to a peer, call out answers). Or teachers have children repeat aloud things they want to remember (e.g., "One plate, one spoon") or talk about what they will write before doing it.

■ During much of the day, children are expected to watch or be quiet. During group time teachers call on one child at a time to respond, making all the others wait, during which they disengage mentally or become disruptive.

Comments on listening, speaking, and understanding:

—Using *decontextualized language* requires children and adults to use more explanation and description. Also, as children will have to rely on printed language alone when reading, experience with decontextualized language provides valuable preparation.

—Young children's language development progresses most when they are actively engaged in verbal interaction and teachers encourage them to extend their comments. Yet classroom research suggests that limited teacher-child interaction occurs and that children are active verbal participants in these interactions less than half the time (Dickinson 2001b). Because many children have ground to make up in vocabulary and other language skills and/or English fluency, teachers need to find ways for children to be talked *to* less and talked *with* more. For example, in a language-intensive alternative to show-and-tell, each child tells a partner about a topic (e.g., "Tell your friend what you like to do when you get home from school") and then the two switch roles. From this routine, children not only learn to take turns talking and listening—a good self-regulation challenge for preschoolers—but also spend far more time as active verbal participants than they do in a conventional show-and-tell format (Bodrova & Leong 2006).

Developmentally Appropriate Practice, 3d Edition

Developmentally appropriate	In contrast

Planning Curriculum to Achieve Important Goals (cont.)

Book reading and motivation

Every day, teachers read aloud to children, in both small and large groups when possible. To promote children's engagement and comprehension, teachers use strategies such as reading with expression and asking questions ("What do you think he'll do now?").

■ Teachers do not regularly read to children. Or when they read, they fail to enhance children's enjoyment and engagement (e.g., they do *not* read expressively, draw children into the story, or help them connect it to their own experiences).

■ Teachers often interrupt story reading to address unrelated teaching goals, which disrupts the narrative flow and thus reduces children's comprehension and enjoyment.

To enhance children's vocabulary, teachers choose read-aloud books with rich vocabulary, and they provide simple explanations or synonyms for words likely to be new to children. Teachers read both storybooks and information books.

■ Teachers rarely read aloud books that are vocabulary-rich and varied enough to enhance children's word knowledge. Teachers read only storybooks.

Teachers strive to have books (which can be homemade) in each child's home language; when possible, they have someone read those books aloud (e.g., in person during a classroom visit, recorded on audiotape).

■ For some children's home language, no books or other printed materials are available.

Teachers place books in an inviting, comfortable library area and in other places conducive to their enjoyment and use. There is a good variety of high-quality books (e.g., suitable for children of preschool age and reflecting the gender, cultural, racial, and social diversity of the group; storybooks and information books; varying reading levels). Children can listen to audiobooks and follow along in the printed book.

■ The classroom offers children only a small quantity and/or limited variety of books.

■ For the most part, books are kept out of reach (either handled only by teachers or available only at children's request), and thus children cannot freely explore them.

Comments on book reading and motivation:

—When adults read aloud to young children, the children are motivated to become readers themselves (Sulzby & Teale 2003). Information books and storybooks introduce children to different kinds of vocabulary and concepts as well as writing styles. In addition, some children—often boys—find information books related to their interests (e.g., space exploration, transportation) more motivating than stories.

—The language of conversation differs significantly from the language of text. Thus, being proficient in conversational English is not a sufficient foundation for facing the vocabulary demands of text that children will encounter as they progress through school (Cummins 1994).

—Building a wider ("school") vocabulary is important for all children—far more so for those who have been exposed to only a limited conversational vocabulary outside of school. Adults can spur substantial vocabulary growth by reading aloud, especially when they explain unfamiliar words along the way. In addition, by having children retell and reenact stories, supporting pretend play, talking about words, and employing other kinds of cognitively challenging talk, teachers can contribute significantly to children's language development (Dickinson & Smith 1994; Snow, Burns, & Griffin 1998; Dickinson & Tabors 2001).

Developmentally appropriate	In contrast

Planning Curriculum to Achieve Important Goals (cont.)

Phonological awareness

Teachers introduce engaging oral language experiences (e.g., songs, poems, books, word games) that include rhyming and alliteration, which feature sound patterns and give preschoolers a foundation of phonological awareness. They encourage children to add their own verses and variations. Teachers assess and take into account where each child is in phonological awareness and tailor instruction accordingly.

■ Teachers give little or no attention to promoting children's phonological awareness. Or they do not tailor learning experiences according to what children need to progress.

■ Teachers spend too much time on structured phonological awareness activities, continuing even after losing children's interest or children have mastered those skills.

Teachers understand the typical trajectory of phonological skill development for preschool children—rhyming, alliteration, syllable segmenting, onset/rime blending and segmenting. Teachers add challenge to learning experiences as children make progress along the skills continuum.

■ Teachers continue to focus on beginning phonological skills such as rhyming and alliteration long after children have mastered them.

■ Teachers jump to structured lessons on phonics or blending phonemes or other learning experiences requiring higher levels of phonological awareness before children have mastered the prerequisite skills and concepts.

Comments on phonological awareness:

—Phonemic awareness is the understanding of and ability to manipulate the smallest sounds of the spoken language (e.g., /t/ in contrast to /d/); it is one of the strongest predictors of success in learning to read and write. The broader concept, phonological awareness, is the understanding that spoken language is composed of smaller chunks, such as words, syllables, and word beginnings (onsets) and endings (rimes).

—The foundation for acquiring phonemic awareness is laid during preschool both as children engage in planned activities that move them along the phonological skills continuum and in the natural course of speaking, listening, and being read to.

Writing

Teachers plan activities that give children a motivation to engage in writing ("How about we write a menu for your restaurant?"). They focus on capturing children's ideas, recording their dictated words in charts, stories, or messages to parents or others, then read the dictation back (using their finger to indicate the words so the child can follow along).

■ Teachers do not engage children in dictating stories, letters, and messages.

| Developmentally appropriate | In contrast |

Planning Curriculum to Achieve Important Goals (cont.)

Writing (cont.)

Teachers help children understand that the written marks represent the children's speech. They encourage children to write the sounds they hear in words they are trying to spell; teachers accept children's *developmental spellings.*

■ Heavy emphasis is put on "correctness" (e.g., correction of errors in children's handwriting and/or spelling) in children's early writing efforts.

Teachers encourage and assist children in their own efforts to write. They display children's writing. They display alphabet charts in the classroom, so children can remind themselves of letter sounds and shapes if they need to.

■ Teachers are reluctant to tell children about print conventions or provide correct spellings even when children request the information.

■ Teachers have young preschoolers trace letters on worksheets and do other rote tasks to improve their handwriting.

Teachers provide writing materials in various interest/play areas and in a designated space where children can always find a variety of materials for their writing.

Teachers encourage children to write for various purposes (e.g., signs, letters, and other messages to communicate with others; lists, observational records/notes).

■ Teachers control access to writing materials (to prevent messes or misuse), and children must request them. Children rarely have opportunities to write on their own.

Comments on writing:

—*Developmental spelling* refers to young children's attempts to use what they already know about letters and sounds to write words. Research indicates that encouraging developmental spelling is highly effective in promoting children's understanding of the relationship between letters and sounds (Templeton & Bear 1992). Further, it enables children to write independently long before they are ready for a formal reading or spelling program, and it does not impede children's ability to learn to spell accurately.

Letter, word, and print knowledge

Teachers create a print-rich environment in which lots of print not only is present but is also used in ways that show print's many purposes, such as conveying important messages, helping children find materials, and enhancing their dramatic play (e.g., through signs, lists, menus).

■ Print is scarce or not placed where children can readily see and refer to it.

■ Purposeless print clutters the environment (e.g., labels on many familiar objects) to the extent that children tune out the print.

Developmentally appropriate	In contrast

Planning Curriculum to Achieve Important Goals (cont.)

Letter, word, and print knowledge (cont.)

Teachers draw children's attention to letters and their sounds and use various strategies to help children grasp the alphabetic principle and relate print to spoken language (e.g., noting that several of their names start with the letter M and asking them to point to the names).

■ Teachers rarely point out letters, letter sounds, or words to children.

■ Teachers spend too much time teaching the alphabet and neglect other important goals; for example, they do relatively little talking with children, or they interrupt children's play and other engaged activities to identify letters or ask children about them.

Teachers draw children's attention to print conventions. For example, while reading a Big Book aloud, the teacher moves his finger under the line of print from left to right; or as he records the child's dictation, the teacher mentions that he is using an uppercase letter to start the sentence.

■ Teachers do not expect preschoolers to learn anything about print features and conventions and do nothing to begin to acquaint children with them.

■ Teachers hold children to too high a standard in following print conventions, frequently calling attention to their errors.

Comments on letter, word, and print knowledge:

—The *alphabetic principle* is the idea that written spellings represent the sounds of spoken words in reading and writing. Children's failure to grasp and employ the alphabetic principle is one of the main stumbling blocks to their progress in reading. Moreover, children vary widely in how readily they grasp the alphabetic principle and how much explicit teaching they need; some children need more instruction to grasp it, while other children pick it up quickly and would be bored and frustrated by such instruction.

—Children's alphabet knowledge, phonological awareness, and concepts of print at kindergarten entry are among the strongest predictors of later success in learning to read. There are many engaging, interesting, and effective ways for teachers to help children acquire these skills. As noted in the comments on **Writing**, encouraging developmental spelling promotes children's understanding of the relationship between letters and sounds.

Building knowledge and comprehension

To broaden children's knowledge and vocabulary, teachers use a variety of strategies such as reading stories and information books rich in new concepts, information, and vocabulary; planning field trips and inviting class visitors to tell children about their work or interests; and providing experiences through technology ("virtual field trips").

■ The books that teachers read to children cover a limited range of familiar topics and use mostly common, known words.

■ Teachers use materials and experiences primarily to entertain children or to occupy their time, overlooking many opportunities for learning.

| Developmentally appropriate | In contrast |

Planning Curriculum to Achieve Important Goals (cont.)

Building knowledge and comprehension (cont.)

Teachers engage children with questions and comments to help them recall and comprehend what is happening in a story and make connections between the book and their own life experience (e.g., "Max's aunt is coming to visit. What kinds of things do you like to do when a neighbor or relative comes to visit you?").

■ Teachers read books to the whole group most of the time. They do not engage children in conversation about the book—before, during, or after—for fear that they will lose control of the group.

■ Much of reading time is spent correcting children's behavior ("Sit on your bottom," "It's listening time now"). The narrative flow is interrupted, and children lose attention.

Teachers are comfortable with the slight diversions that occur when children share connections that are relevant to them.

■ Teachers permit some children's comments or interruptions and ignore or correct others'.

Comments on building knowledge and comprehension:

—*Dialogic* reading, which involves children in conversation about the book being read aloud, is one of the most effective strategies for promoting children's vocabulary development and comprehension.

—Children of diverse backgrounds, including English language learners, may have a difficult time grasping what they read or what is read to them, not simply because of the language barrier but because of their different life experiences. Teachers can help to bridge these gaps by becoming familiar with children's backgrounds and prior knowledge and drawing connections between these and the text or other classroom experiences.

—Open-ended and "distancing" questions are most effective in promoting comprehension and vocabulary; these questions require children to think beyond the story events and relate the events to something that happened to them in the past or might happen in the future.

Mathematics

Teachers recognize children's interest in making sense of their world with mathematics. They build on children's intuitive, informal notions and encounters relating to math, making a point of supplying mathematical language and procedures. In other words, teachers "mathematize" children's everyday encounters. For example, they help children learn and practice math skills and concepts during block building, play with games and manipulatives, movement activities, and computer time.

■ Teachers' own negative feelings about mathematics cause them to avoid teaching it.

■ The preschool day is marked by many missed opportunities for children to learn important mathematics content. Teachers fail to see the importance of introducing math concepts and infusing math vocabulary and methods into children's experiences (instead relying on what children may figure out on their own in play).

Developmentally appropriate	In contrast

Planning Curriculum to Achieve Important Goals (cont.)

Mathematics (cont.)

Using various learning contexts (e.g., small-group, large-group, one-on-one), teachers provide focused mathematics time that is interesting and meaningful to children, and they also find opportunities to integrate math learning experiences with other curriculum areas and throughout the preschool day.

■ There is no focused time provided for mathematics teaching and learning in small or large groups.

■ Teachers think they integrate mathematics throughout the day, but little time is actually devoted to mathematics teaching and learning.

■ Teachers do integrate mathematics into other learning experiences, but the integration is superficial (e.g., counting days on the calendar during opening group).

To promote **reasoning** and **problem solving**, teachers engage children in thinking about solutions to everyday situations (e.g., balancing a block structure, dividing crackers fairly) and in interesting, pre-planned mathematics activities. They talk about the problem, draw children into the process of investigating and solving it, and ask how children came up with their solutions.

■ Teachers focus heavily on children getting "the right answer" to a problem. Instead of teachers giving children time and guidance to assist their reasoning and problem solving, teachers tell children the answers or solve problems for them.

■ Teachers stand back and leave children to solve problems on their own without adult assistance or support, therefore missing important opportunities to scaffold children's mathematical thinking and reasoning.

Because mathematics is a discipline in which mastering the next concept/skill requires having understood earlier, foundational concepts/skills, the curriculum reflects a research-based progression of topics.

■ The mathematics curriculum covers too many content areas superficially, and children do not have the opportunity to master the foundational concepts and skills needed to move forward.

■ There is no organized mathematics curriculum.

The curriculum includes the major content areas of mathematics (NCTM 2006) and emphasizes the three areas that are most important for preschoolers: **number and operations**, **geometry/spatial relationships**, and **measurement**.

Teachers actively foster children's understanding of whole numbers (including counting, one-to-one correspondence, and number relationships) and of beginning operations (joining and separating sets). They engage children in thinking about and working with geometric/spatial relationships and manipulating two-dimensional and three-dimensional shapes.

■ Teachers consider mathematics too abstract for young children and underestimate preschoolers' ability to understand and master important foundational mathematics concepts and skills.

■ Teachers focus only on teaching children to count.

■ Teachers provide only low-level, repetitive experiences, such as counting the days on the calendar or identifying a few two-dimensional shapes.

Developmentally Appropriate Practice, 3d Edition

Developmentally appropriate	In contrast

Planning Curriculum to Achieve Important Goals (cont.)

Mathematics (cont.)

Comments on mathematics:

—Recent research (e.g., Duncan et al. 2007) finds that what preschoolers know and can do in mathematics is an important predictor of their later success in school (not only in mathematics but across the curriculum). Even before preschool entry, a mathematics achievement gap exists between children from middle-class families and those from low-income families (Lee & Burkam 2002). Reducing this gap as early as possible is important to low-income children's further progress.

—Because many preschool teachers themselves are not knowledgeable about mathematics content, learning sequences, and effective teaching strategies, a validated mathematics curriculum is a useful tool.

Science

Recognizing preschoolers' curiosity about the world around them, teachers focus on the uses and processes of science in children's everyday lives. They provide interesting experiences and materials that convey key scientific concepts (e.g., weight, light, cause and effect), as well as skills (e.g., predicting, observing, classifying, hypothesizing, experimenting, communicating).

■ Science in the classroom is no more than a few items for children to look at (e.g., plants on a windowsill, stones on the "nature table") or an occasional demonstration that children see as magic (e.g., making a volcano with baking soda and vinegar). Teachers do not use the items or events to expand children's knowledge or introduce children to scientific inquiry/methods.

■ Teachers may transmit factual information on scientific topics, but they do not engage children in "doing science." Or the science curriculum is only about exploration, and children do not acquire foundational concepts and knowledge.

The curriculum includes concepts not only from **life science/nature** but also from **physical science** (e.g., rolling and sliding objects on ramps) and **earth science** (e.g., soil and rocks). Teachers use a variety of strategies to help children develop important scientific concepts and skills.

■ The curriculum is limited to one area of science or to a few isolated topics with which the teacher feels comfortable. Other areas receive scant attention, even when children ask questions and show interest in them.

Comments on science:

—In science learning, children need both open and focused exploration. During open exploration, the children as a group build a foundation of common experiences with a phenomenon. They also begin to build a common language for talking about what they are noticing, which is important as they move into more focused investigation (Worth & Grollman 2003).

—In children's science experiences, recording and documenting their investigations play a vital role. Much of science is about noticing changes, finding patterns, and looking at relationships, so children need to keep in mind what has been going on over time. Documentation and recording help to make that process visible and allow children to go back to the beginning of a change or see a pattern over time (Chalufour & Worth 2003; 2005).

Developmentally appropriate	In contrast

Planning Curriculum to Achieve Important Goals (cont.)

Technology

Teachers make thoughtful use of computers and other technology in the classroom, not to replace children's experience with objects and materials but to expand the range of tools with which children can seek information, solve problems, perform transformations (e.g., rotating geometric shapes), and learn at their own pace. Software is selected to emphasize thinking and problem solving.

■ Children spend a great deal of the preschool day on computers and/or watching television or videos.

■ Computer software is primarily devoted to drill or to games with only a recreational purpose.

■ Teachers avoid use of computers and other technology in the classroom.

Teachers locate computers to foster shared learning and interaction—children talking about what they are doing, cooperating in solving problems, and helping one another. Teachers encourage children to use technology (e.g., cameras, video and audio recorders) to document their experiences and work. They invite children's exploration of the various operations and actions possible with the technology.

■ Computers are located in an area outside the main learning environment (e.g., in a computer lab), so children have limited access. Or computers are in an accessible location, but teachers insist that only one child at a time work at the computer.

■ Teachers insist that children stick with a defined task or routine ("Press this key, then this one, then wait until I come check").

The program provides enough equipment that a child can become engaged in a technology project in a sustained, deep way. Both boys and girls have equal opportunity to use computers.

■ The program doesn't provide any technology or provides so little that children get only very brief turns using a piece of equipment in order to allow everyone to have a chance. Computer use is dominated by boys.

Social competence; social studies

The curriculum uses children's familiar, everyday experiences as the foundation for their social studies learning. Teachers plan experiences and use the daily life of the classroom to foster that learning.

■ Teachers may convey facts relating to social studies, but the information is too remote from children's experience or too fragmented to be meaningful and interesting to them.

■ Rather than integrating learning experiences, teachers address each social studies standard individually with a separate activity or experience, and/or they separate social studies from other curriculum areas.

Developmentally appropriate	In contrast

Planning Curriculum to Achieve Important Goals (cont.)

Social competence; social studies (cont.)

In later grades, social studies will include geography, history, and civics/political science; preschoolers can begin learning basic concepts in these disciplines. For example, learning to make or read simple maps of the classroom areas helps children to acquire some of the foundational skills and concepts of geography. Using a timeline of the day or week is a precursor of using timelines in the study of history.

Teachers actively foster children's understanding of democratic processes and attitudes in concrete, experiential ways that young children are able to understand, such as making and discussing rules, solving together the problems that arise in the classroom community, and learning to listen to others' ideas and perspectives.

■ Teachers introduce social studies concepts that are too abstract for preschoolers, such as scale in mapping or chronological historical time.

■ Teachers do not provide experiences that introduce children to basic concepts and ideas foundational for later learning in social studies.

■ Teachers are the only decision makers in the classroom; they do not engage children in sharing ideas and solving their problems together.

■ Teachers attempt to teach about democracy but in ways that are too abstract for young children to relate to.

Comments on social competence and social studies:
—Early childhood teachers work to promote children's development of social competence throughout the day and across all areas of the curriculum. Social studies appears in this section (alongside social competence) because in early childhood, children's knowledge of social studies builds on and is integrated with the development of their social skills. Moreover, important aspects of the social studies curriculum are taught and learned through the everyday events of the classroom. For example, teachers foster preschoolers' abilities to participate in group decision making, establish rules and consequences, express opinions in a group setting, collaborate with others, and respect the rights of others in the classroom.

Creative arts

Creative/aesthetic development

Teachers give children daily opportunities for creative expression and aesthetic appreciation. Children explore and enjoy various forms of dramatic play, music, dance, and visual arts. Whether or not there are specialist teachers for the arts, classroom teachers meaningfully integrate the arts into children's learning experiences. If there are specialists, teachers interact with them and consult them as resource experts.

■ Art, music, and dance/movement activities occur only once a week or even more sporadically. The arts are disconnected from the goals and activities of the rest of the program.

Developmentally appropriate	In contrast

Planning Curriculum to Achieve Important Goals (cont.)

Creative/aesthetic development (cont.)

Adults help children explore and work with various art and music media and techniques; they introduce concepts and vocabulary to extend children's experiences in the arts.

■ Teachers spend time preparing children for special performances for families and others, rather than supporting active participation in the arts for the sake of children's own creative expression, knowledge, and appreciation of the arts.

Teachers display children's art, as well as the work of artists, in the classroom and elsewhere in the program setting. Children have opportunities to experience music, art, and dance out in the local community. Children have the opportunity to experience the arts of various cultures, especially their own and those present in their neighborhoods.

■ The music and art in the environment reflect only the teachers' own culture(s) and tastes and do not include the arts of the local community or the backgrounds of the children and their families.

■ The environment is heavily decorated with depictions of commercial media characters or other simplified, cartoon-like images.

Comments on creative/aesthetic development:
—Teachers can use a variety of strategies to increase young children's awareness and appreciation of the arts in their own cultural and local communities and beyond. These include bringing the arts into the classroom (e.g., displaying prints of fine art and books that include art reproductions); inviting community artists to visit or going to their studios; and taking field trips to galleries, museums, performances, and public art displays.

Visual arts

Classroom teachers or specialist art teachers give children opportunities to explore various art materials (e.g., markers, paints, clay) to use in creative expression and representation. They talk with children about their art. Teachers have children revisit projects and media, giving them opportunities to revise and expand their ideas and refine their skills.

■ To avoid mess, teachers provide only a very limited selection of art materials or allow children to use materials only under highly teacher-controlled conditions.

■ Teachers introduce only a few art media and methods that they enjoy or know.

Teachers do not provide a model that they expect children to copy. However, they demonstrate new techniques or uses of the materials to expand children's options.

■ Emphasis is on the products children make, and teachers typically provide a model that children are to reproduce (thus, children's products all look identical). They often give children tasks such as coloring in forms on printed pages, and they emphasize "coloring inside the lines." Teachers "fix" children's work if it does not meet expectations.

Developmentally appropriate	In contrast

Planning Curriculum to Achieve Important Goals (cont.)

Visual arts (cont.)

Comments on visual arts:

—Preschoolers' efforts at representation show their thinking and the effort they put into trying to depict objects and people with marks on the page. Drawing, in particular, is a child's first step toward writing. They often can describe their creations verbally in far greater complexity ("This is a cat, and here are his whiskers, and this is his tail") than they are able to achieve in their drawings, which may consist of only simple shapes and lines. Listening to what they have to say about their artwork can give teachers insights into children's thoughts and feelings.

Music and movement

Teachers have a repertoire of songs to sing with children for their enjoyment and for mastering recall of both melody and lyrics. They provide musical instruments for children to use. Teachers include songs and instruments from various cultures, especially those of the children in the group. Music is integrated with other curriculum areas, such as literacy (e.g., for teaching phonological awareness) and mathematics (e.g., for counting beats or building spatial awareness).	■ Teachers rarely return to a song or dance once they have shared it with children, so children are unable to build up a repertoire of music with which they are familiar. ■ Teachers offer only the kinds of music they know best and enjoy. They don't sing or play themselves because they "can't carry a tune," implying to children that making music is only for those with "talent." ■ Music is not integrated with other curriculum areas.
The joy of music is central in the experiences teachers share with children. In ways that don't interrupt that enjoyment, teachers highlight elements such as pitch, duration, tempo, and volume, and they engage children in varying and exploring these elements.	■ Teachers approach music in a didactic way, teaching specific terms and elements but not giving children integrated, enjoyable experiences in music. ■ Having a "performance orientation," teachers tend to single out those children most clearly gifted or trained and criticize or ignore the creative efforts of the rest.
Teachers encourage children to engage in full-body activities that require rhythm and timing, such as swinging; teachers join them in such movement.	■ Opportunities for moving to music are limited to clapping and other hand movements that children can do while sitting. Teachers do not get up and move with children.

Comments on music and movement:

—Most young children are uninhibited, enthusiastic performers and lovers of music and movement, both of which enrich children's lives and learning in many ways. These should be a focused part of the day and also be integrated with other content areas. For example, music can help children learn phonological awareness, patterns, and counting. In addition, music helps English language learners learn new words and brings their cultures into the classroom.

Developmentally appropriate	In contrast

Assessing Children's Development and Learning

Strategic and purposeful

Assessment is done for four specific, beneficial purposes: planning and adapting curriculum to meet each child's developmental and learning needs, helping teachers and families monitor children's progress, evaluating and improving program effectiveness, and screening and identification of children with potential disabilities or special needs.

■ No systematic assessments of children's progress or achievements are done.

■ Assessments are done, but results are not used to provide information about children's degree of understanding or to adapt curriculum to meet their needs. Doing the assessment takes an excessive amount of teachers' time and attention away from interacting with children.

■ Single-test assessment is used for high-stakes decision making (e.g., entry, special education referral).

Teachers use developmental screening, typically upon program entry, to identify children who might have a learning or developmental problem. When screening identifies the possibility of a special need, appropriate referral to a specialist for diagnostic follow-up or other intervention occurs.

■ Developmental screening does not occur, or it (and the post-screening follow-up) occurs so late in the year that children go for months without receiving needed intervention or support.

■ Teachers diagnose or label a child after only a screening or one-time assessment. Test results are used to group or label children (e.g., as "unready" or "special needs").

Decisions that will have a major impact on children (e.g., entry, grouping) are based on multiple sources of information. Sources include observations by teachers and specialists and also information from parents.

■ Eligible-age children are denied entry to preschool based on a one-time readiness or achievement test, defined as measuring what the child already knows and can do. Readiness or achievement tests are used as the sole criterion to recommend that children not go on to kindergarten or be placed in special classrooms.

■ Children are judged on the basis of inappropriate and inflexible expectations for their academic, social, or self-help abilities (e.g., whether they know shapes and colors or can sit still for a story).

Preschool assessments address key goals in all developmental domains (physical, social, emotional, cognitive) and in the areas of physical education and health, language and literacy, mathematics, science, social competence, and creative arts.

■ Programs and teachers don't think about which goals are important in each area, so their assessments look at trivial skills and facts (e.g., naming the days of the week).

■ Assessment focuses on certain areas (e.g., math and literacy) and not others, ignoring the interconnectedness among domains.

| Developmentally appropriate | In contrast |

Assessing Children's Development and Learning (cont.)

Systematic and ongoing

Developmentally appropriate	In contrast
There is an assessment plan that is clearly written, well-organized, complete, comprehensive, and well-understood by directors, teachers, and families.	▪ No plan for assessment exists. ▪ The plan for assessment is not shared with or is not understood by the teachers who must execute it or the families whose preschoolers are assessed.
Regular health and developmental screenings are done by appropriate personnel to identify children who may need more in-depth, diagnostic assessment. Screening focuses on children's health needs and possible developmental delays.	▪ Screenings are not frequent enough in view of children's rapid growth and development in the preschool years. ▪ When a child appears to be having difficulty (i.e., is outside the typical performance range), no individual assessment is done. ▪ Teachers make diagnoses that should be done by specialists.
Information is collected at regular intervals throughout the year.	▪ Assessments are rare and/or random. ▪ Children's performance is assessed at the end of the year, when it's too late to affect learning outcomes.
Teachers have the time, training, and materials they need to do assessment properly and accurately.	▪ Teachers are burdened with assessment requirements but not provided with adequate tools or appropriate professional development to use them accurately. Thus, assessing is a waste of teachers' and children's time.

Integrated with teaching and curriculum

Developmentally appropriate	In contrast
Assessments are consistent with the developmental and learning goals identified for children and expressed in the preschool curriculum.	▪ Assessments look at goals not in the curriculum or content not taught to the children. ▪ Assessments narrow and/or distort the curriculum (e.g., only assessing literacy skills or what will later be tested for accountability purposes).
Teachers use assessment to refine how they plan and implement activities. Teachers develop short- and long-range plans for each child and the group based on children's knowledge, skills, interests, and other factors.	▪ There is no accountability for what children are doing and little focus on supporting their learning and development.

Developmentally appropriate	In contrast

Assessing Children's Development and Learning (cont.)

Integrated with teaching and curriculum (cont.)

Developmentally appropriate	In contrast
Teachers look at what each child can do independently but also assess collaborative work with peers and adults. Teachers assess as the child participates in groups and during other scaffolded situations.	■ Children are assessed only as individuals. Thus, teachers miss information about what children can do as members of a group or what tasks are just beyond their current capabilities and would benefit from adult support.
Teachers assess children on an ongoing basis (i.e., observe, ask, listen in, check) during daily activities, including play. They document children's learning and development, including in written notes, photographs, audio recordings, and work samples. They use this information both in shaping their teaching moment by moment and in planning learning experiences.	■ Teachers don't determine where each child is in learning a new skill or concept, so they give every child the same learning experiences as every other child. ■ Assessment results (observation notes, work samples, etc.) go straight into a folder and are filed away. They are not reflected on to inform teachers how to help or challenge individual children.
Information about each child's learning and development is used to evaluate teaching effectiveness, which may lead to changes in schedule, curriculum and teaching strategies, room set up, resources, and so on.	■ Assessment results show that problems exist but do not indicate what needs to be changed. Or nothing changes because "that's how we've always done it" or it would be expensive or inconvenient for the program and teachers.

Comments on assessment integrated with teaching and curriculum:
—As much as possible, assessment should be woven into the act of teaching and interacting with children. However, there are times when the teacher needs to set up a special situation (e.g., clinical interview, structured task) designed to reveal a child's specific skill or understanding to get a fuller, more accurate picture of the child's thinking and abilities.

Valid and reliable

Developmentally appropriate	In contrast
Assessments are used only for acceptable purposes, where research has demonstrated they yield valid and reliable information among children of similar ages, cultures, home languages, and so on. Only assessments demonstrated to be valid and reliable for identifying, diagnosing, and planning for children with special needs or disabilities are used for that purpose.	■ The program uses tests or other measures for which inadequate evidence of validity and reliability exists for the population assessed or for some segment(s) of that population.

Developmentally Appropriate Practice, 3d Edition

Developmentally appropriate	In contrast

Assessing Children's Development and Learning (cont.)

Valid and reliable (cont.)

Assessments include teachers' observations of what children say and do during play and other classroom experiences, as well as other documentation of children's development and learning (e.g., photographs of block constructions, easel paintings) collected during their daily activities.

■ Teachers use methods not suited to preschool children (e.g., paper-and-pencil tests). Assessment is primarily administered separate from children's usual activities.

Assessments are matched to the ages, development, and background of the specific children. Methods include accommodations for children with disabilities.

Teachers use a variety of methods/tools, recognize individual variation among learners, and allow children to demonstrate their competence in different ways.

■ Assessment assumes background knowledge that some or all of the children don't have. Methods prevent a child from demonstrating what he actually knows and is able to do (e.g., asking "Which block is red?" in English when the child speaks only Spanish).

Teachers gather information from families, especially about preschool children's health and development, interests, and family life.

■ Families are not considered a valid source of information.

Comments on valid and reliable assessment:
—Today's preschoolers are highly diverse, with an increasing number of English language learners. In order to properly assess this population, assessment measures must take linguistic background into account and be free from cultural bias (NAEYC 2005b). Using a variety of approaches to assess is especially important with English language learners and children who are less familiar with the culture reflected in formal assessment measures. Some indicators and sources of information may reveal more of a child's skills and abilities than others.

Communicated and shared

Teachers and families regularly share information in ways that are clear, respectful, and constructive. They make decisions together regarding learning goals and approaches to learning that are suitable for the individual child. Families are regularly informed about how their children are doing in all developmental domains.

■ Families are not kept informed about assessment results and children's progress. Teachers/programs make important decisions unilaterally (e.g., family finds out after the fact that their child has been assessed for special needs).

■ Programs provide families with information in ways that are not respectful or useful to them (e.g., not in their home language).

Developmentally appropriate	In contrast

Assessing Children's Development and Learning (cont.)

Communicated and shared (cont.)

Within the limits of appropriate confidentiality policies, teachers exchange information about each child across ages/grades (e.g., preschool teachers with kindergarten teachers), so children are prepared for the next challenge, and the next teacher knows each child's history.

■ Assessment information is not used to help ease transitions for children from one setting or group to another or on to kindergarten.

Establishing Reciprocal Relationships with Families

Teachers actively work to create a partnership with each family, communicating regularly to build mutual understanding and trust and to ensure that children's learning and developmental needs are met. Teachers solicit parents' knowledge about their children and input about their goals and concerns, and they use this information in ongoing assessment, evaluation, and planning.

■ Teachers communicate with parents only about problems or conflicts, and thus parents have little relationship with teachers and also feel isolated from their child's experiences. Teachers convey the impression that only they—not family members—really know about the child.

Teachers and parents work together in making decisions about how best to support children's development and learning or how to handle problems or differences of opinion as they arise. Teachers listen to parents, seek to understand their goals and expectations for their children, and respect the family's personal and cultural preferences.

■ Teachers blame parents when children have difficulty in the classroom. They encourage parents to punish children at home for infractions at school.

■ The director and/or teachers always give in to parents' demands, even if these are not to the benefit of the child or the other children in the group.

Developmentally appropriate	In contrast

Establishing Reciprocal Relationships with Families (cont.)

Parents are welcome in the early childhood setting at all times. Family members have opportunities to participate in ways that are comfortable for them, such as observing, reading to children, or sharing a skill or interest. Parents' work schedules are accommodated in the planning of participation opportunities as well as teacher-parent conferences and family activities.

■ Parent visits to the classroom are seen as intrusive, and program policies discourage visiting. Parents' presence in the classroom is so rare that their visits tend to be disruptive for the children.

■ Opportunities for parent participation, teacher-parent conferences, meetings, and other events for families occur only on rigid schedules. Conferences and meetings are held only during the day when many employed parents are unavailable.

With parents who do not speak English, teachers/administrators seek strategies to facilitate communication, such as hiring bilingual staff or using translators at conferences or meetings.

■ Program staffs take no action to enable families with limited English proficiency either to understand written or spoken communications directed to them or to ask questions and convey ideas or concerns they may have regarding their child or the program.

■ Because of the challenges and potential difficulties that may arise in meetings and other communication with family members who speak little or no English, program staffs avoid having meetings, conferences, and other planned events with families.

Comments on establishing reciprocal relationships with families:

—In some cultures, teachers are so highly respected that they are given absolute authority over everything educational. For families from such cultures, the partnership idea is a strange and uncomfortable concept, so teachers need to be patient and let the relationship evolve gradually into a more collaborative, two-way partnership.

—Preschool is a different kind of educational setting for many parents, no matter what culture they come from. Challenges to partnering with the teacher can come when parents think about their own experiences as students in formal schooling settings. It is up to teachers to help parents understand the differences between their school experience and developmentally appropriate early childhood settings. It is also up to teachers to understand the perspectives families bring to the situation, especially when these seem to be at odds with developmentally appropriate practice. That's what makes a two-way exchange—when both parties can share their perspectives and respectfully talk about their differences. It is the teacher's responsibility to initiate such conversations as well as be receptive when parents do so.

the
kindergarten
year

6

Developmentally Appropriate Practice in the Kindergarten Year—Ages 5–6

An Overview

Heather Biggar Tomlinson*

Experienced kindergarten teachers often reflect that kindergartners, despite wide individual variation, have common attributes such as enthusiasm for learning, an increased ability to integrate information and inhibit impulses, and a captivating interest in interacting with others, all of which makes them ready for a new phase in their education. As originally conceived, kindergarten was a preparatory year of schooling, designed primarily to support children's social and emotional adjustment to group learning.

However, the increased number of children attending preschool and child care programs at younger ages combined with the increased academic demands of the early years of school have greatly transformed the role of kindergarten. More than a preparatory year—about 95 percent of kindergarten age children in America are enrolled in some type of kindergarten program (NCES 2008)—kindergarten is now generally considered the first year of school.

The age at which children are eligible (or required) to begin kindergarten varies from state to state. Kindergarten primarily serves 5-year-olds, but the age range can span from 4¾ to 7¼ years (Berk 2006a). Sometimes families feel compelled or are encouraged to hold their children out of kindergarten until they are older and can cope with the academic, emotional, and physical demands required of kindergartners, a practice known as "redshirting." About 10 percent of families defer kindergarten entry (NCES 1997), so there are many 6-year-olds in kindergarten classrooms (despite the fact that age of entry into kindergarten has not been shown to be a major factor in school performance; NICHD 2007).

There is a major and well documented shift in cognition that has been found to occur between ages 5 and 7 (Piaget 1952; White 1965; 1970; Sameroff & McDonough 1994). Before this shift occurs, children are developmentally more

---

*In writing this chapter, the author drew extensively from four chapters authored by Stephen Sanders (physical education), Martha Bronson (social and emotional competence), Susan Golbeck (cognitive skills), and Laura Berk (learning and development of the kindergarten child) from the NAEYC book *K Today: Teaching and Learning in the Kindergarten Year* (Gullo 2006b). The full citation for each of those chapters appears in the references.

like preschoolers than like school age children; throughout and after the shift, children show increased levels of personal responsibility, self-direction, and logical thinking. The change that occurs has been marked throughout time and across cultures as "achieving the age of reason" (Whiting & Edwards 1988).

The changes associated with this "5 to 7 shift" affect development across physical, social and emotional, cognitive, and language domains. They also affect children's "approaches to learning," another important domain of development that includes children's *enthusiasm* for learning (their interest, joy, and motivation to learn) and their *engagement* in learning (their focused attention, persistence, flexibility, and self-regulation) (Hyson 2008).

Experiences at home and in early childhood programs can either support or undermine children's enthusiasm for and engagement in learning. In this respect, kindergarten is a critical year. At its best, kindergarten experiences nurture positive approaches to learning and prepare children for the more rigorous academic expectations of the primary grades. In these circumstances, teachers can nurture kindergartners' positive approaches to learning by implementing an engaging curriculum and teaching methods that draw children in and challenge them to reflect, try out their ideas, and tackle meaningful problems.

Pressured by expectations for student performance on a narrow range of skills, teachers may inadvertently discourage kindergartners' interest in learning and fail to provide time to develop qualities such as persistence and flexibility. By carefully reviewing the curriculum and teaching methods with children's approaches to learning in mind, teachers can help ensure that children are neither overwhelmed by nor bored with the curriculum and teaching practices. By stoking children's enthusiasm and engagement, teachers support children to enter the primary grades not only academically prepared but also with positive learning attitudes and effective learning behaviors.

Because of the great individual variation among kindergartners and the wide age range that often exists in a kindergarten classroom, teaching practices must be responsive to developmental, individual, and cultural variation (as is true for every other grade, as well). Although most 5-year-olds are developmentally more like preschoolers than like older children, kindergartens are usually housed institutionally with elementary schools. Teachers have to strike a fine balance in meeting the needs of children's varied capacities and vertically aligning curricula with both preschool and first grade.

In spite of the challenges, and because of the many opportunities for teaching and learning, it's a very exciting period for children and their teachers.

Physical development

Kindergartners are fascinated with learning what their bodies can do—how fast they can run, how high they can jump, how skillfully they can move. They are becoming more sophisticated in their movements, more coordinated in their physical endeavors, and increasingly competent in physical skills such as balance and eye-hand coordination. They use movement to express their feelings, manipulate objects, and learn about their world. They delight in physical accomplishment.

Motor skills are the result of a dynamic developmental system: jointly contributing are kindergarten children's longer, leaner bodies; their motivation to attain new goals; their advancing cognition; their improved ability to cooperate with peers; and opportunities for extensive practice (Thelen & Smith 1998). As children participate in small-group games with reciprocal roles, they integrate previously acquired motor skills into more complex actions. Kindergartners need teachers to guide them in making choices about physical activity and in acquiring and refining skills. The ideal time for children to develop basic physical skills (e.g., throwing, catching, kicking, skipping, and balancing) is from ages 2–7—during their "fundamental" movement phase (Gallahue 1995, 131–3).

Most 2- and 3-year-olds attempt to throw, catch, or jump, but their movements are rela-

tively crude and uncoordinated. At 4 and 5, most children have matured to an elementary skill stage. They have greater control over their movements, although they still look awkward and their movements are not yet fluid. (Many adults never exit the elementary stage in basic activities such as throwing and catching.) By age 6, many children have the developmental potential to be at a mature stage in most fundamental movement skills. This means that they can integrate all the parts of a particular pattern of movement into a well coordinated, mechanically correct act appropriate to the demands of the task.

As with all areas of development, no two children are alike. Some kindergartners will come close to or reach the mature level for some skills, while others will need more guidance and practice. In general, girls tend to be more advanced than boys in fine motor skills and in gross motor skills that require precision such as hopping and skipping. Boys tend to do better with skills that require force and power such as running and jumping (Berk 2008).

Although they will delight in movement programs, most kindergartners are not yet ready for the skills and pressures of organized sports such as soccer or gymnastics. Activities designed for youth or adults that are pushed on kindergartners can be both frustrating and unsafe for them. They usually are not able to achieve a consistently high level of competence in a sport until they have had instruction in specific skills (e.g., climbing, throwing a ball, jumping) and opportunities over time and contexts to practice.

Gross motor development

In the gross motor area, kindergartners run more quickly and smoothly than before and can change directions easily. They throw and catch with increasing involvement of their whole body, shifting their weight with the release of the ball and varying the force of their throw in accord with where they want the ball to land. When a ball is thrown to them, kindergartners

© Marilyn Nolt

can anticipate its place of landing by moving forward, backward, and sideways and by "giving" with their body to absorb the force of the ball (Roberton 1984; Cratty 1986).

By the end of the year, kindergarten children should be able to do things such as walking and running using mature form, traveling forward and sideways in a variety of patterns, changing direction quickly in response to a signal, demonstrating clear contrasts between slow and fast movement, rolling sideways without hesitating or stopping, tossing a ball and catching it before it bounces twice, kicking a stationary ball using a smooth continuous running step, and maintaining momentary stillness while bearing weight on various body parts (Gallahue 1995; Sanders 2002).

Fine motor development

A child's attention span usually lengthens during kindergarten, and control of the hands and fingers improves, both of which lead to greater enjoyment of and involvement in fine motor activities. Many kindergartners initially struggle with tasks that require detail, patience, steadiness, and fine motor coordination, such as writing, drawing, and cutting with precision. By the end of the year, however, they will have benefited from activities that allow practice in these areas and that better develop hand muscles, such as writing, drawing and painting, working with clay, and constructing with Legos. They improve in activities such as sorting small objects; stringing beads; zipping, buttoning, and tying various articles of clothing; using scissors; pouring milk or juice at snack; and setting the table. Children with disabilities improve in fine motor skills with the help of assistive technology such as Velcro shoes and weighted bowls and utensils.

Writing is an especially important area of fine motor development at this age, as children develop an increased desire to communicate through written expression. Most kindergarten children are adept at gripping a crayon or pencil as a result of experimentation during the preschool years. They may have tried different forms of pencil holding, gradually learning the grip and angle that maximizes stability and writing efficiency (Greer & Lockman 1998). By age 5, children use an adult pencil grip when writing and drawing—a milestone that results from the child's own active reorganization of behavior. In their efforts to write, kindergartners gradually improve in their renditions of the letters.

Promoting physical development in kindergarten

Early childhood educators have always placed great importance on children's learning about and with their bodies through play and being outdoors (Brooks 1913). But we now understand that, in the case of physical development, children also need to learn through instruction; they do not develop physical skills through play alone (Manross 1994; 2000). In other words, sending children out to recess and encouraging them to participate in free play does not guarantee that they will develop physical skills and healthy attitudes, competencies, and habits. Teachers (and specialists, where available) working with kindergarten children should teach basic physical skills and then offer play-based opportunities so children can experiment and be creative with the skills they are learning.

National recommendations state that kindergartners need at least 60 minutes (not more than 30 minutes at a time) of moderate to vigorous physical activity on all or most days of the week (NASPE 2004; USDHHS & USDA 2005; NASPE 2008a). Today, many children get such exercise only at shool. Scheduling bouts of physical activity interspersed with sedentary activities helps reduce inattentiveness and misbehavior (Mahar et al. 2006; NASPE 2008b).

The role of kindergarten teachers in physical education is to create positive and success-based environments in which children can develop fundamental motor skills through play-based learning activities. The teacher and the school can strive to create an environment that includes the following:

• inside and outside physical activity areas with adequate space for children to move freely and safely without bumping into each other,

- opportunities for daily, high-quality movement instruction with plenty of time for practice—exclusive of the outdoor play time that should also occur, and

- appropriate equipment so that each child benefits from maximum participation.

The ideal environment offers children opportunities to develop both fine and gross motor skills. Kindergartners have opportunities to learn and practice fine motor skills in the course of classroom activities such as writing, drawing, doing puzzles, and working with manipulatives. However, learning and practicing gross motor skills requires open space, such as a large room, a gym, or a spacious hallway or outdoor area so that children can throw, kick, strike, run, and skip. There must also be enough equipment so that many children can participate in similar physical education activities at the same time (i.e., every child has a ball to dribble, or every child has a jump rope to practice jumping). If space is a problem, setting up physical education stations (supervised by adults such as student teachers or trained parent volunteers) can allow children to move from place to place to practice a variety of skills.

A physical education center—a semipermanent space similar to a reading or science center—can also provide space for children to practice gross motor skills. Here, small groups of children can practice developing a specific movement skill, deepen their understanding of movement and movement concepts, and use their physical education skills in ways that link to other areas of the curriculum. For example, in a center where children are learning about moving through space, they might plot a route on a map they have created, construct a miniature obstacle course using playdough and props, or measure various lengths of jumps and leaps using rope segments or tape measures.

When introducing motor development activities to children, teachers can foster the growth of children's physical education skills by focusing first on large body movements, such as throwing or kicking, and then designing

tasks for gradual and sequential learning. For example, tasks such as working on puzzles and perfecting cutting skills help develop better eye-hand coordination, which in turn improves the ability to catch or bounce a ball. Tasks should have a definite purpose, progress logically, and be structured to yield high rates of success.

Breaking down motor skills into small, doable actions—a form of scaffolding—allows everyone to participate, even if participation is partial for some. For instance, if a child cannot grasp a racket to strike a balloon, she might be encouraged to strike the balloon with her hand. Also, it is helpful to provide cues and suggestions that help children refine specific skills. Many children have difficulties understanding verbal instruction (or understanding directions in English) and may do better when they can watch someone practicing the skill they are being asked to do.

Presenting multiple skills and offering appealing choices (e.g., partners, equipment, space, and activities) and challenges help maintain children's interest as they learn. Activities should be open-ended so children can experiment with and explore materials and their abilities. Offering a variety of tasks, materials, and learning centers helps children practice specific skills and learn to use different types and sizes of equipment. Movement and skill activities should involve everyone in the class and should promote inclusion and cooperation rather than exclusion and competition. Teachers who foster a sense of community, emphasizing that everyone can participate and has strengths, will find delighted responsiveness from most children. However, not all children will be performing the same task at the same time or with the same skill level. As with other domains, teachers should individualize or modify a task based on the abilities and interests of each child.

Kindergarten teachers not only can help children develop an immediate foundation in physical skills; they also can instill healthy habits that will affect children's well-being for a lifetime.

Social and emotional development

Social and emotional competence matters a great deal in school and in life. Skill in basic areas of social and emotional competence has pervasive and long-lasting consequences, such as success in school, avoiding criminal behaviors, and social and psychological adjustment throughout the life span (e.g., Schultz et al. 2001; Raver 2002; McClelland, Acock, & Morrison 2006). As kindergartners, children are expected to regulate their emotions and behavior appropriately under most circumstances. They are expected to be able to delay, defer, and accept substitutions for their preferred goals without becoming aggressive or overly frustrated. They are also expected to cope well with challenges in the environment or to new events (Sroufe 1995).

Social development

The ability to form and sustain relationships with others, both with adults and children, is central to a child's social development—not to mention his happiness. Kindergarten children are intensely interested in interacting with their peers, and for the most part, they do well in engaging cooperatively, getting along, and forming friendships. Social skills relate not only to the obvious correlates such as peer acceptance, but also to broader well-being, such as success in school (McClelland, Acock, & Morrison 2006) and future adjustment (Kupersmidt & Coie 1990).

Some kindergarten children do struggle in the social arena, though; they may be overly shy, aggressive, or generally unable to regulate their emotions and behavior in prosocial ways. Kindergartners who are rejected by their peers are likely to have long-term problems, including difficulties in friendships later in childhood and even adulthood and academic difficulties in school (Cowen et al. 1973; Achenback & Edelbrock 1991).

Prosocial behavior. Prosocial behavior includes cooperating, resolving conflicts with peers in peaceful, positive ways, following classroom rules and adult requests, and other helpful actions (Shonkoff & Phillips 2000). Teachers of young children have always valued these skills in creating a classroom environment where all children can thrive. Recently there has been a surge of interest in fostering prosocial skills in order to cope with the growing number of serious behavior problems sometimes seen in schools, including kindergarten classrooms (Gartrell 2004).

Kindergartners are better able than younger children to apply an internal control that uses rules, strategies, and plans to guide behavior. They begin to internalize standards and monitor their own actions and tend to seek permission to transition to another activity (Schunk 1994; Wood 2007). A sense of conscience continues to build, and children may feel guilty when they violate standards, wanting instead to be "good." Older kindergartners are more able to act responsibly and to hold themselves accountable for their behavior, but they can be unpredictable, behaving well at home and poorly at school or vice versa, being oppositional at times, and wanting to test limits more frequently (Whiting & Edwards 1988; Wood 2007). Adults may see a regression to temper tantrums, complaining, and acting out later in the year, making the consistency of rules and consequences even more important than it was earlier in the year.

Kindergartners overall are more able to interact cooperatively than younger children; they like to be helpful and follow rules. They can use negotiation and reciprocity to some degree to settle disputes, although they still benefit from adult modeling and guidance in applying these skills. They do best with following rules and showing cooperative behaviors in environments with clear and simple expectations and consistent rules and consequences.

In addition to being more skilled at dealing with potential conflicts by sharing and taking turns, kindergarten children can, given guidance and opportunity, use proactive strategies to organize, direct, and sustain interactions with

© Ellen B. Senisi

others (Bronson 1994; Bodrova & Leong 2008). These include making initial suggestions about what to do ("*Let's pretend the baby has to go to the hospital*"), continuing suggestions about how to proceed ("*Now let's say the baby is all better and we take her home*"), assigning roles or resources to the participants ("*You take the thermometer, and I'll use the stethoscope*"), and laying out the rules or constraints of a proposed activity ("*The doctor has to say it's okay for the baby to go home*"). These proactive strategies allow children to have more complex interactions with fewer conflicts.

Children who exhibit positive behaviors such as cooperation and conflict resolution skills tend to show better overall social skills and have more friends (Howes 1988; Katz & McClellan 1997). They also are more likely to be well adjusted, good at coping, and able to manage their emotions and behavior in ways appropriate to the situation (Eisenberg & Mussen 1989).

Sociability. As in other periods of early childhood development, a child's secure, warm attachment with an adult or adults in kindergarten is the foundation for constructive development and learning across all domains. Relationships with parents or other family adults are most important, but teacher-child relationships are also very powerful and can be a buffer in times of stress. Kindergartners, even more than children of other ages, especially seek and tune into teachers' approval and want to be viewed as being good (Wood 2007).

Kindergartners learn best when they feel valued, needed, and loved by the teacher, are confident the teacher will meet their basic needs promptly, and can count on the teacher to interact with them in intimate, playful, and personal ways (Hyson 2004). When the teacher and the classroom atmosphere reflect these qualities, children are able to devote the necessary energy to the developmental and learning tasks at hand.

Research shows that in early childhood classrooms in which teachers provide high-quality emotional and instructional support to children, along with helpful feedback and a structured, predictable environment, children develop better social skills than children in other classrooms (Rimm-Kaufman et al. 2005; Wilson, Pianta, & Stuhlman 2007). Furthermore, children who have warm and supportive teachers demonstrate greater prosocial behavior, empathy, self-regulation, and social competence (Eisenberg & Fabes 1998). Having a positive relationship with the teacher in kindergarten is correlated with school success during that year, and it predicts future school achievement as well (Hamre & Pianta 2001; Pianta et al. 2008).

As children's interest in friendship building intensifies throughout the kindergarten year, their communication skills and understanding of others' thoughts and feelings improve, and thus, their skills in interacting with other children improve. Cooperative play—in which children orient toward a common goal, such as building a block structure or acting out a make-believe theme together—increases during their preschool years. Likewise, kindergarten children also engage in solitary and in parallel play—in which a child plays near other children with similar materials but does not interact (Howes & Matheson 1992). Teachers may wonder whether a child who often plays alone is developing normally. Most kindergartners who tend to play by themselves enjoy it, and their solitary activities are positive and constructive (e.g., painting, looking at books, working puzzles, building with blocks). Such children are usually well-adjusted, and when they do play with peers, they show good social skills (Coplan et al. 2004).

A few children, however, may retreat into solitary activities when they would rather be playing with classmates but have been rejected by them. Some are temperamentally shy children whose social fearfulness causes them to withdraw (Rubin, Burgess, & Hastings 2002). Others are immature, impulsive children who find it difficult to regulate their anger and aggression. Ongoing observations will inform the teacher as to whether there is cause for concern about a child's sociability and a need for intervention.

The ability to make and keep friends increases the joy and pleasure in life and has important correlates, both contemporary and long-term. For example, having close friendships tends to foster positive attitudes toward school and correlates with better academic performance, perhaps because these rewarding relationships energize cooperation and initiative in the classroom (Ladd, Birch, & Buhs 1999; Ladd, Buhs, & Seid 2000). Young children with gratifying friendships are also more likely to become psychologically healthy and competent adolescents and young adults (Bagwell et al. 2001; Bukowski 2001).

Like older children, kindergartners seek compatibility in their friendships, often choosing friends who are similar not just in gender but also in age, socioeconomic status, ethnicity, personality (sociability, helpfulness, aggression), and school performance (Hartup 1996). However, children who attend ethnically diverse schools and live in integrated neighborhoods often form friendships with peers of other ethnicities (Quillian & Campbell 2003).

One of the most noticeable features of kindergartners' sociability is their preference for play with peers of their same sex, which strengthens over early childhood; by age 6, children play with same-sex peers 11 times more than they play with other-sex peers (Maccoby & Jacklin 1987; Martin & Fabes 2001). Children tend to choose play partners whose interests and behaviors are compatible with their own. Social pressure also plays a role; children pick up a wealth of gender stereotypes in early childhood ("*Trucks are for boys,*" "*Only girls can be nurses*"), which certainly contributes to gender segregation.

For most kindergartners, friendships involve at least a degree of sensitivity, caring, emotional expressiveness, sharing, cooperation, and joy—qualities that promote emotional understanding, empathy, sympathy, and posi-

tive social behavior (Hartup 1996; Vaughn et al. 2001). However, sometimes friendships are argumentative and aggressive, which interferes with children's adjustment. Kindergartners with conflict-ridden peer relationships are less likely than others to have lasting friendships and more likely to dislike school and to achieve poorly (Dodge et al. 2003; McClelland, Acock, & Morrison 2006). Shy or self-centered children also are likely to have few or no friends (Ladd 1999). Teachers' efforts to help less socially adept children develop and maintain friendships will do much to bring joy, confidence, and success into their lives.

Self-concept. The development of self-concept, which becomes better established in kindergarten, occurs within the context of children's maturing awareness of the social environment. Kindergartners develop their emerging self-concept in part by comparing themselves with peers, usually comparing against one classmate at a time. When asked to describe themselves, kindergartners typically focus on observable characteristics: their name, physical appearance, possessions, and everyday behaviors (Harter 1996). They also mention typical emotions and attitudes, such as "I'm happy when we get to run outside" or "I don't like to be with kids I don't know"—statements that suggest a budding grasp of their own unique personality (Eder & Mangelsdorf 1997).

Kindergartners readily internalize adult evaluations. Positive messages from adults about their growing knowledge, skills, and prosocial behaviors, as well as respect, warmth, and positive guidance, enhance children's self-concept. On the other hand, repeatedly negative messages contribute to early signs of self-criticism, anxiety about failing, and weakened motivation that can seriously interfere with learning and academic progress (Burhans & Dweck 1995).

In kind, children cannot yet sort out the precise causes of their successes and failures, instead developing a global self-image. They tend to view all good things as going together: A person who tries hard is also a smart person

who is going to succeed. As a result, most kindergartners are "learning optimists," who rate their own ability very highly, underestimate the difficulty of tasks, and are willing to exert effort when presented with new challenges (Harter 2003). These attitudes contribute greatly to kindergartners' initiative during a period in which they must master many new skills.

Emotional development

Kindergartners grow in the complexity of their emotional experiences, their ability to interpret the emotional cues of others, and their awareness that each person has an inner life of beliefs, opinions, and interpretations of reality different from their own (Wellman, Cross, & Watson 2001; Bronson 2006). As a result, and with modeling and guidance, children come to interact in increasingly intentional, sympathetic, skilled, and positive ways with others. A variety of factors contributes to these expanded skills, including the development of the frontal lobes of the cerebral cortex, cognitive and language development, a solidifying self-concept, conversations with adults and peers about mental states, make-believe play, and the patient guidance and reasonable expectations of adults.

Research in school settings shows that when prekindergarten, kindergarten, and primary grade children have warm, caring relationships with the teacher, these relationships foster their development and learning (Pianta, Hamre, & Stuhlman 2003). However, research finds that some teachers, especially those in poor-quality child care settings, are emotionally insensitive and detached (Cost, Quality & Child Outcomes Study Team 1995). The tendency to deny or ignore children's emotional development most hurts those with special vulnerabilities, such as children with special needs and those growing up in poverty (Peth-Pierce 2000; Raver & Knitzer 2002). Vulnerable children who lack a foundation of emotional security also are at risk for eliciting further criticism and harshness because they show inappropriate behavior that is hard for teachers and peers to respond to in positive ways; this cycle decreases such

children's chances of social and academic success (Hyson 2004).

For most children, however, age 5 is generally a time of happiness. "Life is good," a kindergartner might say (Wood 2007). The kindergarten teacher can enhance that happiness and help the child grow emotionally when he develops a bond with the child, designs activities to meet emotional needs, encourages open expression of feelings, helps develop positive feelings such as joy and satisfaction, and is aware of the child's unique emotional responses to various tasks and situations (Hyson 2004).

Emotional understanding and empathy. When adults are warm, encourage children's emotional expressiveness, and show sensitive concern for their feelings (modeling sympathy), children are more likely to react in a concerned way to the distress of others (Koestner, Franz, & Weinberger 1990; Strayer & Roberts 2004). Likewise, teachers who convey the importance of kindness and intervene when a child displays inappropriate emotion (such as taking pleasure in another's misfortune) help that child respond to others' distress with sympathy (Eisenberg 2003).

Given an emotionally secure foundation, kindergarten age children gain a considerable understanding of emotion. Children at ages 5 to 6 are developing a greater understanding of others' minds and emotions (Denham & Kochanoff 2002; Perner, Lang, & Kloo 2002) and can correctly judge the causes of emotions in many cases ("*She's mad because she thought it was her turn*"). They also can predict the consequences of many emotions with reasonable accuracy (an angry child might hit someone; a happy child is more likely to share). Furthermore, kindergartners show advancing skills in thinking of ways to relieve others' negative feelings, such as giving a hug to comfort someone or sharing a favorite toy when someone is sick.

These skills in understanding and empathizing, in turn, greatly help children get along with others. It is related to kindergartners' kind, friendly, and considerate behavior; willingness to make amends after harming another; and

peer acceptance (Dunn, Brown, & Maguire 1995; Eisenberg & Fabes 1998; Fabes et al. 2001).

About 3 percent of kindergartners, mostly boys, are highly aggressive. These children, who strike out at others with verbal and physical hostility, are limited in their ability to take another's perspective and are less empathic and sympathetic than other children. They need teachers to intervene by helping them to reinterpret others' behaviors in more positive ways (e.g., that being hit by a ball was an accident, not an attack) and to learn new coping strategies in the face of negative emotions (Tremblay 2000; Pettit 2004).

Self-regulation of emotions. Self-regulation is an internal ability to intentionally control our emotions and behavior as the situation demands. It involves children either making themselves not do something, such as not blurt out an answer, or making themselves do something even when the desire is not there, such as stop playing and clean up the puzzle pieces (Bodrova & Leong 2008). Self-regulation pertains to three aspects of development: emotions (discussed here), thoughts—in particular, attention (discussed in "Cognitive Development" below)—and behaviors (discussed in both sections). Compared with younger children, kindergartners are typically more able to regulate the ways they express emotions as they interact with other people (Eisenberg, Fabes, & Losoya 1997).

During preschool, given the right modeling of self-regulation, as well as patience, warmth, and guidance from adults, children, with effort, do improve in their ability to self-regulate their behaviors. Yet they do not all improve to the same degree, and children enter kindergarten with varying levels of self-regulation skills. Some are quite good at delaying gratification and thinking about the consequences of their actions, while others struggle. Teachers rate "difficulty following directions" as their number one concern about children because they say that more than half of their children have difficulty in this area of self-regulation (Rimm-Kaufman, Pianta, & Cox 2001).

Being able to adjust one's emotional state to a comfortable level of intensity is an important skill for engaging productively in tasks, interacting in positive ways with others, and succeeding in school (Howse et al. 2003). As experienced kindergarten teachers will attest, this skill is important for success with peers and academics. With age and experience, children become more able to control their impulses, which allows them to become more accepted and liked by other children (Eisenberg & Fabes 1992). Social competence is, in turn, associated with an ability to manage how one acts and to show few problem behaviors (Caspi 1998). Furthermore, children who develop these skills in the early years get on a positive trajectory, and they tend to have better peer acceptance and the ability to regulate their emotions as adults (Sroufe, Carlson, & Shulman 1993).

Children with highly emotionally volatile temperaments have greater difficulty regulating their feelings; they require extra adult support in developing self-regulation skills (Kochanska & Knaack 2003). Hyson (2004) delineates five major benefits of gains in emotion regulation: Children (1) reach the goals they desire, (2) feel better having more control, (3) experience mastery and competence, (4) become part of the culture and are accepted more readily, and (5) become more socially competent and able to direct attention to others.

Promoting social and emotional development in kindergarten

Kindergarten teachers can support children's social and emotional development in myriad ways, three of which are discussed below. The common denominator in enhancing development and learning in these areas is having a warm, positive relationship with the teacher and family members.

Prosocial behavior and attitudes. Relationships are the context that supports children's internalization of the rules and values in their world. This internalization reveals itself as kindergartners show more and more prosocial behaviors—cooperating, resolving conflicts peacefully, following classroom rules, and other positive actions. Teachers strengthen children's prosocial tendencies when they model prosocial behaviors; call attention to prosocial statements made by children; give explicit instructions about helping, sharing, and like behaviors; and reward these behaviors when they occur (Eisenberg & Mussen 1989). Effective teachers monitor children's interactions in the classroom, knowing that both negative and positive behaviors occur and that other children imitate the bad as well as the good. Some indirect methods of monitoring peer interaction include "stage setting" (providing time, space, materials, and arrangements of materials for positive and appropriate interactions) and "coaching" (suggesting positive social interaction and problem-solving strategies as needed in the context of ongoing interactions between children) (Hoffman 1983).

In addition to creating a warm, responsive emotional climate, teachers can foster prosocial attitudes by interpreting social situations in ways that show sympathy and caring. For example, when a teacher responds to an accident by saying, "Oh, Jacob's juice spilled; let's help him clean it up," children learn to be sympathetic and helpful to others. Modeling caring behaviors accompanied by a general prosocial lesson ("*We must help people who are hurt*") promotes these attitudes in children.

Kindergarten children are beginning to understand the feelings of others, and they are more likely to develop prosocial dispositions when their teacher connects behaviors with their consequences ("*He is sad because you wouldn't let him play the game with you*") and rules with reasons ("*We don't push others on the steps because somebody might fall*"). Teachers can also encourage cooperative interactions by suggesting sharing, taking turns, or other ways of negotiating disputes. Encouraging children to take responsibility for tasks that serve the classroom community also helps to promote prosocial attitudes. When teachers expect children to contribute to the common good, children internalize these expectations.

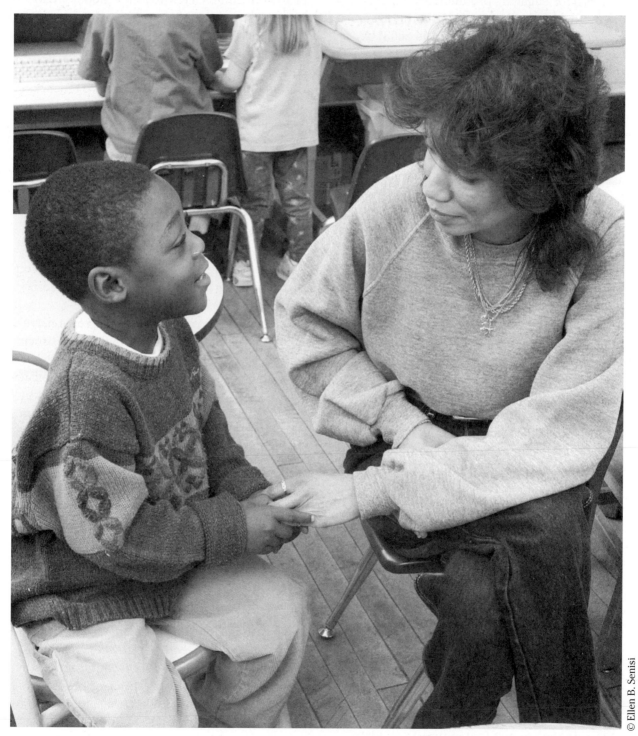

© Ellen B. Senisi

Developmentally Appropriate Practice, 3d Edition

Social interaction skills. Children learn how to interact with others from their early close relationships. When a teacher is caring and responsive to children's interests and feelings, she creates an atmosphere that fosters social development. Children are more likely to cooperate with and model a teacher with whom they have a positive relationship (Birch & Ladd 1998; Hyson 2004; Pianta & Stuhlman 2004). When children can rely on the teacher to care about them as individuals, validate their interests and feelings, and support their efforts to regulate themselves, they are more likely to develop trust, feel secure, and be ready to interact confidently with the social and physical environment.

Teachers must be careful to show a positive attitude toward *all* children—kindergartners notice when an adult likes or dislikes particular children. Because adults' attitudes and interaction styles influence children's own attitudes and behaviors, it is important that teachers act as positive role models—for example, showing interest in and kindness toward others and having respect for others' ideas, points of view, and emotions.

Because interactions with peers are critical for social learning, teachers must make sure to provide children ample time and opportunities for those interactions, such as space, materials, and encouragement for dramatic play, cooperative work, and problem-solving activities, conversations, and group discussions. They should also help children who need assistance to find play partners and should teach children proactive strategies for entering and participating in social activities. Part of the teacher's role is to monitor children's social activities and provide positive ways of solving problems, settling disputes, and keeping interactions fair and inclusive, without interfering unnecessarily (Katz & McClellan 1997). Teachers also model and teach the use of language to communicate ideas and emotions, negotiate differences, and treat others respectfully.

Self-regulation skills (emotional and behavioral control). The development of emotional and behavioral control—self-regulation—is a skill that should be taught to all children, not just those who demonstrate behavioral problems (Vieillevoye & Nader-Grosbois 2008). A teacher provides the foundation of support for children's control over emotions and behavior by creating a safe, warm, and supportive atmosphere that enables them to feel secure and capable of emotional control. She helps children maintain self-control by providing language that children can internalize and use for self-guidance, by helping them understand the relationship between their goals and the behavior strategies they use to reach those goals, and by allowing opportunities and supports for sustained dramatic play, which enhances their self-regulation skills (Yang 2000; Bodrova & Leong 2008). Teachers help children learn and rehearse strategies for negotiating social problems before they occur.

When a kindergartner's control fails, the teacher should focus on problem solving with the child (and, in some cases, the other children who were involved in the incident) and on helping him consider what else he could have done. The incident becomes a learning opportunity, and the child gains experience in making choices and using more effective strategies, which will help him the next time he needs his self-control, rather than just curbing behaviors for which he might get caught and punished.

Guidelines and rules for children's behavior should be simple and consistent and should include rationales so children can understand that rules are designed to help and protect them and all members of the classroom community. Kindergarten children are mature enough to participate in discussions about classroom problems, and they can help generate ideas about possible solutions and rules. Such discussions help children understand why guidelines are necessary and give them a sense of control and responsibility. Having opportunities to set and monitor their own rules contributes to young children's increasing capacity for regulating themselves rather than having to be regulated by adults (Bodrova & Leong 2008).

Teachers also should discuss emotions with children. When children learn to talk about what they and others are feeling, possible causes for the feelings, and what might be done about them (*"How do you think he felt when you wouldn't let him be in the game? How could you make him feel better?"*), children become able to separate emotions from action, reflect on their actions, and exercise more self-control.

The ways in which adults organize the environment also affect children's ability to exercise control. Children are more likely to learn self-regulation and be effective problem solvers if they are given a considerable amount of choice and control over their own activities (Ryan & Deci 2000). It is important to minimize sources of frustration, overstimulation, and stress in the environment that might be more than children can handle. Teachers also can provide visual and tangible reminders about self-regulation; for example, providing a coin for children to toss to settle an argument or decide who gets the next turn on the computer (Bodrova & Leong 2008).

Play, particularly complex dramatic or make-believe play, is a crucial vehicle allowing children to develop and practice self-regulation skills. Such play allows children to gain understanding of their emotions, as well as the feelings of others, as they act out situations that induce strong emotions and resolve those feelings. It also provides practice in remaining within a prescribed role and play scenario and in establishing, negotiating, and following their own rules—and thus it promotes self-regulation skills more powerfully than adult-directed play.

This is not to say that play should be without adult guidance and support. In fact, children often require adult modeling and scaffolding to help them learn to engage in the sustained, complex play that is most beneficial to their development. However, once opportunity and guidance have been provided, teachers should remove themselves, as children tend to show more complex and beneficial social play in the absence of adults (Kontos & Keyes 1999; Leong & Bodrova 2005).

Dramatic play experiences are especially advantageous for impulsive children, who are behind their peers in self-regulatory development (Elias & Berk 2002). To foster self-regulation skills, teachers should make sure children have ample opportunity, materials, and encouragement to engage in play, such as make-believe play and play with made-up rules (Yang 2000; Elias & Berk 2002; Bodrova & Leong 2008).

Cognitive development

Compared with younger children, kindergartners show more flexibility in their thinking, greater ability to conceptualize categories, advances in reasoning and problem solving, and gains in knowledge of the world, ability to pay attention, and use of memory. In short, kindergartners' thinking is reorganizing, gradually becoming more systematic, accurate, and complex. This transition—from preschool thought to the style of thinking more typical of middle childhood—is the "5 to 7 shift" mentioned in the beginning of the chapter (Sameroff & McDonough 1994; Flavell, Miller, & Miller 2001; Newcombe 2005). It stems from a congruence of major changes in the brain and greater societal expectations and opportunities.

Brain development and a key shift in thinking abilities

New research in cognitive neuroscience shows that, given healthy environments, a child's neurological system develops dramatically during the early childhood years (Halfon, Shulman, & Hochstein 2001). The first five to seven years of life are a sensitive period for brain development; the brain is especially responsive to stimulation, which prompts a massive wiring of neurons and sculpting of brain regions. The brain is more malleable than it will be later, making kindergarten an optimum time for learning and effective intervention with all children.

When children have appropriately stimulating surroundings, including interaction with responsive caretakers, rapid brain growth

occurs during this time; from preschool to kindergarten, the brain grows steadily, increasing from 70 percent to 90 percent of its eventual adult weight (Thatcher et al. 1996). In addition to gains in size, the brain undergoes much reshaping and refining. There is a thickening of the coating of the nerve cells in the brain's cerebral cortex and "pruning" of neural networks that are not being used, allowing active portions of the brain to become more powerful. Such changes enable the child to better meet the particular demands of the environment. Profound changes also occur in the frontal lobes of the cerebral cortex, areas devoted to regulating thought and action.

At about age 5, children have nearly twice as many connections between neurons (synapses) as adults in some brain areas, including the frontal lobes. This overabundance of communication channels supports the brain's "plasticity," or high capacity for learning. It helps ensure that the child will be able to acquire basic human abilities even if some brain areas happen to be damaged. As the child interacts with others and the environment and learning occurs, the synaptic connections of the neurons become increasingly elaborate and committed to specific functions (Huttenlocher 2002; Nelson 2002).

The frontal lobes are important because they govern the inhibition of impulse, orderly memory, and the integration of information—capacities that facilitate reasoning and problem solving, as well as emotional self-regulation. All these skills improve considerably in the kindergarten child.

The interaction of these brain developments and stimulating, supportive environments leads to children's thought patterns becoming more systematic and organized. This is evident in the way children explore new situations, acquire concepts, respond to directions, play games, approach problems, and carry out everyday activities. By the end of kindergarten, children are more aware of patterns and regularities. They also begin to redefine confusing problems and combine concepts they previously used only alone. Kindergartners begin to recognize event sequences in many ways—as they appear in stories, in the physical world, in biological cycles within the physical world, in daily routines within the classroom, and in larger societal routines.

Kindergartners also demonstrate an emerging awareness of part/whole relationships. This development becomes more evident in the next few years as children's attention to stories and the complex connections between plot lines and characters' emotions as motivating factors grows. This awareness of part/whole relations is also evident in mathematics and science, in spontaneous comments such as "I see five fish—two blue ones and three yellow ones."

During kindergarten, children's thinking typically becomes less rigidly fixed and egocentric; it better accounts for multiple perspectives, is more flexible, and is beginning to be able to transform ideas and representations (Dunn 1988; Halford & Andrews 2006; Harris 2006). In the physical domain, children can now grasp that the same object or set of objects can look very different depending on the observer's vantage point. In the social domain, children are better able to make inferences about what another person knows or feels. For example, if a child sees someone try to trick someone else, the child might infer that the child being tricked is unaware of what is happening.

In a variety of situations, children begin to see multiple sides of an issue. Unlike preschoolers, who assume that other people see things as they do, 5-year-olds begin to recognize that their own perspective on a situation may differ from someone else's—although this is an emerging ability that should not be expected on a regular basis. They may struggle to predict precisely what it is that someone else sees, but they are not surprised that another's view is different from their own. For example, a child may turn a book around so a friend can see it better. She begins to (but again, will not consistently) recognize that what her father would like as a gift is not what she would like. This awareness reflects an emerging ability to consider more information at one time.

An increase in flexible thinking is evident in other ways, as well. Children can mentally rearrange or transform information—they are less bound by the first thing they see or hear. For example, a kindergartner can figure out a couple of ways to combine blocks to create a structure of a particular shape. Or sometimes children can temporarily put aside their own feelings and be sensitive to the needs of another, especially if that person is a friend or loved one—and if there is no conflict with the child's own needs and desires.

This flexibility of thinking is apparent in geometric, spatial, and mathematical thinking. Children begin to apply visual spatial strategies and mental images to solve problems in the everyday world. Children understand that they can divide things, such as a cookie, so that everyone can have some—one thing becomes many. And they understand that a tangram with ten separate pieces can be returned to its original appearance by putting the pieces together again—many things become one. This idea of applying visual spatial strategies applies to stable objects, such as puzzles and their parts, and to things that move through space. With a bit of exploring, for example, children may be able to predict the expected pathway of a cone-shaped object rolling down an incline. They might discover that shadows are influenced by the orientation of the light source.

A child's skill in using these mental transformations will expand and improve throughout the course of middle childhood, but significant changes begin to appear in kindergarten. They continue to learn best with hands-on exploration of materials and with repetition.

In comparison with preschoolers, 5- and 6-year-olds are more likely to look for conceptual categories rather than just simple associations. For example, they understand that when they are looking for cereal in the grocery store, they probably will not find it in the dairy aisle. They also have a greater ability to think about their own thinking—that is, to engage in metacognition. To demonstrate, as anyone who has shared a secret with a kindergartner knows, the child is able to recognize (with excitement!) that he knows something that someone else does not know (*"Let's surprise Ms. Plum by bringing cupcakes and lemonade for her birthday on Friday"*). They can reflect on how they know something (*"How do you know the plant will wilt if we don't water it all week?"*), make connections with other things they've learned (*"What does this remind you of that we examined last week?"*), and predict and plan for the future (*"What instructions should we give Mr. Sweenie to take good care of our pet rabbits during winter break?"*).

A description of kindergartners' cognitive development and learning must include at least a brief account of their progress in two domains emphasized in the kindergarten curriculum—mathematics (discussed in this section) and literacy (discussed in "Language and Literacy Development" below).

For each grade the National Council of Teachers of Mathematics has defined key learning goals (termed "curriculum focal points") based on children's abilities and mathematics educators' judgment about what children at that grade—in this case, kindergartners—need to learn to have a strong foundation for continued progress in math (NCTM 2006).

Research in math and literacy has contributed to our knowledge of what children of this age group are capable of learning and doing in these domains. To some extent, typical accomplishments in the kindergarten year reflect the expectations and instructions prevalent in many U.S. schools; they also reflect kindergartners' cognitive and perceptual abilities and their eagerness to learn to read and write and make sense of their world in spatial and numerical ways. Unfortunately, the potential for great gains in academic areas during the kindergarten year are not equally realized by all children. Children from low-income families and diverse cultural, linguistic, and racial backgrounds are at particular risk for not advancing in academic areas; as many as one-third of children entering kindergarten are already behind their peers (Carnegie Corporation of New York 1998). The

Math in Kindergarten "Curriculum Focal Points"

Number and Operations: Representing, comparing, and ordering whole numbers and joining and separating sets

Children use numbers, including written numerals, to represent quantities and to solve quantitative problems, such as counting objects in a set, creating a set with a given number of objects, comparing and ordering sets or numerals by using both cardinal and ordinal meanings, and modeling simple joining and separating situations with objects. They choose, combine, and apply effective strategies for answering quantitative questions, including quickly recognizing the number in a small set, counting and producing sets of given sizes, counting the number in combined sets, and counting backward.

Geometry: Describing shapes and space

Children interpret the physical world with geometric ideas (e.g., shape, orientation, spatial relations) and describe it with corresponding vocabulary. They identify, name, and describe a variety of shapes, such as squares, triangles, circles, rectangles, (regular) hexagons, and (isosceles) trapezoids presented in a variety of ways (e.g., with different sizes or orientations), as well as such three-dimensional shapes as spheres, cubes, and cylinders. They use basic shapes and spatial reasoning to model objects in their environment and to construct more complex shapes.

Measurement: Ordering objects by measurable attributes

Children use measurable attributes, such as length or weight, to solve problems by comparing and ordering objects. They compare the lengths of two objects both directly (by comparing them with each other) and indirectly (by comparing both with a third object), and they order several objects according to length.

Source: Reprinted with permission from *Curriculum Focal Points for Prekindergarten through Grade 8 Mathematics: A Quest for Coherence,* copyright © 2006 by the National Council of Teachers of Mathematics. All rights reserved. The *Curriculum Focal Points* document may be viewed in its entirety at www.nctm.org/focalpoints.

failure to achieve affects middle-class children as well (Zill & West 2001)—when education programs are not high quality, when families are not supported and involved, and when teachers are not well prepared and supported. The achievement gap that may evolve or widen in the kindergarten year distressingly leads to an ever-widening long-term gap in achievement (Carnegie Corporation of New York 1998).

As described in the following sections, children's advancing reasoning and problem solving, demonstrated in the various curricular areas, is supported by gains in knowledge of the world, attention, and memory.

Reasoning and representational thinking

Both brain development and experience contribute to give older children a larger memory span, and thus they are better able to hold in mind and consider, at times, two or more dimensions of an object or event at once (Case 1998; Cowan et al. 1999). Kindergartners' advances in reasoning are initially fragile, and they may revert to earlier and more simplistic ways of thinking, including considering only one dimension at a time (AAAS 2008). Consequently, the kindergarten child's thinking sometimes seems limited and inflexible, and at other times quite advanced.

This move toward more complex thinking shows up in many ways. In everyday activities such as drawing pictures, for example, a 4- or 5-year-old often depicts people and objects separately, ignoring their spatial arrangement. Older kindergartners may be able to coordinate these two aspects so the drawing depicts both the features of objects and the objects' spatial relationship to one another. In creating stories, a similar progression takes place. Younger children focus on only a single character's actions and emotions; older children can combine two characters' actions and emotions in a single plot (Case & Okamoto 1996).

Because of variations in their experiences, interests, and goals, children display better developed thinking on some tasks than on

others (Sternberg 2002). In this respect, culture is profoundly influential. For example, a child who comes from a cultural group in which children are expected to be quiet and learn through observing adults would have difficulty demonstrating her competence in a classroom where she is expected to speak up and address the adult in reciprocal conversation. But she might well have impressive competence in areas where she has ample experience, such as sorting and counting household items, caring for younger siblings, or collaborating with an adult in preparing a family meal. What is valued as "intelligent" behavior varies considerably from one cultural group to another (Sternberg & Grikorenko 2004).

Self-regulation and attention

Self-regulation skills, as previously mentioned, have both emotional and cognitive aspects. One of the most important aspects of self-regulation in the cognitive domain relates to a child's ability to focus attention. The ability to not give in to distraction, to listen to what others are saying, and to focus on a given task for a productive length of time is crucial for success in school (for all ages, not just kindergarten). Self-regulation in kindergarten has been shown to correlate with achievement in math and reading, independent of a child's general level of intelligence (Blair & Razza 2007).

Kindergartners in well structured and supported classrooms can often work for 15 to 20 minutes at a time on a quiet, seated activity (Wood 2007). Their improved ability to focus and manage their attention contributes to transformations in their reasoning. Development of the frontal lobes of the cerebral cortex leads to greater cognitive inhibition—an improved ability, while engaged in a task, to prevent the mind from being distracted and straying to alternative thoughts (Bush, Luu, & Posner 2000). The capacity for cognitive inhibition, which already increases throughout the preschool years, improves dramatically beginning at about age 5 or 6 (Dempster 1993; Sameroff & McDonough

1994; Harnishfeger 1995). This increased ability enables children to focus more intently on the types of tasks they will encounter often in school. Still, kindergartners tend to have a limited attention span compared with older children or adults—unless they are pursuing self-chosen activities that are highly motivating to them. With the support of adults, kindergartners are also increasingly capable of planning; they can think out a short, orderly sequence of actions ahead of time and allocate their attention accordingly (Hudson, Sosa, & Shapiro 1997).

Memory

The combination of brain growth and improved use of memory strategies eventually improve children's ability to recall information. However, kindergartners are not yet good at deliberate use of memory strategies unless teachers help them. When asked to recall items, such as a list of toys or groceries, children might rehearse on one occasion but not on another, and even when they do rehearse, their recall rarely improves. At this age, applying a memory strategy initially requires so much effort and attention that children have little attention left for the memory task itself (Schneider 2002). Nonetheless, teachers can help children improve memory skills by prompting the use of strategies such as rehearsing information, organizing it into categories, or simply alerting children to the need to remember something.

Although they show limited memory for unrelated or non-meaningful information, kindergartners show good memory for information that is meaningful to them (Ely 2005). For example, at about ages 4½ to 5, children can give chronologically organized, detailed, and evaluative accounts of personal experiences, as this kindergartner illustrates: "We went to the lake. Then we fished and waited. I caught a big catfish! Dad cooked it. It was so good we ate it all up!" Increased memory capacity—when combined with teacher-guided opportunities to practice personal storytelling and other skills—is a manifestation of growing cognitive skills.

Promoting cognitive development in kindergarten

For all children to thrive academically and to reduce the achievement gap, schools and teachers should implement high-quality curricula and teaching strategies, embed teaching and learning in caring, nurturing relationships, and engage and empower families (Carnegie Corporation of New York 1998). One study of ethnically diverse, low-income families showed that increases in family involvement in school predicted improvements in children's literacy and mathematics skills (Dearing, Kreider, & Weiss 2008). Teachers should offer inviting, well organized classrooms and should establish warm and trusting relationships with children to create the conditions that foster children's thinking abilities. Emotional security frees children to devote energy to the cognitive tasks they encounter in the classroom. Organization of instruction allows for taking advantage of teachable moments in planned and systematic ways (Clements 2001).

Children continue to build on their early knowledge areas, and teachers who are sensitive to what children already know and think can help them refine and add to that base. Often these expanded ideas can be linked to specific curriculum content. For example, learning in science can be linked to children's own ideas about the physical world (Gelman & Brenneman 2004). If a child explains that we sleep "because it's nighttime," the teacher can build on that belief to explore the biological needs and rhythms of humans and other living organisms. Teachers also should help children connect concepts. Children can relate number concepts to geometry, for instance, by counting the sides of shapes or measuring the length of a rug, which strengthens their understanding of mathematics as a coherent *system* (Sarama & Clements 2006). The key for teachers is to understand the concepts themselves and also to understand how each child makes sense of the world and what interests him.

One way to support cognitive development is by asking children thought-provoking questions ("*How do you get to the cafeteria from here?*" or "*How could we remember how many we have?*") and making comments ("*I wonder how many big blocks it would take to cover the rug*" or "*Our plant didn't grow as much this week as before; I wonder if we did something differently*") that encourage children to think and reflect. Questions might focus on descriptions of events and changes in the physical and social world or on thought processes themselves, since kindergartners now have some capacity for metacognition. These questions encourage "thinking about thinking," directing children's attention to awareness of how they know something and how they might remember or solve a problem.

Teachers also promote cognitive development when they encourage children to record and document their knowledge by using various representational methods, such as words and gestures, writing, and drawing and by making diagrams, graphs, and models. Children are most highly motivated when sharing a message that is important to them. In such instances, children are likely to notice when their message is not getting across and perhaps grasp that it needs to be modified, though they are not yet skilled in knowing how to change the message to communicate more effectively. An important focus in the kindergarten year is enhancing children's understanding of the many ways that we use representations to communicate and share knowledge. A teacher might invite children to describe through words or actions something seen on a field trip to the zoo, create a page for a memory album, and build a model of the zoo (Golbeck 2006).

As with children of all ages, kindergartners learn from their interactions not only with adults but also with peers. Children frequently test their ideas with peers and learn a lot from the reactions they receive. Sometimes the child's peers understand him and respond positively to his ideas; sometimes they do not. Teachers greatly promote kindergartners' cognitive development by recognizing the value of peer interactions for kindergartners' cognitive growth and by designing learning environments

and planning experiences that encourage children to interact and collaborate.

Finally, children need to be able to make choices. Choices empower children to be active thinkers who challenge themselves. Teachers who offer children choices do not give up control, nor are they passive. Rather, they look for ways to be active participants in children's learning processes, while ensuring that the children are also active and engaged. Overall, the kindergarten year requires teachers to provide a nuanced balance for optimal cognitive development. On the one hand, there should be plenty of play, child choice, and verbal interaction; on the other, there should be adult-guided activities that are engaging to children and adaptable to their varying readiness. Kindergartners learn best under conditions in which adults guide and support their active efforts, with a gradual and measured introduction of more formal lessons.

It is also worth noting that most kindergarten age brain growth occurs in the course of everyday experiences as adults offer young children age-appropriate play materials and stimulating, enjoyable daily routines and social interaction: a shared meal, a picture book to discuss, a song to sing, or an outing at the park or another type of field trip. The resulting growth readies the brain for later, more advanced brain development, such as that necessary for reading comprehension, solving mathematical problems, or investigating scientific hypotheses (Shonkoff & Phillips 2000; Huttenlocher 2002). Hurrying a young child into mastering skills that depend on extensive training—such as advanced reading and comprehension, musical performance, or sports—runs the risk of overwhelming the brain's neural circuits and reducing its sensitivity to the experiences needed for healthy brain development (Bruer 1999).

Language and literacy development

From infancy on, most children learn from the adults around them that listening and talking are enjoyable activities that often help them in getting what they need. Early on, they learn how to use language to communicate what they want or need and how to take turns in conversation. By kindergarten age, they have learned extraordinary amounts. Not only do they listen to conversation (and music) for pleasure, but they also listen and speak (and sing) with attention. They know the sounds of their home language and can identify sounds in their environment.

Kindergartners become increasingly knowledgeable about the features of language. For example, they have a good sense of the concept of *word*. When an adult reading a story stops to ask, "What was the last word I said?" children almost always answer correctly (Karmiloff-Smith et al. 1996). They know sentence structure and use correct grammatical structures most of the time in increasingly complex ways (Seefeldt 2005). They show awareness of the need for "style shifting" in language use; for example, they use different language in the classroom than on the playground (Strickland 2006).

Most children of this age can maintain a topic of discussion over many speaker turns with both peers and adults (Tager-Flusberg 2005). In addition to being capable of such conversations, many kindergartners will also speak up in small groups and before the whole class. They ask and answer questions and like to both explain and have things explained to them. Further, their communication becomes more precise; for example, they are better able to describe one object among a group of similar objects in a way that distinguishes it.

Kindergartners know the meanings of a substantial and growing number of words. In the early grades, children learn about 20 new words each day (Anglin 1993). Of course, these gains depend on being in language-rich environments where children are exposed to a reasonably wide range of words; where they hear and participate in rich conversations; and where books, stories, and other forms of written expression are valued and enjoyed. A 6-year-old's vocabulary is typically about 10,000 words (Bloom 1998)—again, if he is exposed to a language-rich environment. Because of large socioeconomic

differences in language used in the home, some children begin kindergarten with far more limited knowledge of language and word meanings (Hart & Risley 1995; Snow, Burns, & Griffin 1998), and the gap continues to widen over time.

Oral language is the foundation for literacy learning, which also begins in infancy and not in kindergarten, as is commonly thought; language and literacy develop in tandem (Strickland 2006). Two things make a big difference in children's progress in these two areas: knowledge about the world and knowledge about print and books (RAND 2002). In particular, children advance in language and literacy areas with shared adult-child reading experiences in which adults (parents and teachers) explore the idea and uses of print, have conversations with children about a book's content and meaning, and convey the value of books for the pleasure, information, and empowerment they bring.

Also essential for becoming a skilled reader is a solid base of knowledge and conceptual development. Not only for the sake of improving reading comprehension but for wider curricular purposes as well, teachers work to expand children's content and vocabulary knowledge by providing interesting objects, nonfiction and fiction books, and encounters with the broader world (e.g., field trips and virtual field trips that are now possible through technology). Meaningful projects and investigations enable children to expand and use their knowledge, as well as gain research skills from searching books, asking adult experts, or using the Internet. Teachers focus children's attention by asking questions that encourage children to observe carefully, make comparisons, or review their past experiences.

One ability strongly linked to mastering reading is phonological awareness (Whitehurst 1999); that is, noticing the sounds of spoken language—speech sounds and rhythms, rhyme and other sound similarities, and, at the highest level, phonemes, the smallest units of speech that make a difference in communication (hence the term *phonemic awareness*). Phonemic aware-

ness does not occur automatically for most children, but they acquire it when teachers purposefully support it and provide the assistance that each child needs (which varies considerably from one individual to another). Phonics, which is not the same as phonological or phonemic awareness, is a system of teaching how letters and combinations of letters correspond to sounds of spoken language and is typically introduced in kindergarten or first grade. At around age 5, children start making great strides in phonological awareness (this continues until about age 8)—an awareness also reflected in kindergartners' increasing sensitivity to incorrect pronunciation (Foy & Mann 2003).

By the time they enter kindergarten, children who have had quality literacy experiences in the preschool years have acquired some basic knowledge about print. For example, they are likely to understand that print performs a variety of functions, recognize print in the environment, distinguish separate words, and realize that English print is read left to right and top to bottom. They know letters by name and have begun to connect some letters with sounds. They are ready to go farther in mastering the alphabetic principle (i.e., the systematic relationship between letters and sounds).

Continuing in a print-rich and conversation-rich environment, kindergartners often make great strides in their reading skills over the course of the year. They become more comfortable and interactive with books and read-aloud times and often enjoy partner reading, where more able readers pair up with beginning readers (as long as both play an active role) (Wood 2007). They tend to do best in phonics groups that include others at similar skill levels, however.

They also like it when adults read aloud to them, and they benefit from hearing predictable books—books with few words, a good deal of repetition, and pictures that reinforce the story. These types of books help them practice decoding words. Kindergartners have generally learned that books have titles, authors, and illustrators and that pictures can convey ideas

but cannot be read (Strickland & Schickedanz 2004). They begin to develop the concept of *story structure* and even come up with their own theme stories with classmates—favorite themes include families, pets, babies, school, seasons or holidays, and of course, themselves (Seefeldt 2005; Wood 2007). Books aside, kindergartners have fun with their newfound abilities to understand some signs, posters, labels, and charts.

As reading comprehension and fine motor skills progress, kindergartners also move forward in writing skills. Engaging children in writing helps them learn about print and the written words that they will increasingly learn to read and spell. Further, when children write—even at a very basic level—they begin thinking of themselves as writers, and this idea is a powerful catalyst to their advancing in literacy and self-expression. As young children experiment with writing, teachers have many opportunities to convey basic information about print. Kindergarten children recognize and can produce recognizable letters and words, usually writing first in uppercase letters. They often tell stories through the use of drawings, incorporating print into the drawing or painting to express their ideas.

They might begin the writing process by using a beginning consonant letter to stand for a word in their stories, such as to label a drawing (e.g., "F" for *family*) or to string together to compose a sentence (e.g., "HIMH" for *here is my house*). They are likely to use developmental or emergent word spellings as well, showing attempts to associate sounds with letters; for example, writing "kak" for *cake* or "bfl" for *butterfly*. More and more, they are eager to learn to spell words correctly and often ask teachers and peers how to spell words as they write. Kindergartners progress to more conventional spelling with experience (Seefeldt 2005). They usually write with irregular spacing between their letters and words.

Overall, there are two paramount goals for kindergarten teachers in promoting children's literacy in effective and appropriate ways. The first is to inculcate a solid familiarity with the

structure and uses of print, basic phonemic awareness, and ability to recognize and write most letters of the alphabet. The second is to instill interest in and reliance on print, since children's future learning depends in large part on their ability to get knowledge from books and other print sources (Burns, Griffin, & Snow 1999). The box (below) delineates more specifically what the expert panel convened by the National Research Council indicated teachers might expect regarding kindergartners' reading and writing skills.

English language learners

In 2000, about 18 percent of U.S. residents reported speaking a language other than English at home (U.S. Census Bureau 2003). Spanish accounts for almost 80 percent of the non-English languages, but more than 460 languages are spoken by English language learners nationwide. The dramatic rise in ethnic and linguistic diversity in the United States means more and more children in kindergarten and other early childhood programs speak a language other than English as their first language. Because many

---

Literacy: What Happens in Kindergarten

Book and print awareness. To be successful readers, children must understand how books and print work. In kindergarten, they should know the parts of a book and their functions, that the print on the page represents words that can be read aloud, and that there are various forms and purposes of print, such as letters, signs, and storybooks.

Phonological awareness. With support, kindergartners deepen their ability to think about the sounds of spoken words (*phonological awareness*). Teachers can help them develop an awareness of the smallest meaning units (*phonemes*) that make up a spoken word (e.g., an /r/ sound changes *ice* to *rice*). This is a crucial step in understanding the alphabetic principle that phonemes are what letters stand for, and toward being able to read.

Language, comprehension, and response to text. Kindergartners need a chance to build their general knowledge background in order to make sense of the wonderful books they will encounter. They need help increasing their repertoire of words and context so they can understand a book on volcanoes, a fairy tale about silkworms, or an essay about Inuits. They also need encouragement in following their interests in order to want to practice reading. One important

goal of kindergarten is to motivate children to relate to books and print as a meaningful part of their lives. Rich classroom discussions, thoughtful question-and-answer exchanges, fun activities relating to texts, and high-quality storybook readings are important avenues through which children become real readers.

Letter recognition, decoding, and word recognition. By the end of kindergarten, children should be able to name without much effort most letters of the alphabet, regardless of order and whether written in upper or lower case. They should begin to recognize some very common words by sight.

Spelling and writing. Early in the year, kindergartners will still be scribbling and drawing pictures. With ample opportunity during the year to practice writing and with access to paper, writing utensils, and materials for making books (e.g., staples, tape), they make good progress in independent writing. By the end of the year, kindergartners can write most letters in upper and lower case. They have a growing repertoire of conventionally spelled words but still use their own invented spelling for many words.

Source: Adapted from National Research Council, *Starting out right: A guide to promoting children's reading success,* eds., M. Susan Burns, Peg Griffin, and Catherine E. Snow (Washington, DC: National Academies Press, 1999).

---

consider kindergarten the beginning of "real school," the language issue tends to become more critical at kindergarten age for families of English language learners and their teachers.

Young children are adept at learning more than one language, but the process of learning two (or more) languages simultaneously may look different and occur at different rates than for children learning only one language. Many children learning a second language exhibit a silent period, in which they stop speaking almost altogether in order to focus intently on listening to the new language they are working to acquire. Children (and adults) using more than one language sometimes use words and phrases of both languages in an intermingled way. Neither the silent period nor mingling languages for a time is an indication of confusion or a problem, but rather typically indicates active learning and navigation, often savvy navigation, between the two or more languages.

Compared with those learning only in English, children with limited proficiency in English are more likely to experience long-term academic success when they receive systematic, deliberate exposure to English combined with ongoing opportunities to learn important concepts in their home language (Thomas & Collier 2002). If English replaces the home language and children do not have an opportunity to continue to learn in the language they know, their future linguistic, conceptual, and academic development in English is at risk (Espinosa 2008).

A national longitudinal study found that English language learners who attend English-only mainstream programs beginning in kindergarten show large decreases in reading and math achievement by grade 5 and are more at-risk for dropping out of school when compared with their peers who participated in language support programs such as bilingual education (Thomas & Collier 2002).

Promoting language and literacy development in kindergarten

Children's language development is profoundly affected by early conversational and literacy experiences, and kindergartners vary greatly in such experiences (Hart & Risley 2003). For example, children's exposure to hearing books read aloud to them—an important predictor of children's language development—varies depending on the quantity of books in the home, the literacy level of adults in the family and their interest in reading, access to a children's library, and so forth. Before starting kindergarten, a child from an average middle-class family has been read to for a total of 1,000 hours, whereas a child from an average family living in poverty has been read to for only 25 hours (Neuman 2003). As a result, kindergartners from chronically low-income families often arrive at the kindergarten door with a disadvantage based on their different experiences. As an illustration, their vocabularies are, on average, one-fourth the size of their middle-class peers' (Lee & Burkam 2002).

In light of the wide variation in language, conversation, and literacy experiences with which children enter kindergarten, it is important to note that language-rich (and literacy-rich) kindergarten environments are crucial for narrowing gaps and reducing at-risk children's chances of academic failure. There is a great deal teachers can do to foster language skills, which includes listening and speaking, using vocabulary to build comprehension, and cultivating awareness of the sounds of language.

First, a word on teaching children whose home language is not English. There is a great need for more bilingual teachers who can promote both English and children's home languages. However, in many contemporary classrooms, teachers do not speak the language(s) used by children in their classrooms—and often these are numerous (Ray, Bowman, & Robbins 2006). This mismatch could be less than ideal in supporting children's language development, but it doesn't have to be. The critical issue is the teacher's attitude and effort toward promoting dual-language development.

When the atmosphere in the classroom and the school is one of valuing each child's home language, children tend to be less inhibited and

can thrive in their language development and learning (Strickland 2002). Teachers support the language development of English language learners when they take the time to show appreciation for the child's home language by, for example, correctly pronouncing the child's name, learning at least a few words in the home language, celebrating the unique contributions of the child's culture, and playing music in the child's home language.

Teachers can also add to the richness of their own curriculum by (1) introducing nursery rhymes, songs, or vocabulary in the child's languages to the entire class, (2) enlisting the resources and members of the community, and (3) engaging the parents of English language learners and incorporating their talents, skills, and interests into the curriculum (Espinosa 2007).

Demonstrating respect for the language, as well as for cultural traditions, values, and preferred interaction styles, sends a clear message to children that using words or phrases in more than one language is welcomed. It also sends a message to families: Not only are their culture and language valued, but building language skills and vocabulary in more than one language benefits—and does not harm—children's development and engenders later academic success (Espinosa 2007; 2008).

Teachers might promote language development for English language learners through the use of pictures and props, physical demonstration (either pretend or actual) of actions and requests, and pairing words heard in stories with words written on a chalkboard. Explicitly teaching reading comprehension will help children as they learn science, mathematics, social studies, and other subject matter areas. Teachers should be sure to help with comprehension by summarizing what was heard; using brief, simple explanations of new vocabulary words; modeling how to think out loud ("*This sounds confusing to me. Let's read it again*"); and asking questions to see how much children have understood and learned (Colorín Colorado 2007).

For all kindergarten children, principles of developmentally appropriate practice are especially salient in the area of language development. For example, teachers need to plan for and provide a balance between adult-guided and child-guided experiences in the kindergarten day. Opportunities to learn and practice listening and speaking skills should occur in a variety of formats. At whole-group time, for instance, the teacher asks several children who have worked on a project together to tell the others about a problem they encountered and how they solved it. A collaborative small-group investigation of worms promotes children's language as well as their science knowledge and reasoning. As an individual activity, the teacher makes available a variety of audiobooks for children to listen to when they wish.

It is important for teachers to combine language learning with other curricular areas, such as mathematics, science, and physical development. Language gains will influence comprehension of these other areas, and knowledge of other areas will enhance vocabulary and communication skills.

And last, teaching language development and learning should occur through a scaffolded approach, in which teachers model good listening and communication skills, peers work together and teach each other, and the schedule allows for times of guided, independent practice.

Strickland (2006) suggests various strategies and activities teachers might use to promote language and literacy learning. Reading aloud and then setting aside time for children to respond to what they have heard and fostering extended conversations about the story or related personal experiences encourage listening and speaking skills as well as comprehension. Explaining new vocabulary words introduced by the book is a good way to enhance that comprehension as well as build vocabulary.

Enhancement of language skills and vocabulary knowledge also occurs when teachers provide materials and opportunity for children to engage in dramatic play. Having various thematic topics for class discussion and study

(e.g., transportation, how things grow) can help organize children's thoughts and vocabulary, as well. Phonemic awareness skills can be fostered by listening for and making rhymes, listening to similarities in the beginning sounds of words, and counting the number of syllables in a word. A literacy learning center in the classroom should not only have plenty of books but also include audiobooks to be listened to with headphones.

The creative, effective ways to scaffold reading and writing experiences for kindergartners are limitless for intentional teachers. Reading to children, facilitating discussion about book content, and providing opportunities for children to respond to what they have heard is a foundation for enhancing kindergartners' love of reading and literature. Repeated readings of favorites allow for deepened understanding of the events in the story as well as the vocabulary and concepts conveyed. Teachers can compose charts or lists stemming from a book or topic of study, with the children helping by dictating their ideas. And teachers can use the opportunity to comment on conventions of written language, such as capital letters and punctuation. They can foster letter recognition, phonemic awareness, and understanding of sound/letter correspondence by focusing on children's names, naming letters in books that teach the alphabet, making rhymes, and identifying beginning sounds of words. Having children dictate or write stories and illustrate them is a rich activity that gives children the sense of being writers.

Regardless of the specific activity or strategy, good teachers will be promoting language skills throughout the kindergarten day. It is best

© Ellen B. Senisi

to differentiate instruction—that is, to allow children at different levels to gain new knowledge and skills within the same lesson or activity. Moving from the easy to the difficult and the known to the unknown through a range of experiences and opportunities ensures that all children will make progress in their language skills, regardless of where they start (Strickland 2006).

Easing the transition into and out of kindergarten

For many children, two of their most dramatic transitions occur around kindergarten—first participation in a group program and, at the end of kindergarten, entry into the primary grades. In addition, many kindergartners also transition within the school day to an after-school program or an out-of-home caregiver. When all adults caring for a child—teachers, family members, care providers—work together to create positive, communicative relationships, transitions can be smooth for the child (and adults) instead of stressful.

The two major points of transition—entering kindergarten and leaving kindergarten—are discussed below.

Transitioning into kindergarten

About 56 percent of 3- and 4-year-old children in the United States are enrolled in a preschool program of some kind, whether a private setting, a community-based organization, Head Start, or a public school prekindergarten class (NCES 2008). This means that almost as many children—44 percent—enter kindergarten without having a preschool experience to prepare them in some way to participate and learn in the kindergarten group setting.

The transition experience for all participants—the child, the family, and the teacher—will differ depending not only on the child's individual characteristics and cultural experiences but also on his or her experience or lack of experience in a preschool setting. For adults and children alike, change is stressful. But for young children who have limited experience and few well developed coping strategies, change can be very upsetting. Adult relationships (between teachers and families and among teachers) will make all the difference in how children experience the transition.

The home-school connection. When children enter kindergarten, they essentially become citizens of two cultures—home and school. They must learn to navigate the new etiquette, rules, and conditions of the classroom, which are different from those at home, regardless of ethnicity or cultural background (Lam & Pollard 2006). As active, participatory learners, they learn to make sense of and adapt to the new environment in creative and dynamic ways, some children more quickly and easily than others. The amount of stress and the time required to make a successful adjustment can be lessened significantly when teachers and administrators plan and work together with parents to make adjusting as easy as possible for the child.

Communication is critical, including about cultural issues such as the interplay between the values and expectations at home and those of the school. Today, as most teachers know, cultural variety is the American norm. Children develop and learn within a cultural context, using that context to understand the world, what behavior is appropriate, and how to show what they know and can do.

Children can most easily show their accomplishments in environments with which they are comfortable and familiar. They experience easier transitions and feel more successful when the skills, abilities, and understandings they construct in their family and community are congruent with the expectations of the classroom. Likewise, families will feel better prepared and more able to support their child if they know what is expected—within the context of and in relation to what happens at home—and that their own traditions and expectations are valued (Rhodes, Enz, & LaCount 2006).

If children's developmental accomplishments, which are culturally bound events, go unrecognized, their adjustment to school may

be very difficult. For example, a child may be very competent and effective at communicating in the home language but not yet proficient in English, and the teacher may fail to recognize the child's language competence. On the other hand, confidence and self-esteem can blossom when the teacher recognizes the child's competence and looks for evidence of it in the classroom—in either language.

When children enter school, their self-esteem comes to include perceptions of their families by teachers and others at school. Having the sense that teachers respect and value their family strengthens a child's sense of self-esteem and competence. Fully knowing children and responding to their individuality are possible only if parents are active partners in the educational process. This informed responsiveness happens when teachers and parents communicate frequently and respectfully and parents feel welcome in the school at all times. If children's culture and background are rejected—or worse, treated as a deficit or somehow less worthy than the primary culture of the classroom—children's healthy development and capacity to learn face a serious threat.

Even when cultural cues are very similar between the home and school environment, there are myriad differences between the culture of a classroom environment—the rules, values, and expectations of that group setting—and that of a home—the rules, values, and expectations unique to each family. Families usually feel as anxious as their children do about school transitions, and children sense their stress. If parents feel less anxious, then their children are likely to face the change with more confidence and enthusiasm.

Transitions tend to be more successful when teachers and families develop respectful, reciprocal relationships founded on good communication, and then they can work together to help children negotiate the changes. Teachers might reach out to each family through visits, phone calls, or e-mails, as well as with resources such as brochures and newsletters in each family's home language that help families know

what to expect (Duda & Minick 2006). In these two-way relationships, teachers tell parents about plans, expectations, and observations, and they seek out parents' concerns, hopes, and goals for their children. Good teacher-family relationships have endless benefits for children, one of which is making the transition into school easier.

The program-to-program (preschool-to-kindergarten) connection. Differences in program content, teaching strategies, and expectations of children between preschool and kindergarten settings are not only normal but desirable. Programs *should* vary depending on the age of children and the needs and interests of individual children and families. Nevertheless, when the kindergarten program is developmentally appropriate, children's transitions from preschool (and later to a developmentally appropriate first grade) will be smoother and more successful.

The preschool and kindergarten settings may differ starkly with respect to the length of the day, class size, and the instructional style or room setup. The greater the disparity in developmental expectations and teaching practices between preschool and kindergarten, the more potential stress there is for the child making the transition. When kindergarten is a lot more like second or third grade, with desks and workbooks, than it is like preschool, with blocks and dramatic play props, the change is so sharp that many children have difficulty adapting. When such a stark contrast exists, it is not the case that the preschool teacher should introduce inappropriate academic instruction to help her group of children "get ready" for kindergarten, but rather that all teachers involved should work to better align the programs (Pianta & Kraft-Sayre 2003).

This is not solely a teacher responsibility, however; administrators at both the preschool and kindergarten levels have a responsibility to align programs and to ensure they support teachers in implementing developmentally appropriate curricula. Directors and principals should support teachers in designing environments that allow children to choose some activ-

ities, in having materials and space available to allow for healthy growth across all domains of development and learning, and in using practices that benefit young children, such as positive guidance, appropriate individual and group instruction, and good daily transition practices.

At the teacher level, classroom-to-classroom connections are very important. Too often there is an expectation that responsibility for a smooth transition into kindergarten lies with preschool or Head Start teachers—that they should make sure children are "ready to learn" when they enter kindergarten. It is equally the responsibility of the kindergarten teacher to communicate with those teachers and administrators to smooth the way.

For example, kindergarten teachers might invite local Head Start teachers, children, and parents to visit their classrooms to observe, meet the teacher and current students, and ask questions. If children are coming from too many programs to realistically arrange such visits, the kindergarten teacher could develop a letter for the preschool teachers, outlining kindergarten activities, the structure of a typical day, how routines are handled, favorite songs or books, and perhaps include classroom and playground photos.

Such cooperation is advantageous, not only for the child but also for the kindergarten teacher, because children are better prepared and less fearful. Also, teachers have a chance to learn from each other, enhance their classrooms, broaden professional contacts, and feel good about meeting the developmental needs of the children in their care. Transitions will be easiest when there is good communication between preschool and kindergarten administrators and between kindergarten and preschool teachers.

More teacher-initiated activities to ease the transition into kindergarten can be adapted from the activities discussed below.

Transitioning out of kindergarten

Many kindergartners move on to a first grade where expectations are radically different from what they have experienced—so different that the transition is sometimes called "hitting the wall." In the face of such a drastic shift, children who previously loved going to school may quickly lose their enthusiasm for school and learning. They may become anxious and intimidated. Such a turn of events is distressing and problematic because the adjustment from kindergarten to first grade can have long-lasting effects on school success (Entwisle & Alexander 1998) as well as happiness, so a good transition is important. Kindergarten teachers can play an important role in helping children better adjust.

Downer, Driscoll, and Pianta (2006) explain the value of taking a "developmental/ecological" approach to the transition, as compared with a skills-only approach. In a skills-only approach, teachers focus only on the child's current abilities and skills, such as the number of letters she can write at the end of kindergarten. In this view, the major considerations in determining the child's readiness are age and certain skills—to the exclusion of program quality, instructional practices, or the teacher-child relationship.

In contrast, the developmental/ecological approach considers all the interconnected factors that influence development and learning, including the family, school, peers, and community in which the child lives. It acknowledges that young children learn in uneven and episodic ways; a kindergartner may know or be able to do something one day and not the next, or may be able to do it at school but not at home or vice versa. It considers not only the child's readiness to move on to first grade but also the school's readiness to work with each new child who enters its classrooms, regardless of the child's skills or background. Schools that take a developmental/ecological approach understand that communication and information sharing are instrumental in supporting children and families in making the transition to first grade.

Communication and information sharing can take many forms and should occur between teachers and families and also among teachers (or among administrators). Downer, Driscoll,

and Pianta (2006) provide many ideas for easing the transition. For example, kindergarten teachers can prepare parents and other family members by hosting family nights, arranging meetings about what to expect in the coming school year, providing transition packets or handouts, and organizing back-to-school nights at both the beginning and end of kindergarten as an orientation about expectations. Teachers should initiate communication with families and should be responsive when families contact them.

Kindergarten teachers can establish connections with first grade teachers by observing the first grade classroom to learn about the curriculum and routines, discussing and agreeing on a common assessment tool, and meeting together to share information about individual children. This knowledge allows teachers to better prepare children for the new environment.

Positive, honest comments that get children excited about the new opportunities and challenges that await them in primary school are appropriate and helpful. Children need time to talk about their feelings, and they need sensitive adults to listen and help prepare them for the exciting and positive changes that are a natural part of growing up (Hyson 2004).

The kindergarten teachers might also, time and resources permitting, arrange a group visit to a first grade classroom, have children practice first grade behaviors or routines, invite first-graders to read to the kindergarten children, arrange a joint summer activity, and encourage their children to ask questions about what they've seen or heard. They also can reassure children that they will stay in touch by sending letters or making visits in the next year, which will greatly hearten these kindergartners, who likely have become warmly attached to their teachers.

With all that kindergarten (and other) teachers have to do, these ideas are not meant to add to an already full plate. Rather, they are meant to increase simplicity from the continuity that should emerge and to allow for deeper relationship building with the children, which will strengthen and make easier every aspect of implementing the curriculum, from emotional to academic domains.

Using these strategies, with a particular focus on communication, should lessen the negative impact of transition and perhaps even make transition points times of joy and celebration.

Developmentally Appropriate Practice in
the Kindergarten Year—Ages 5–6

Examples to Consider

The framework of developmentally appropriate practice derives from
what the early childhood field knows from research and experience
about how children develop and learn. Major points from this knowledge base are highlighted in the position statement and summarized in the
overview in chapter 6. As no learning tool clarifies understanding better than
examples, the chart below presents many examples of practices to consider.

The chart addresses developmentally appropriate practice in five areas
important in the teacher's role: creating a caring community of learners, teaching to enhance development and learning, planning curriculum to achieve
important goals, assessing children's development and learning, and establishing reciprocal relationships with families. The set of examples offered here is
not exhaustive, and the goal is not to describe best practice comprehensively.
We have tried to capture major aspects of practice that one sees in excellent
kindergarten classrooms and, by contrast, in those kindergartens that in some
respects have not achieved a high level of quality. Neither is the aim to issue a
prescriptive formula to be rigidly followed. Instead, the examples are meant to
encourage readers to reflect on their practice. Establishing a habit of thoughtful reflection is essential in working with young children because of their varying family backgrounds, preferences, and needs.

In the chart's left column, under the heading "Developmentally Appropriate,"
are examples of practices consistent with available research and that most
in the field agree promote young children's optimal learning and development. The examples in the "In Contrast" column are intended to aid reflection by helping readers see clearly the kinds of things that well-intentioned
adults might do but that are not likely to serve children well. Many of the "In
Contrast" examples are very prevalent in early childhood settings. A few of
those practices are dangerous or would cause children lasting damage. Others
are unlikely to harm children significantly but also are less likely to promote
their optimal development. Sometimes context affects whether a practice
should be used or adapted.

Where they appear, the comments sections expand on the practice examples presented in the chart cells above them. Some of the comments speak to

cultural factors to consider when determining what practices to use. Other comments elaborate on a practice that is briefly described in a column, and some indicate the research finding on which it is based.

Finally, most of the examples are phrased as descriptions of what teachers do or fail to do. For the "In Contrast" examples, however, that wording is not meant to imply that deficient or questionable practices are necessarily teachers' fault. Most teachers are working hard and doing their best—but often constrained by very challenging circumstances, including large class size, limited resources, and administrative requirements. The hope of this chapter is to help them in their efforts.

Developmentally appropriate	In contrast

Creating a Caring Community of Learners

Fostering positive relationships

Teachers are warm, caring, and responsive. They are encouraging to children and respectful to their families. They come to know children well and make reaching out to families a priority.	■ Teachers do not see the importance of forming relationships with children and families. Or large class sizes make it very difficult for teachers to know children and families well.
	■ Teachers devote time and attention to those children who present challenging behaviors, while others are overlooked. Some children are repeatedly singled out for discipline. Others receive little attention because they are quiet or speak limited English.
Teachers model positive interaction with others and encourage prosocial behavior. All children in the class are provided opportunities to get to know and work with each other, and friendships are encouraged. Teachers actively involve children in conflict resolution.	■ Classrooms are managed rigidly with little opportunity for interaction. Children who need assistance forming friendships are not given teacher support. Teasing and rejection in the classroom go unchecked, and procedures are not in place to deal with bullying.
	■ Teachers rely heavily on a directive approach to classroom conflicts rather than helping children learn conflict resolution skills. Adults typically react after the fact but do not give thought to preventive measures that would reduce conflict.

Developmentally appropriate	In contrast

Creating a Caring Community of Learners (cont.)

Fostering positive relationships (cont.)

Teachers include all children in the social aspects of the classroom. For example, children with special needs and children with limited social skills are provided with resources and encouragement. Teachers act to promote a sense of positive self-identity for all children in the classroom.

■ Children who need assistance interacting with others lack support, resulting in social isolation. Interaction with children who have special needs is largely left to specialists.

Teachers design all classroom activities to allow for the full participation of all children, including those who are not fluent in English.

■ English language learners cannot understand or take part in some classroom activities because teachers fail to make modifications or provide assistance to make their full participation possible.

Comments on fostering positive relationships:

—Supporting social and emotional growth is one of the most important aspects of the kindergarten year, yet it is sometimes overshadowed by curricular goals and the need to maintain order in the classroom. The capacity to form and sustain positive social relationships is crucial for social development and overall success in school (Bronson 2006). Children who are neglected or rejected by peers are negatively affected academically as well as socially and emotionally.

—When teachers form warm and caring relationships with children, they in turn help to foster greater prosocial behavior. And when children are able to form positive relationships with peers, their overall attitudes toward school and learning improve.

Building classroom community

Teachers act to create a cohesive community of learners by establishing common ground in the classroom. Children have opportunities to act as leaders and helpers with specific tasks; all children are given a chance to participate and are drawn into class activities in a variety of ways. Class meetings are used to solve and prevent problems and provide a forum for discussion.

■ The classroom environment and tone are rigid, and the organization (or disorganization) of the classroom limits children's interaction with one another. Children are required to stay in their seats throughout much of the day.

A variety of opportunities for peer interaction are offered throughout the day and throughout the week. Children work with partners as well as in small- and whole-group situations. Teachers encourage peer-to-peer scaffolding and assistance when possible.

■ Teachers rely heavily on whole-group settings, with children remaining at their places. There is little opportunity for peer interaction.

■ Teachers do not encourage children to work problems out independently or with peers.

Developmentally appropriate	In contrast

Creating a Caring Community of Learners (cont.)

Building classroom community (cont.)

Teachers respect the diversity of the classroom community, providing activities and initiating discussions that explore the cultures and languages represented in both the class and the larger society. The class explores similarities and differences among people in ways that engender respect and appreciation without singling out individual children. The environment promotes all children's positive self-identity, including cultural identity.

■ Diversity in the classroom is ignored, as is cultural variety in the larger society. Teachers do not make an effort to avoid presenting stereotypes in the classroom and do not adequately intervene when teasing or rejection occur. No thought is given to fostering positive self-identity.

■ Diversity is addressed but in ways that single out individual children in the classroom as representative of entire cultures or groups. This leads children to see themselves as outsiders to the class as a whole.

Teachers promote children's sense of community involvement beyond their classroom—in the school or center as a whole, the neighborhood, or town/city. For example, children make a sign to alert the other classes in the building about an upcoming event, collect clothing for a local shelter, take walks in the neighborhood, and note what shops and services are available to the local community.

■ No effort is made to build a sense of the group as a community or to link classroom matters to those of the larger community and society.

Comments on building classroom community:

—A climate of respect for all members of the classroom community is crucial for children's wellbeing in kindergarten. In such an environment, all children feel accepted and have a sense of belonging. Conversely, when children insult or reject others, not only are they devaluing those they reject, they also are not learning the important prosocial skills they need to function and succeed in school and in society.

—Providing opportunities for collaboration and learning from one another strengthens a sense of the classroom as community when children see their impact on the group as a whole. And when activities reflect the diversity of the homes, neighborhoods, and daily lives of the class, all children increase their awareness and appreciation of differing cultures and abilities. Children learn to recognize that they can enjoy and work with others from many backgrounds.

Developmentally appropriate	In contrast

Teaching to Enhance Development and Learning

Environment and schedule

Teachers carefully plan the physical layout of the classroom, providing several discrete areas in the room where children can interact with peers and materials. If children have desks, they are grouped together to form small tables or circles.	■ Teachers give insufficient thought to the physical environment of the classroom. Desks often are set up in rows, limiting children's interaction with peers.
Teachers and assistants provide a safe environment and attentive supervision.	■ Supervision is lax. Health care personnel are not stationed at the school at all times. ■ Teachers are overly cautious in the classroom, restricting children's activities. Teachers and aides often help children with tasks they could do or could learn to do on their own instead of challenging children to learn new skills.
Teachers foster a learning environment that encourages exploration, initiative, positive peer interaction, and cognitive growth. They choose materials that comfortably challenge children's skills. The classroom includes spaces for children to keep their work and personal belongings; a place for group meetings; a variety of spaces for working, such as learning centers and tables of different sizes; a comfortable library area and other quiet places for independent work or conversation with friends; places to store materials; and displays of children's work.	■ The environment is disorderly, with little structure or predictability. Consequently, children's behavior is frantic or disengaged. The noise level is stressful for children and adults, making it hard to focus or have a conversation. ■ The arrangement of the environment severely limits children's opportunities to pursue engaging learning experiences. For example, children generally have to ask teachers for materials rather than finding materials readily accessible. ■ The environment, materials, and experiences reflect only a single culture or in other respects provide too little variety, interest, or choice for children (e.g., all games are at one level of difficulty).
The daily schedule includes periods of activity and movement and also quiet and restful times. Half-day kindergarten includes a morning snack, and full-day kindergarten includes a morning and afternoon snack as well as lunch.	■ Children are bustled from one activity to the next with little downtime and frequently become overtired, overstimulated, and distracted. Snack time is overlooked or rushed, and/or snacks have limited nutritional value.

Developmentally appropriate	In contrast

Teaching to Enhance Development and Learning (cont.)

Environment and schedule (cont.)

Teachers allocate extended periods of time in learning centers (60 minutes or more in full-day and at least 45 minutes in half-day kindergarten) so that children are able to get deeply involved in an activity at a complex level. The classroom includes a dramatic play area to which all children have frequent access. Children have ample time and opportunity to investigate what sparks their curiosity. Schedules are set but not rigid— if children are highly engaged in an activity, the teacher may choose to extend it.

■ Frequent transitions and excessive emphasis on rituals such as "doing the calendar" every day or lining up to go outside take up too much time, often interrupting children's engagement in learning activities. This prevents children from gaining maximum benefit from sustained investigations, construction, dramatic play, or other such activities. The schedule is rigidly followed with activities tightly scripted.

Comments on environment and schedule:

—An important way to help kindergartners feel secure is to focus on smooth transitions between learning experiences. These times can be challenging for young children, who may either be eager to rush on to the next activity or be engrossed in what they are doing and reluctant to start a new task.

—Requiring kindergartners to sit still for extended periods of time is usually counterproductive. One useful strategy to help children retain their energy and focus is to break up an extended block of time into several different learning experiences and formats. For example, a language arts block could begin with a brief large-group instruction and discussion of new concepts, time for children to work in small groups or individually, as the teacher observes and offers individual help as needed, and finish with a whole-group teacher read-aloud.

Teaching methods

Teachers provide a variety of engaging learning experiences and hands-on materials. Materials include books, writing materials, math-related games and manipulatives, natural objects and tools for science investigations, CDs and musical instruments, art materials, props for dramatic play, and blocks (and computers, if budgets allow).

Materials are chosen for how well they support the overall curriculum and goals of the classroom.

■ Learning materials are primarily workbooks, worksheets, flash cards, and other materials that do not engage children's interest, promote their self-regulation, or involve them in problem solving and other higher-order thinking skills.

■ The same materials are available week after week. Children have few new choices and little variety in materials and activities.

■ Teachers choose materials based on entertainment value and popular culture fads, such as stickers from a new movie. Candy and other sweets are often used as incentives.

Developmentally Appropriate Practice, 3d Edition

Developmentally appropriate	In contrast

Teaching to Enhance Development and Learning (cont.)

Teaching methods (cont.)

Teachers use a variety of learning contexts throughout the day and throughout the week in order to guide children's learning. These include a whole-group setting, small groups, learning centers, and daily routines.

■ Teachers overuse one or two learning formats in the course of the day and make little or no use of others. For example, teachers give children very little time in interest areas or fail to use the small-group format when it would be the most effective approach.

■ Group work tends to be didactic, with teachers being largely unresponsive to children's ideas and contributions.

Teachers use a variety of instructional strategies to suit particular learning goals, specific situations, and the needs of individual children. These strategies can include encouraging children; offering specific feedback; modeling skills or positive behavior; creating or adding challenge; giving a cue, hint, or other assistance; telling information directly; and giving directions. Such approaches are used within any learning context and during child-guided activities.

■ Teachers have a hands-off approach during much of the day. Beyond setting up the materials, teachers' involvement in center time is limited to observation; teachers step in only to mediate conflicts that arise. Interactions with children during less structured times are very basic, such as giving directions.

■ Teachers make excessive use of direct instruction methods (e.g., giving directions, presenting information), which are useful for some purposes but not effective as the predominant strategy in teaching young children. Children spend long periods of time on seatwork that does not extend their learning.

In addition to teacher-guided lessons and activities, there is time allotted each day for child-guided experiences, including play. These may be during center time or other parts of the day. Teachers support children's deep engagement in these experiences by adequately scheduling time, providing interesting materials, and thoughtfully intervening and assisting as needed (e.g., helping a shy child gain access to a group).

■ Teachers are too passive in the classroom, planning too few adult-guided learning experiences and rarely taking action, even when children's behaviors are aimless or disruptive. When children are engaged in play and interest centers, teachers contribute little or nothing to their play and learning. Teachers use play as a reward for acceptable behavior or for children who finish their "work."

■ Too little time (or none at all) is allotted for child-guided activities, and teachers do not recognize how important it is for children to guide some of their own activities. They frequently interrupt and undermine children's immersion in and management of their own activities.

Developmentally appropriate	In contrast

Teaching to Enhance Development and Learning (cont.)

Teaching methods (cont.)

Teachers frequently engage children in planning or in reflecting on their experiences, discussing a past experience, and working to represent it (e.g., drawing, writing and dictating, making charts). Such opportunities let the teacher discover what children are thinking and encourage children to deepen and refine their own concepts and understanding. Teachers frequently document children's answers to monitor comprehension and learning across the year.

■ Feeling pressured to cover the standard curriculum and believing that returning to the same topic or experience is a waste of time, teachers present a topic or experience only once and fail to provide opportunities for revisiting and reexamining experiences, which would make fuller, more refined understanding possible.

Teachers provide many opportunities for children to learn to collaborate with others and work through ideas and solutions as well as develop social skills, such as cooperating, helping, negotiating, and talking with other people to solve social problems. Children work collaboratively to answer questions, such as those encountered in studying mathematics or science.

■ Children have few opportunities for meaningful social interaction with other children, especially in half-day kindergarten programs where teachers feel pressed for time.

■ Though teachers may recognize the social dimension of children's interactions, they do not see this dimension as integral to children's cognitive development and learning. Thus, teachers rarely make use of children's interactions and relationships in addressing learning goals.

Comments on teaching methods:
—Children learn best when they are deeply engaged. Both when they themselves primarily shape the activity (as in play) and in thoughtfully planned activities guided by adults (as in a large-group read-aloud or a small-group science activity), children are often highly engaged and learning.
—For a discussion of the purposes behind each classroom format (small group, large group, etc.), see the position statement and chapter 1.

Communication and language use

Teachers talk often and warmly with every child—getting to know children, building positive relationships with them, and gathering information about them.

■ Teachers' speech is mostly one way, much more often *telling* children things than conversing with or listening to them.

■ Teachers usually speak to children as a group. For the most part, teachers address individual children only to admonish or discipline them.

Developmentally Appropriate Practice, 3d Edition

| Developmentally appropriate | In contrast |

Teaching to Enhance Development and Learning (cont.)

Communication and language use (cont.)

When talking with children, teachers take into account children's capabilities as listeners, recognizing that there is a wide range of individual variation in kindergartners' verbal skills and ability to focus attention. Teachers communicate information in small units, tie new information to what children already know, check for understanding, and invite questions or comments to engage their interest.

■ Teachers talk at length or read aloud for long periods; they expect attentiveness during these times, but children often become restless or tune out.

■ Teachers put a high priority on children being silent unless addressed; they ignore or correct children for talking or for not waiting to be called on.

■ Teachers talk down to children or answer for children who are sometimes slow to respond (e.g., English language learners).

When children are talking, teachers take into account their capabilities as speakers, giving children time to express themselves and responding attentively to their speech. Teachers share with children the role of setting the topic and purpose of talk.

■ Adult agendas dominate classroom conversations. Teachers often view children's talk as interruptions of the adults' talk or work.

■ Teachers don't respect children as speakers (e.g., asking questions without really meaning children to answer).

Teachers encourage children's efforts to communicate. They make it a priority to involve English language learners in meaningful interactions at whatever level the children are able. Teachers allow children time to think about how they want to respond to a question or comment (*wait time*).

■ Teachers are so focused on the shortcomings of kindergartners' language skills that they neglect or miss the messages children are attempting to communicate.

■ Teachers insist on children's speaking only in English or only with proper grammar, correcting them every time they diverge from standard English usage.

Teachers engage individual children and groups in real conversations about their experiences and projects as well as current events. Teachers encourage children to describe their work products or explain their thinking, and teachers express interest in children's opinions, observations, and feelings.

■ Teachers interrupt children and dominate conversations instead of taking conversational turns.

■ Teachers don't talk in depth with children, often underestimating children's complexity of thought because they can't yet communicate it fully.

Developmentally appropriate	In contrast

Teaching to Enhance Development and Learning (cont.)

Communication and language use (cont.)

Developmentally appropriate	In contrast
Teachers use wide-ranging vocabulary in their talk to and with children, including words that are unfamiliar to them. When teachers use words unfamiliar to a child, they give sufficient information for the child to grasp the meaning. With an English language learner, teachers provide *nonverbal* cues to enable the child to learn what the new words mean (e.g., using gestures, pointing to objects or pictured items).	■ Teachers talk down to children both in terms of content and oversimplified speech, using relatively limited vocabulary in their conversational exchanges. ■ Teachers use a fairly rich vocabulary, but when they use words unfamiliar to children, teachers do not give sufficient information for children to grasp the meaning.
Teachers talk with *all* children, making it a priority to talk often with children who are learning English and those with delayed language development or limited vocabulary.	■ Teachers don't make extra effort to talk with children who are shy or hesitant, have communication difficulties, or are in the process of learning English. ■ Teachers pay so much attention to English language learners (and draw their peers' attention to them, as well) that those children feel unusual or outside the community of learners.

Comments on communication and language use:

—By their interest in and responsiveness to what children say, teachers help initiate children to the back-and-forth sharing of conversation, and they enhance the complexity of children's language and the size of their vocabulary.

—For teachers to draw special attention to English language learners may be problematic if those children are from cultural groups in which getting singled out for attention, even positive attention, is not desirable.

Motivation and positive approaches to learning

Developmentally appropriate	In contrast
Recognizing children's natural curiosity and desire to make sense of their world and gain new skills, teachers consistently plan learning experiences that children find highly interesting and engaging and that contribute to their development and learning.	■ Most classroom experiences either are uninteresting and unchallenging or are so difficult and frustrating that they undermine children's intrinsic motivation to learn. Teachers do not use what they know about the children to inform curriculum in order to better reflect their interests. ■ Seeking to motivate children, teachers rely heavily on external rewards (stickers, privileges, etc.) or chastise children for their mistakes or shortcomings.

Developmentally Appropriate Practice, 3d Edition

Developmentally appropriate	In contrast

Teaching to Enhance Development and Learning (cont.)

Motivation and positive approaches to learning (cont.)

Teachers use verbal encouragement in ways that are genuine and related to what the child is doing. They acknowledge the child's effort and work with specific comments ("You've been working very hard on your drawing," "I see from your chart that you ate peanut butter and jelly three times for lunch last week").

■ Teachers make such frequent use of nonspecific praise ("Good job!" or "What a nice block tower") that it becomes meaningless either to provide useful feedback or to motivate the child. Children may also become focused on pleasing the teacher rather than on the learning experience itself.

■ Teachers' feedback consists mostly of negative comments and correction of errors.

Comments on motivation and positive approaches to learning:
—Genuine, positive feedback promotes children's intrinsic motivation. However, many kindergarten classrooms focus heavily on a system of tangible rewards, giving out small prizes and treats for good behavior or for mastering skills. There are some cases where using a reward system for a limited time may help children (e.g., with certain special needs or challenging behaviors). For most children, though, such a system focuses their attention on the rewards rather than on the learning experience itself and thus is a shortsighted strategy that undermines internal motivation.

Guidance

Teachers model and encourage calm, patient behavior and facilitate children's development of self-regulation by supporting them in thinking ahead, planning their activities, and considering strategies to solve social problems.

■ Teachers are uncontrolled in their own behavior (e.g., showing irritation, stress, impulsive responses) with children and with other adults.

■ Not knowing what kindergarten children are capable of, teachers do not involve children in thinking through and solving problems and learning to regulate their own behavior, emotions, and thinking.

Teachers offer opportunities for positive interactions through a range of teacher-supported, child-guided experiences (e.g., dramatic play, exploring books, manipulatives). Teachers focus on helping children to become self-regulated. They monitor children's interactions, and when children present challenging behavior, adults help them to resolve conflicts by teaching them communication, emotional regulation, and social skills.

■ Children flit from one activity to another, simply reacting in the moment rather than being planful or reflective. Or activities are highly teacher-directed, so children remain too adult-regulated and don't develop self-regulation skills.

Developmentally appropriate	In contrast

Teaching to Enhance Development and Learning (cont.)

Guidance (cont.)

Teachers set clear limits regarding unacceptable behaviors and enforce these limits with explanations in a climate of mutual respect and caring. Teachers attend to children consistently, not principally when they are engaging in problematic behaviors. Class meetings and group discussions are often used to talk about and set rules together.

■ Teachers do not set clear limits and do not hold children accountable to standards of acceptable behavior. The environment is chaotic. Teachers do not help children learn classroom rules or let them participate in setting rules, so children have difficulty incorporating the rules as their own.

■ Teachers spend a great deal of time punishing unacceptable behavior, refereeing disagreements, and repeatedly putting the same children in time-out or disciplining them in other ways unrelated to their actions. These strategies attempt to control children rather than promote children's self-regulation, conflict resolution skills, and social problem solving.

When a child consistently displays challenging behaviors, teachers identify events, activities, interactions, and other contextual factors that occur with the behavior and may provoke it. Then, to help the child progress toward more acceptable behavior, teachers (in collaboration with families) make modifications in the activities and environment and give the child adult and peer support.

■ Teachers and school administrators push to get children with challenging behaviors excluded from regular kindergarten classrooms and placed in special programs.

■ Children with special needs or behavioral problems are isolated or reprimanded for failure to meet group expectations, rather than having teachers provide them with learning experiences that are at a reasonable level of difficulty.

Comments on guidance:

—The age range of kindergarten children within a single classroom can be wide, from as young as age 4 to as old as age 7. Children's levels of self-control and self-regulation can be similarly varied. In addition, children's experience of being part of a social group will vary considerably, depending on their prior care and preschool education, if any. Teachers may find that some children are able to assimilate prosocial behavior modeled by adults easily, while others may need more systematic, positive behavior support.

—It will help most children improve their self-regulation skills if teachers form caring relationships with them, organize the environment to promote positive interactions, and model and support prosocial behavior. However, kindergarten is often the first setting in which children who have special needs related to aggressiveness or who show other serious challenging behaviors may be identified. Because early interactions set the course for those later in school, it is important that teachers implement an individualized behavior support plan with the child's family and school specialists, if necessary, for the benefit of the child.

—For more on self-regulation in the kindergarten year, see chapter 6.

Developmentally appropriate	In contrast

Planning Curriculum to Achieve Important Goals

Curriculum essentials

Comprehensive scope; important goals

The curriculum addresses key goals in all areas of development (physical, social, emotional, cognitive) and in the domains of physical education and health, language and literacy, mathematics, science, social studies, and creative arts.

■ Curriculum goals are narrowly focused on a few learning domains (e.g., literacy and math) without recognition that all areas of a child's development and learning are interrelated and important.

In each area, the curriculum is consistent with high-quality, achievable, and challenging early learning standards, such as those adopted at the state level. Curriculum is informed by recommendations from the relevant professional organization.

■ Curriculum content lacks intellectual integrity and is trivial and unworthy of children's attention.

The curriculum is designed to help children explore and acquire the key concepts ("big ideas") and the tools of inquiry for each discipline in ways that are effective for kindergarten children (e.g., language experiences exploring sound/letter relationships, hands-on science activities).

■ The curriculum is developed by extending expectations for first grade downward, rather than by reflecting what kindergarten children are capable of—thus, expectations may be too high. Alternatively, expectations are set too low or are otherwise not a good fit with the children.

Coherence and integration

Teachers are knowledgeable about the sequence and pace that development and learning typically follow as children build understandings and skills in each content area. For example, teachers' understanding of the progression of concepts and skills involved in joining sets (addition) enables them to introduce the concepts to children in a coherent way and to scaffold children's progress from each idea and ability to the next.

■ Because the standards on which the curriculum is based include too many topics or learning objectives, learning experiences touch on topics only superficially, and children are unable to gain real understanding of any single topic.

■ Teachers fail to recognize the sequences of learning in the discipline areas and how these apply to children in this age range.

| Developmentally appropriate | In contrast |

Planning Curriculum to Achieve Important Goals (cont.)

Coherence and integration (cont.)

Teachers integrate ideas and content from multiple domains and disciplines through themes, projects, play opportunities, and other learning experiences so that children are able to develop an understanding of concepts and make connections across disciplines. For example, in discussing a certain kind of pattern in math, teachers draw children's attention to the same pattern in songs.

■ Children's learning is seen as occurring in separate content areas, and times are set aside to teach each subject without integration. Teachers fail to connect curriculum topics in ways that are meaningful to children. As a result, learning is often fragmented, and children are less likely to generalize ideas and apply them across content areas.

■ Teachers use a "holiday curriculum" or choose other themes based only on their initial appeal to children (even when the topics do not provide opportunities for learning important content and skills).

Effective implementation

The curriculum, which exists in written form, provides teachers with a useful and flexible framework for planning learning experiences and materials and for seeing how those experiences can fit together to accomplish the school's stated goals.

■ If there is a prescribed curriculum (published or adopted by a district or school), teachers do not have the flexibility or the capability to make adaptations in the curriculum to optimize its interest and effectiveness with the particular children in the group.

Teachers refer to and use the curriculum framework as they plan what they will do with children, so classroom experiences are coherent. Teachers plan and implement experiences to help children achieve important developmental and learning goals.

■ Teachers do not consider the curriculum framework in their planning. Children's learning experiences do not follow a logical sequence. Curriculum goals are unclear or unknown.

In planning and implementing learning experiences, teachers draw on their knowledge of the content, awareness of what is likely to interest children of that age, and understanding of the cultural and social contexts of children's lives. Teachers value children's input and let it shape curriculum as appropriate (e.g., letting children suggest topics for project work).

■ Teachers rigidly follow a prescribed curriculum plan without attention to individual children's interests and needs or the specific and changing context (e.g., studying weather change because it is in the October curriculum, even though a national election is about to occur). Teachers stick with their previously planned topics regardless of circumstances or events (e.g., a child's uncle is performing in a local concert). No effort is made to let children's interests inform classroom activities.

Developmentally appropriate	In contrast

Planning Curriculum to Achieve Important Goals (cont.)

Effective implementation (cont.)

Teachers plan curriculum that is responsive to and respectful of the specific contexts of children's experiences. Culturally diverse and nonsexist activities and materials are provided to help children develop positive self-identity, relate new concepts to their own life experiences, and respect differences and similarities. For example, books and pictures include people of different races, ages, and abilities and of both genders in various roles.

■ Children's cultural and linguistic backgrounds and other individual differences are ignored or treated as deficits to be overcome. Insufficient resources are allocated to help children who speak English as a second language.

■ Multicultural curriculum reflects a "tourist approach" in which artifacts, food, or other aspects of different cultures are presented without meaningful connections to the children's own experiences. Teachers point out a culture's traditions in ways that convey these are exotic or deviations from the "normal" majority culture (thus, the children of this culture feel like outsiders).

Teachers assess each child's progress toward the school's stated curricular goals, and they reflect on their practice to monitor the effectiveness of their teaching. They make changes to their teaching practice (environment, schedule, methods, etc.) as necessary to improve effectiveness for the group and for individual children.

■ Teachers do not regularly make use of assessment information to inform curriculum decisions.

Teachers connect curriculum topics with children's interests and with what children already know and can do. Young children learn best when the concepts, vocabulary, and skills they encounter are related to things they know and care about, and when the new learnings are themselves interconnected in meaningful ways.

■ Meaningful, connected learning is not a priority in the curriculum planning. Curriculum is not integrated across multiple learning domains.

Comments on effective implementation:
—Kindergarten teachers often do not have any say in the curriculum that is chosen by their school, district, or state. Despite this fact, teachers have the most important role to play in how effectively curriculum is implemented. In order to fully realize the curriculum's potential, teachers must have a clear idea of how learning experiences within the curriculum fulfill standards-based learning goals. By giving careful consideration to which standards are addressed by daily activities, teachers are able to better adapt curriculum in practice.

Developmentally appropriate	In contrast

Planning Curriculum to Achieve Important Goals (cont.)

Physical development

Health and fitness

Teachers acquaint children with healthy habits in eating and exercise and introduce basic concepts of body functioning and physical health. Snacks are nutritious; sweets are never offered as an incentive. Teachers reinforce good hygiene habits.

■ Foods with low nutrition value and with high sugar or fat content are served. Children spend too much time sitting and do not get adequate exercise.

Comments on health and fitness:
—Children as young as kindergarten age are becoming obese in ever larger numbers. Even when children aren't dangerously overweight, being overweight at all negatively impacts children's current and future health, as a cycle of inactivity, tiredness, and decreased ability in and enjoyment of physical activity is established. It also affects children socially, as they may be excluded from active interactions with their peers.

Gross motor development

Children spend little time sitting; they are able to move around throughout much of the day. They have plenty of opportunities to use large muscles in balancing, running, jumping, climbing, and other vigorous movements, both in their play and in planned movement activities. Children play outdoors every day and have specialized instruction in physical education on a regular basis.

■ Children's opportunities for large muscle activity are limited, and there is no regularly scheduled time for specialized instruction in physical education. Recess time is limited, or there are no opportunities for gross motor activities when the weather is poor.

Adults teach children the pleasure and importance of physical activity, as well as body and spatial awareness and key movement skills (e.g., catching, jumping, balancing). Teaching of physical skills is sequential and adapted to accommodate children's various skill levels and special needs. Equal encouragement is given to girls and boys. Physical activities are integrated into various learning experiences throughout the day.

■ Teachers or other qualified adults are uninvolved during recess and free play times, except to provide basic supervision. Adults make little effort to involve less-active children and those lagging in physical skills or coordination and to help them develop the skills and confidence to engage in gross motor activities. Accommodations are not made to include children with special needs.

■ Physical activity areas have very limited equipment, so children lack variety of choices and/or must often wait quite a while to get a turn.

Developmentally appropriate	In contrast

Planning Curriculum to Achieve Important Goals (cont.)

Gross motor development (cont.)

Comments on gross motor development:

—Kindergarten children need structured instruction in physical activity, unstructured time to play and exercise large muscles, and integration of physical activities throughout the day. However, less and less time in contemporary kindergarten classrooms is spent on planned acquisition of physical skills. In some districts, positions for specialist teachers in physical education have even been subject to budget cuts, and daily specialized instruction is rare. Unfortunately, this reduction comes at a time when it's more important than ever for children to be active, as our society becomes increasingly overweight.

—In light of reduced physical education programs and the needs of kindergarten children, many classroom teachers need to integrate physical development and learning into the day's activities. They need to familiarize themselves with the kindergarten standards in early physical education and plan activities to foster skill acquisition and link to learning in other domains. The PE Central website (www.pecentral.org) offers suggestions for classroom teachers who want to use physical activity to teach academic content, either in the classroom or in an outdoor play area.

Fine motor development

Teachers provide opportunities throughout the day for children to develop fine motor skills through working with suitable materials (e.g., pencils and markers, puzzles, playdough, beads, paper and scissors, small plastic interlocking blocks, buttons and zippers on clothing). As needed, teachers help children acquire such skills through scaffolding their efforts. Modifications and accommodations are made for children with physical disabilities.

■ Teachers give children fine motor tasks that are too difficult or hold them to an unrealistically high standard in executing tasks (e.g., expecting them to write letters with precision when they lack the necessary small muscle control).

■ The tools and fine motor experiences that teachers provide have insufficient variety to allow children at many different levels to progress in eye-hand coordination and motor control (e.g., there are only fat markers or brushes for the children to use). Assistive technology is not available for children with special needs.

Teachers provide opportunities and support for children to develop and practice self-help skills, such as putting on jackets, serving themselves snack or meals, washing hands, and cleaning up materials. Adults are patient when there are occasional spills, accidents, and unfinished jobs.

■ To save time and mess, adults often perform routine tasks for children. Children cannot get materials as needed, but must always ask adults for them.

■ Adults shame children or display irritation when spills or other accidents happen.

Developmentally appropriate	In contrast

Planning Curriculum to Achieve Important Goals (cont.)

Fine motor development (cont.)

Comments on fine motor development:

—Although kindergarten children have longer attention spans than preschoolers and can focus more on fine motor tasks like writing and drawing, they often find it difficult to exert the necessary patience, time, and effort. Offering play-based activities with fine motor components (e.g., board games with game pieces and squares to land on) and especially open-ended learning opportunities (e.g., exploring and sorting a shell collection) is especially important in building children's abilities and tolerance for fine motor activity.

—Teachers need to take gender into consideration; in general, girls at the kindergarten level have more facility at fine motor tasks than boys (Berk 2008). This should be a factor in the selection of materials for fine motor activities—for example, manipulatives can include not only beads for stringing but also small interlocking blocks for construction, and both boys and girls can be encouraged to engage with all materials.

Language and literacy

Listening, speaking, and understanding

Developmentally appropriate	In contrast
To enhance children's listening skills, teachers create regular opportunities for children to actively listen to and converse with others and work together in small groups on projects or problem solving. They provide opportunities for students to listen and respond to stories and information books, follow directions, and listen attentively to others during group discussions.	■ Teachers focus on getting children to listen only for classroom management purposes. ■ Teachers stress the need for children to pay attention to them, providing little or no opportunity for response and discussion. They value passive rather than active engagement.
Teachers provide opportunities for oral response to stories and information books. Children are encouraged to describe events, retell stories or parts of stories, and give simple directions to others.	■ Little attention is given to intentional focus on developing children's speaking abilities in various situations. Children are largely viewed as the passive recipients of information. ■ Focused, guided opportunities for response and interactive discussion are limited.
Teachers engage in conversations with both individual children and small groups. Whenever possible these are sustained conversations (with multiple conversational turns, complex ideas, and rich vocabulary) and include decontextualized speech (talk about children's experiences beyond the here and now).	■ Teachers mostly ask children questions that call for brief or simple responses rather than elaborated speech. ■ Conversations with children are limited to the current context ("I'd like to hear about your picture").

Developmentally appropriate	In contrast

Planning Curriculum to Achieve Important Goals (cont.)

Listening, speaking, and understanding (cont.)

Teachers attend to the particular language needs of English language learners and children who are behind in vocabulary and other aspects of language learning. They engage the child more frequently in sustained conversations and make extra efforts to help them comprehend.	■ Teachers talk mostly with verbally skilled children, neglecting the children who most need language help—children who are shy or hesitant, have communication difficulties, or are in the process of learning English. ■ When teachers talk to a child behind in language learning, they don't show the patience and attentiveness that the child requires in order to become a successful conversational partner.
Teachers support English language learners in their home language (e.g., by gathering books and tapes/CDs in each child's language, involving family members and other speakers of the language in various ways) as well as promoting their learning of English.	■ Teachers provide no support for children in maintaining their home language. ■ A policy (sometimes imposed from above) specifies that children and teachers use only English in the classroom.
Teachers help children use communication and language as tools for thinking and learning. For example, during group time teachers provide ways for every child to talk (e.g., talk to a peer, call out answers). Or teachers have children repeat aloud things they want to remember (e.g., "One plate, one spoon") or talk about what they will write before doing it.	■ During much of the day, children are expected to watch or be quiet. During group time teachers call on one child at a time to respond, making all the others wait, during which they disengage mentally or become disruptive.

Comments on listening, speaking, and understanding:

—Using *decontextualized language* requires children and adults to use more explanation and description. Further, children will have to rely on printed language alone when reading, and experience with decontextualized language provides valuable preparation.

—Young children's language development progresses most when they are actively engaged in verbal interaction and teachers encourage them to extend their comments. Because many children have ground to make up in vocabulary and other language skills and/or English fluency, teachers need to use approaches in which children are talked *to* less and talked *with* more.

Developmentally appropriate	In contrast

Planning Curriculum to Achieve Important Goals (cont.)

Book reading and motivation

Everyday, teachers read aloud to children, in both small and large groups when possible. Books are accessible in a library area and other places conducive to their enjoyment and use. There is a good variety of high-quality books (e.g., suitable for kindergartners and reflecting the gender, cultural, racial, and social diversity of the group; storybooks and information books; varying reading levels). Children can listen to audiobooks and follow along in the printed book.

▨ The classroom offers children only a small quantity and/or a limited variety of books.

▨ For the most part, books are kept out of reach (i.e., handled only by teachers or available only at children's request), and thus children cannot freely explore them.

Teachers provide multiple copies of familiar kindergarten-level texts. Children are encouraged to return to books that have been read aloud to them for independent "browsing." Special time is regularly set aside for independent reading of self-selected familiar texts.

▨ Books in the literacy center rarely change. Multiple copies of books are unavailable for individual reading or reading with a partner.

▨ Children are encouraged to read books on their own when time allows, but teachers do not set aside time for independent reading.

Teachers engage children in discussions about topics of interest and importance to them in books. Taking notes on individuals' comments and questions, teachers follow up on these in small groups or one-on-one.

▨ Teachers do most of the talking when books are discussed.

▨ When teachers ask questions, these are frequently at the recall level rather than at levels requiring children to make inferences, think critically, and express themselves through the use of new knowledge and vocabulary.

Comments on book reading and motivation:
—Fostering young children's interest in books and reading has an important positive influence on reading achievement. The more children read, the better they get at reading—and the more they want to read (Meiers 2004).

Phonological/phonemic awareness

Teachers introduce engaging oral language experiences (e.g., songs, poems, books, word games) that enhance kindergartners' phonological and phonemic awareness. Teachers assess and take into account where each child is in developing phonological awareness and tailor instruction accordingly.

▨ Teachers give little or no attention to promoting phonological or phonemic awareness. Or they fail to tailor learning experiences according to what children need to progress.

▨ Teachers spend too much time on structured phonemic awareness activities, continuing with such instruction even after children have mastered those particular skills.

Developmentally appropriate	In contrast

Planning Curriculum to Achieve Important Goals (cont.)

Phonological/phonemic awareness (cont.)

Teachers continue to build on children's demonstrated understandings of phonological/phonemic awareness. For example, teachers move from phoneme identity ("What sound is the same in *sit, sip,* and *sun*?") to phoneme categorization, or identifying the word in a set of words that has a different sound ("Which word doesn't belong: *doll, dish, toy*?").

■ Teachers do not build on a logical progression of phonological and phonemic skills and concepts.

■ Teachers do not differentiate instruction to give students extra support where needed and offer appropriate challenges to those who are ready to move on.

Comments on phonological/phonemic awareness:

—Research has shown that children's awareness and ability to manipulate the sounds of spoken words—specifically, their phonemic awareness—is a strong predictor of their later success in learning to read (National Reading Panel 2000). Because many children do not automatically acquire such awareness and because it is vital for further progress, teaching phonemic awareness is a key role of the kindergarten teacher.

Writing

Teachers encourage and assist children in their own efforts to write (using letters, words, drawings) for different purposes such as signs, letters, lists, journals, and records of observations.

■ "Writing" is limited to completing workbook pages.

Teachers give children frequent opportunities to draw and write about topics that interest them. Emphasis is placed on helping children share their ideas through written communication. Teachers display children's writing, even if there are errors, for the ideas and expression they demonstrate.

■ Written composition for the purpose of expressing ideas is limited. Teachers view writing primarily as handwriting practice and copying, and they stress correct form and legibility above expression and communication.

■ Teachers control access to writing materials, and children must request them. Children rarely have opportunities to write on their own.

Children are encouraged to use conventional spelling for common or familiar words and also to apply their developing knowledge of sound/letter correspondences to spell independently (i.e., developmental spelling).

■ Correct spelling is highly valued. Little is done to encourage children's applications of their knowledge of sound/letter relationships in conjunction with the development of conventional spelling.

Comments on writing:

—*Developmental spelling* refers to young children's attempts to use what they already know about letters and sounds to attempt to write words. Research indicates that encouraging developmental spelling promotes children's understanding of the relationship between letters and sounds (Templeton & Bear 1992). Research also finds that developmental spelling does not interfere with children later becoming accurate spellers.

Developmentally appropriate	In contrast

Planning Curriculum to Achieve Important Goals (cont.)

Letter, word, and print knowledge

Much of the environmental print in the classroom is generated by and with children. It is purposeful and used by children in functional ways. For example, children refer to lists of helpers' responsibilities and things to do as part of their daily routines. Teachers encourage them to return (independently) to and reread charts that were developed collectively by the group.

■ Purposeless print clutters the environment (e.g., labels on many familiar objects) to the extent that children tune the print out.

■ Print is scarce or not placed where children can readily see and refer to it.

Teachers use various strategies to help children recognize that the sequence of letters in written words represents the sequence of sounds in spoken words. During shared writing, teachers model and/or engage children in figuring out sound/letter relationships in order to spell words. They track the print from left to write to reinforce the sequence of sound/letter relationships and encourage children to take risks and apply what they know about sounds and letters to form words.

■ Teachers do not actively engage children in making connections between the sounds of spoken language and the letters that represent them.

■ Teachers spend too much time focusing on the connections between letters and sounds.

■ Teachers are unaware of individual children's knowledge of sound/letter relationships because they do not collect and analyze students' written work samples.

Comments on letter, word, and print knowledge:

—Some children enter kindergarten knowing letters and sounds, recognizing some words, and understanding a good deal about print; others have considerably less of this knowledge. Teachers need to find out where all children are in their literacy learning and then differentiate instruction to help each student make optimal progress.

—As noted in comments on **Writing**, encouraging developmental spelling promotes children's understanding of the relationship between letters and sounds.

Building knowledge and comprehension

To broaden children's knowledge and vocabulary, teachers use a variety of strategies such as reading stories and information books rich in new concepts, information, and vocabulary; planning field trips and inviting class visitors to tell children about their work or interests; and providing experiences through technology ("virtual field trips").

■ The books that teachers read to children cover a limited range of familiar topics and use mostly common, known words.

■ Teachers use materials and experiences primarily to entertain children or to occupy their time, thus overlooking many opportunities for learning.

Developmentally appropriate	In contrast

Planning Curriculum to Achieve Important Goals (cont.)

Building knowledge and comprehension (cont.)

Children are prompted to link content (in text or in class instruction and discussion) to their own background experience while expanding their knowledge base. Teachers use questions and prompts that require children to problem solve and use new vocabulary.

■ Teachers give little attention to helping children connect new words or concepts to what they already know.

To help students develop comprehension strategies and monitor their own understanding, teachers engage them in guided discussion when listening or reading. They ask children to make predictions about story events, retell or dramatize stories, and notice when text does not make sense.

■ Teachers' questioning during and after read-aloud activities is restricted to low-level, recall questions. They rarely ask children to give their opinions about an event or character in the story or to respond to open-ended questions.

■ Teacher follow-up to reading activities is largely confined to assigning worksheets.

Comments on building knowledge and comprehension:

—Children of diverse backgrounds, including English language learners, may have a difficult time grasping what they read or what is read to them, not simply because of the language barrier but because of their different life experiences. Teachers can help to bridge these gaps by becoming familiar with children's backgrounds and prior knowledge and drawing connections between these and the text or other classroom experiences.

—Children are better able to comprehend stories and other text when they are taught to make connections between what they know and what is being read to them. Children also learn vocabulary most effectively when teachers actively engage them in grasping word meanings (e.g., by explaining new words in everyday language, relating words to contexts and to other words children do know).

—Open-ended and "distancing" questions are most effective in promoting comprehension and vocabulary; these questions require children to think beyond the story and relate the events to something that happened to them in the past or might happen in the future.

Mathematics

Teachers recognize children's desire to make sense of their world through mathematics. They build on children's intuitive, informal notions and encounters relating to math, making a point to supply math language and procedures. In other words, teachers "mathematize" children's everyday encounters. For example, they help children learn and practice mathematics skills with block building, play with manipulatives, games, movement activities, and computers.

■ Teachers' own negative feelings about mathematics cause them to avoid teaching it.

■ The kindergarten day is marked by many missed opportunities for children to learn important mathematics content. Teachers fail to see the importance of introducing math concepts and infusing math vocabulary and methods into children's experiences (instead relying on what children may figure out on their own during play and other activities).

Developmentally appropriate	In contrast

Planning Curriculum to Achieve Important Goals (cont.)

Mathematics (cont.)

Every day, teachers provide focused math time that is interesting to children, using various instructional contexts (e.g., small-group, large-group, individual) and find opportunities to integrate mathematics learning with other curriculum areas.

- So much time is devoted to literacy instruction that planned mathematics experiences are given short shrift.
- Teachers teach math only to the whole group.

Because mathematics is a discipline in which mastering new concepts/skills requires having mastered earlier, foundational concepts/skills, the curriculum reflects a research-based progression of topics, and children gain an understanding of current concepts before they are moved on to a new topic.

- The mathematics curriculum covers too many content areas superficially or doesn't follow a logical sequence; thus, children do not have the opportunity to master the foundational concepts and skills needed.
- There is no organized mathematics curriculum.

Teachers build on children's current knowledge, making sure that children consolidate their understanding of a concept before moving ahead (e.g., children understand the link between number and quantity before moving on to addition or subtraction problems).

- Teachers move along in the curriculum, even when children do not understand what has been covered.
- Teachers spend too much time reviewing the same content over and over, boring children who have mastered it and are ready for new challenges.

Teachers use a variety of strategies to engage children in **reasoning**, **problem solving**, and **communicating** about mathematics (e.g., teachers talk about the problem, draw children into the process of investigating and solving it, and ask how they came up with their solutions).

- Teachers focus heavily on children getting "the right answer" to a problem. Instead of giving children time and guidance to assist their reasoning and problem solving, teachers tell children the answers or solve problems for them.
- Teachers stand back and leave children to solve problems on their own without any adult assistance or support, thus missing many opportunities to help children learn to think and reason mathematically.

The curriculum includes the major content areas of mathematics (NCTM 2006) and emphasizes the three that are most important for kindergartners: **number and operations**, **geometry**, and **measurement**. Teachers actively foster children's understanding of number and operations (representing, comparing, and ordering whole numbers; joining and separating sets). They engage children in thinking about and working with geometric/spatial relationships (describing shapes and space, ordering and comparing lengths of two objects).

- Teachers focus only on teaching children about numbers and counting.
- Teachers provide low-level, repetitive experiences, such as counting the days on the calendar or identifying common two-dimensional shapes (circle, triangle, square).

Developmentally appropriate	In contrast

Planning Curriculum to Achieve Important Goals (cont.)

Mathematics (cont.)

Comments on mathematics:

—Economically disadvantaged children tend to enter kindergarten significantly behind their middle-class peers in understanding basic number concepts such as the relationship between number and quantity. With very few exceptions, all children are capable of learning complex mathematics. However, children from more affluent homes have more opportunities to learn math (e.g., through playing board games or using manipulatives) in situations at home or in preschool where adults make connections between children's experiences and mathematical language and concepts. In kindergarten, math teaching that focuses on building understanding of foundational concepts and skills is essential, or children will fall further behind in later grades.

—Covering too many topics interferes with children's gaining deep understanding of the concepts and skills important to prepare them for next steps in the mathematics learning. Consequently, the National Council of Teachers of Mathematics (2006) indicates that although each grade's curriculum should include all the major content areas of mathematics, there should be certain areas of focus each year. The emphases indicated in the columns above are based on the NCTM work.

Science

Teachers focus on kindergarten children's natural curiosity to emphasize inquiry in science experiences. Children are encouraged to observe and to ask questions about the natural world and to think about what might happen during various scientific processes. Teachers provide materials and offer experiences that teach about important scientific concepts and skills.

The curriculum includes concepts not only from **life science/nature** but also from **physical science** (e.g., wheels, swings, levers) and **earth and space science** (e.g., sand and soil, the moon). Teachers use a variety of strategies to help children develop important scientific concepts and skills.

■ Teachers slight science under pressure to cover other subjects in the curriculum. Teachers may transmit factual information on scientific topics, but they do not engage children in "doing science."

■ The science curriculum is only about exploration, and children do not acquire foundational concepts and knowledge.

■ The curriculum is limited to one area of science or to a few isolated topics with which the teacher feels comfortable. Other areas receive scant attention, even when children ask questions and show interest in them.

Comments on science:

—Many kindergarten classrooms do not teach science in a meaningful, sustained way. Due to pressures such as the emphasis on literacy and math in accountability testing, science curriculum may be short changed. Even when science is integrated into the curriculum, kindergarten children often encounter only a limited range of topics (e.g., studying some aspects of the natural world but not physics). Further, for rich, in-depth learning experiences, children need opportunities for hands-on experimentation.

Developmentally appropriate	In contrast

Planning Curriculum to Achieve Important Goals (cont.)

Technology

Teachers make thoughtful use of computers and other technologies in the classroom, not to replace children's experience with objects and materials but to expand the range of tools with which children can seek information, solve problems, understand concepts (e.g., rotating or transforming geometric shapes onscreen to gain a better grasp of them), and move at their own pace. Software is selected to emphasize thinking and problem solving.

▉ Children spend a great deal of class time on computers and/or watching television or videos.

▉ Computer software is primarily devoted to drill or to games with only a recreational purpose. Use of computers is a privilege, allocated as a reward or taken away as a punishment.

▉ Teachers avoid use of computers and other technology in the classroom.

Teachers locate computers to foster shared learning and interaction—children talking about what they are doing, cooperating in solving problems, and helping one another. Teachers encourage children to use technology (e.g., cameras, video and audio recorders) to document their experiences and work. They invite children's exploration of the various operations and actions possible with the technology. Technology is used to document children's learning.

▉ Computers are located only in an area outside the main learning environment (e.g., in a computer lab), so children have limited access to them.

▉ Computers are in an accessible location, but children are never given the opportunity to work with partners or a small team on computer activities. Or due to a lack of equipment, children are always required to work in at the computer with three or four peers (and consequently never gain individual experience with the technology).

▉ Teachers do not adjust use of technology for children's different comfort levels and abilities (e.g., a math game is set at the same level for everyone). Children must progress at a single pace, even if some children struggle to keep up and some are bored and ready for the next thing.

The program provides enough equipment that a child can become engaged in technology-based activities in a sustained, deep way. Boys and girls have equal access and opportunity to use technology.

▉ The school doesn't provide any technology, or provides so little that children get only very brief turns using a piece of equipment in order to allow everyone to have a chance. Boys dominate use of computers.

Developmentally appropriate	In contrast

Planning Curriculum to Achieve Important Goals (cont.)

Social competence; social studies

Kindergarten social studies curriculum is organized into broad topics of study. The content connects to children's lives, and study is integrated with other learning domains.

■ Teachers may convey facts relating to social studies, but the information is too remote from children's experience or too fragmented to be meaningful and interesting to them.

■ Rather than integrating learning experiences, teachers address each social studies standard individually with a separate activity or experience, and/or they separate social studies from other curriculum areas.

Teachers introduce projects and/or units that include basic aspects of geography, history, and civics/political science, and they draw connections between social studies knowledge and methods and everyday situations and events (e.g., having children vote on a decision such as the name of the class newsletter they produce together).

■ Teachers do not provide experiences that introduce children to basic concepts and ideas foundational for later learning in social studies. Or they lecture children on topics (e.g., values and ideals of civic engagement) without discussion and room for comment or disagreement.

Teachers actively foster children's understanding of democratic processes and attitudes in concrete, experiential ways that children are able to understand, such as making and discussing rules, solving together the problems that arise in the classroom community, and learning to listen to others' ideas and perspectives. When possible, children are involved in conflict resolution in the classroom through such vehicles as class meetings.

■ Teachers are the only decision makers in the classroom; they do not engage children in sharing ideas and solving their problems together. Children are never involved in conflict resolution or group decision making.

■ Teachers attempt to teach about democracy but in ways that are too abstract for young children to relate to (e.g., discussing the different branches of government).

Comments on social competence and social studies:

—Children have a wide variety of life experience before entering kindergarten. While many have attended preschool, the type and quality of programs range widely; many children have no experience in educational group settings whatsoever. At the beginning of the year, some children will find merely sitting in a group and listening to others a challenge. As the year progresses, teachers' thoughtful planning to bolster children's social competence is interwoven with the social studies curriculum.

—Social studies appears in this section with social competence because up through the early grades, important aspects of the social studies curriculum are taught and learned through the everyday events of the classroom. For example, teachers foster kindergartners' abilities to participate in group decision making, establish rules and consequences, express opinions in a group setting, collaborate with others, and respect the rights of others in the classroom.

Developmentally appropriate	In contrast

Planning Curriculum to Achieve Important Goals (cont.)

Creative arts

Creative/aesthetic development

Classroom teachers (on their own or working with specialists) help children explore and work with various art and music media and techniques. Teachers convey an open, adventurous attitude toward the arts ("How about trying this?") that encourages children to explore available media and try new approaches and movements. The arts are integrated with other areas of the curriculum.

■ Art and music are taught as separate subjects once a week or less, and specialists do not coordinate closely with classroom teachers.

■ Teachers spend time preparing children for special performances or exhibits for families or the public rather than supporting children's active participation in the arts for the sake of their own creative expression, knowledge, and appreciation.

Teachers display children's art, as well as the work of artists, in the classroom and elsewhere in the program setting. Children have opportunities to experience music, art, and dance in the community.

■ Teachers emphasize the finished product or performance and single out for praise those children who are particularly gifted or trained in one of the arts.

■ The music and art in the environment reflect the teachers' own culture(s) and tastes but do not include the arts of the local community or the backgrounds of the children and their families.

■ The environment is heavily decorated with depictions of commercial media characters or other simplified, cartoon-like images.

Comments on creative/aesthetic development:
—Creativity and creative expression are not limited to the arts, but the arts are an excellent venue for fostering new ways of thinking. Kindergarten children love to explore with a wide variety of materials; when teachers include means for creative expression throughout the curriculum, children's interest in the subject matter is heightened. At the same time, teachers need to recognize that arts activities themselves fulfill important learning goals and have intrinsic value.

Developmentally Appropriate Practice, 3d Edition

Developmentally appropriate	In contrast

Planning Curriculum to Achieve Important Goals (cont.)

Visual arts

Classroom teachers or specialized art teachers make available a wide variety of art media for children to explore and work with. They talk with children about their art. Teachers have children revisit projects and media, giving them opportunities to revise and expand their ideas and refine their skills.

■ Art materials are available, but children are not supported in moving beyond the exploration level.

■ Teachers introduce only the few art media and methods that they enjoy or know.

Teachers demonstrate new techniques or uses of materials to expand what children can do with them. When demonstrating techniques, teachers present information appropriate to children's developmental level (e.g., kindergartners are shown how black and white pastels can make gray but aren't expected to use shading in their pictures).

■ Children are allowed to use materials only under tightly controlled conditions. Or children have no conditions imposed on their artistic expression, as teachers believe this limits creativity; the result is a chaotic classroom in which children do not learn useful techniques.

Teachers do not provide a model that they expect children to copy.

■ Teachers provide a model and/or expect children to follow specific directions resulting in similar products. Emphasis is on group-copied crafts rather than individual artistic creations, and artworks are produced primarily to be pleasing to adults.

Comments on visual arts:

—In how they depict objects, people, relationships, and emotions on the page, children reveal their thoughts and feelings. Listening to what they have to say about their art can give teachers special insight. They often can describe their creations verbally in far greater complexity ("This is my sister, who has brown hair and laughs a lot") than they are able to achieve in their drawings.

—Teachers promote creative expression when they offer open-ended art experiences, in which children use their imaginations, for example, to consider a familiar story ("What do you suppose the Cat in the Hat's own house looks like?") (Jalongo & Isenberg 2006).

Developmentally appropriate	In contrast

Planning Curriculum to Achieve Important Goals (cont.)

Music and movement

Teachers have a repertoire of songs to sing with children, who are mastering recall of both melody and lyrics. These include songs with predictable melodies and lyrics, as children enjoy repetition, and such songs give them opportunities to learn about pitch, rhythm, and melody.

Teachers provide musical instruments for children to use. Songs and instruments from various cultures, especially those of the children in the group, are included.

■ Teachers rarely return to a song or dance once they have shared it with children, so children are unable to build up a repertoire of familiar music. Teachers do not introduce repetitive songs, and they do not sing with the children.

Whether or not there are specialist teachers for music, it is integrated with other areas of the curriculum, such as literacy (e.g., for teaching new vocabulary or phonological awareness) and mathematics (e.g., for counting beats or building spatial awareness).

■ Music is not integrated with other curriculum areas.

The joy of music is central in the experiences teachers share with children. In ways that don't interrupt that enjoyment, teachers highlight elements such as pitch, duration, tempo, and volume and engage children in varying and exploring these elements.

■ Teachers approach music in a didactic way, teaching specific terms and elements but not giving children integrated, enjoyable experiences in music.

■ Teachers have a "performance orientation" and tend to single out those children most clearly gifted or trained in singing, dancing, or playing instruments and criticize or ignore the creative efforts of the other children. Teachers focus on performances to the exclusion of other musical curriculum.

Teachers introduce movement activities that engage kindergartners in recognizing and following rhythms. They give children opportunities to incorporate movement with music, both in responding to recorded music and in independent creation of music. Teachers encourage children to engage in full-body activities that require rhythm and timing (e.g., swinging).

■ Opportunities for moving to music are limited to clapping and other hand movements, which children can do while sitting. Teachers do not get up and move with children.

Comments on music and movement:
—Kindergartners enjoy call-and-response and echo songs. They can follow melodies and are able to grasp concepts such as higher or lower pitch, duration of sound, or tempo. Around age 5 or 6, children are learning to do two things at once, such as marching in a circle while playing a rhythmic instrument. Such music and movement experiences are also an important part of children's oral language learning, as they contribute to children's ability to separate syllables and analyze sounds.

Developmentally Appropriate Practice, 3d Edition

Developmentally appropriate	In contrast

Assessing Children's Development and Learning

Strategic and purposeful

Assessment is done for four specific, beneficial purposes: planning and adapting curriculum to meet each child's developmental and learning needs, helping teachers and families monitor children's progress, evaluating and improving teaching effectiveness, and screening and diagnosis of children with disabilities or special learning or developmental needs.

- ▦ No systematic assessments of children's progress or achievements are done.

- ▦ Assessments are done, but results are not used to provide information about children's degrees of understanding or to adapt curriculum to meet their needs. Doing the assessment takes an excessive amount of teachers' time and attention away from interacting with children.

- ▦ Single-test assessment is used for high-stakes decision making (e.g., entry, special education referral).

Teachers use assessments in identifying children who might have a learning or developmental problem (in screening), typically at the beginning of the kindergarten year. When assessment identifies the possibility of a special need, appropriate referral to a specialist for diagnostic follow-up or other intervention occurs.

- ▦ Developmental screening does not occur, or it (and the post-screening follow-up) occurs so late in the year that children go for months without receiving needed intervention or support.

- ▦ Teachers diagnose or label a child after only a screening or one-time assessment. Test results are used to group or label children (e.g., as "unready" or "special needs").

Decisions that will have a major impact on children (e.g., entry, grouping, retention) are based on multiple sources of information. Sources include observations by teachers and specialists and also information from parents.

- ▦ Eligible-age children are denied entry to kindergarten based on a one-time readiness or achievement test—that is, a test measuring what the child already knows and can do.

- ▦ Overemphasis on assessing "readiness" or "achievement" causes some families to hold their kindergarten-age child out of school an extra year (red-shirting).

- ▦ Children are judged on the basis of inappropriate and inflexible expectations for their academic, social, or self-help abilities (e.g., whether they can write their name or go all day without a nap).

Developmentally appropriate	In contrast

Assessing Children's Development and Learning (cont.)

Strategic and purposeful (cont.)

Kindergarten assessment addresses key goals in all developmental domains (physical, social, emotional, cognitive) and in the areas of physical education and health, language and literacy, mathematics, science, social studies, and creative arts.

■ Programs and teachers don't think about which goals are important in each domain/area or how concepts and skills build on one another, so their assessments look at a limited set of skills in isolation.

■ Assessment focuses on certain domains/areas (e.g., math and literacy) and not others, ignoring important disciplines such as science, social studies, and social-emotional skills.

Comments on strategic and purposeful assessment:

—When a "readiness test" is an assessment of what sort of kindergarten experiences children are ready for and the results inform practice, then such a test can be both useful and appropriate (Gullo 2006a). Such assessments of children prior to kindergarten can play a useful role in helping teachers to plan kindergarten programming for the group and/or for individual children.

—Using a test to determine whether children are "ready" for kindergarten is inappropriate and can lead to detrimental decisions such as denial to kindergarten, required attendance in "developmental" instead of "regular" kindergarten, and retention in kindergarten or required attendance in a transitional year before first grade (Gullo 1994).

—Delaying children's kindergarten entry does not seem to help children and may actually be detrimental (Mehaffie & McCall 2002).

Systematic and ongoing

There is an assessment plan that is clearly written, well-organized, complete, comprehensive, and well-understood by administrators, teachers, and families.

■ No plan for assessment exists.

■ The plan for assessment is not shared with or is not understood by the teachers who must execute it or the families whose kindergartners are assessed.

Regular health and developmental screenings are done by appropriate personnel to identify children who may need more in-depth, diagnostic assessment (e.g., vision and hearing screening upon kindergarten entry). Disabilities or other specific concerns not apparent at younger ages are a particular focus.

■ Screenings are not frequent enough in view of children's rapid growth and development as kindergartners.

■ When a child appears to be having difficulty (i.e., is outside the typical performance range), no individual assessment is done.

■ Teachers make diagnoses that should be done by specialists.

| Developmentally appropriate | In contrast |

Assessing Children's Development and Learning (cont.)

Systematic and ongoing (cont.)

Developmentally appropriate	In contrast
Information is collected at regular intervals throughout the year.	■ Assessments are rare and/or random. ■ Children's performance is assessed at the end of the year, when it's too late to affect learning outcomes.
Teachers have the time, training, and materials they need to do assessment properly and accurately.	■ Teachers are burdened with assessment requirements but not provided with adequate tools or appropriate professional development to use them accurately. Thus, assessing is a waste of teachers' and children's time and is likely to give misleading results.

Integrated with teaching and curriculum

Developmentally appropriate	In contrast
Assessment is consistent with the developmental and learning goals identified for children and expressed in the kindergarten curriculum.	■ Assessments look at goals not in the curriculum or content not taught to the children. ■ Assessments narrow and/or distort the curriculum (e.g., assessing in kindergarten only what will later be tested for accountability purposes).
Teachers use assessment to refine how they plan and implement activities. Teachers develop short- and long-range plans for each child and the group based on children's knowledge and skills, interests, and other factors.	■ There is no accountability for what children are doing and little focus on supporting their learning and development.
Teachers assess children on an ongoing basis (i.e., observe, ask, listen in, check). They collect and later reflect on documentation of children's learning and development, including written notes, photographs, recordings, and work samples. They use this information both in shaping their teaching moment by moment and in planning learning experiences.	■ Teachers don't determine where each child is in learning a new skill or concept, so they give every child the same learning experiences as every other child. ■ Assessment results (observation notes, work samples, etc.) go straight into a folder and are filed away. They are not reflected on to inform teachers how to help or challenge individual children.
Information about each child's learning and development is used to evaluate teaching effectiveness. This may lead to changes in schedule, curriculum and teaching strategies, room set up, resources, and so on.	■ Assessment results show that problems exist but do not indicate what needs to be changed. Or nothing changes because "that's how we've always done it" or it would be expensive or inconvenient for the school and/or teachers.

Developmentally appropriate	In contrast

Assessing Children's Development and Learning (cont.)

Integrated with teaching and curriculum (cont.)

Teachers look at what each child can do independently but also assess collaborative work with peers and adults. Teachers assess as the child participates in groups and during other scaffolded situations.

■ Children are assessed only as individuals. Thus, teachers miss information about what children can do as members of a group or what tasks are just beyond their current capabilities and would benefit from adult support.

Comments on assessment integrated with teaching and curriculum:
—As much as possible, assessment should be woven into the act of teaching and interacting with children. However, there are times when the teacher needs to set up a special situation (e.g., clinical interview, structured task) designed to reveal a child's specific skill or understanding to get a fuller, more accurate picture of the child's thinking and abilities.

Valid and reliable

Assessments are used only for acceptable purposes, where research has demonstrated they yield valid and reliable information among children of similar ages, cultures, home languages, and so on.

Only assessments demonstrated to be valid and reliable for identifying, diagnosing, and planning for children with special needs or disabilities are used for that purpose.

■ The school uses tests or other measures for which inadequate evidence of validity and reliability exists for the population assessed or for some segment(s) of that population.

Assessments include teachers' observations of what children say and do during center time, play, projects, discussions, movement games, and other learning experiences, as well samples of students' work and performance during teacher-guided tasks (e.g., categorizing words by their phonemes).

■ Teachers use methods not suited to kindergarten children (e.g., paper-and-pencil tests).

Assessments are matched to the ages, development, and backgrounds of the specific children. Methods include accommodations for children with disabilities.

Teachers use a variety of methods/tools, recognize individual variation among learners, and allow children to demonstrate their competence in different ways. They help children begin to reflect on their own learning.

■ Assessment assumes background knowledge that some or all of the children don't have. Methods prevent a child from demonstrating what he actually knows and is able to do (e.g., assessing addition with only a paper-and-pencil test when some children could accurately solve the problems with manipulatives).

Developmentally appropriate	In contrast

Assessing Children's Development and Learning (cont.)

Valid and reliable (cont.)

Teachers gather information from families about children's health and development, including the skills, knowledge, and interests that children show at home.

■ Families are not considered a valid source of information.

Comments on valid and reliable assessment:
—Today's kindergartners are highly diverse, with an increasing number of English language learners. In order to properly assess this population, assessment measures must take linguistic background into account and be free from cultural bias (NAEYC 2005b). Using a variety of approaches to assessment is especially important with such children, as some indicators and sources of information may reveal more of a child's skills and abilities than others.

Communicated and shared

Teachers and families share information in ways that are clear, respectful, and constructive. Teachers and families make decisions together regarding learning goals and approaches to learning that are suitable for the individual child. Families are regularly informed about how their children are doing in all developmental domains.

■ Families are not kept informed about assessment results and children's progress. Teachers/ programs make important decisions unilaterally.

■ Schools provide families with information in ways that are not respectful or useful to them (e.g., written in educational jargon).

Within the limits of appropriate confidentiality policies, teachers exchange information about each child across ages/grades (e.g., kindergarten teachers with first grade teachers) and across areas (e.g., regular classroom teachers with "specials" teachers), so children are prepared for the next challenge and the next teacher knows each child's history.

■ Assessment information is not used to help ease transitions for children from one classroom and teacher to another.

Developmentally appropriate	In contrast
Establishing Reciprocal Relationships with Families	

Teachers, administrators, and school staff work to foster supportive relationships with families throughout the school year. Teachers solicit parents' knowledge about their children and input about their goals and concerns, and they use this information in ongoing assessment, evaluation, and planning. Families are offered venues for communication with teachers, such as e-mail, a notebook that travels between home and school each day, and parent conferences.

■ Teachers and staff discount families' input, viewing them as of secondary importance in their children's education. Family members feel intimidated by teachers and by school policies, which makes them reluctant to become involved in school matters.

Teachers listen to parents, respecting differences in culture and goals while guiding families to participate in formal school procedures. When problems arise that necessitate communication with home, teachers see families as partners in finding solutions rather than obstacles. Teachers view children's education as a joint responsibility between parents and teachers.

■ Teachers view parental noninvolvement in school affairs as evidence that families do not care about their children's education, rather than taking into account cultural and linguistic differences or factors such as job schedules. When children have problems in the classroom, teachers assume that the home environment must be to blame.

■ Communication with parents is used mainly to convey negative news.

■ The administration and teachers are too quick to accommodate parents' requests, even when these run counter to what is best for the child.

Families are welcome to visit the classroom as arranged with teachers, and they are encouraged to do so. Family members are offered opportunities to participate through various means, such as volunteering or observing in the classroom, accompanying children on field trips, and attending school events. Parents' work schedules are accommodated to the extent possible when planning events, conferences, and activities.

■ Families are not welcome in the school and parents are not encouraged to visit. Teachers are difficult to contact directly, and families are dissuaded from participating by a bureaucratic school culture.

■ Opportunities for parent participation, teacher-parent conferences, meetings, and other events for families occur only on rigid schedules. Conferences and meetings are held only during the day when many employed parents are unavailable.

Developmentally appropriate	In contrast

Establishing Reciprocal Relationships with Families (cont.)

With parents who do not speak English, teachers/administrators seek strategies to facilitate communication, such as hiring bilingual staff or using translators at conferences or meetings.

■ Teachers and school staff take no action to enable families with limited English proficiency to understand written or spoken communications directed to them or to ask questions and convey any concerns they may have regarding their child or the program. Written communications are never translated. Families and children are penalized for incomplete or missing forms though families cannot complete them due to language barriers.

■ Because of the challenges and potential awkwardness that may arise in meetings and other communication with family members who speak little or no English, teachers and school staff avoid having meetings, conferences, and other planned events with families.

Comments on establishing reciprocal relationships with families:

—Kindergarten teachers have a special opportunity and responsibility to establish positive, supportive school-family relationships at the outset of children's formal school experience. The quality of interaction between a child's kindergarten teacher and family helps to form a family's overall connection with school.

—Some cultures give teachers absolute authority over a child's education. When working with families from such cultures, teachers will need to let the relationship evolve gradually until those families become comfortable partnering with teachers.

the
primary
grades

Developmentally Appropriate Practice in
the Primary Grades—Ages 6–8

An Overview

Heather Biggar Tomlinson

The early grades are a time for children to shine—they gain increasing mastery in every area of their development and learning. They explore, read, reason, problem solve, communicate through conversation and writing, and develop lasting friendships. They delight in their new intellectual prowess, social skills, and physical abilities. When all goes well, teachers can take advantage of the fit between developmentally appropriate classroom practice and primary grade goals to instill in children a lifelong love of learning.

Primary grade children benefit when teachers focus on each child holistically. Children prosper with warm and sensitive teaching; integrated learning; ongoing, authentic assessment; a blend of child-guided and teacher-guided activities; and the strong support and involvement of their families. They look for ways to apply their enhanced reasoning, problem-solving, and other cognitive skills. They are increasingly aware of how they compare with peers and care a great deal about social approval. Activities that create strong, positive emotional connections—such as cooperative, process-oriented projects—enhance their learning. Similarly, they find learning experiences that build on their interests and engage them (e.g., role-playing) more meaningful, complex, and memorable (Sylvester 1995; Hyson 2008).

As with younger children, progress in one domain of development continues to influence and be influenced by progress in other domains; that is, development and learning do not occur in neat compartments. Children at this age learn best and achieve optimally when the curriculum is intellectually challenging and also emphasizes positive relationships between teachers and children and, of course, students' engagement in the learning experiences (Myers & Pianta 2008).

One of the most important goals for this age group is developing an enthusiasm for learning. During the primary grades, it is essential for children to learn to read, but it is equally important for them to develop the *desire* to read. Similarly, it is as important for children to be *motivated* to solve mathematics

problems as it is for them to learn how to add and subtract or measure with a ruler. Teachers build children's motivation when they show they care about each child's needs and interests, demonstrate genuine enthusiasm for the subject at hand, and capitalize on teachable moments within the planned curriculum.

Unfortunately, as teachers know, things do not always go well for children in school. Even children who emerge from preschool and kindergarten as very enthusiastic learners sometimes lose interest or become frustrated during their primary years. In the primary grades, children encounter learning tasks that are more difficult and require greater persistence and effort than those they have previously faced. In addition, as children begin to more accurately compare their performance with their peers', they may see themselves as lacking in one or more domains. Teachers need to create many opportunities for primary grade children to experience success, because this age group can become easily discouraged.

Threats to children's motivation and progress at this age include overemphasis on mastery of some skills (usually reading or mathematics) and excessive practice of already mastered skills, both of which dampen children's enthusiasm and motivation to use the knowledge and skills they have previously acquired (Hyson 2008). Children younger than 8 or 9 are still learning in uneven and episodic ways and cannot always perform on demand; that is, while they may demonstrate new knowledge or a new skill one day, they may not be able to show it on demand the next day and may react negatively if pressured. In addition, learning experiences in which children are passive (at the expense of engaged, direct-experience learning) tend to yield rote memorization rather than real gains in concept development, problem-solving abilities, complex thinking skills, and real-world application of new knowledge (NEGP 1997).

If children show signs of discouragement or disengagement or if they give up when faced with challenging tasks, teachers need to respond—by intentionally planning experiences to build or reignite children's positive approaches to learning. Children are more likely to regain their earlier enthusiasm and engagement if teachers tap into each child's interests, encourage children to persist, support them as they try new academic tasks, teach them to plan ahead, demonstrate different ways of solving problems, and build the kind of relationship with them that helps young learners feel secure (Hyson 2008).

Teacher challenges and pressures. Primary grade teachers may face particular challenges because of the pressures on them to narrow achievement gaps and improve the academic performance of all children. Mandatory proficiency testing in language arts and mathematics, the results of which reflect on teachers and schools as well as children, begins in the third grade in the United States and has led to roughly one-third less instructional time spent on learning in other disciplines (Center on Education Policy 2008).

Primary grade classrooms typically are part of larger institutions and complex educational systems with many levels of administration and supervision. Those responsible for planning and implementing curriculum include principals, curriculum supervisors, superintendents, and local and state school boards. Thus, primary grade teachers may have little control over the curriculum or policies they are expected to carry out. Because of the accountability pressures, school boards or administrators may require teachers to use a curriculum that is narrowly focused on the specific areas to be tested. Incorporating developmentally appropriate practices that promote children's overall development and learning, rather than simply teaching test material, can be a real challenge in the present environment (Rushton & Juola-Rushton 2008).

Even when teachers understand the importance of using a balanced approach to literacy and mathematics instruction, they may not get the administrative support to do so (Snider & Roehl 2007). For example, often teachers are not afforded the time and resources to participate

in the ongoing professional development experiences they need to stay current on best practices (Nielsen, Barry, & Staab 2008).

Using focused instruction within an integrated curriculum. Regardless of the challenges, teachers have an obligation to implement best practices with the children they serve. Best practices for children in first, second, and third grades include balancing children's need for focused instruction about a specific subject area or concept with children's need to build on what they already know and to make connections between concepts and domains of learning—that is, to experience an integrated curriculum.

To respond to the pressure to cover the curriculum, primary grade teachers may try to fit everything in by tightly scheduling blocks of time for each subject. But this approach grows out of a misguided, adult-imposed scheme, rather than from the way young children learn and construct their understandings. Primary grade children do not distinguish learning by subject area ("Now I'm learning a math concept," "Now I'm building my vocabulary"). In fact, the brains of children in this age span are *looking* for meaningful connections when presented with new information (Bransford, Brown, & Cocking 2003).

Still, scheduling blocks of time—to study in depth a new concept or skill within an integrated curricular framework—is necessary and productive. Even more so than in kindergarten, children in the primary grades are eager for and need explanations; expository information; direct instruction about a new concept, word, or event; and opportunity to practice a new skill. Having time to focus on a subject helps children learn about and describe the world, structure their knowledge of the world, test assumptions, and solve problems (Bredekamp & Rosegrant 1992). By setting aside time for focused instruction to work on specific new knowledge and skills, teachers enable children to add to and deepen their budding understandings and abilities (Beck & McKeown 2007; Wahlstrom & Louis 2008).

Whatever they are studying, children at this age learn best through concrete experiences;

they need to see connections, and they seek coherence and relevance across domains. When teachers encourage children to build connections across disciplines, they simultaneously foster intellectual growth, social connection, and a joy in learning, making progress deeper and more extensive. An integrated curriculum taps children's interests and senses while enhancing learning across all domains. The purpose of integrating content is not only to make school more enjoyable and interesting, which promotes enthusiasm and a love of learning; it also is to support children's ability to connect new learning to prior knowledge, which has the effect of expanding children's memory and reasoning capacity (Bredekamp & Rosegrant 1995; Hyson 2008).

Integration of curriculum is accomplished in several ways. The teacher may plan a project around a topic of interest to the children that relates to learning goals, addressing them through periods of focused instruction as well as child-selected activity. For example, children may be interested in the ocean because they live near it; depending on instructional goals, teachers can use this topic to advance language and literacy, math, science, social studies, and artistic and music skills.

By participating in cooperative projects and presentations describing what they have learned, children develop social and emotional skills. A focused topic also provides rich opportunities for dramatization, which can enrich language and self-regulation. Children might even create a "published" version of their work by printing and binding a report, promoting fine motor skills. Such a project requires children's sustained effort and involvement over many days and perhaps weeks. Whatever the project or activity, when children have the opportunity to study or focus on a specific new concept in some depth and then to apply what they have learned, they make gains in every domain, from language to science to emotional development (AAAS 2008; Hyson 2008; Spada & Lightbown 2008).

The rest of this chapter describes major aspects of development and learning that occur

from ages 6 to 8 and the implications for teaching. Of course, such a brief summary can only scratch the surface. The necessity of leaving much out is even more striking for the primary grades than for the other age group chapters. Space does not allow explaining with any depth how to teach children to read, write, learn about whole numbers or fractions, understand melting and freezing, or acquire myriad other important primary skills and concepts, much less distinguishing how different teaching should look across first, second, and third grade. Books on these topics fill libraries.

Rather, the aim of this overview is to summarize in very broad terms what is known about primary grade children's development and learning and to offer implications of this knowledge for curriculum and teaching strategies during school's earliest years.

Physical development

Physical health and well-being is foundational to learning across all other domains; children need, at a minimum, adequate shelter, nutrition, sleep, and exercise to concentrate, learn, and interact well with others. During the early school years, children enjoy becoming even more independent and confident as they refine their motor skills and become more adept physically. With teaching and opportunity to practice, they can learn to ride a bike, jump rope, play a sport or an instrument, write, swim, and rollerblade.

Although the rate of children's physical growth is slower than during the previous five years of life, development is relatively steady—with occasional growth spurts. At this age, children have improved use of all their different body parts, which allows for better gross and

© Ellen B. Senisi

Developmentally Appropriate Practice, 3d Edition

fine motor skills, and they are more aware of their body positions and movements.

Overall growth and physical maturation

On average, children grow two to three inches and gain three to five pounds per year during this phase of development. The average 6-year-old in the United States weighs about 45 pounds and is just over 3½ feet tall (Craig & Baucum 2002).

That said, considerable variation exists. Measurements of 8-year-olds around the world show a range of nine inches in height between the shortest and tallest children (Ruff 2002), and in the United States, school age children are evidence of that diversity. Furthermore, environmental factors throughout a child's life will have played an important role in a child's growth: Access to nutritious foods and adequate activity and exercise interact with genetics to determine growth rates. For most of this age span, boys and girls are of relatively equal size and strength; by age 8, some girls might experience a preadolescent growth spurt and overtake boys in size, although probably not in strength.

Much of children's growth during these years occurs in the extremities and in the face, which elongates to accommodate permanent teeth. The presence or absence of front teeth becomes a social and developmental milestone. Six-year-olds are often missing their two front teeth, and by age 8, in spite of some facial elongation, many children have front teeth that seem too big for their face. The body lengthens and broadens as bones grow longer, contributing to the elongation of the extremities, which can make children appear leggy.

Muscle mass also increases in both boys and girls, but they are by no means physically mature in terms of skeletal and ligament development.

During these years, there is a growth spurt of the brain. By age 8, the brain is about 90 percent of its adult size, and head growth slows. The surface area of the frontal lobes of the cortex, which control thought and emotion, increases somewhat as neurons continue to branch out and become more efficient. The functions and structures of the two halves of the brain—working together and as well as separately—have become more consolidated (Nelson 2002).

By about age 6, binocular vision—the ability of the eyes to work together—is usually well established, aiding children's participation in reading and closer-focus work. They have improved ability to track from left to right, for example. However, many children experience nearsightedness or farsightedness at this age (teachers may notice a child covering or closing one eye), so large print is still necessary (Craig & Baucum 2002; Wood 2007).

Health and fitness

The noticeable but incomplete physical gains in terms of height, muscle mass, and use of the body intersect with primary grade children's inclination to try new and increasingly challenging physical activities, leaving them prone to accidents and injury.

On the other hand, primary grade children generally experience better health—fewer infections and illnesses such as colds, stomachaches, and ear infections—than preschoolers and kindergartners (Starfield 1992). By the primary grade years, most children have developed fairly good immunity because of previous exposures. Of course, environmental conditions, nutrition, and other individual factors such as allergies or other chronic illnesses play a big role in children's health, too.

Children at this age living in poverty continue to be at higher risk for a number of health problems—from environmental factors such as exposure to lead-based paints; poor-quality medical care; or inadequate shelter, hygiene, or nutrition. These health factors negatively affect all domains of development; for example, when basic nutritional needs are not met, children are less able to concentrate and their performance in school suffers (Yu & Hannum 2007).

American children are increasingly at risk physically because of the growing and historic prevalence of childhood obesity. In 2003, almost 20 percent of children ages 6–11 were overweight, representing a fourfold increase since

the 1960s (Craig & Baucum 2002; Land 2008). Being overweight in childhood predicts obesity in adulthood, and it contributes to heart disease, high blood pressure, childhood diabetes, and other physical ailments—and as a result, in certain cultural contexts, children can suffer teasing, embarrassment, and unhappiness. Children who experience healthy, nutritious diets and regular physical activity that promotes flexibility, muscle endurance and strength, and cardiovascular fitness are less at risk for obesity. They are more likely to experience healthy functioning of the heart, lungs, muscles, and blood vessels (Craig & Baucum 2002).

Gross motor development

Before the primary grades, children's major gross motor (locomotive) skills, such as running and jumping, are generally well established. When they enter the primary grade ages, they refine these skills, becoming more purposeful and controlled in their movements. They have greater coordination of their bodies in space, such as with balance tasks, and learn to sequence a series of movement skills; for example, they can learn to do a cartwheel or learn the steps to a relatively simple dance (Mayesky 2002).

Younger primary grade children still have a fairly slow reaction time, but their reaction time and accuracy improve over these years, allowing them to become more competent at skills such as throwing and catching a ball, which should be at a mature phase by age 7 (Pica 2004). At age 7, most boys can throw a ball about 34 feet, and by age 10, can throw it twice as far. (Hand-eye and foot-eye coordination are not fully developed until age 9 or 10.)

Boys tend to throw farther than girls, but research shows that this difference is dependent on opportunities to practice (Williams, Haywood, & Painter 1996). In fact, on average, girls are slightly ahead of boys physiologically in this age range—but gender differences in motor skills are mostly insignificant, with boys and girls developing at a similar pace given similar opportunities (Craig & Baucum 2002; Pica 2004). Their interests are similar at the beginning of the age range but begin to diverge by age 8 or so (Pica 2004).

Most children in the primary grades are delighted by their improving skills, independence, and abilities, and this delight often translates into physical risk taking. They have fun climbing trees, rollerblading down a hill, or using a log to cross a stream. They become more interested in active team sports such as kickball and soccer, since they not only have better physical coordination and endurance but also the more sophisticated cognitive and social awareness that allows for cooperation and following rules. However, they tend to be unaware of the dangers they may solicit by their daredevil behavior, even more so because their bones, muscles, and ligaments are still not mature, leaving them more vulnerable to injury.

Because of their high need for movement at this age, some children, especially boys, may become more fatigued by long periods of sitting than by active motion such as running or bicycling. First-graders will still tire quickly, but they also tend to recover quickly (Pica 2004).

Individual differences in children's approaches to physical activity are evident at this age, and children become more aware of how their skills compare with their peers'. As a result, some children may decide that they are not athletic and cease to try to do well in physical activities, which has further negative effects on their physical development.

Fine motor development

Depending on prior opportunities, children may enter the primary grades with reasonably developed fine motor skills. During the primary grades, children practice and refine their fine motor development, and they become more capable of doing fine motor work without the neurological fatigue that younger children often experience. Noticeably, children's writing and drawing skills become more controlled and precise. Considerable individual variation exists, however; it is not abnormal for a child to be unable to draw, say, a recognizable diamond shape until about age 8 (Craig & Baucum

2002). Overall, during this time, girls are ahead of boys in this area of development (Haywood & Getchell 2005). By age 7 or 8, some children, especially those who have had considerable practice, are capable of creating products that rival work done by adults in intricate, detailed tasks such as sewing or origami.

Promoting physical development in the primary grades

Although primary grade children gain greater control over their bodies and can sit for longer time periods, they nevertheless have lots of energy, are far from mature physically, and need to be active. Movement activities are just as important in the primary grades as they are in the earlier years (Pica 2004). Physical action is essential not only to refine developing skills—such as batting a ball, skipping rope, or balancing on a beam—but also to keep up children's energy levels. Movement promotes critical thinking skills, verbal and communication skills, and problem-solving abilities (Pica 2004) and enhances self-confidence.

Ideally, primary grade children experience daily movement activities with their classroom teacher and receive regular instruction and learning extensions from a physical education specialist (Pica 2004). They learn best with verbal prompts, feedback on their performance, and encouragement (Patterson & Van Der Mars 2008).

Children in this age range become increasingly sensitive to social comparison of all kinds, including physical abilities, and it is especially difficult for them to lose. They enjoy playing with one another, but they become increasingly self-conscious as they start to value peer approval as much as adult approval.

Because of children's growing inclination to compare themselves with others, adults need to avoid pushing hypercompetitive activities for children in this age range. However, for many reasons, including the links among self-esteem, peer approval, physical competence, and healthy habits, adults should encourage participation in sports and other physical activi-ties that promote cooperation and validation (Grineski 1993; Pica 2004).

If competition is a factor at all, it should be at an individual level; adults can encourage children to compete with their own earlier performances or to meet their own goals. Because many children of this age also are great risk takers and may suffer injuries while their bones and muscles are still maturing, adults should minimize or very closely monitor children's participation in sports with the potential for serious injury, such as football and strenuous dance or gymnastics (Lord & Kozar 1996; Radelet et al. 2002).

Children with disabilities that affect gross motor development (including physical impairments, hearing or visual impairments, and mental retardation) often share their classmates' interest in sports and movement but are frequently left out of these activities (Foley, Bryan, & McCubbin 2008). Yet physical education is well suited for children with special needs and may even be more beneficial for them than for their typically developing peers, even though there may be additional challenges. Movement programs can enhance their coordination, listening and expressive skills, conceptual learning, and perhaps most important, their body image (Pica 2004).

It is important that teachers make accommodations and adaptations so that all children can participate in an activity and achieve the success that will contribute to their confidence. Participation allows children to relate better to their peers and have their movements and contributions accepted and valued by the group; it also promotes following rules and taking turns (Hibben & Scheer 1982).

To promote success, adaptations may be necessary. For example, teachers might make music a part of the program because children with special needs often show high responsiveness to music (Isenberg & Jalango 2002). A child whose movement is restricted, such as by spina bifida or cerebral palsy, may be able to tap a crutch or sway her head instead of stomping her foot. Playgrounds and outdoor equipment should be accessible for children with disabili-

© Terri Gonzalez

ties. Similarly, modified equipment, such as racing wheelchairs or skis, can enable special needs children to participate fully in physical activities with their peers.

In general, it can be helpful to use a multisensory approach that allows children to use their body, voice, eyes, and ears and to use an incremental approach for teaching new movement skills (Pica 2004). Encouraging the other children to include physically challenged peers in their play is also an important avenue for improving motor (and social) development (Diamond, Hong, & Tu 2008).

Social and emotional development

The gains in complex cognitive capacity, maturing language and communication skills, and self-regulation that take place during the primary grades influence children's increasingly multifaceted social and emotional skills. They develop more nuanced and complex understandings of how their behavior affects others, their roles in society, and the importance of showing caring attitudes in their relationships. Their peer relationships in particular are more elaborate and influential.

Along with the home, religious institutions, and the community, primary grade schools (and before- and after-school programs) are among the key settings in which children learn about what is often referred to as character development. Therefore, the primary grade years are an important time not only to support children's intellectual development but also to help them develop the ability to work collaboratively with peers; express respect and appreciation for diversity, empathy, and caring for other people; function responsibly; and gain positive approaches to learning such as curiosity, initiative, risk taking, and persistence.

Having social skills and healthy emotional states are crucial developments affecting children's success and happiness in almost every aspect of school and life.

Social development

Primary grade children need environments characterized by good conversation, joy and excitement over accomplishments, and laughter and by teachers who are tuned in to children's needs, moods, interests, and abilities. At this age, children are very interested in their peers' opinions and abilities, both for social comparison and for the sake of making friends. They are better able than before to cooperate and engage each other in extended conversations and rich social interactions. A lack of social skills can interfere with academic learning and have long-term negative consequences for children's adjustment in school and later life (Burton 1987; Klomek et al. 2008).

Sociability, teacher relationships, friendships, and aggression. Like younger children, primary grade children flourish in environments in which they feel supported and safe and have close emotional attachments to the pivotal adults in their lives, including teachers. Close teacher-child attachments and supportive social environments are important not only for enhancing self-esteem and shaping a positive self-concept but also for promoting school adjustment, academic achievement, and social skills (Pianta & Stuhlman 2004; Hamre & Pianta 2005; Myers & Pianta 2008).

In a study of classrooms where teachers were observed to be respectful of children, positive, and sensitive and where feedback engaged the children and expanded learning, children displayed significantly better social competence than children in other classrooms (Wilson, Pianta, & Stuhlman 2007).

Children at risk for behavioral problems and children with developmental delays or disabilities may be especially affected by the quality of the teacher-child relationship, benefiting tremendously from teachers who promote both closeness and independence. One study showed that children who tended to act out, show aggression, or act impulsively in kindergarten had much improved behaviors by third grade if they had close relationships with their teachers (Silver et al. 2005).

Research suggests that the quality of teacher-child relationships is quite variable across classrooms, meaning that children are not always experiencing the type of supportive relationships with teachers they need (NICHD 2002).

During these years, children's gender identification becomes very strong. Unlike preschoolers, children by age 6 clearly understand that their gender is a permanent characteristic that does not vary depending on their clothes or behavior. During the early school years, children's sense of their own gender becomes connected to culturally accepted roles and expectations, and it more strongly influences their behavior and choice of friends. In the primary grades, peers of the same gender have a stronger influence on behavior than those of a different gender (Stearns, Dodge, & Nicholson 2008). Children show a marked preference for same-gender playmates and an almost stereotypic rejection of the opposite sex, saying things such as "Boys (or girls) have cooties."

Children of primary grade age now are more capable of playing cooperative, rule-regulated games and sticking to the rules. Establishing productive, positive social and working relationships with others close to their age gives children the foundation for developing a sense of social competence.

During the early school years, children usually develop their first reciprocal friendships. Preschoolers typically define friendship as doing things together, whereas primary grade children's friendships are marked by genuine give and take, negotiation of differences, shared experiences, and the beginnings of mutual trust. Most children have at least one unilateral friendship at this age—although it is not unusual for a child not to have a friendship that includes real give and take (George & Hartmann 1996).

Peer groups also are important for 6- to 8-year-olds, although not as important as they will be for older children. The structure of peer groups is flexible; children tend to enter and leave social circles easily at this age, such that groups are fluid and permeable in most cases (Craig & Baucum 2002; Pica 2004). Groups usually have few operating rules; conformity becomes much more important as children get older, by ages 10 to 12 (Craig & Baucum 2002).

Some children show relational aggression—for example, being mean to, deceiving, or excluding another child—as early as preschool, continuing into the primary grades and beyond. Relational aggression has most often been studied in girls (Rigby 2004; Bowie 2007), but boys, too, use this form of aggression. There is some evidence that girls with better social skills may actually be more aggressive in relationships than girls with poorer social skills (Carpenter & Nangle 2006). Cultural mores, family expectations, and media exposure influence the use and frequency of physical and relational aggression in primary grade children, and more research is needed on the roles of gender, culture, and ethnicity to understand the various manifestations of aggression in young children (Ostrov, Gentile, & Crick 2006; Brown et al. 2007).

Other children show a tendency to physically bully others, be bullied by others, or both, any combination of which has grievous consequences for the children at the time and for their future. Bullies, most often boys, are often disliked and avoided by classmates and adults alike and are often inaccurate in perceiving others' intentions and likely behaviors, which starts in motion or perpetuates a negative spiral toward isolation and rejection (Hubbard & Coie 1994; Lansford et al. 2006; Kenny et al. 2007). Boys who frequently bully others at age 7 or 8 are, in adolescence or early adulthood, at higher risk for depression, suicidal thoughts, violent behavior, psychopathology, and other problems (Raine et al. 2006; Klomek et al. 2008).

Between 15 and 30 percent of children are chronic victims; ironically, as many as half of the victimized children are also bullies, and these are the most disliked children (Kochenderfer-Ladd 2003). Victims tend inadvertently to reinforce bullying behavior by behaving passively, giving in to demands, crying, or assuming defensive postures (Boulton 1999). They may be children who are frail in appearance, temperamentally inhibited, overly

dependent on adult protection, or otherwise vulnerable (Snyder et al. 2003). Victims, like bullies, are lonely, become depressed, often do poorly in and avoid school, and are generally rejected (Kochenderfer-Ladd & Wardrop 2001). Without help, children who are persistently bullied endure a terribly painful cycle of further impaired emotional self-regulation and social skills that only encourages more bullying.

Teachers who view bullying as a normal part of growing up jeopardize classroom harmony and individual children's well-being. Separating bullies from their victims and teaching both groups alternative coping mechanisms can greatly reduce the incidence of undue aggressive behaviors (Kochenderfer-Ladd & Pelletier 2008). Teaching children when to seek help or intervention—as children are often encouraged to resolve conflicts on their own—can provide helpful guidance (Newman 2008). Similarly, child bystanders might be encouraged to intervene in safe ways. Helping victims improve their opinions of themselves, especially through having a close friend to whom they can turn for help, does wonders.

Self-concept and self-esteem. The cognitive growth that occurs between ages 5 and 7 not only affects children's understanding of other people's perspectives but also affects their understanding of self (Harter 1990). Primary grade children also tend to start comparing themselves with their peers. While preschool children typically describe themselves in terms of their behavior or preferences ("I play with my dog" or "I like jello"), school age children describe themselves in terms of their traits and competencies ("I am good at soccer" or "I am shy"). Younger primary grade children hold at least three images of themselves, according to their academic, social, and physical competence. As they mature, they judge themselves in a more balanced way ("I'm good at playing the piano, but I'm not good at singing"). By age 8, these images blend into a more singular, generalized image of self that children can verbalize, including whether they like themselves and how much (Sameroff & McDonough 1994).

During the primary grade years, children's self-esteem—their estimation of their self-worth and either pride or shame in their competence—becomes more realistic and accurate. Like kindergartners, many first-graders have a more positive self-assessment than is sometimes warranted, which is helpful as they tackle new learning challenges; but accuracy improves as children get older (Eccles et al. 1993). They begin to understand the limits of their own abilities, and they also become more prone to social comparison, comparing themselves with others both favorably and unfavorably. This information becomes part of their self-concept and can affect their motivation for an activity. For example, children learn whether they excel in science or art or soccer, and such realizations, which are affected by feedback from teachers and other adults, can influence life decisions.

In the social context, children with a negative image of themselves are likely to be more aggressive and disliked by peers, further exacerbating their low self-esteem. By depriving children of interaction with peers—an important agent of socialization in childhood—this cycle of low self-esteem and social isolation may have very negative long-term consequences. A large body of research provides powerful evidence that children who fail to develop minimal social competence and who experience rejection or neglect by their peers are at significant risk of dropping out of school, becoming delinquent, and experiencing mental health problems in adulthood (e.g., Mikami & Hinshaw 2006; Lansford et al. 2007; Klomek et al. 2008). Research also demonstrates that adult intervention and coaching can help children develop better peer relationships (Asher & Williams 1987; Burton 1987; Dodge 2007).

The ability to work and interact effectively with peers is one dimension of the major social-emotional developmental task of the early school years—development of a sense of mastery or competence. For primary grade children,

© Ellen B. Senisi

the urge to master the skills of esteemed adults and older children is as powerful as the urge to stand and walk is for 1-year-olds. Erikson (1963) describes this major developmental challenge as the child's struggle between developing a sense of "industry" versus feelings of inferiority. To develop this sense of competence or industry, primary grade children need to acquire the knowledge and skills recognized as important by their culture. Contemporary mainstream American culture emphasizes academic competencies, foremost of which are literacy skills and, to a lesser degree, math and science.

Toward the goal of mastery, school age children are willing to practice skills, persisting for longer than they would have as preschoolers. When children do not succeed in acquiring the competencies needed to function in the world, they are likely to develop a sense of inferiority or inadequacy that may seriously inhibit their future performance—and happiness. At the same time, children who do not do well in school can certainly develop a healthy respect for themselves, particularly when their family, peer group, or subculture values other achievements more than academics (Craig & Baucum 2002).

Experiences that shape self-concept and self-esteem are especially important during the early school years because children's self-esteem influences their behavior. And as children get older, their self-concept becomes more difficult to change. For example, if children have a negative image of themselves as learners, they generally exert less effort in school. When children are pressured to acquire skills too far beyond their current ability or are judged competitively—receiving low grades on their work or hearing constant correction—their motivation to learn as well as their self-esteem may be impaired. A major cause of negative self-image for children this age is not succeeding in school—for example, failing to learn to read or being assigned to the lowest-ability math group.

In short, children develop a solid basis for self-esteem when adults help them develop efficacy in the valued skills of the culture, especially literacy, mathematics, language, and social skills (Weissbourd 1996).

Emotional development

Emotions, both positive and negative, are the main force guiding behavior and learning from infancy through adulthood. Genetic and environmental factors—everything from temperament to culture to relationships—influence the pathways emotions follow (Hyson 2004). With support, children in the primary grades become increasingly adept at reading others' emotions and managing their own.

Emotional understanding and empathy. A skill central to allowing primary grade children to develop and maintain relationships with adults and peers is the ability to infer others' thoughts, expectations, feelings, and intentions. In the younger years, children have a largely egocentric perspective of the world that focuses on "life according to me." During the primary grades, they become increasingly able to consider others' feelings and perspectives.

At 6, many children are still not very good at accurately understanding another's perspective or motives, although they do usually know when another person's thoughts differ from their own. By 7 or 8, however, they usually have more awareness of the other's feelings and perspective, and they understand that people think about what others are thinking (Craig & Baucum 2002). Also by around 7 or 8, children understand that they can feel two emotions at the same time ("I like Sophie, but I don't like the way she is bossy sometimes"). By age 8, they are better able to empathize with other people and can accept with varying degrees of graciousness the idea of giving special consideration to those in greater need (Berk 2008).

It is not until later that a child can infer what another person might be thinking and what that other person might be thinking about the child's own thoughts ("Ava is mad at me, and she knows that I know she's mad"). It is also later, between ages 9 and 12, that children begin holding more developed concepts about the obligations of friendship, such as loyalty or trust (Craig & Baucum 2002). Awareness of others' emotions and motives may play a role in the reduction of aggressive, disruptive, and anx-

ious behaviors among primary grade children (Hoglund, Lalonde, & Leadbeater 2008).

Development of self-regulation skills (emotional and behavioral control). Self-regulation, or self-control, is the ability to contain and manage one's own behavior without relying on others for impulse control. It is an internalized mechanism that develops through instruction and support, much the way math or literacy must be learned, and is a central ability to success in school and life. Without it, a child has trouble following the teacher's directions and rules, interacting successfully with peers, and experiencing a feeling of competence—troubles that contribute to feelings of low self-esteem (Landy 2002). Development in this area extends from children's current functioning into their adult life, influencing health, friendships, and mastery in later life (Hampson 2008).

The process of becoming self-regulated requires internalizing an understanding of what behaviors are considered acceptable and desirable as opposed to unacceptable and wrong, a process that occurs gradually over the course of all of early childhood. By age 6, most children, provided with opportunities to learn and practice these skills, have a foundation in being able to manage their thoughts, words, and actions. However, they still need teaching and practice in the area of self-regulation for optimal learning and development.

Bodrova and Leong (2005b) identify some principles and practices that promote development in this area in the early grade school years. First, all children, and not just "problem" children, should be taught how to self-regulate, which is as much a skill requiring teacher support as is learning to read or to add or subtract. Second, because children in this age range are concrete learners, they should have visual or tangible reminders of rules. For example, when children have a tendency to blurt things out during group time, teachers can use a play microphone or "talking stick" to indicate which speaker has the floor. And third, children at this age are mature enough to engage in discussions about the rules or to help create rules, which

gives them an investment in upholding them, for others (hence a newfound interest in tattling) and ultimately for themselves.

Also, role-playing and dramatization (especially of stories that include character conflicts or moral dilemmas) can enhance self-regulation and prevent some conflicts; such an exercise helps a child come up with alternatives to, say, hitting, which is usually an impulsive reaction rather than a premeditated plan (Dodge 2008). Primary grade teachers who can find ways to stimulate those activities—by providing props and ideas for characters, for example—enrich children's skills and learning in self-regulation as well as negotiation, empathy, rule development, and more.

Another major developmental achievement for children in this age range is an evolving sense of conscience, but they tend to be rigid in terms of interpreting and applying rules—for both themselves and others. They may expect visitors to follow the rules of the home or classroom as strictly as they do (Landy 2002). They may feel guilty if they break a rule. If they have not complied with an adults' rule—which happens less frequently than it used to—they often may attempt to negotiate their way out of having broken it. For example, a child who wants to stay outside and play may try to argue, "Mr. Barnes said it was okay" or "he won't mind." Primary grade children continue to modify and revise their values and standards in their efforts to manage themselves.

By third grade, children are highly attuned to and have internalized to a great degree adults' and society's expectations of them (a process that continues throughout the school years). For example, while growing up in poverty is correlated with negative impacts on academic achievement and later problems (Brooks-Gunn, Klebanov, & Duncan 1996; Landy 2002), they are not inevitable. When low-income children live in homes or communities in which expectations for academic performance and educational attainment are high, children perform better on standardized tests than they do when neighborhood or societal expecta-

tions are low (Emory et al. 2008). This is not to diminish in any way the serious and debilitating challenges presented by poverty, but rather to highlight the extent to which children by second or third grade can adapt to and internalize expectations.

Promoting social and emotional development in the primary grades

Because these are formative years for children's development of self-concept and self-esteem, it is important for teachers to create environments in which all children will thrive and develop a positive self-image. They can do this by, for example, creating cooperative and harmonious environments, minimizing competition between children, taking advantage of children's intrinsic motivation to learn, and using strategies that strengthen children's engagement and joy in the process of learning, while minimizing

children's focus on external recognition or adult praise (Hyson 2008). (Praise and encouragement are essential but not in lieu of enhancing internal motivation.)

Because a major goal of the primary grades is to tap into children's strong motivation for mastery, teachers are wise to give children the opportunities and support they need to develop skills, while keeping in mind that children all too easily can feel that they have failed (especially in various curricular areas such as reading and math) and become discouraged. Teachers might tailor lesson plans to individual children to help them take the next challenging, but achievable, step so that all children experience success and mastery.

Before problems and conflicts arise, it can be helpful to role-play problem situations and call on children to establish some of the basic classroom rules. (Teachers need to set limits on children's rule setting, however, since they

Peer Tutoring in the Primary Grades

Peer tutoring is an effective and efficient strategy based in our understanding that children's cognitive development and social development often go hand in hand. Across grades K–12, peer tutoring has been found to increase academic achievement and motivation, as well as cognitive and social skills (Utley & Mortweet 1997; Kalkowski 2001). The benefits of peer tutoring have been particularly evident among students in grades 1–3, among children with mild disabilities, and for children from poor and less educated families (Rohrbeck et al. 2003).

The major goals in peer tutoring are to provide students with more one-on-one instruction and more opportunities to apply their learning in the classroom (Access Center 2008). In most programs, students are paired by their teacher: One child performs as the tutor or coach, while the other child is assigned as the tutee. In these pairs, students creatively and independently apply learning strategies that ultimately help them to expand their own knowledge base and develop a deeper understanding of concepts. Peer tutoring is also use-

ful in encouraging children to engage in positive interactions with each other and in increasing children's self-esteem and social skills (Utley & Mortweet 1997; Fuchs et al. 2001).

Teachers have great flexibility in how they structure the process. They may decide to pair children of similar skill sets and ages, or they may purposely assign pairs with varying ages and skill sets. Teachers also may differ in whether they assign structured or unstructured activities. Another variation occurs when teachers have children exchange their tutor/tutee roles after a certain amount of time has passed (Access Center 2008).

Through peer tutoring, primary grade children receive individual attention and opportunities to apply various learning strategies, and teachers are able address a wide range of learning abilities and engage all students simultaneously. These qualities, in turn, create a more cooperative classroom that increases appropriate social engagement among students and decreases the likelihood for disruptive classroom behavior (Utley & Mortweet 1997; Kalkowski 2001).

can be too harsh when deeming punishments.) Primary grade children also should have input on how to enforce the rules necessary for congenial group living. Involving children in some aspects of the social environment is effective for children at this age—who are rule conscious and relatively good at self-regulation—whereas punishing, criticizing, or making pointed comparisons between children generally undermines their motivation and pleasure in being in the classroom.

Because blossoming peer relationships and social skills play such a pivotal role in learning and development in this age range, teachers should try to promote social competence for each child. That is not to say that teachers can or should control all aspects of children's relationships with peers, but they do influence children's budding social skills and even their forming of friendships.

For example, when teachers provide opportunities and support for cooperative small-group projects in which children work together, they help to promote children's comfort level with one another and, potentially, their likelihood of becoming friends. Besides fostering positive peer relationships that directly benefit each child, such collaborative work also contributes to children's cognitive and language development and their ability to take on and solve problems (Forman, Minick, & Stone 1993).

Cognitive development

Children in the primary grades make great strides in cognitive development. A gradual but significant shift in cognitive abilities occurs in most children between about ages 5 and 7, such that children under 5 think and reason differently than those 7 and older (Piaget 1952; White 1965; Piaget & Inhelder 1969; Sameroff & McDonough 1994; Case & Okamoto 1996).

Between 5 and 7, children become more proficient and flexible in their use of mental representations and begin to acquire the ability to think about things more dimensionally and to solve a wider range of problems, a finding that

holds in studies of children around the world (Rogoff et al. 1975). Children this age enjoy reading, spelling, printing activities, board games, and computer games. They are interested in nature, simple science experiments, collecting and sorting, learning about weights and the value of coins, creating a finished product from their work, and discerning the line between fantasy and reality, as with magic tricks or the tooth fairy.

During the primary years, the brain continues to develop. Changing cognitive capacities at this age are in part the result of processes such as lateralization, wherein the two hemispheres of the brain start to function more efficiently as learning occurs. Brain lateralization further improves with maturation of the corpus callosum (the tissue connecting the two halves of the brain), and this speeds mental processing of information (Harris 1986). Also during this period, the synapses of the brain (the connections that transmit information from one neuron to another) go through "pruning," a process of eliminating neurons that are not often activated, which scientists speculate improves efficiency (Chugani 1996; Dana Alliance on Brain Initiatives 1996).

After age 7, most children will have achieved some or all of this important brain restructuring. This brain development, it is important to note, is the result of an interaction between the biological changes occurring at this time of life and the experiences that children have in the environment. In effect, brain development shapes and is shaped by learning (Bransford, Brown, & Cocking 2003).

The changes in brain structure and processes are important not only in and of themselves but also because they influence how children interact with the environment—and how people in the environment interact with children. There are changes in the expectations, demands, and structuring by adults of the social and cultural context within which children live (Vygotsky 1978). Adults from all different cultures expect more of children in this age group as compared with when they were younger; around ages 5 to 7, children experience more

responsibilities and more adult-like chores and roles (Rogoff et al. 1975).

The changes that occur in children's cognition during these years equip them to perform the mental operations required for reading, mathematics, and other content learning in the early grades. These changes affect not only their academic and intellectual functioning but also social cognition, moral reasoning, and language abilities. However, individual and cultural differences contribute to wide variation in children's abilities.

Concept acquisition and reasoning

By first grade, most children exhibit more flexible, multidimensional thinking. Changes in children's cognition occur gradually and unevenly, and children will occasionallyand temporarily revert to earlier ways of thinking. Primary grade children continue to need lots of hands-on, experiential learning (AAAS 2008). When presented with a new concept, primary grade children need physical actions or direct experiences to help them grasp the idea, much as adults need vivid examples and illustrations to grasp unfamiliar concepts (Pica 2004).

Although children in second or third grade can solve some abstract problems (such as determining place value), they are not yet able to grasp highly complex, abstract concepts or learn by text or direct instruction alone. While they can symbolically or mentally manipulate concrete concepts, it will be some time before they can mentally manipulate abstract ideas; for example, use certain mathematical algorithms, grasp dates in history, or fully comprehend the irreversibility of death. Accordingly, while children can use symbols such as words and numerals to represent objects and relations, they still need concrete reference points.

Unlike younger children, whose reasoning is often from the particular to the particular, primary grade children gradually gain the ability to engage in syllogistic logic. By age 8 or 9, for example, most children know that if stick A is longer than stick B, and B is longer than stick C, then A is also longer than C, at least when they encounter such problems in reality rather than as hypothetical situations. Similarly, primary grade children are better able to engage in spatial reasoning. For instance, 5- and 6-year-olds are confused about left/right directionality when facing a person. By age 7 or 8, most children can mentally reverse the directions and understand left and right from a perspective other than their own (Berk 2008).

Children's capacity for classification—the ability to group objects by common attributes—extends during these years to the ability to use more than one attribute to classify and understand class inclusion; that is, the capacity for an object to be a member of more than one group simultaneously. To a greater extent than kindergartners, primary grade children understand part/whole relationships. They understand that with a group of four cats and five dogs, for example, there are more animals than dogs.

During the primary grades, children typically master seriation and sequencing. Seriation is the ability to place objects in order by length, weight, or size. Sequencing requires the ability to hold two pieces of information simultaneously—noting that an object is both larger than one object and smaller than another. These abilities are examples of children's increasing capacity to decenter from a single focus and consider multiple perspectives. In other words, thinking becomes more multidimensional.

Although primary grade children have largely move beyond the egocentrism of their preschool thinking, a form of egocentrism particular to reasoning emerges during this period: Children can become fixated on the validity of their own hypotheses and will change the facts to fit a hypothesis rather than modify the hypothesis because the facts do not support it. For example, if a 7-year-old comes to believe that he is not a good athlete because he has not scored any goals on the soccer field, he may hold fast to this belief despite specific evidence to the contrary. Children get better at separating evidence from theory as they get older (Kuhn & Dean 2004).

As primary grade children increasingly become able to understand the viewpoints of others and focus on several aspects of a problem at one time, they become able to reverse their thinking. They can mentally go through a series of steps and then reverse them or understand that one operation can undo another; for example, that subtraction can undo or reverse addition. These capabilities have important implications for the kinds of problems that children can solve.

Although considerable individual variation exists and abilities depend on exposure through teaching (Fuchs et al. 2008), children in the primary grades generally develop a true understanding of measurement and mathematical problems. By age 6 or 7, most children's understanding of one-to-one correspondence and number is complete. For instance, they realize that the number of cookies (eight, say) does not change when the cookies are rearranged, distributed, or divided into different subsets (5 + 3, 6 + 2, and so on). These concepts develop in some predictable order (e.g., number followed by mass, length, area, and weight, respectively).

Executive functioning

By the primary grades, children are expected to and are ready to start learning on demand, according to Vygotsky and his followers (Elkonin 1972; Zuckerman 2003). This means children must be able to focus their attention, remember things on purpose, and be able to compare the process and findings of their own learning with teacher expectations (Bodrova

© Ellen B. Senisi

& Leong 2007). Many of the changing cognitive abilities and developments in the brain, particularly in the prefrontal cortex, that allow a child to learn on demand are the higher mental functions executive functioning or cognitive control. Executive functioning includes abilities such as planning, organization, being able to shift thought or attention, inhibiting distracting thoughts, and sustained and sequenced behavior; it also involves "working memory," or the ability to hold information actively in mind while performing tasks (Mahone & Silverman 2008).

These are all self-regulatory skills that allow someone to make use of appropriate strategies to complete a job, such as building a model car or creating a classroom habitat for worms. These higher mental functions are indeed skills to be cultivated, not just the result of becoming older, like getting in new teeth, which requires no effort or application. The abilities are just beginning to emerge in the early primary grades and, like other skills, they should be taught, are dependent on one's motivation, and improve with practice (Nelson, Thomas, & de Haan 2006; Bodrova & Leong 2007; Mahone & Silverman 2008).

Self-regulation of thought and attention. Many classroom activities and real-world tasks require children to selectively focus attention on relevant information—whether through listening, watching, or reading—while simultaneously filtering out irrelevant information that distracts from the activity at hand.

Starting around age 6, children do improve in their ability to focus attention on demand and to ignore distracting information—although teachers and parents should recognize that this is a skill that is not fully developed until adolescence (Ridderinkhof et al. 1997; Casey, Durston, & Fossella 2001). Whereas 6- and 7-year-olds will continue to struggle with focusing attention on what matters most versus what is irrelevant, 8-year-olds and older children will have somewhat less trouble with this (Rueda et al. 2004).

This growing skill allows children to engage in sustained work, and they appreciate having time to finish their work now that they can concentrate for somewhat longer periods (Wood 2007).

Of course, the ability to pay attention relates to children's ability to learn various subjects. For example, in the area of literacy, being able to focus on information that matters and ignore what does not helps children correctly formulate complex sentences and recall in an organized way information they have heard from a story (Purvis & Tannock 1997). Problems paying attention can lead to learning difficulties, such as an inability to remember or even recognize words previously learned (Cutting et al. 2003).

Planning and organization. To solve problems requiring a series of steps—in other words, to plan—one has to postpone action in order to weigh alternatives, organize task materials, and remember each step in the right order (Berk 2009). Children who are able to form and carry out a plan are more likely than others to develop other advanced cognitive skills (Hyson, Copple, & Jones 2006). But planning is not necessarily easy. Activities that may seem commonplace and effortless for adults (such as baking a cake or completing a three-digit subtraction problem) actually involve many steps that must occur in a certain sequence. Planning for and completing these activities involve first thinking about all the necessary steps ahead of time and then allocating attention appropriately (Scholnick 1995).

Because of primary grade children's enhanced ability to classify and sort, they may do quite well at organizing materials (e.g., for baking a cake). However, they might have trouble knowing by themselves the order in which things should be done or how to break down the steps into individual actions. With subtraction, for example, children have to know that they must always subtract the bottom row from the top row (rather than, say, smaller digit from larger digit), work across columns from right to left, and "borrow" before subtracting from a column with too few.

Primary grade children show an interest in time, and their concepts of time are improving but still are not mature. Not until after age 8 are children reasonably accurate in placing events

in time sequence. They can generally categorize past, current, and future events, but they are not yet able to use dates to sequence historical time—another example of their ability to reason about concrete, but not abstract, concepts (Thornton & Vukelich 1988; Barton & Levstik 1996). Therefore, it is not always possible for a primary grade child to plan ahead without considerable guidance from an adult.

Memory. Being able to retain and recall new information is essential for success in school, and children's maturing capacity to use working memory in the primary grades greatly assists with their learning. For example, with reading, children's freedom from using repetition and great effort to remember word meanings allows them to move toward comprehension (Cutting et al. 2003; Beck & McKeown 2007). Most information-processing theorists attribute primary grade children's improved ability to solve problems to their increased capacity to store information and retrieve it from memory. Their increased memory capacity, use of memory strategies, and awareness of mental processes (metacognition, metamemory) allow them to be more reflective and interested in reviewing their work.

Before age 6, children usually don't think about the process of thinking, instead focusing on the outcomes of their thinking. Between ages 7 and 10 and continuing into adolescence, children begin to understand their own capacity to construct knowledge, select and transform information, and distinguish between and select various memory strategies (Schwanenflugel, Henderson, & Fabricius 1998; Flavell 2000; Kuhn 2000).

Children younger than age 9 rarely use memory organization strategies on their own (Bjorklund 1988), but teachers can actively promote primary grade children's expanding ability to think about their own memory functioning—that is, their metamemory. They might teach children to reorganize a list of words so that like words are clustered together (e.g., apples, pears, and bananas are all fruits; koalas, pandas, and grizzlies are all bears), making them more meaningful (Cutting et al. 2003). Or they might encourage using mental imagery, so that chil-

dren remember unusual material by creating a picture in their mind (Craig & Baucum 2002). One simple but effective strategy is for teachers to simply remind children, "This is something you will need to remember."

During the primary grade years, children show improved capacity in both short- and long-term memory, although again these capacities are not yet mature. For example, the adult capacity for short-term memory is seven chunks or bits of information (words, numbers, phrases, etc.); preschoolers can hold only two or three chunks, while 7-year-olds can usually retain five. By the beginning of third grade, children usually are well on their way toward automatic retrieval by memory (e.g., of number combinations as their major strategy to solve mathematics problems) (Fuchs et al. 2008).

Once information is in short-term memory, it must be transferred to long-term memory if it is to be retained. Information in short-term memory is in danger of being forgotten, of course, especially when new information interferes. This is why children need time and opportunities to consolidate new learning before the next concepts are introduced. When the curriculum moves along at too rapid a pace, it is not surprising that children cannot remember what has already been taught and that topics have to be re-taught (an all too common occurrence in American schools).

During the primary grade years, children become better able to employ memory strategies such as rehearsal (repeating information to remember it) and organization (grouping information into similar categories). Children begin to apply these memory strategies more systematically (e.g., distinguishing vowels from consonants or remembering the multiplication tables) as the demands of school increase. The primary grade child is better able than a younger child to retain decontextualized information, but adults help greatly by structuring the memory tasks, making them meaningful, and guiding children to systematically use memory strategies.

Children's improved memory during this age period is in large part a result of their

increasing body of accumulated knowledge and concepts. In other words, children's experiences and memories provide categories or structures to which they can more readily connect new experiences. As adults are aware, when we know a lot about a topic, we find new information on this topic more meaningful and easier to retain and retrieve. Information-processing theorists believe that school-age children's improved memory capacity is due largely to the fact that primary grade children have accumulated more knowledge to which to connect new information or experiences than their younger counterparts. This theoretical perspective argues that children's limited concrete thinking is not just the result of age-related constraints on cognition, it is also a lack of prior knowledge in the content area (Metz 1995).

Moral development

The cognitive changes that have occurred by about age 7 have important implications for children's moral development. As their reasoning improves and their ability to understand multiple perspectives increases, children become better able to think about and reflect on rules of behavior and to understand right and wrong. With this advance in social understanding, children have the basis for beginning to grasp and allow for others' intentions.

© Ellen B. Senisi

At age 5 or 6, most children are in a period of moral realism in which they consider breaking any given rule equally bad, giving no consideration to a person's intentions. For example, a child in this stage would view breaking a stack of plates by accident as being as bad as or worse than breaking a single plate on purpose (Craig & Baucum 2002). By about age 7, children are more able to view rules as relative; they realize that not all rules are the same and breaking a rule is not always wrong. They are better able to consider a person's intention when deciding whether an action is right or wrong, good or bad (Piaget 1965; Irwin & Ambron 1973). Children at this age also begin to make more accurate judgments about what is true and false, but they often rigidly apply their newfound understanding of justice and fair play (Elkind 1981).

Around age 6, most children begin to internalize moral rules of behavior and thus develop what we think of as "conscience." This internal monitoring of their own conduct enables them to function more independent of adult supervision and to be trusted to take on more responsibility. However, children's behavior at this age often shows that they find it difficult to live with and by their new self-monitoring and that they need adult assistance. For example, they may interpret accidents or chance occurrences as punishments for their misbehavior ("I lied about going to my friend's house, so she got sick"). Likewise, children's newly developed conscience is often excessively strict; children of 6 or 7 typically treat every little mistake as a major crime, deserving of terrible punishment or dire consequences. Adults can help children assess mistakes realistically and find ways to correct them.

Children of this age are very concerned with fairness. They watch adults closely and are sensitive to perceived infractions and inequitable actions. Before 6 or 7, children insist that fairness requires absolute equality in treatment; for example, everyone should receive the same amount of snack food. By 6 or 7, they begin to consider merit in decisions about fairness; for example, they understand that someone who worked extra hard might deserve a special treat. By age 8, because they are better able to empathize with other people, they tend to accept the idea of giving special consideration to those in greater need (Berk 2008).

The stages of moral development and their age guidelines are by no means absolute or rigidly fixed. Children can go back and forth between levels of judgment for some time, and they may be more capable of a higher-level judgment for one type of situation than another. For example, they might not be willing to invite a child they don't like over to play, but they would be willing to help that person if he were injured (Eisenberg 1989a; 1989b).

Children are more likely to show advanced moral reasoning if adults reason with them and help them to understand the rationale for the rules. Sensitive adults help children this age develop empathy by appealing to children's respect for fairness and rules in their interactions with others or when they must deny a child's request; for example, "If I allow you to do that, I would be unfair to the others. If we all do it the same way, it will be fair for everyone" (Furman 1980; 1987).

Developments in children's moral reasoning are not automatic, and a wide variation exists among individual children as a product of their experience and the adult guidance they receive. For example, children from various cultural groups may differ in their reactions to specific moral situations. Cultures value aspects of moral development differently and to varying degrees. In Latino families, research has consistently found moral education (*la educación*) of children to be among the top childrearing goals. An "educated child" (*un niño educado*), in the Latino culture, refers to a child who possesses qualities reflective of high morals and politeness. To shape children's moral behaviors and attitudes, Latino parents will often engage in *consejos*, spontaneous homilies or words of wisdom, with their children (Valdes 1996; Halgunseth, Ispa, & Rudy 2006).

Despite their developing conscience and improving ability to work quietly for longer peri-

ods, 6-, 7-, and 8-year-olds still need supervision and the support of trusted adults. As a result, teachers should not expect children of this age group to supervise themselves in school or after school for extended time periods. Teachers and parents can provide opportunities for children to assume responsibility but should not expect primary grade children to display adult levels of self-regulation.

Promoting cognitive development in the primary grades

Compared with preschoolers and kindergartners, school age children are more logical and flexible in their thinking, have more knowledge of the world, have improved memory, and can better sustain their attention. But compared with adults, 6-, 7-, and 8-year-olds are novices in virtually every cognitive area, and their thinking and reasoning reflect this shallow level of prior knowledge.

Children in the primary grades enjoy challenges that test their growing skills as long as they can achieve success with the challenges. Children can become perfectionistic (Wood 2007), but teachers can support children by helping them enjoy the process of the task and feel good about effort exerted, rather than focusing on praise for the product (Hyson 2008). Children may show a type of egocentrism in their logic where they change the facts to fit their hypothesis, but they are not being deliberately obstinate in holding on to their views. Rather, they are working through a developmental phase in their reasoning skills. Teachers can help them correct misconceptions by patiently questioning assumptions or creating ways to test hypotheses.

To find a good balance between challenging children and ensuring their success, teachers will find national benchmarks or key learning goals helpful. Consider mathematics as an example. For each grade, the National Council of Teachers of Mathematics (NCTM) has defined key learning goals (termed "curriculum focal points") based on children's abilities and mathematics educators' judgment about what chil-

dren at that grade need to learn to have a strong foundation for continued progress in math (NCTM 2006). NCTM's curriculum focal points (excerpted here for the primary grades) are especially useful for prioritizing and organizing mathematics curriculum and instruction.

The focal points document was developed in an attempt to bring consistency, coherence, and focus to the mathematics curriculum in the United States, which is often described as "a mile wide, and an inch deep." The report is not a curriculum; instead it describes the specific concepts and skills that should be addressed at each grade level. More so than other subject areas, mathematics is a sequential discipline in which earlier understandings provide an essential foundation on which later skills and concepts build.

No matter what the subject area, teachers should keep learning concrete, relevant to children's everyday lives, and connected to previously learned material. A new concept must have a tangible referent, something real and familiar. Children are more likely to learn about, say, measurement and distance if the task is fun and imaginative yet based in their reality; for example, determining how far a ladybug has moved across the table (Tyminski et al. 2008). Likewise, a unit on water will mean more to children when they can relate it to their own lives. They may experiment with its properties in various conditions (e.g., in the freezer, on the countertop, after two minutes in the microwave), measure its weight in different amounts (a cup, a bucket, a bathtub), or determine the amounts needed by the cactus on the desk versus the African violet on the window sill.

All of these tasks would be more meaningful than, say, discussing water's subatomic particles—which would have no meaning in children's daily lives. A child in the early grades is still several years away from being able to reason about a hypothetical situation or an abstract concept.

Teachers can promote cognitive development by using periods of focused instruction about a specific new skill or concept within inte-

Developmentally Appropriate Practice, 3d Edition

Math for the Primary Grades "Curriculum Focal Points"

Grade 1

Number and Operations and Algebra: Developing understandings of addition and subtraction and strategies for basic addition facts and related subtraction facts.
Children develop strategies for adding and subtracting whole numbers on the basis of their earlier work with small numbers. They use a variety of models, including discrete objects, length-based models (e.g., lengths of connecting cubes), and number lines, to model "part-whole," "adding to," "taking away from," and "comparing" situations to develop an understanding of the meanings of addition and subtraction and strategies to solve such arithmetic problems. Children understand the connections between counting and the operations of addition and subtraction (e.g., adding two is the same as "counting on" two). They use properties of addition (commutativity and associativity) to add whole numbers, and they create and use increasingly sophisticated strategies based on these properties (e.g., "making tens") to solve addition and subtraction problems involving basic facts. By comparing a variety of solution strategies, children relate addition and subtraction as inverse operations.

Number and Operations: Developing an understanding of whole number relationships, including grouping in tens and ones.
Children compare and order whole numbers (at least to 100) to develop an understanding of and solve problems involving the relative sizes of these numbers. They think of whole numbers between 10 and 100 in terms of groups of tens and ones (especially recognizing the numbers 11 to 19 as 1 group of ten and particular numbers of ones). They understand the sequential order of the counting numbers and their relative magnitudes and represent numbers on a number line.

Geometry: Composing and decomposing geometric shapes.
Children compose and decompose plane and solid figures (e.g., by putting two congruent isosceles triangles together to make a rhombus), thus building an understanding of part-whole relationships as well as the properties of the original and composite shapes. As they combine figures, they recognize them from different perspectives and orientations, describe their geometric attributes and properties, and determine how they are alike and different, in the process developing a background for measurement and initial understandings of such properties as congruence and symmetry.

Grade 2

Number and Operations: Developing an understanding of the base-ten numeration system and place-value concepts.
Children develop an understanding of the base-ten numeration system and place-value concepts (at least to 1000). Their understanding of base-ten numeration includes ideas of counting in units and multiples of hundreds, tens, and ones, as well as a grasp of number relationships, which they demonstrate in a variety of ways, including comparing and ordering numbers. They understand multidigit numbers in terms of place value, recognizing that place-value notation is a shorthand for the sums of multiples of powers of 10 (e.g., 853 as 8 hundreds + 5 tens + 3 ones).

Number and Operations and Algebra: Developing quick recall of addition facts and related subtraction facts and fluency with multidigit addition and subtraction.
Children use their understanding of addition to develop quick recall of basic addition facts and related subtraction facts. They solve arithmetic problems by applying their understanding of models of addition and subtraction (such as combining or separating sets or using number lines), relationships and properties of number (such as place value), and properties of addition (commutativity and associativity). Children develop, discuss, and use efficient, accurate, and generalizable methods to add

(continued on page 280)

Math for the Primary Grades "Curriculum Focal Points" (cont.)

(continued from page 279)

and subtract multidigit whole numbers. They select and apply appropriate methods to estimate sums and differences or calculate them mentally, depending on the context and numbers involved. They develop fluency with efficient procedures, including standard algorithms, for adding and subtracting whole numbers, understand why the procedures work (on the basis of place value and properties of operations), and use them to solve problems.

Measurement: Developing an understanding of linear measurement and facility in measuring lengths.
Children develop an understanding of the meaning and processes of measurement, including such underlying concepts as partitioning (the mental activity of slicing the length of an object into equal-sized units) and transitivity (e.g., if object A is longer than object B and object B is longer than object C, then object A is longer than object C). They understand linear measure as an iteration of units and use rulers and other measurement tools with that understanding. They understand the need for equal-length units, the use of standard units of measure (centimeter and inch), and the inverse relationship between the size of a unit and the number of units used in a particular measurement (i.e., children recognize that the smaller the unit, the more iterations they need to cover a given length).

Grade 3

Number and Operations and Algebra: Developing understandings of multiplication and division and strategies for basic multiplication facts and related division facts.
Students understand the meanings of multiplication and division of whole numbers through the use of representations (e.g., equal-sized groups, arrays, area models, and equal "jumps" on number lines for multiplication, and successive subtraction, partitioning, and sharing for

division). They use properties of addition and multiplication (e.g., commutativity, associativity, and the distributive property) to multiply whole numbers and apply increasingly sophisticated strategies based on these properties to solve multiplication and division problems involving basic facts. By comparing a variety of solution strategies, students relate multiplication and division as inverse operations.

Number and Operations: Developing an understanding of fractions and fraction equivalence.
Students develop an understanding of the meanings and uses of fractions to represent parts of a whole, parts of a set, or points or distances on a number line. They understand that the size of a fractional part is relative to the size of the whole, and they use fractions to represent numbers that are equal to, less than, or greater than 1. They solve problems that involve comparing and ordering fractions by using models, benchmark fractions, or common numerators or denominators. They understand and use models, including the number line, to identify equivalent fractions.

Geometry: Describing and analyzing properties of two-dimensional shapes.
Students describe, analyze, compare, and classify two-dimensional shapes by their sides and angles and connect these attributes to definitions of shapes. Students investigate, describe, and reason about decomposing, combining, and transforming polygons to make other polygons. Through building, drawing, and analyzing two-dimensional shapes, students understand attributes and properties of two-dimensional space and the use of those attributes and properties in solving problems, including applications involving congruence and symmetry.

Source: Reprinted with permission from *Curriculum Focal Points for Prekindergarten through Grade 8 Mathematics: A Quest for Coherence,* copyright © 2006 by the National Council of Teachers of Mathematics. All rights reserved. The *Curriculum Focal Points* document may be viewed in its entirety at www.nctm.org/focalpoints.

Developmentally Appropriate Practice, 3d Edition

grated curriculum studies and long-term projects (lasting weeks or months) that enable children to gain deeper knowledge and understanding of a topic. Trying to cover every topic of study quickly leads to shallow learning. Rather, encouraging the primary grade child to pursue a topic—or an interest or hobby—in some depth supports concept development. Children can develop "expertise" in any area that is of intellectual interest to them—stars, rocks, state flags—and the habits of mind they develop from deep study in one area are broadly applicable to learning in other areas. By providing challenging, high-quality choices in the topics of study, teachers help children persist and stay engaged, enhancing their learning (Brophy 2004).

When guiding children in a task, teachers should remember to be specific. For example, teachers sometimes direct children to "pay attention," meaning to ignore distractions and focus on the task at hand. The problem with such directions is that they require children to read between the lines, so to speak, and infer what specifically the teacher wants them to pay attention to. If a child doesn't succeed at the task, perhaps the child was paying attention but was focusing on the wrong aspect of the task. A child who reads, "We wents to the store to buys a apple" and declares the sentence correct may be responding to the meaning of the sentence, because the class did go to the store to buy apples, rather than considering the grammatical errors in the sentence (Bodrova & Leong 2007). Teachers can help children focus their attention by being specific about where it is that children should focus their thoughts and efforts.

Adults should not expect children in the primary grades to be fully aware of their thought processes yet; they can help them advance in planning, attention, memory, and other cognitive processes by engaging children in cooperative or shared activities that allow them to perform at the next higher level of functioning, by using verbal reminders and prompts, and by using writing and drawing activities to improve self-reflection (Zuckerman 2003; Bodrova & Leong 2007).

Language and literacy development

Closely tied to cognitive development are changes in children's language and communication capacity. The huge expansion of language development during the preschool and kindergarten periods is followed by a dramatic transition in the primary grades—the movement from listening, speaking, and emerging reading skills to "real" reading and written self-expression. During these years, children's receptive vocabulary increases not just by listening but also by reading, and their expressive vocabulary expands from spoken to include written communication.

Depending on their prior experiences and exposure to vocabulary and printed materials, children enter the primary grades with a range of abilities in these areas. But no matter the starting point, children's development in this period in the cognitive, social, and approaches to learning domains intersect to make language and literacy an exciting arena for children and teachers alike.

Vocabulary knowledge and communication skills

Although there are wide variations due to prior language experience, by age 8 many children have doubled their 6-year-old vocabularies to some 20,000 words, and by the end of elementary school they have increased fourfold (Berk 2008). Children learn new words at a far more rapid rate than before—almost 20 words per day when they are in an environment where they continually hear new words, listen to and read books, and see language and literacy valued and celebrated. Vocabulary knowledge increases in part because of children's improved perspective-taking skills and better understanding of part/whole relationships. These abilities enable them to understand parts of words and to apply that understanding to a new word. For example, children might deconstruct the use of the prefix *un-* (as in *undo* or *unlock*) and practice creating their own *un-* words.

Oral conversation is the source for most vocabulary learning for younger children, but by the primary grade years, this source is less effective than it once was because everyday conversations rarely contain uncommon words (Cunningham & Stanovich 1998). Instead, hearing books with advanced words read aloud, participating in discussion of the meaning of new or less familiar words, and interacting with these words in various contexts are richer sources of word learning (Coyne et al. 2004). Children more easily learn words that are concrete and easy to picture, but they also can and should learn more abstract words (e.g., adverbs) with adult support (Penno, Wilkinson, & Moore 2002; Beck & McKeown 2007). (Although children's vocabulary expands and their speech is fluent, they still struggle with some syntactical complexities of language, such as passive voice. Until the age of 8 or 9, children might misinterpret the sentence "The boy was hit by the ball," for example, as meaning that the boy hit the ball.)

There is a clear gap in the rate of vocabulary learning, however, between children from middle-class or professional families and those from low-income families. Several studies of first-graders, for example, show that those from families of higher socioeconomic status know at least twice as many words as those from lower socioeconomic status, and this disparity does not go away without focused attention (White, Graves, & Slater 1990; Juel et al. 2003). Yet all primary grade children have the capacity and motivation to make big gains in language development and literacy skills if they have the learning experiences necessary to do so.

Children's greatly expanded vocabulary, along with their new awareness that the same word can have multiple meanings, has implications for social interactions. The ability to take multiple points of view vastly expands the child's communication skills. Engaging in conversation about their learning also strengthens children's abilities to communicate, express themselves, understand, reason, and solve problems. Children gain greater control of language and subsequently use it to think and to influence others' thinking. Better language

skills are generally associated with better social skills with peers, such as using less physical aggression and being better able to collaborate (Dickinson, McCabe, & Sprague 2003; Werner, Cassidy, & Juliano 2006).

Primary grade children engage in interactive, reciprocal conversations with adults and other children and effectively use the power of verbal communication, including humor. Unlike preschoolers, whose humor tends to be limited to silliness and bathroom jokes, 6-, 7-, and 8-year-olds typically love the kinds of jokes, puns, tongue twisters, and riddles that reflect their new language capacities—knock-knock jokes are a common favorite. During these years, children also use language (e.g., nicknames, teasing, or secret words) to include or exclude others from their social circle. As receivers of teasing, joking, or sarcastic language, they are highly sensitive and easily hurt by words (Wood 2007).

Reading and writing

Vocabulary knowledge is important not only because of its conversational and social implications but also because it affects comprehension (RAND Reading Study Group 2002). "Comprehension is the reason we read," write Matteson and Freeman (2006, 51). By first grade, children are likely to have a reading vocabulary of 300 to 500 words (including sight words and easily sounded out words), can correctly decode regular one-syllable words, and recognize irregularly spelled but common words such as *where* and *two*. By third grade, children can not only decode more advanced words, read aloud with fluency, and point out words that are causing comprehension difficulty, they also can infer word meanings from prefixes, suffixes, and roots they have been taught (Snow, Burns, & Griffin 1998).

It is not word knowledge alone that matters, however. Also important is being able to retrieve word meaning readily—as opposed to having to struggle to remember what a word means, which jeopardizes comprehension (Stahl & Fairbanks 1986; Perfetti & Hart 2002).

Younger primary grade children read and understand fiction and nonfiction, can understand simple written instructions, and can describe in their own words what new information they have learned from the text. Third-graders can summarize fiction and nonfiction readings and identify themes, read longer fiction texts and even chapter books independently, and can distinguish between fact and opinion, main idea, and supporting fact (Snow, Burns & Griffin 1998). They incorporate what they've read in their fantasy play, deepening the meaning and contexts of new information.

In other words, during the primary grades, most children become real readers. And perhaps most important, many children across these years come to thoroughly enjoy reading and seek out reading activities voluntarily.

The natural extension of all the new information fueling the minds, imaginations, and spirits of these primary grade children is self-expression through writing. By first grade, children are creating their own written texts for others to read—stories, journal entries, notes to friends, and the like. They use invented spelling (spelling based on phonics) as necessary, but they are already conscious of getting it right; they want to spell words correctly and can use basic conventional punctuation and capitalization. They produce fairly readable first drafts and do some self-correcting.

By second grade, they use improved spelling based on previously having studied the word and represent the complete sound of the word when spelling independently, make reasonably good judgments about what to include in written text, and show sensitivity to formal English language patterns (e.g., using proper verb forms). Third-graders can produce a variety of written products including reports, responses to literature, journal entries, and letters. They can pull and combine information from multiple sources to inform their writing, use more elaborate descriptions and figurative language, and can edit and revise their own work, focusing on spelling and mechanics as well as clarity of meaning (Snow, Burns, & Griffin 1998).

To get a sense of how primary grade children progress in reading and writing areas, consider what the expert panel convened by the National Research Council (Burns, Griffin, & Snow 1999) indicated should be happening in first and second grade in these areas (see "Literacy: What Happens in First and Second Grade" on page 284). The progress in these areas continues in comparable fashion in third grade. By the end of that year, children can read appropriate texts aloud with fluency and comprehension, can ask about words and concepts they don't understand, and can decode unfamiliar words. They read increasingly longer books independently, with a goal of about 20 minutes a day outside of school. They know more and more words and examine the basis of their hypotheses and opinions. They use more elaborate descriptions and dialogue in their writings. They use nonfiction resources to find information but often need help paraphrasing and giving credit for sources. They can provide helpful suggestions to improve each other's work.

English language learners

The number of young children who speak a language other than English at home is growing at an increasingly fast clip; demographers estimate that approximately 40 percent of school-children will be English language learners in 2030 (Roseberry-McKibbin & Brice 2005; Lee et al. 2008). Asians and Hispanics are the fastest growing groups, and schools report that 80 percent of their current English language learners speak Spanish at home (Roseberry-McKibbin & Brice 2005; Pre-K Now 2008b).

As clearly demonstrated in countries throughout the world, young children have great capacity to acquire bilingual and even multilingual competence. Research strongly supports the benefits of bilingualism in language, literacy, and cognitive development: Bilingual children perform better than monolingual speakers on measures of analytical ability, concept formation, cognitive flexibility, and metalinguistic skill (Hakuta, Ferdman, &

Literacy: What Happens in First and Second Grade

First Grade	*Second Grade*
Continuing phonemic awareness and letter/print knowledge. Children will have acquired experience with phonemes in spoken language and with written letters. Their understanding of the uses and purposes of books and other types of text continues to increase. Some children will need additional practice in these areas in first and second grade.	
Decoding, word recognition, and oral reading. The emphasis is on moving from pretend reading to conventional reading and relying less on others and more on oneself to read. By the end of first grade, each child should be able to read aloud with comprehension and reasonable fluency, at least by the second reading. First-graders can accurately decode any phonetically regular one-syllable word, and they rely on the alphabetic principle to attack unknown words. They can usually recognize common but irregularly spelled words such as *have* or *said*.	**Decoding, word recognition, and oral reading.** By the end of the year, second-graders should be able to read and comprehend fiction and nonfiction appropriate to their level. They can accurately decode phonetically regular, two-syllable words and nonsense words. They use their phonics knowledge to sound out unknown words, including multi-syllable words. They can read longer, more complex sentences of written language with fluency and expression.

Diaz 1987; Roseberry-McKibbin & Brice 2005). NAEYC encourages teachers to support children's literacy in English *and* the home language in order to promote both language skills and academic achievement (NAEYC 1996).

It is not possible to say what a "typical" child who speaks a language other than English at home might look like in terms of language and literacy development in the primary grades—status and progress depend on myriad interacting factors, including:

• how long the child has lived in the United States;

• whether other family members speak and read in the home language, English, or both;

• the family's goals for the child;

• the child's proficiency in the home language;

• previous classroom- or program-based instruction in English (40 percent of Hispanic preschool and kindergarten age children partici-

pate in early education programs, compared with 59 percent of Caucasians and 64 percent of African Americans; Pre-K Now 2008b); and

• the type of support and structure the child experiences in the current classroom.

What we do know is that children learning English show common characteristics in their learning patterns, and we know teaching strategies generally help or hurt their language development.

Children learning a second language sometimes mix up grammar rules or use words from both languages in the same sentence. Also, some children will go through a silent period when first introduced to a second language, which can last several months. Both of these occurrences are normal when learning a second language (ASHA 2008).

Teachers should know that English language learners tend to make greater gains in the English language the more they experi-

Literacy: What Happens in First and Second Grade (cont.)

First Grade	*Second Grade*
Spelling and writing. By the end of first grade, children should correctly spell three- and four-letter short-vowel words. They can compose fairly readable first drafts of stories, letters, journal entries, and so forth, and pay some attention to planning, drafting, punctuation, and corrections. They use developmental or invented spelling (e.g., "iz" for *is*) to exercise independence and analytical thinking about their growing knowledge of phonemes and confidence in the alphabetic principle. They also learn correct spellings through well designed instruction.	**Spelling and writing.** Children correctly spell more previously learned words and represent all sounds when spelling new words, which they may do inconsistently. They are rapidly becoming writers, using formal language patterns such as quotes and proper verb forms in their writings. They know what kinds of information to include when they write and can productively discuss how to improve the piece. With help, they can write informative, well structured reports, paying attention to spelling and mechanics. When available, they use computers to compose their writing.
Language, comprehension, and response to text. By the middle of first grade, children should be readily talking and writing about what they read. They are learning how to summarize, locate main ideas, and make connections (both factual and emotional) to other readings and with life in general. They are beginning to draw inferences from text, such as understanding what is not explicitly stated, why something is funny, and what might happen next. They are becoming comfortable and taking joy in the ideas, information, and language that print brings them.	**Language, comprehension, and response to text.** Children read voluntarily for their own purposes and interests. They look to reading to answer their questions and are becoming well acquainted with the purposes of various print resources, from atlases to chapter books to weather reports. They read independently every day outside of school. They show an expanding repertoire of language and vocabulary. They can interpret information from diagrams and graphs and remember the facts and details. They respond creatively to what they've read through dramatizations, oral presentations, and fantasy play. They can answer how and why questions and explain new concepts in their own words. They can identify nouns, verbs, and other parts of speech.

Source: Adapted from National Research Council, *Starting out right: A guide to promoting children's reading success*, eds., M. Susan Burns, Peg Griffin, and Catherine E. Snow (Washington, DC: National Academies Press, 1999).

ence grade-level schooling in their primary language (Thomas & Collier 2002). Likewise, a review of the research by the U.S. Department of Education's 2002 National Literacy Panel on Language-Minority Children and Youth concluded that being literate in one's home language is an advantage as children learn to read and write (August & Shanahan 2006). Beyond

language and literacy development, a bilingual approach also improves content knowledge in various academic areas: High-quality, long-term programs that promote bilingualism are the most effective in shrinking the achievement gap between English language learners and native English-speaking children in the primary grades and beyond (Thomas & Collier 2002).

In addition to support in their home language, English language learners need specific instruction in English, beyond what English-proficient children experience, to clarify similarities and differences between languages. In the absence of focused spelling instruction in English, for example, children fall back on spelling knowledge they have acquired in their home language; when English-specific elements of spelling are taught, bilingual children quickly overcome "errors" brought from knowledge of their home language (San Francisco et al. 2006).

Teachers should also be aware of practices that can deter the learning of language and literacy skills by English language learners. For example, when children experience an abrupt submersion in an English-only environment, they are at risk of "semilingualism"—inadequate proficiency in both languages that contributes greatly to school failure, especially among low-income Hispanic children (August & Garcia 1988). And when teachers view children's bilingualism as a problem rather than as a rich strength on which to build, these young learners are less likely to experience the instruction, confidence, and encouragement they need to thrive (Gay & Howard 2000; Monzó & Rueda 2001; Souto-Manning & Dice 2007).

Promoting language and literacy development in the primary grades

No matter how good a book, curriculum, or computer program may be, nothing is as important as good teaching to instill a love of reading and writing. Effective primary grade teachers do a number of things to promote listening, speaking, vocabulary knowledge, reading, and writing skills. They create an overall literate environment in which children have access to a variety of materials to read; use focused instruction, trade books, and games; adjust the intensity of instruction based on a child's needs; link reading and writing activities; and create varied opportunities for sustained practice, such as in individual, partner, and group activities (Burns, Griffin, & Snow 1999).

Imagine a classroom in which a teacher reads and works on vocabulary with a small group of children at one table while another group browses books independently in the classroom library corner, another group practices using newly learned words in sentences or short stories, and still another works together on a journal entry. After 20 minutes or so, a timer goes off and each group rotates to the next literacy station. When each group has participated in every activity, the teacher brings the class back together for 10 minutes to review and hear from children what they learned (Slack 2008). This scene demonstrates how individual, small-group, and whole-group activities can intersect to benefit primary grade children in developing and practicing new language and literacy skills.

Small-group activities seem to work especially well (Dickinson 2001a; Kosanovich et al. 2006; Matteson & Freeman 2006). Forming small groups whose composition of children continuously changes to accommodate the different learning paths of readers is a particularly effective method teachers can use for attending to individual needs (Foorman & Torgesen 2001; Iaquinta 2006). Depending on the instruction goals, a teacher might create similar-skill or mixed-skill groups. Mixed-skill groups tend to work best when the teacher is present to facilitate (Slack 2008).

Whole-group activities work well for introducing a new skill or concept, modeling (visually or verbally) an exercise, debriefing or summarizing previous instruction, or practicing a skill that each child already has, to at least some degree. It is important to keep everyone engaged in whole-group sessions by, for example, having children vote on an answer by show of hands, answer in unison, or practice a task briefly with another child (Slack 2008).

Regularity of language and literacy activity is essential: Teachers should make sure that one or more adults read with children every day (Dickinson 2001a). Vocabulary instruction should be intentional rather than assumed as a result of book reading or conversation, and

© Ellen B. Senisi

teachers should select readings that include new, varied, and challenging vocabulary (Dickinson 2001a; Matteson & Freeman 2006; Beck & McKeown 2007).

Some children enter the classroom at a disadvantage when it comes to language and literacy experiences. But when teachers pay special attention to enhancing the vocabulary and reading and writing skills of these children, they see encouraging gains (Biemiller & Boote 2006; Beck & McKeown 2007). Reading books aloud is key to increasing their vocabulary knowledge (as with all primary grade children)—but not just any books will do. Most primary grade books include mainly words that children already know from conversation; teachers should select trade books for reading aloud that are beyond children's current independent reading level. These books usually have complex structures and more advanced vocabulary than the books children can read by themselves (Beck

& McKeown 2007). Teachers might offer direct explanation of the meaning of unfamiliar words as the story is read and might repeat readings, although more than two or three readings can lead to boredom (Biemiller 2004).

To extend vocabulary knowledge for children from low-income families or children who are otherwise at risk for school failure, additional activities beyond reading aloud can promote rich word learning: Teachers should spend additional instruction time on words that emerging readers would not otherwise learn, targeting sophisticated, high-utility words that children may find hard to picture, including verbs (e.g., *dazzle*), adverbs (*cautiously*), and nouns (*commotion*). Teachers should have children engage in constructive activities with these words and use them in different contexts. Also, they should focus instruction on target words not just before but also after reading and discussing a story. Additional reinforcement for children to learn

© Ellen B. Senisi

target words should continue over subsequent weeks. This type of rich, focused instruction has been shown to lead to twice as many words learned by disadvantaged children as those only hearing books read aloud (Beck & McKeown 2007).

To support English language learners in developing their English language learning, reading, and writing skills, August and Shanahan (2006) suggest that teachers should:

- provide focused instruction on English phonemes that are not present in children's home language;

- focus (if students are literate in their home language) on differences between that language and English, with less attention given to elements that are similar;

- provide extra practice in reading words, sentences, and stories;

- use cognate (similar) words in the home language as synonyms when teaching vocabulary;

- identify and clarify difficult words and passages; and

- consolidate knowledge of the text by summarizing (see Irujo 2007).

Technology can be helpful, but it must be used in interactive ways and practice should occur with real audiences; children won't learn a new language in a vacuum (Zehr 2007). Finally, wherever possible, teachers should find appropriate ways to use the child's home language in the classroom as a way to underscore appreciation for the home language, strengthen existing language skills, and highlight the importance of language skills in general.

Developmentally Appropriate Practice in the Primary Grades—Ages 6–8
Examples to Consider

The framework of developmentally appropriate practice derives from what the early childhood field knows from research and experience about how children develop and learn. Major points from this knowledge base are highlighted in the position statement and summarized in the overview in chapter 8. As no learning tool clarifies understanding better than examples, the chart below presents many examples of practices to consider.

The chart addresses developmentally appropriate practice in five areas important in the teacher's role: creating a caring community of learners, teaching to enhance development and learning, planning curriculum to achieve important goals, assessing children's development and learning, and establishing reciprocal relationships with families. The set of examples offered here is not exhaustive, and the goal is not to describe best practice comprehensively. We have tried to capture major aspects of practice that one sees in excellent primary classrooms and, by contrast, in those classrooms that in some respects have not achieved a high level of quality. Neither is the aim to issue a prescriptive formula to be rigidly followed. Instead, the examples are meant to encourage readers to reflect on their practice. Establishing a habit of thoughtful reflection is essential in working with young children because of their varying family backgrounds, preferences, and needs.

In the chart's left column, under the heading "Developmentally Appropriate," are examples of practices consistent with available research and that most in the field agree promote young children's optimal learning and development. The examples in the "In Contrast" column are intended to aid reflection by helping readers see clearly the kinds of things that well-intentioned adults might do but that are not likely to serve children well. Many of the "In Contrast" examples are very prevalent in early childhood settings. A few of those practices are dangerous or would cause children lasting damage. Others are unlikely to harm children significantly but also are less likely to promote their optimal development. Sometimes context affects whether a practice should be used or adapted.

Where they appear, the comments sections expand on the practice examples presented in the chart cells above them. Some of the comments speak to

cultural factors to consider when determining what practices to use. Other comments elaborate on a practice that is briefly described in a column, and some indicate the research finding on which it is based.

Finally, most of the examples are phrased as descriptions of what teachers do or fail to do. For the "In Contrast" examples, however, that wording is not meant to imply that deficient or questionable practices are necessarily teachers' fault. Most teachers are working hard and doing their best—but often constrained by very challenging circumstances, including large class size, limited training, inadequate staff:child ratios, limited resources, and administrative requirements. The hope of this chapter is to help them in their efforts.

Developmentally appropriate	In contrast

Creating a Caring Community of Learners

Fostering positive relationships

Teachers are warm, caring, and responsive. They help children learn how to establish positive, constructive relationships with others. They support children's forming of friendships and provide opportunities for them to play and work together. Communication with families is a priority.	▉ With heavy emphasis on structured instruction in academic areas, particularly literacy and math, teachers give little or no attention to social-emotional dimensions. ▉ Teachers do not see the importance of forming relationships with children and families. Or large class sizes make it very difficult for teachers to know children and families well.
Teachers know each child well and design the curriculum, environment, and teaching methods based on their knowledge of individual children's abilities and developmental levels, as well as where each child is in acquiring the skills and concepts important in a given area.	▉ The curriculum, environment, and teaching are essentially the same for all children in the classroom, without adaptation for the identities, interests, or work of individual children.
Teachers ensure that children with disabilities or special learning needs are included in the classroom socially and intellectually as well as physically. Necessary supports are in place to meet children's individual needs within the group context. To the extent possible, children with disabilities receive the extra support and services they need within their regular classroom.	▉ Children with disabilities or special learning needs are assigned to a class, but a great deal of their instruction occurs with special teachers outside the classroom. Even when they are with the rest of the group, children with special needs may not have access to all areas and activities. For example, parts of the playground may not be available to children with physical disabilities.

Developmentally Appropriate Practice, 3d Edition

Developmentally appropriate	In contrast

Creating a Caring Community of Learners (cont.)

Fostering positive relationships (cont.)

Teachers design all classroom activities to allow for the full participation of all children, including those who are not fluent in English.

■ English language learners cannot understand or take part in some classroom activities because teachers fail to make modifications or provide assistance to make their full participation possible.

Comments on fostering positive relationships:

—The capacity to form and sustain positive social relationships is important for social development and overall success in school (Bronson 2006). Children who are neglected or rejected by peers are often negatively affected academically as well as socially and emotionally.

—When teachers form warm and caring relationships with children, they in turn help to foster greater prosocial behavior and academic success. When children are able to form positive relationships with peers, their overall attitudes toward school and learning improve.

Building classroom community

The classroom is seen as a setting where children learn to work collaboratively, often working in groups to explore common goals. Teachers discuss significant issues with children and respect their viewpoints, while guiding them to a greater understanding of other people's lives.

■ Teachers rely on comparison and competition between students, undermining a sense of cohesiveness in the classroom. Groupings are always based on ability, and games are often overly competitive. Chronic tattling, scapegoating, teasing, and bullying are not seen as serious issues and go unchecked. A culture of respect is lacking, and teachers do not take action when hurtful behaviors or remarks occur.

Teachers promote children's sense of community involvement beyond their classroom—in the school or center as a whole, the neighborhood, or the town/city. For example, children make a sign to alert the other classes in the building about an upcoming event, collect clothing for a local shelter, take walks in the neighborhood, and note what shops and services are available to the local community.

■ No effort is made to build a sense of the group as a community or to link classroom matters to those of the larger community and society.

■ Classroom groups are not maintained long enough for children to become comfortable working together. Or they are unchanged for long periods, preventing children from interacting with everyone in the classroom.

Developmentally appropriate	In contrast

Creating a Caring Community of Learners (cont.)

Building classroom community (cont.)

Peer interaction is common in the classroom, and teachers provide many opportunities for children to work together. Children often solve problems or engage in activities in small groups or with partners. Even whole-group instruction is usually interactive. When possible, teachers encourage children to assist peers and may set up situations free of pressure where peers model or scaffold skills for others.

■ Most of the time, teachers address the whole group.

■ Teachers emphasize the need for children to do their own work independently at all times and do not provide opportunities for them to work together on cooperative activities or learn from one another.

Children learn to respect individual and cultural differences, and they acquire important skills and knowledge to enable them to function in society. Teachers bring each child's home culture and language into the shared culture of the school so that children gain a sense of belonging and form a positive self-identity. Through literature and social studies, for example, teachers help children understand values such as respect for others, equality, and personal freedom and the impact of biases in society on groups of people.

■ Cultural, linguistic, and other differences among children are devalued or ignored. Some children do not see their race, language, or culture reflected in the classroom, making it difficult for them to feel like part of the group.

■ Teachers draw attention to differences among children, including cultural and linguistic differences, to such an extent that some children are made to feel that they do not fit in.

Comments on building classroom community:

—A climate of respect for all members of the classroom community is crucial for children's success in the primary grades. In such an environment, all children feel accepted and have a sense of belonging. Conversely, when children insult or reject others, not only are they devaluing those they reject, they also are not learning the important prosocial skills they need to function and succeed in school and society.

—Providing opportunities for collaboration and learning from one another strengthens a sense of the classroom as community as children see their impact on the group as a whole. And when activities reflect the diversity of the homes, neighborhoods, and daily lives of the children in the class, children's awareness and appreciation of differing cultures and abilities increase. Children learn to recognize that they can enjoy and work with others from many backgrounds.

Developmentally Appropriate Practice, 3d Edition

Developmentally appropriate	In contrast

Teaching to Enhance Development and Learning

Environment and schedule

Teachers arrange tables or flexible groupings of desks to enable children to work alone or in small groups.	■ Children sit in desks throughout the day and year, which is not conducive to small-group projects and other positive interactions with peers. ■ Children are assigned a seat for the entire year and are rarely moved.
Teachers provide a safe environment and age-appropriate supervision as children are gradually given more responsibility. For example, second- and third-graders at times are allowed to navigate the school independently, but teachers always know where children are and what they are doing.	■ Teacher supervision is lax, and preventable injuries occur as a result. Health care personnel are not stationed at the school at all times. ■ Teachers fail to intervene when some children are too aggressive and hurt others.
Teachers anticipate and prevent situations in which children might be hurt, while supporting children's risk-taking behavior within safe boundaries (e.g., using tools or doing jobs and errands in the building).	■ Teachers are overly concerned for health and safety, leading them to severely restrict children's risk-taking behavior, thus failing to help children develop a sense of appropriate confidence, judgment, and personal responsibility for their own health and safety.
Teachers foster a learning environment that encourages exploration, initiative, positive peer interaction, and cognitive growth. They choose materials that comfortably challenge children's skills. A variety of spaces are provided in the classroom, including comfortable work areas where children can interact and work together and also places for silent or shared reading, working on construction projects, writing, playing math or language games, and exploring science.	■ The environment is disorderly, with little structure or predictability. Consequently, children's behavior is frantic or disengaged. The noise level is stressful for children and adults, making it hard to focus or have a conversation. ■ The arrangement of the environment severely limits children's opportunities to pursue engaging learning experiences. For example, children generally have to ask teachers for materials rather than finding materials readily accessible. ■ The environment, materials, and experiences reflect only a single culture or in other respects provide too little variety, interest, or choice for children (e.g., all books are at one reading level).

| Developmentally appropriate | In contrast |

Teaching to Enhance Development and Learning (cont.)

Environment and schedule (cont.)

Teachers organize the daily schedule to allow for alternating periods of physical activity and quiet time. They allocate ample time for children to become deeply engaged in investigating problems or creating products (e.g., writing, constructing models). Teachers give children advance notice of transitions and, when possible, allow them to complete what they are working on before moving to the next thing.

■ The organization of the schedule is rigid and arbitrary, with discrete and often insufficient periods of time devoted to each subject area. Children are required to sit still for long periods of time and are reprimanded when they cannot do so.

■ Transitions are disruptive and too frequent, often interrupting children's work and wasting time that could better be used for learning.

Teachers plan the curriculum, schedule, and environment so that children can learn through active involvement in various learning experiences with each other, with adults, and with a variety of materials.

■ Teachers do not spend sufficient time preparing the classroom environment or planning for groups and individuals. Children have little or no opportunity to work on projects, engage in activities of their own choosing, or use materials creatively. There is little or no time allotted for recess.

Comments on environment and schedule:

—Primary grade curriculum requires that children master a great deal of knowledge and skill, especially in the areas of reading and mathematics. Under pressure to ensure that children achieve learning outcomes, teachers may require students to sit still for extended periods of time. This is difficult and counterproductive for active young children, leading to boredom and frustration and potentially reducing comprehension and learning.

—One useful strategy to help children retain their energy and focus is to break up an extended block of time into several different learning experiences and formats. For example, a required 90-minute language arts block could begin with large-group instruction and discussion of new concepts, switch to some children in small groups for guided reading while others read silently or in pairs, continue with individual work while the teacher observes and offers individual help as needed, and finish with a whole-group teacher read-aloud.

Teaching methods

Teachers provide a variety of materials and activities that are relevant to children's lives in order to actively engage them in a range of learning experiences. Materials for children to explore and work with include construction materials, games, books and writing tools, computers, art media, and scientific equipment and are readily available.

■ Available materials are limited primarily to textbooks, workbooks, and pencils. Few manipulative objects or hands-on materials are available to assist children in building their understanding of math and science concepts, such as multiplication, floating and sinking, gears and levers, or the relationship between form and function.

Developmentally appropriate	In contrast

Teaching to Enhance Development and Learning (cont.)

Teaching methods (cont.)

Teachers use grouping as a deliberate teaching strategy and make it a key part of their planning. Classroom groups vary in size and composition, depending on the activity and children's needs. Children have opportunities to work in small heterogeneous groups, as well as homogenous groups, for various purposes. Children also have opportunities to create their own informal groupings. The composition of these groups is flexible and temporary, changing with the learning experience.

■ Teachers do not help children make good use of time to work independently (e.g., writing, sustained silent reading) or on group projects.

■ Although children who have difficulty working independently become frustrated or disruptive, teachers fail to intervene.

To help children learn and develop, teachers use a variety of active, intellectually engaging strategies, including posing problems or pointing out discrepancies, asking thought-provoking questions, adding complexity to tasks, and engaging in reciprocal discussion in which they take children's ideas seriously. Teachers also model, demonstrate, and explain, as well as provide information, direct instruction, coaching, and other assistance that children may need to progress.

■ Instructional strategies involve limited individual teacher-child interaction. Teachers lecture to the whole group and require children to spend long periods of time on seatwork that does not extend their learning. Teachers introduce new content or skills to children through worksheets with little prior explanation, discussion, or connection to previous learning. When speaking to individual children, teachers are usually just repeating directions rather than engaging children in substantive conversation or discussion.

Teachers are aware of the continuum of learning in each curriculum area (e.g., literacy, mathematics, science, social studies) and adapt instruction for individual children who are having difficulty and also for those who are capable of more advanced levels of competence.

■ Teachers do not modify their focus or teaching strategies when children's learning is beyond or behind predetermined expectations and benchmarks. Teachers do not feel accountable to help all children succeed.

By observing and interacting with individual children and small groups during learning experiences, teachers maximize their understanding of each child's current capabilities and what that child is capable of doing with and without adult support.

■ Because children do much seatwork or independent work on problems, in which teachers monitor only right or wrong answers, teachers have little idea about how each child processes problems or what that child's specific areas of difficulty and competence are. As a result, teachers do not know how to help children who do not understand or how to further challenge children who get the problem right.

Developmentally appropriate	In contrast

Teaching to Enhance Development and Learning (cont.)

Teaching methods (cont.)

To help children acquire new skills or understandings, teachers select instructional strategies, taking into consideration the intellectual demands of the learning task in relation to the participating learners. For example, the teacher might first allow the children to explore materials being introduced; next demonstrate a new technique; and then give structure or cues, such as steps to include in solving the problem. For a more advanced group, the teacher might give only the problem and the resources to solve it.

■ Teachers do not intervene when some children get frustrated and fail to learn key concepts and skills or when others are bored and progress far more slowly than they could.

■ Teachers are uninvolved in children's projects, play, or other learning experiences, providing minimal guidance or support. Teachers are passive, failing to take action when necessary, assuming that children will develop intellectual and social skills (e.g., negotiation, problem solving, conflict resolution) on their own without adult assistance.

Teachers recognize the importance of both child-guided and adult-guided learning experiences. In supporting children's deep engagement in creative experiences and child-guided activities, teachers find opportunities to enhance children's thinking and learning.

■ Teachers are passive in the classroom, rarely taking action even when children's behaviors are aimless or disruptive. When children are engaged in child-guided activities, teachers contribute little or nothing to children's exploration and learning.

■ Teachers do not recognize how important it is for children to guide some of their own activities, such as building structures or creatively exploring with science materials, and the adults frequently interrupt and undermine children's immersion in and managing of their own activities.

Teachers guide children in evaluating their own work and participating in determining where improvement is needed. Some work is corrected in small groups, in which teachers and children give feedback and children edit their own or each other's work. Errors are viewed as opportunities for learning. Teachers analyze children's errors and use the information to plan instruction.

■ Teachers correct children's work, but the results are not used to inform curriculum and teaching decisions; children are informed of their weaknesses but are not helped to do better. During most work times, children are expected to work silently and alone on worksheets or other seatwork. Children rarely receive encouragement or even permission to help each other in their work.

■ Feeling pressured to cover the curriculum and believing that returning to the same topic is a waste of time, teachers assume that if they have presented information or provided an experience once, children have learned the content.

| Developmentally appropriate | In contrast |

Teaching to Enhance Development and Learning (cont.)

Teaching methods (cont.)

Teachers provide many opportunities for children to plan, anticipate, reflect on, and revisit their own learning experiences. They engage children in discussion and representation activities (e.g., writing, drawing maps, constructing models), which helps children refine their own concepts and thinking and also helps the teachers develop a better understanding of children's thinking. Teachers use children's own hypotheses about how the world works to engage them in problem solving and experimentation.

■ Expecting children to respond correctly with one right answer most of the time, teachers view children's naive or partial hypotheses as wrong answers rather than as clues to their thinking or measures of the effectiveness of instructional strategies. Not realizing how much learning young children are capable of, teachers do not engage children in dialogues that take their ideas seriously.

Teachers and children together select and develop sustained, in-depth project work to be carried out by small groups who report back to the larger group. Teachers consider ways to pursue vital curriculum goals through these activities, which typically grow out of or expand on children's interests. To extend children's ideas, challenge their thinking, and further develop their social skills, teachers encourage involvement in collaborative learning and group problem solving, both of which require children to share their own perspectives, listen to the views of others, and negotiate shared goals and strategies.

■ Teachers offer little opportunity for collaborative work with peers, limiting social interaction in the classroom. Projects are not used as a means of engaging children in meaningful work toward integration of curriculum goals and objectives. Rather, projects are seen as "filler" for occupying or entertaining children. Teachers adopt a passive role as children work on projects.

■ Children have opportunities to work in small groups, but activities are unsystematic, disorganized, or fragmented. Any type of "hands-on" activity is assumed to be valuable, even if unconnected to curriculum goals, meaningful content, or children's needs and interests. The positive social aspect of peer interaction in small groups is overlooked.

Comments on teaching methods:
—Creative, hands-on exploration is an invaluable teaching approach in the early primary grades. Such experiences accompany or augment teacher-guided instruction to foster greater overall engagement in the subject matter.
—For a discussion of the purposes behind each classroom format (small group, large group, etc.), see the position statement and chapter 1.

Developmentally appropriate	In contrast

Teaching to Enhance Development and Learning (cont.)

Communication and language use

Teachers talk often and warmly with every child—getting to know children, building positive relationships with them, and gathering information about their interests and abilities.

■ Teachers' speech is mostly one way; adults much more often *tell* children things rather than talking with or listening to them.

Teachers engage in many one-on-one conversations with individual children.

■ Teachers usually speak to children as a group. For the most part, teachers address individual children only to admonish or discipline them.

■ Teachers dominate conversations with children instead of taking conversational turns.

Teachers provide numerous opportunities throughout the day for children to discuss their experiences, feelings, and the content they are learning. Teachers engage individual children, small groups, and the whole group in discussions about their learning experiences and projects, as well as current events. They encourage children to describe their work products or their thinking, and teachers express interest in children's opinions, observations, and feelings.

■ Teachers don't talk in depth with children, underestimating their complexity of thought.

■ Teachers talk at length to the whole group, offering few opportunities for discussion or children's input.

Teachers allow children time to think about how they want to respond to a question or comment (*wait time*), then listen and respond attentively to children's responses. Teachers encourage children's verbal interaction and expression of their own ideas.

■ Teachers show lack of respect for children as speakers (e.g., asking them questions without giving children time to answer thoughtfully).

■ Teachers stop children as they speak in order to correct their grammar, so much that children become reluctant to speak up.

Teachers intentionally employ a variety of strategies to expand children's vocabulary and word knowledge. For example, they introduce and explain new words in context as they occur during the natural course of the day ("You must be *exhausted* after recess. You're breathing hard and look like you're tired and need a rest").

■ Teachers talk down to children, both in terms of content and oversimplified speech, using relatively limited vocabulary in their conversational exchanges.

■ Teachers use a fairly rich vocabulary, but when they use a word unfamiliar to children, they rely on a dictionary definition that does not make sense to children, and they do not give sufficient information for children to grasp the word's meaning.

Developmentally Appropriate Practice, 3d Edition

Developmentally appropriate	In contrast

Teaching to Enhance Development and Learning (cont.)

Communication and language use (cont.)

Developmentally appropriate	In contrast
Teachers help children make connections among related words to expand their vocabulary ("Susanna holds a *grudge* against Marta. She is still mad that Marta wouldn't sit with her at lunch. She *grudgingly* agrees to talk to Marta").	■ Teachers miss opportunities to link words to connected families of words.
Teachers make it a priority to involve English language learners in meaningful verbal interactions at whatever level children are able. In talking with them, teachers help build children's English language proficiency by using nonverbal prompts, gestures, props, and repetition.	■ Teachers insist on children's speaking only in English, correcting them every time they use their home language or mingle the two.
Teachers talk with *all* children, making it a priority to talk often with children who are learning English and those with delayed language development or limited vocabulary.	■ Teachers don't make extra effort to talk to children who are shy or hesitant, have communication difficulties, or are in the process of learning English. ■ Teachers pay so much attention to English language learners (and draw their peers' attention to them as well) that those children feel unusual or outside the community of learners.

Comments on communication and language use:
—When introducing children to a new word, teachers need to describe how it is typically used and/or explain it in everyday language ("Today we're going to make *observations*. That's a word scientists use for looking very closely at something and writing down what you see, so you can eventually find out what it looks like or how it works").

Motivation and positive approaches to learning

Developmentally appropriate	In contrast
Teachers draw on children's eagerness to make sense of the world and to acquire competence by engaging them in interesting and challenging learning experiences.	■ A preponderance of experiences that are uninteresting and unchallenging or too difficult and frustrating undermines children's intrinsic motivation to learn.

Developmentally appropriate	In contrast

Teaching to Enhance Development and Learning (cont.)

Motivation and positive approaches to learning (cont.)

Teachers encourage children to set high but achievable goals for themselves and to tackle challenging problems and tasks. For example, when children impose low thresholds for their own performance ("I can't write a story. I can only write four sentences"), teachers lead them to raise their sights and reach a higher standard ("I'm curious to know what happens next in this story. Tell me about it, and I'll help you write it down if you need me to").

■ To get children to participate in activities or to complete assignments, teachers rely on external rewards (e.g., stickers, gold stars, candy, privileges, grades on every piece of work) or punishments (e.g., detention, no recess time).

Teachers use verbal encouragement in ways that are genuine and related to what the child is doing. They acknowledge and encourage the child's effort and work with specific, objective comments ("You really put a lot of detail into your story, and it sounds like you had a real adventure").

■ Teachers make such frequent use of nonspecific praise ("Good job!") that it becomes meaningless either to provide useful feedback or to motivate the child. Children may also become focused on pleasing the teacher rather than on the learning experience itself.

■ Teachers' feedback consists mostly of negative comments and correction of errors.

Comments on motivation and positive approaches to learning:
—As children get older, their self-evaluations of their own skills and abilities become more accurate. At the same time, schooling becomes increasingly demanding and challenging. This combination can sometimes foster in a child a negative view of her capabilities in the face of more difficult schoolwork. Genuine and concrete encouragement from teachers is powerful motivation, as a teacher's positive and negative feedback directly shapes a child's image of herself as a student.

Guidance

Teachers offer opportunities that promote initiative, cooperation and other prosocial behaviors, perseverance, task orientation, and self-regulation by providing many engaging activities, encouraging individual choices, allowing ample time for children to complete work, and ensuring numerous opportunities for one-on-one time with the teacher or with close friends.

■ Teachers lecture about the importance of appropriate social behavior and use punishment, public humiliation, or deprivations (e.g., no recess) to enforce rules. They do not make time for private conversations with children, and only the most able students finish their work in time to pursue special interests or interact with other children.

■ Virtually all activities are highly teacher-directed, so children remain too adult-regulated and don't develop self-regulation skills.

| Developmentally appropriate | In contrast |

Teaching to Enhance Development and Learning (cont.)

Guidance (cont.)

Teachers promote children's development of respect for others, conscience, and self-control through positive guidance techniques: involving children in establishing clear and reasonable rules for social living and conflict resolution, enforcing consistent consequences for unacceptable or harmful behavior, and meeting with an individual child having problems or with the child and parents together to discuss solutions. Teachers keep misbehavior in perspective, recognizing that every infraction does not warrant attention and identifying those that can be used as learning opportunities.

Teachers provide many daily opportunities for children to develop social skills (e.g., helping, cooperating, negotiating, solving peer conflicts by talking). Teachers facilitate the development of social skills, considered a central part of the curriculum. They intervene promptly when children engage in antisocial behavior and provide timely coaching in development of social skills for those children neglected or rejected by peers.

■ Teachers do not involve children in setting clear limits and standards of acceptable social behavior. Teachers place themselves in an adversarial role, spending considerable time threatening children for lack of impulse control and punishing infractions.

■ Teachers do not hold children accountable to acceptable standards of behavior and ignore unacceptable behavior, leaving some children to become bullies and others, victims. Classrooms lack clear limits on unacceptable behavior and put disproportionate responsibility on children to solve all their own social problems; this leaves the classroom without order and the teacher without authority.

■ Children have few opportunities to practice social skills or develop positive peer relationships in the classroom because they are always seated and doing silent, individual work or are involved in teacher-directed group work. Social interaction occurs almost entirely on the playground, where adults rarely interact with children except to admonish them to behave.

■ Teachers believe that if they ignore unacceptable behavior it will decrease, so they fail to take action when children are not developing social skills. For example, children who are persistently taunted or teased by classmates are told to ignore the taunts or to "work it out yourselves."

■ Children with persistent challenging behaviors are not referred for evaluation by specialists or provided with proper assistance.

Developmentally appropriate	In contrast

Teaching to Enhance Development and Learning (cont.)

Guidance (cont.)

Comments on guidance:

—In the early primary grades, children increasingly learn to internalize expectations for appropriate behavior. The way teachers set up the classroom and the types of activities and experiences that children engage in dramatically affect children's relations with peers and adults. Children develop and consolidate self-regulation skills much more effectively through positive interactions within a healthy, orderly environment than they do by being subject to directives regarding proper behavior.

—Many antisocial behaviors can be prevented or stopped through prompt and careful intervention by teachers. However, when serious challenging behavior persists, aggression may stem from a more difficult, underlying problem. Bullying is one of the most serious problems in schools today, with lasting negative consequences for both victims of bullying and bullies themselves. In such cases, it is important for teachers to work with families and specialists to create an individualized education plan for the child's current and future school career.

—For more on self-regulation in the early primary grades, see chapter 8.

Planning Curriculum to Achieve Important Goals

Curriculum essentials

Comprehensive scope; important goals

Developmentally appropriate	In contrast
The curriculum addresses key goals in all areas of development (physical, social, emotional, cognitive) and in the domains of physical education and health, language and literacy, mathematics, science, social studies, and creative arts.	■ Curriculum goals are narrowly focused on a few learning domains (e.g., literacy and math) without recognition that all areas of a child's development and learning are interrelated and important.
In each area, the curriculum is consistent with high-quality, achievable, and challenging early learning standards, such as those adopted at the state level. Curriculum is informed by recommendations from the relevant professional organization.	■ Curriculum content lacks intellectual integrity and is unworthy of children's attention. Alternatively, the curriculum covers some key topics but is designed mainly to help children do well on formal assessment measures, such as standardized tests.
The curriculum is designed to help children explore and acquire the key concepts ("big ideas") and the tools of inquiry for each discipline in ways that are effective for children in the early primary grades (e.g., experiences reading varying types of text, hands-on science activities using real equipment).	■ The curriculum is developed by extending expectations for higher grades downward rather than by reflecting what early primary grade children are capable of—thus, expectations may be too high. Alternatively, expectations are set too low or are otherwise not a good fit with the children.

Developmentally appropriate	In contrast

Planning Curriculum to Achieve Important Goals (cont.)

Coherence and integration

Teachers are knowledgeable about the sequence and pace that development and learning typically follow as children build understandings and skills in each content area. For example, teachers' understanding of the progression of mathematics concepts and skills involved in addition or subtraction enables them to introduce children to these in a coherent way and to scaffold children's progress from each idea and ability to the next.

■ Because the standards on which the curriculum is based include too many topics or learning objectives, learning experiences touch on topics only superficially, preventing children from gaining real understanding of any single topic.

■ Teachers do not know or understand the sequence of learning in the discipline areas or how it applies to children in this age range (e.g., expecting children to perform two-digit subtraction with regrouping before they fully understand place value).

Teachers integrate ideas and content from multiple domains and disciplines through themes, projects, creative opportunities, and other learning experiences so that children are able to develop an understanding of concepts and make connections across areas. For example, for a science project about worms, children might draw a picture of a worm's habitat and write down their observations of the worms they studied outside.

■ Children's learning is always seen as occurring in separate content areas, and content is never integrated. Teachers fail to connect curriculum topics in ways that are meaningful to children. As a result, learning is often fragmented, and children are less likely to generalize ideas and apply them across content areas.

■ Units of study are based on themes or topics that are limited in scope and depth (e.g., talking about the moon without reference to the sun), rather than using a curriculum based on characteristics of children's development and learning, the content and skills (including thinking skills) they need to acquire, and what they find deeply engaging.

Effective implementation

The curriculum, which exists in written form, provides teachers with a useful, flexible framework for planning learning experiences and materials and for seeing how those experiences fit together to accomplish the school's stated goals.

■ If there is a prescribed curriculum (published or adopted by a district or school), teachers do not have the flexibility or the capability to make adaptations in the curriculum to optimize its interest and effectiveness with the particular children in the class.

Developmentally appropriate	In contrast

Planning Curriculum to Achieve Important Goals (cont.)

Effective implementation (cont.)

Teachers actually refer to and use the curriculum framework as they plan what they will do with children, so classroom experiences are coherent. Teachers plan and implement experiences to help children achieve important developmental and learning goals.

■ Teachers do not consider the curriculum framework in their planning. Children's learning experiences do not follow a logical sequence. Curriculum goals are unclear or unknown.

In planning and implementing learning experiences, teachers draw on their knowledge of the content, awareness of what is likely to interest children of that age, and understanding of the cultural and social contexts of children's lives. Teachers value children's input and let it shape curriculum as appropriate (e.g., letting children suggest topics for their writing or science projects).

■ Teachers rigidly follow a prescribed curriculum plan without attention to individual children's interests and needs, the school's specific context (e.g., the region, student body, community characteristics), or any events that occur. For example, the teacher focuses only on the topic designated for the week even though a marathon is going to pass right by the school.

Teachers plan curriculum that is responsive and respectful of the specific contexts of children's experiences. Culturally diverse and nonsexist activities and materials are provided to help children develop positive self-identity, relate new concepts to their own life experiences, and learn to respect differences and similarities. For example, books and pictures include people of different races, ages, and abilities and of both genders in various roles.

■ Children's cultural and linguistic backgrounds and other individual differences are ignored or treated as deficits to be overcome. Insufficient resources are allocated to help children who speak English as a second language.

■ Multicultural curriculum reflects a "tourist approach" in which the artifacts, food, or other aspects of different cultures are presented without meaningful connections to the children's own experiences. Some children's cultural traditions are noted in ways that convey that they are exotic or deviations from the "normal" majority culture (and thus the children feel like outsiders).

Teachers regularly assess each child's progress toward the school's stated curricular goals, using both formal and informal assessment measures. Teachers monitor student learning and use assessment results to determine whether and how to change their teaching practices (environment, schedule, methods, etc.) to improve effectiveness for the class and for individual children.

■ Teachers do not regularly make use of assessment information, whether of children's learning or self-assessment of teaching practices, to inform their curriculum decisions.

Developmentally appropriate	In contrast

Planning Curriculum to Achieve Important Goals (cont.)

Effective implementation (cont.)

Teachers connect curriculum topics with children's interests and with what children already know and can do. Young children learn best when the concepts, vocabulary, and skills they encounter are related to things they know and care about and when the new learnings are interconnected in meaningful ways.

■ Meaningful, connected learning is not a priority in the curriculum planning. Curriculum is not integrated across multiple learning domains.

Comments on effective implementation:

—Teachers often do not have a say in the curriculum that is chosen by their school, district, or state. Despite this fact, teachers have the most important role to play in how effectively curriculum is implemented. In order to fully realize the curriculum's potential, teachers must have a clear idea of how learning experiences within the curriculum fulfill standards-based learning goals. By giving careful consideration to what standards are addressed by daily activities, teachers are able to better adapt curriculum in practice.

Physical development

Health and fitness

Teachers acquaint children with healthy habits and introduce basic concepts of body functioning and physical health. Sweets are never used as an incentive, and teachers reinforce good hygiene habits.

■ The school serves foods with low nutrition value and high sugar or fat content. Vending machines with candy, soft drinks, and other unhealthy foods are available to children. Children spend too much time sitting and do not get adequate exercise.

Comments on health and fitness:

—Childhood obesity is an increasingly critical problem in elementary school. While teachers in the early primary grades generally don't serve snacks, it is not uncommon for teachers and others to use sweets and candy as incentives or special treats. This is not a healthy habit; not only does it promote unhealthy eating and views toward food, but it also emphasizes external rewards. When such treats are given out by authority figures, the practice gains legitimacy for children and families.

Developmentally appropriate	In contrast

Planning Curriculum to Achieve Important Goals (cont.)

Gross motor development

Children do not spend extended time sitting; they are able to move around at frequent intervals. They have plenty of opportunities to use large muscles in balancing, running, jumping, climbing, and other vigorous movements, both during recess and in planned movement activities.

Children play outside every day and have specialized instruction in physical education on a regular basis.

Adults teach children the pleasure and importance of physical activity, as well as body and spatial awareness and key movement skills (e.g., catching, balancing). Teaching of physical skills is sequential and should be adapted to accommodate children's various skill levels; equal encouragement is given to boys and girls. Physical activities are integrated into various learning experiences whenever possible. Equipment and activities are adapted and/or modified to allow for active participation by children with disabilities and special needs.

■ Children have little opportunity for gross motor activity, and there is no regularly scheduled time for specialized instruction in physical education. Recess time is limited, or there are no opportunities for gross motor activities when the weather is poor.

■ Children are not allowed to play independently during recess but must follow structured adult-directed activities (e.g., everyone plays kickball during the entire recess period). All rough-and-tumble play is banned, without regard to whether such play is actually aggressive or not. Alternatively, children are not monitored during recess beyond the most basic supervision.

■ Adults make little effort to involve less-active children or those lagging in physical skills or coordination and to help them develop the skills and confidence to engage in gross motor activities. Accommodations are not made to include children with special needs.

■ Physical activity areas have very limited equipment, so children lack variety of choices and/or must often wait quite a while to get a turn. There is no adequate outdoor area for gross motor activity.

Comments on gross motor development:

—In many elementary schools today, less time is being spent on planned acquisition of physical skills. In some districts, positions for specialist teachers in physical education have even been subject to budget cuts, and daily specialized instruction is rare. Unfortunately, this reduction comes at a time when it's more important than ever for children to be active, as our society becomes increasingly overweight.

—In light of reduced physical education programs and the needs of school-age children, many classroom teachers need to integrate physical development and learning into the day's activities. They need to familiarize themselves with the grade level standards in early physical education and plan activities to foster skill acquisition and link to learning in other domains. The PE Central website (www.pecentral.org) offers suggestions for classroom teachers who want to use physical activity to teach academic content in the classroom, in an outdoor play area, or on field trips.

Developmentally appropriate	In contrast

Planning Curriculum to Achieve Important Goals (cont.)

Fine motor development

Teachers provide opportunities for children to develop and refine fine motor skills, especially in relation to writing and drawing experiences. Teachers provide assistance with handwriting, recognizing that some children may need more support than others in this area. Besides writing and drawing, teachers offer other activities involving fine motor skills, such as using art materials and tools (e.g., scissors, scientific equipment and tools, computers). As needed, teachers help children acquire such skills through scaffolding their efforts. Assistive technology is available for children with disabilities so they can participate as fully as possible in the classroom.

■ Teachers give children fine motor tasks that are too difficult or hold them to an unrealistically high standard in executing tasks. Teachers give negative evaluations to children whose efforts are unrefined.

■ The tools and fine motor experiences that teachers provide have insufficient variety to allow children at many different levels to progress in eye-hand coordination and motor control. Assistive technology is not available for children with special needs.

Teachers recognize that children are increasingly capable of functioning independently (e.g., they can keep track of school supplies and personal belongings), but they still offer occasional assistance when a child truly needs it. Adults are patient and encouraging when children need extra time to finish tasks involving more fine motor control.

■ To save time and prevent mess, teachers do not allow children to get materials on their own; children must always ask for what they need.

■ Adults shame children or display irritation when spills or other accidents occur or when children cannot finish their work quickly.

Comments on fine motor development:

—Though school age children are increasingly able to focus on fine motor tasks such as writing and drawing, the activities can still pose a challenge. With the pressure of curriculum content to cover, teachers may feel impatient when some children take much longer than others on tasks that require more fine motor control. Also, when children struggle to write numbers or letters, teachers may underestimate what the child really knows. Allowing children sufficient time to complete their work and giving them additional help with writing are important ways to differentiate instruction and allow children to work to their full potential.

—Gender is still a consideration in the early primary grades, as girls generally have more facility at fine motor tasks than boys do (Berk 2008). This should be a factor in the selection of materials for fine motor activities as well as when individualizing instruction on such tasks as writing.

Developmentally appropriate	In contrast

Planning Curriculum to Achieve Important Goals (cont.)

Language and literacy

Listening, speaking, and understanding

Teachers engage in conversations with both individual children and small groups. Whenever possible, these are sustained conversations (with multiple conversational turns, complex ideas, rich vocabulary). Teachers and children talk about children's experiences outside of school, what they are reading, and the topics the class is studying across the curriculum.

■ Teachers mostly ask children questions that call for brief or simple responses rather than elaborated speech.

■ Teachers use limited vocabulary in conversations with children or do not take time for conversation during the day.

To enhance children's listening skills, teachers create regular opportunities for them to actively listen to and converse with others and work together in small groups on projects or problem solving. Teachers give students opportunities to listen and respond to stories and poetry, follow directions, and listen attentively to others during group discussions.

■ Teachers focus on children's listening for classroom management purposes only.

■ Teachers stress children's ability to pay attention but provide little or no opportunity for response and discussion. Passive rather than active engagement is valued.

Teachers go beyond simply telling children to listen; they teach them the skills needed for careful listening. For example, when children need direction in order to complete a particular activity, teachers model and show examples of what is to be done. Then they ask children to review the procedures before they begin on their own. Participation in retelling activities after read-aloud sessions is used to encourage active listening and to help children monitor their own listening comprehension.

■ Teachers view listening as equivalent to hearing rather than as a set of cognitive skills and behaviors similar to those used for understanding and interpreting written texts.

■ When giving instructions or reading aloud, teachers rarely take the opportunity to guide children through the process of making sense of what they hear or explaining what they heard to others. Self-questioning when things don't initially make sense is not modeled or emphasized.

Teachers attend to the particular language needs of English language learners and children who are behind in vocabulary and other aspects of language learning. They frequently engage these children in sustained conversations and make extra efforts to help them comprehend.

■ Teachers talk mostly with verbally skilled children, neglecting the children who most need language help—children who are shy or hesitant, have communication difficulties, or are learning English.

■ When teachers talk to a child who is behind in language learning, they don't show the patience and attentiveness that the child requires in order to become a successful conversational partner.

Developmentally appropriate	In contrast

Planning Curriculum to Achieve Important Goals (cont.)

Listening, speaking, and understanding (cont.)

Teachers support English language learners in their home language (e.g., by gathering books and tapes/CDs in each child's language, involving adult speakers of the language in the classroom) as well as promoting their learning of English.

▨ Teachers provide no support for children in maintaining and developing their home language.

▨ A policy (sometimes imposed from above) specifies that children and teachers use only English in the classroom.

Teachers use reading to engage children in response activities that involve them in speaking purposefully to the group. For example, children might be asked to identify the problem in a story and then offer suggestions for solving the problem. The group might counter with questions about the solution, promoting an active dialogue.

▨ Most opportunities for speaking involve what is known as IRE—teacher **I**nquires, children **R**espond, teacher **E**valuates. In such an interaction, the teacher asks a question that often has an explicit reference in the text. Children's answers are largely based on recall of specifics from the text. The teacher gives a positive response if the answer is correct; if it is incorrect, the teacher moves on to another child until the expected answer is given.

Teachers help children use communication and language as tools for thinking and learning. For example, during group time teachers provide ways for every child to talk (e.g., talk to a peer, call out answers). Or teachers have children repeat aloud things they want to remember (e.g., "One plate, one spoon") or talk about what they will write before doing it.

▨ During much of the day, children are expected to watch or be quiet. During group time teachers call on one child at a time to respond, making all the others wait, during which they disengage mentally or become disruptive.

Comments on listening, speaking, and understanding:
—The quantity and complexity of children's vocabulary is one of the strongest predictors of reading comprehension (Smith 1997), which is a major goal of the primary grade years. Children's language development progresses most when they are actively engaged in verbal interaction, when teachers encourage them to extend their comments, and when teachers intentionally introduce and teach new vocabulary words. Because many children have a great deal of ground to make up in vocabulary and other language skills and/or English fluency, teachers need to find ways for children to be talked *to* less and talked *with* more. For example, during large-group instruction, teachers might introduce a new concept or skill, then have children turn to a partner and talk about it or discuss the idea as a whole group.

Motivation for reading

Special time is regularly set aside for children to choose and read books on their own, and a well-stocked reading corner is maintained for this purpose. Working closely with the school librarian or children's librarian at the public library, teachers ensure that there is a good selection of books, both stories and information books, and that the collection is regularly refreshed with new books.

▨ Children have access to only a small quantity and/or limited variety of books.

▨ For the most part, books are kept out of reach (either handled only by teachers or available only at children's request) and thus children cannot freely explore them.

Developmentally appropriate	In contrast

Planning Curriculum to Achieve Important Goals (cont.)

Motivation for reading (cont.)

Teachers read aloud to children each day. For those books and books that children read in heir own, teachers engage children in discussions about content of interest and importance to them. Taking notes on individuals' comments and questions, teachers follow up on these in small groups or one-on-one.

■ Teachers do most of the talking when books are discussed.

■ Teachers' questions in book discussions with children do not engage them in making inferences, thinking critically, or expressing themselves through use of new knowledge and vocabulary.

Comments on motivation for reading:

—The more children read, the better they get at reading—and the more they want to read (Meiers 2004). During the primary grades, children must master conventional reading—a task that requires lots of hard work. When children are motivated to learn to read, they are more likely to put in the needed effort and persist when confronting challenges along the way. Using school resources and public libraries, teachers must make sure to offer children a rich variety of engaging reading materials, including information books for children's specific interests, to expand all children's background knowledge and vocabulary.

Phonemic awareness/phonics

Teachers value and teach phonics systematically as part of a complete reading and language arts program. Teachers encourage children to write and spell notes, e-mails, journals, and messages using what they know about sounds and letters.

■ Phonics is emphasized to the exclusion of engaging children with writing, literature, and other important aspects of a balanced reading program.

■ Insufficient attention is devoted to helping children learn phonics, even though some children may need extra support.

Teachers assess the needs of the individual students and tailor instruction to meet specific needs. If a phonics program with a fixed sequence of lessons is in use in the school, teachers have the flexibility to adapt it to individual student needs.

■ Highly prescriptive plans for phonics instruction are used. Teachers cannot (or do not) make adaptations based on what children know.

Comments on phonemic awareness/phonics:

—Research shows that phonemic awareness and phonics strongly predict success in learning to read (National Reading Panel 2000). *Phonemic awareness* is the ability to manipulate the sounds of spoken words. *Phonics* is a component of reading instruction that teaches children the principles of sound/letter relationships, how to sound out unknown words, and exceptions to the general principles. Children who arrive in first grade without phonemic awareness will need more explicit and intensive instruction and then explicit instruction in phonics.

Developmentally appropriate	In contrast

Planning Curriculum to Achieve Important Goals (cont.)

Writing

Teachers give children frequent opportunities to write about topics of personal interest and content themes they are studying. Teachers engage children in creating original texts using the complete writing process: prewriting, drafting, revising, proofreading, and editing. They use a variety of teaching strategies, including modeling, sharing, and examining children's writing samples in order to draw focus to various aspects of the writing process.

■ Opportunities for children to engage in written composition are limited. Writing topics are almost always dictated by the teacher.

■ Teachers grade children's writing and mark their errors, but they make little effort to help them understand what makes effective writing and how to express and organize their ideas in order to communicate them to others through writing. Heavy emphasis is placed on neatness and correct spelling.

Teachers recognize that writing is a social activity and embed writing instruction in social contexts (e.g., each child is paired with a partner and the children react to each other's work). Through learning experiences and feedback, teachers emphasize that one writes differently depending on the audience.

■ The teacher is the only audience for children's writing and the only one to give feedback on it.

Comments on writing:

—Writing development is closely tied to reading development; writers grow in their ability to write in a particular genre, such as poetry, through being immersed in opportunities to write poetry and look closely at the poetry of others (NCTE 2003).

Word and print knowledge

Teachers use both explicit and informal teaching to help children identify specific features of the language that help them to recognize new words and make sense of what they read. These features are addressed in lessons where meaning is emphasized. For example, teachers help children to "build" new words using the prefix *un-* or the suffix *-ed*. New words are put into sentences to reinforce meaning, and as they read children are encouraged to take note of examples of the features they have learned (these may be added to a chart as they are found).

■ Teachers introduce a list of prefixes and suffixes to children with lists of words that apply. Little attention is given to how such features may affect meaning. Opportunities to extend the learning to children's everyday reading and writing are incidental and limited.

Developmentally appropriate	In contrast

Planning Curriculum to Achieve Important Goals (cont.)

Word and print knowledge (cont.)

Teachers use word study activities that call for active problem solving. They encourage students to look for spelling patterns, form hypotheses, predict outcomes, and test their ideas. These activities encourage students to ask themselves what they know about a new word and how it is similar to words they already know.

■ Teachers do not teach children strategies and encourage a problem-solving approach to recognizing and making sense of the words they encounter.

Building knowledge and comprehension

Teachers read to children from information books and chapter books that introduce complex and rich vocabulary. They briefly explain a new word as it is encountered, and then discuss the new words in greater detail with the children after the reading. Children are encouraged to use the words themselves in conversations.

■ Teachers do not take time to read aloud, assuming that read-alouds are for younger children.

■ Reading is limited to books that children can decode themselves, which have more limited vocabulary.

To broaden children's knowledge and vocabulary, teachers use a variety of strategies such as providing information books and literature rich in new concepts, knowledge, and vocabulary; planning field trips and inviting class visitors to tell children about their work or interests; and providing experiences through technology ("virtual field trips").

■ The books that children are given to read include a limited range of familiar topics and words.

■ Children have access to books with challenging vocabulary and a broad array of topics, but teachers do not help them to make connections with and understand unfamiliar words and concepts.

Teachers use enlarged texts, charts, and children's own reading materials to call attention to organizational features of texts. They model the use of textual features such as tables of contents, page numbers, and chapter headings and subheadings as important strategies for locating information.

■ Teachers tell children to read for information but do little to help them learn and use comprehension strategies that may be transferred to any situation or text (conventional or technological) where they may need to search for information.

To help students develop comprehension strategies and monitor their own understanding, teachers engage them in guided discussion when reading or listening. They ask children to make predictions about story events, retell or dramatize stories, and notice when text does not make sense.

■ Teachers' questioning during and after reading activities is restricted to low-level recall questions. They rarely ask children to give their opinions about an event or character in the story or to respond to open-ended questions.

■ Teacher follow-up to reading activities is largely confined to assigning worksheets.

Developmentally appropriate	In contrast

Planning Curriculum to Achieve Important Goals (cont.)

Building knowledge and comprehension (cont.)

Comments on building knowledge and comprehension:

—Children of diverse backgrounds, including English language learners, may have a difficult time grasping what they read or what is read to them, not simply because of the language barrier but because of their different life experiences. Teachers can help to bridge these gaps by becoming familiar with children's backgrounds and drawing connections between each child's experiences and the readings.

—Children are better able to comprehend stories and other text when they are taught to make connections between what they know and what is being read to them. Children also learn vocabulary most effectively when teachers actively engage them in grasping word meanings.

Mathematics

Developmentally appropriate	In contrast
Teachers recognize and build children's interest in making sense of their world through mathematics. They motivate children to learn math by connecting content to real-life, meaningful problems and situations.	■ Teachers communicate their own negative feelings about mathematics to children, assuming that children, too, will automatically dislike or avoid math. ■ Teachers feel inadequate and avoid teaching mathematics, or they stick strictly to the textbook without making meaningful connections for children.
A well-articulated, coherent mathematics curriculum helps teachers guide students through successively deeper levels of understanding and application of math concepts and skills. The curriculum identifies the important mathematics content to be studied at each grade level.	■ The math curriculum covers too many content areas superficially, and children do not have the opportunity to master the concepts and skills needed to move on to more complex mathematics. ■ There is no organized mathematics curriculum.
Teachers build on children's current knowledge, making sure that children consolidate their understanding of a concept before moving ahead (e.g., before they are expected to add and subtract two-digit numbers, they grasp the place value concept—that a digit's value depends on where it is in the number, such as units, tens, hundreds).	■ Teachers move along in the curriculum, even when children do not understand what has been covered. ■ Teachers spend too much time reviewing the same content over and over, boring children who have mastered it and are ready for more challenge.
Every day, teachers provide focused mathematics time that is interesting and meaningful to children, using various contexts (e.g., small-group, large-group, one-to-one), and find opportunities to integrate math learning experiences with other curriculum areas.	■ So much time is devoted to literacy instruction that planned mathematics experiences are given short shrift. ■ Teachers only teach math to the whole group.

Developmentally appropriate	In contrast

Planning Curriculum to Achieve Important Goals (cont.)

Mathematics (cont.)

Mathematics content is taught in ways that promote problem solving, reasoning, communication, making connections, and designing and analyzing representations (e.g., given a two-digit subtraction problem, children may think of various ways to solve it, describe how they solved it, think of how subtraction connects to division, make a drawing or use manipulatives to represent their solution).

■ Teachers focus heavily on children getting "the right answer" to a problem. Instead of giving children time and guidance to foster their reasoning and problem solving, teachers tell children the answers or solve problems for them.

■ Teachers rely heavily on drill and practice to teach mathematics.

Across the primary grades, the curriculum helps children makes connections between the content area of focus, such as number and operations, and other related areas of mathematics, such as data analysis or algebra.

■ Mathematics topics are taught in isolation from one another, and teachers miss many opportunities to help children deepen understanding by connecting what they know in one area to what they know in another.

Comments on mathematics:

—Covering too many topics interferes with students' gaining a deep understanding of the concepts and skills that are important in preparing them for next steps in the mathematics learning. According to the National Council of Teachers of Mathematics (2006), although a given grade's curriculum should include all the major content areas of mathematics, certain areas should be the focus each year:

First grade: Number and operations (addition and subtraction, whole number relationships including groupings of 10s and 1s); geometry (composing and decomposing shapes)

Second grade: Number and operations (the base-ten system and place value, quick recall of addition and subtraction facts, fluent multi-digit addition and subtraction); measurement (measuring lengths)

Third grade: Number and operations (strategies for multiplication and division, understanding fractions); geometry (describing and analyzing properties of two-dimensional shapes)

—Along with reading, accountability tests at the end of third grade now look at children's proficiency in mathematics. As a result, standardized tests can come to dictate the content of the math curriculum, and teaching can become more like testing—focusing on right answers rather than on deep understanding and broader application. For students to comprehend higher-level mathematics in the later grades as well as algebra, which is a prerequisite for college admission, they must first master the fundamental mathematics content and processes that constitute the primary grade curriculum.

Developmentally appropriate	In contrast

Planning Curriculum to Achieve Important Goals (cont.)

Science

Teachers cultivate and build on children's curiosity to emphasize inquiry in science experiences. Children are encouraged to observe and ask questions about the natural world and to think about what might happen during various scientific processes. Teachers provide materials and offer experiences and explanations that teach about important scientific concepts and skills.

■ Teachers slight science under pressure to cover other subjects in the curriculum. Teachers may transmit and test factual information on scientific topics, but they do not engage children in "doing science."

■ The science curriculum is only about exploration, and children do not acquire foundational concepts and knowledge.

The curriculum includes concepts not only from **life science/nature** but also from **physical science** (e.g., levers, pulleys) and **earth science** (e.g., clouds, rain). Teachers use a variety of strategies to help children develop important scientific concepts and skills.

■ The curriculum is limited to one area of science or to a few isolated topics with which the teacher feels comfortable. Other areas receive scant attention, even when children ask questions and show interest in them.

Comments on science:

—Many elementary school classrooms do not teach science in a meaningful, sustained way. Due to pressures such as the emphasis on literacy and math in accountability testing, science curriculum may be given short shrift. Even when science is integrated into the curriculum, children often encounter only a limited range of topics (e.g., study of some aspects of the natural world but no physics). Further, for rich, in-depth learning experiences, children need opportunities for hands-on experimentation.

Technology

Teachers make thoughtful use of computers and other technologies in the classroom, not to replace children's experience with concrete objects and materials but to expand the range of tools with which children can seek information, solve problems, understand concepts (e.g., using computer software that translates keystrokes or mouse clicks into musical notes to gain understanding that symbols can represent ideas), and move at their own pace. Software is selected to emphasize thinking and problem solving as well as to provide practice opportunities in a motivating format.

■ Children spend a great deal of class time on computers and/or watching television or videos.

■ Computer software is primarily devoted to drill or games with only a recreational purpose. Use of computers is a privilege, given as a reward or taken away as a punishment.

■ Teachers avoid use of computers and other technology in the classroom.

Developmentally appropriate	In contrast

Planning Curriculum to Achieve Important Goals (cont.)

Technology (cont.)

The location of computers in the classroom is conducive to shared learning and interaction—children talking about what they are doing, cooperating in solving problems, and helping one another. Teachers encourage children to use technology (e.g., cameras, websites) to document their experiences and work. They invite children's exploration of the various operations and actions possible with the technology, including interaction with the community and beyond through use of the Internet (e.g., participating in a national Web-based children's science study of bird migrations). Technology is used to document children's learning.

■ Computers are located only in an area outside the main learning environment (e.g., in a computer lab), so children have limited access.

■ Computers are in an accessible location, but children are never given the opportunity to work with partners or a small team on computer activities. Or due to a lack of equipment, children are always required to work in at the computer with three or four peers (and consequently never gain individual experience with the technology).

■ Teachers do not adjust use of technology for children's different comfort levels and abilities (e.g., a math game is set at the same level for everyone). Children must progress at a single pace, even if some children struggle to keep up and others are bored and ready for the next thing.

The program provides enough equipment that a child can become engaged in technology-based activities in a sustained, deep way. Boys and girls have equal access to computers.

■ The school doesn't provide any technology or provides so little that children get only very brief turns using a piece of equipment in order to allow everyone to have a chance. Boys dominate use of computers.

Social competence; social studies

The content of social studies curriculum in the early primary grades connects to children's lives and is integrated with other learning domains. Topics or projects are the focus of in-depth work for an extended period of time. Key knowledge and concepts are learned through a variety of projects and activities involving use of library resources, visits to interesting sites, visitor interviews, discussions, and relevant use of language, writing, and reading skills.

■ Teachers may convey facts relating to social studies, but the information is too remote from children's experience or too fragmented to be meaningful and interesting to them.

■ Rather than integrating learning experiences, teachers address each social studies standard individually with a separate activity or experience. Social studies is always separate from the study of other curriculum areas.

Developmentally appropriate	In contrast

Planning Curriculum to Achieve Important Goals (cont.)

Social competence; social studies (cont.)

The teacher introduces projects and/or units that include aspects of the traditional social sciences of geography, history, economics, and civics/political science. Teachers draw connections between social studies knowledge and methods and everyday situations and events.

■ Teachers do not provide experiences that introduce children to basic concepts and ideas foundational for later learning in social studies. Or they lecture children on topics (e.g., values and ideals of civic engagement) without discussion and room for comment or disagreement.

■ Topics are not sufficiently challenging for children, being restricted to themes such as community helpers.

Teachers actively foster children's understanding of democratic processes and attitudes in concrete, experiential ways that children are able to understand, such as making and discussing classroom rules, solving together the problems that arise in the classroom community, and learning to listen to others' ideas and perspectives. When possible, children are involved in conflict resolution through such vehicles as class meetings.

■ Teachers are the only decision makers in the classroom; they do not engage children in sharing ideas and solving their problems together. Children are never involved in conflict resolution or group decision making.

■ Teachers attempt to teach about democracy but in ways that are too abstract for young children to relate to (e.g., the balance of power in government).

Comments on social competence and social studies:

—The social studies provide many opportunities to develop key skills of social competence, such as planning and working in cooperation with others. The classroom can be seen as a laboratory of social relations where children learn rules of social responsibility and respect for individual differences through structured experiences directed toward those goals.

—Primary grade children often have experiences that extend to other parts of the country and even beyond (through travel, immigration, or technology). As our society becomes ever more global, knowledge of the interconnected relations between groups of people as well as between nations becomes increasingly vital for our children's generation. Yet teachers often overlook such connections by constricting study to very close-to-home topics. Primary grade social studies might include topics relating to the immediate community but extend more broadly, as well.

Developmentally appropriate	In contrast

Planning Curriculum to Achieve Important Goals (cont.)

Creative arts
Creative/aesthetic development

Classroom teachers (on their own or working with specialists) help children explore and work with various art and music media and techniques. Teachers convey an open, adventurous attitude to the arts ("How about trying this?") that encourages children to explore available media and try new approaches. The arts are integrated with other areas of the curriculum.

■ Art and music are only taught as separate subjects occurring once a week or less, and specialists do not coordinate closely with classroom teachers.

■ Teachers spend time preparing children for special performances or exhibits for families or the public rather than supporting children's active participation in the arts for the sake of their own creative expression, knowledge, and appreciation.

Teachers display children's art, as well as the work of artists, in the classroom and elsewhere in the school. Teachers encourage all children to take pride in everything that is created, regardless of individuals' varying skill levels. Children have opportunities to experience music, art, and dance in the community.

■ Teachers emphasize the finished product or performance and single out for praise those children who are particularly gifted or trained in one of the arts.

■ The music and art in the environment reflect the teachers' own culture(s) and tastes but do not include the arts of the local community or the backgrounds of the children and their families.

■ The environment is heavily decorated with depictions of commercial media characters or other simplified, cartoon-like images.

Comments on creative/aesthetic development:
—Creativity and creative expression are not limited to the arts, but the arts are an excellent venue for fostering new ways of thinking. Children love to explore with a wide variety of materials; when teachers include the means for creative expression throughout the curriculum, children's interest in the subject matter is heightened. But teachers need to recognize that arts activities themselves fulfill important learning goals and have intrinsic value separate from other academic domains. As children progress through the early primary years, focus on individual creativity as important in and of itself is increasingly necessary to counter the message that accurate representation is most important or that there is only one right way of doing things.

Developmentally appropriate	In contrast

Planning Curriculum to Achieve Important Goals (cont.)

Visual arts

Classroom teachers or specialist art teachers make available a wide variety of art media for children to explore and work with. Children have the opportunity to manipulate advanced art materials, such as papier mâché or yarn stitching, and to explore new materials as their skills and creativity grow.

■ Teachers introduce only the few art media and methods that they enjoy or know.

■ Children are allowed to use materials only under tightly controlled conditions. Or children have no conditions imposed on their artistic expression, as teachers believe this limits creativity; the result is a chaotic classroom in which children do not learn useful techniques.

Teachers discuss children's art with them. Teachers have children revisit projects and media, giving them opportunities to revise and expand their ideas and refine their skills.

■ Art materials are available, but children are not supported in moving beyond the exploration level.

Teachers demonstrate new techniques or uses of materials to expand what children can do with them. In determining what methods to introduce and demonstrate, teachers consider children's developmental level (e.g., encouraging first-graders to depict a scene in their drawings but not expecting them use perspective).

■ Teachers do not teach children new skills that would help them advance in creative expression.

Teachers do not provide a model that they expect children to copy.

■ Teachers provide a model and/or expect children to follow specific directions resulting in similar products. Emphasis is on group-copied crafts rather than individual artistic creations, and artworks are produced primarily to be pleasing to adults.

Comments on the visual arts:

—In the early primary grades, art often takes a backseat to other curriculum areas, such as math and literacy. However, children benefit from frequent art experiences, both during specialized instruction and from integration of art activities and techniques in the classroom. Children of this age are very aware of physical symbols and how they relate to or represent objects in the world, and the visual arts provide opportunities to explore children's sense of power as symbol makers. Practicing artistic techniques also contributes to greater fine motor control (e.g., when children experiment with controlling the flow of paint while using watercolors).

—Teachers should involve children in complex, meaningful tasks, such as creating short picture books or storyboards for making videos. This type of activity incorporates exploration of narrative text with representational art.

Developmentally appropriate	In contrast

Planning Curriculum to Achieve Important Goals (cont.)

Music and movement

Teachers can introduce songs with parts, rounds, and harmonies, as primary grade children now have mature singing voices and a vocal ability to produce 8–10 pitches. Teachers have a repertoire of songs to sing with children, who are increasingly able to master recall of both melody and lyrics.

Teachers provide musical instruments for children to use. Songs and instruments from various cultures, especially those of the children in the group, are included.

■ Teachers rarely return to a song or dance once they have shared it with children, so children are unable to build up a repertoire of music with which they are familiar. Teachers do not sing with the children.

The joy of music is central in the experiences teachers share with children. In ways that don't interrupt that enjoyment, teachers may introduce printed music for children to follow along.

Whether or not there are specialist teachers for music, it is integrated with other curriculum areas.

■ Teachers approach music in a didactic way, teaching specific terms and elements but not giving children integrated, enjoyable experiences in music.

■ Having a "performance orientation," teachers or specialists tend to single out those children most clearly gifted or trained in singing, dancing, or playing instruments and criticize or ignore the creative efforts of the other children. Teachers focus on performances to the exclusion of other musical curriculum.

Teachers give children time to dance to music and they introduce movement activities that allow children the opportunity to invent their own movement patterns. Children are introduced to some basic dance concepts and given opportunities to incorporate movement and dance with music, both in response to recorded music and in independent creation of music. Teachers encourage children to engage in activities that require rhythm and timing.

■ Children have limited or no opportunity to dance or otherwise move to music. Teachers do not get up and move with children.

Comments on music and movement:

—Primary grade children can handle songs with many elements requiring memory and sequencing skills. They are also able to follow complex instructions relating to sequences of movement and can learn many dance movements. Music and dance are important to children's overall cognitive development and should not be regarded as optional curriculum.

—Children are becoming aware of the relation between printed music and sung notes. As children learn to read, they can read words on the page and sing along to less familiar songs.

Developmentally appropriate	In contrast

Assessing Children's Development and Learning

Strategic and purposeful

Assessment is done for four specific, beneficial purposes: planning and adapting curriculum to meet each child's developmental and learning needs, helping teachers and families monitor children's progress, evaluating and improving program effectiveness, and screening and diagnosis of children with disabilities or special learning and developmental needs.

■ No systematic assessments of children's progress or achievements are done.

■ Assessments are done, but results are not used to provide information about children's depth of understanding or to adapt curriculum to meet their needs. Doing the assessment takes an excessive amount of teachers' time and attention away from interacting with children.

■ Formal assessments such as standardized tests are used as the sole qualifying factor for high-stakes decision making (e.g., entry to the next grade level, referral for special education).

Teachers use assessments for identifying children who might have a learning or developmental problem (i.e., for screening), typically toward the beginning of the school year. When assessment identifies the possibility of a special need, appropriate referral to a specialist for diagnostic follow-up or other intervention occurs.

■ Teachers diagnose or label a child after only a screening or one-time assessment. Test results are used to group or label children (e.g., as "unready" or "special needs").

Decisions that will have a major impact on children (e.g., entry, grouping, retention) are based on multiple sources of information, including both formal and informal assessments. Information comes from observations by teachers and specialists and also from parents.

■ Readiness or achievement tests are used to recommend that children be held back or placed in remedial classrooms.

■ Children are judged on the basis of inappropriate and inflexible expectations for their academic or social abilities (e.g., that all children must be reading conventionally by the end of first grade or be retained).

Assessment in the primary grades continues to address key goals in all developmental domains (physical, social, emotional, cognitive). But it increasingly focuses on the continuum of learning in the academic areas of physical education and health, language and literacy, mathematics, science, social studies, and creative arts.

■ Programs and teachers don't think about which goals are important in each area, so their assessments look at trivial skills and facts (e.g., children's ability to decode nonsense words).

■ In preparation for third grade accountability testing, assessment focuses only on a few domains or areas (e.g., math and literacy) and ignores other important disciplines (e.g., science, social studies).

Developmentally appropriate	In contrast

Assessing Children's Development and Learning (cont.)

Strategic and purposeful (cont.)

Comments on strategic and purposeful assessment:
—To ensure that all children benefit from schooling and continue to make progress toward essential learning goals, ongoing and purposeful assessment is essential. However, in this era of accountability, the stakes involved in primary school assessments are often very high for children, teachers, and schools. Children may be denied entry to a grade level or marked with a label that affects their future educational careers. Teachers and schools may receive incentives such as bonuses or increased funding based on children's achievement test results, while disciplinary actions such as loss of resources, funding cuts, and even job cuts and school closures are increasingly based on lower test scores.

Systematic and ongoing

Developmentally appropriate	In contrast
There is an assessment plan in place that is clearly written, well-organized, complete, comprehensive, and well-understood by principals, teachers, and families.	■ No plan for assessment exists. ■ Assessments are imposed on teachers from above without a clear explanation for why they must be given. ■ The plan for assessment is not shared with and/or is not understood by the families whose children are assessed.
Health and developmental screenings are done (e.g., on a schedule per district and/or state mandates) by appropriate personnel in order to identify children who may need more in-depth, diagnostic assessment. Disabilities or other special learning needs not apparent at younger ages are a particular focus.	■ When a child appears to be having difficulty learning, teachers presume a problem of attention or prior knowledge rather than considering a disability or developmental delay (e.g., child needs glasses). ■ Teachers make diagnoses that should be done by specialists.
Information is collected at regular intervals throughout each year.	■ Assessments are rare and/or random. ■ Children's performance is assessed only at the end of a project, unit, semester, or year, when it's too late to affect learning outcomes.
Teachers have the time, training, and materials they need to do assessment properly and accurately.	■ Teachers are burdened with assessment requirements but not provided with adequate tools or appropriate professional development to accurately use them. Therefore, assessing is a waste of teachers' and children's time.

Developmentally appropriate	In contrast

Assessing Children's Development and Learning (cont.)

Integrated with teaching and curriculum

Developmentally appropriate	In contrast
Assessment is consistent with the developmental and learning goals identified for children and expressed in the primary curriculum.	■ Assessments look at goals not in the curriculum—or content not taught to the children—and often include skills or methods not used in the classroom. ■ Assessments narrow and/or distort the curriculum when teachers "teach to the test."
Teachers use assessment to refine how they plan and implement activities. As children progress through the primary grades, teachers increasingly use assessment results to focus on how best to promote children's acquisition of content in specific subject areas.	■ There is no accountability for what children are doing and little focus on supporting learning and development. Teachers don't use assessment information to determine which teaching approaches are working or how to individualize instruction (e.g., to scaffold children having difficulties or challenge those ready for more).
Assessments are tied to children's daily activities, including during child-guided experiences (e.g., in learning centers or work on projects) and peer-to-peer interactions. Teachers record on-the-spot assessments whenever possible (i.e., observe, ask, listen in, check), using the information to shape their teaching moment by moment with individual children. Teachers also collect diverse types of documentation throughout the year, including written notes, audio and video samples, photographs, and children's work samples. Teachers reflect on this documentation regularly to monitor children's progress.	■ Assessment results (observation notes, work samples, etc.) go straight into a folder and are filed away without being used to inform instruction. ■ Teachers use quizzes or weekly tests that tell only what children get wrong or right but not whether they understood a concept or how they solved a problem.
Teachers look at what each child can do independently but also assess collaborative work with peers and adults. Teachers assess as the child participates in groups and during other scaffolded situations.	■ Children are assessed only as individuals. Thus, teachers miss information about what children can do as members of a group or what tasks are just beyond their current capabilities and would benefit from adult support.

Developmentally appropriate	In contrast

Assessing Children's Development and Learning (cont.)

Valid and reliable

Assessments are used only for acceptable purposes, where research has demonstrated they yield valid and reliable information among children of similar ages, cultures, home languages, and so on.

Only assessments demonstrated to be valid and reliable for identifying, diagnosing, and planning for children with special needs or disabilities are used for that purpose.

■ Test results are used to group or label children (e.g., as "unready") but are not used to provide information about children's degrees of understanding or progress.

■ Assessment materials are used without having been checked for validity and reliability.

Assessments include teachers' observations of what children say and do during class activities (e.g., projects, reading and writing tasks, group discussions, math games or problem solving) and examination of children's work samples, as well as increasingly more formal assessments (e.g., responses to teacher questions, pencil-and-paper tests) separate from other classroom activities.

■ Teachers use methods appropriate for much older children (e.g., multiple-choice tests). Assessment is primarily administered separate from children's usual activities.

Assessments are matched to the ages, development, and background of the specific children. Methods include accommodations for children with disabilities.

Teachers use a variety of methods/tools, recognize individual variation among learners, and allow children to demonstrate their competence in different ways. Teachers involve children in evaluating their own work.

■ Assessments assume background knowledge children don't have. Methods prevent a child from demonstrating what he actually knows and is able to do (e.g., giving directions for math problems in English when the child speaks only Korean).

Teachers gather information from families, including what individual children demonstrate they know and can do at home.

■ Families are not considered a valid source of information.

Comments on valid and reliable assessment:
—Primary grade teachers usually have little say regarding the assessment tools used for accountability purposes. For instructional purposes, teachers thus need to gather information about children from multiple sources and use a variety of different assessment methods. This multifaceted approach is especially important when assessing English language learners, who may possess knowledge and skills that would not be evident from an assessment measure requiring fluency in English.

Developmentally appropriate	In contrast

Assessing Children's Development and Learning (cont.)

Communicated and shared

Teachers and families share information in ways that are clear, respectful, and constructive. Families are periodically informed about how their children are doing in all developmental domains and across academic disciplines. If numerical or letter grades are used, they are accompanied by narrative comments and/or verbal explanations regarding the child's learning.

■ Families are not kept informed about assessment results and children's progress (e.g., family is told late in the year that their child will be held back). Or the meanings and limitations of large-scale assessments are not communicated clearly to parents.

■ Teachers report children's progress to parents only in letter or numerical grades.

Within the limits of appropriate confidentiality policies, teachers exchange information about each child with other teachers in the grade who work with the child (e.g., reading or mathematics specialists), as well as with the child's new teachers in the next grade. This eases children's transition and sets the stage for new challenges in school, as the next teachers know each child's history.

■ Assessment information is not used to help ease transitions for children from one classroom, grade, and teacher to another.

Establishing Reciprocal Relationships with Families

Teachers and administrators view families as partners in the educational process. Families' visits to school are welcomed. Family events and a variety of opportunities for participation in the school and classroom are planned, and these are scheduled with families' needs in mind.

■ The administration does not give teachers adequate time or resources for engaging with parents. The message that schools are for teachers and children, not parents, is conveyed to families. Teachers view parents' roles as supporting—but not participating to help determine—the school's agenda and activities.

Educators and parents share decisions about children's education. Teachers listen to parents, seek information from them about their children, and seek to understand their goals for their children. Teachers work with parents to resolve problems or differences of opinion as they arise and are respectful of cultural and family differences.

■ School personnel do not involve parents in decisions about how best to handle issues concerning their child or to support his or her learning. Teachers and administrators see parents in a negative light, complaining that parents have not raised their children well or blaming children's poor school performance on the home environment.

■ Principals or teachers appease the parents who make demands or complaints, even when the action demanded is to the detriment of some students or the school community.

Developmentally appropriate	In contrast

Establishing Reciprocal Relationships with Families (cont.)

Members of each child's family are encouraged to participate in the classroom in ways that they feel comfortable. For example, family members may take part in classroom activities (sharing a cultural event or language, telling or reading a story, tutoring, or playing games) and/or contribute in behind-the-scenes ways (collecting materials or making learning materials for classroom use, bringing library books on a topic of study, or editing the school newsletter).

■ Teachers and administrators see parents as a source of pressure rather than a resource. A policy for parent participation exists, but it receives little time or effort.

■ The school and/or teacher makes excessive demands on parents' limited time and energy, including a great deal of required assistance with children's homework. Teacher-parent conferences, parent meetings, or other participation opportunities occur only during the day when many employed parents are unavailable.

Teachers and administrators facilitate communication with families who do not speak English, offering resources such as translated handouts and bilingual staff.

■ Teachers and staff do not provide assistance to families with limited English skills to help them understand communications on school matters. Families and children are penalized for incomplete or missing forms though families cannot complete them due to language barriers.

■ Communication with family members who speak little or no English is overlooked or actively avoided. No effort is made to keep these families informed or see that they attend conferences and other planned events.

Comments on establishing reciprocal relationships with families:
—Developing reciprocal relationships with families is important because parent and family involvement in their children's education is a key ingredient for success in the early primary years. Knowledge of children's home lives and cultures helps teachers to make decisions—with parents—working through differences and reflecting on what they know will work best for individual children. Such background information is especially important for reaching out to children and families who may be new to a formal school environment and who may, in many cases, have limited English language skills. Understanding parents' preferences is essential to maintaining the two-way exchange necessary for any successful partnership.

FAQs about Developmentally Appropriate Practice

Teachers, administrators, parents, and policy makers ask all sorts of questions about developmentally appropriate practice. Here we briefly address the most common ones. We recognize that responses to such questions are not static. They evolve with changes in the contexts of early childhood programs and schools, the knowledge base, and the thinking of the many individuals who work in the field. So, NAEYC offers these responses not to give the final word on these questions, but rather to foster further conversations among all early childhood educators.

Do proponents of DAP think there is only one right way to teach?

Developmentally appropriate practice actually means just the opposite—it means shaping the way one teaches to fit the children and to suit the rather different kinds of learning children need to do. For example, you don't teach a child to tie his shoe by encouraging him to work it out by trial and error. You show him what to do a step at a time. On the other hand, you don't get children to come up with their own solutions by telling them a common solution. Individual children vary greatly in their development, prior experiences, abilities, preferences, and interests, and there is no formula that works for all of them or for all situations.

To teach any child effectively, a teacher must use a variety of teaching strategies and make intentional choices about what strategy to use in a particular situation, and when and how to extend and support children's learning. Both child-guided and adult-guided experiences are part of the good early childhood program. Teaching strategies include acknowledging and encouraging children, demonstrating and modeling behaviors and methods, asking questions, creating challenges and modifying their difficulty level, and providing specific information and direction.

Is "Developmentally Appropriate Practice" a curriculum?

No, DAP is not a curriculum. NAEYC provides guidance about what constitutes good curriculum in several of its position statements, particularly that on developmentally appropriate practice (2009, see this volume) and one on curriculum, assessment, and program evaluation (NAEYC & NAECS/SDE 2003). Planning curriculum that is appropriate and effective for children is certainly a key aspect of recommended practice, but no one curriculum is designated as "Developmentally Appropriate Practice."

There are a variety of early childhood curriculum frameworks and approaches that have most or all of the characteristics of high-quality curriculum as defined in NAEYC position statements. An array of published curriculum products reflect diverse theoretical perspectives on learning and development and give the teacher varying amounts of structure or flexibility. Decision makers, administrators, and teachers can refer to the principles of developmentally appropriate practice and apply them in developing or selecting curriculum.

Remember that whatever the curriculum, it can be effective and developmentally appropriate only if teachers have sufficient professional development to support their understanding of that curriculum; know how children learn and develop; and adapt the teaching materials, learning experiences, and strategies to meet the individual needs of each child in the classroom. Curriculum matters, but it cannot take the place of a good teacher.

Are developmentally appropriate programs unstructured?

The notion that there is little or no structure in a DAP classroom is a misconception. In reality the opposite is true. To be developmentally appropriate, a program must be thoughtfully structured to promote all aspects of children's well-being and competence. A developmentally appropriate program is well organized in its schedule and physical environment and uses a planned curriculum to guide teachers as they assist children to accomplish important learning goals. The structure of a developmentally appropriate program is also designed to accommodate and adapt for individual differences. Teachers expect to make changes as needed to address children's interests and promote their progress.

In the developmentally appropriate classroom, there is a predictable but not rigid schedule to the day, and there are clear rules for acceptable behavior. In the course of the day, children have opportunities to choose from a number of learning centers and to participate in a variety of other learning contexts, such as large-group and small-group times. In all of these contexts, the teacher is intentional in using the environment, materials, and teaching strategies to enable children to acquire important knowledge and skills.

Someone told me that in developmentally appropriate classrooms, all children do is play. Is that true?

Research shows that child-guided, teacher-supported play benefits children in many ways. When children play, they engage in many important tasks, such as developing and practicing newly acquired skills, using language, taking turns, making friends, and regulating emotions and behavior according to the demands of the situation. This is why play needs to be a significant part of the young child's day—and part of a developmentally appropriate classroom. Moreover, effective teachers take action to enhance children's play and the learning that goes on in the play context. They engage in one-on-one conversations with children; encourage pretend play with themes, roles, rules, and props; or introduce math talk during block building—which research shows is related to language, literacy, mathematics, and social and emotional development.

At the same time, play is not the only thing that children do in developmentally appropriate classrooms. Children also work in small groups,

listen to stories, meet as a whole group, work on projects, solve problems, participate in routines that are developmentally enriching, and engage in many other learning experiences.

The flip side of the play question also arises: In light of current demands for improving learning outcomes and narrowing the achievement gap, is play still a major component of DAP?

Yes, it certainly is. The 2009 position statement says more about play than any previous statement has done. In fact, as the relevant knowledge base has grown, there is more to say about play—its enormous value, its endangered status in today's media-intensive world, and what teachers can do to enable all children to reach the higher levels of play that are most conducive for promoting self-regulation and other aspects of development and learning.

When does it become developmentally appropriate for an early childhood program to include academics?

It has been said that children are learning "academics" from the time they are born (NAEYC & NAECS/SDE 2003). Even babies and toddlers are beginning—through play, relationships, and informal opportunities—to develop some of the precursors and foundations of the academic disciplines, such as language and literacy, math, science, and other areas. If *academics* is understood to mean such foundational skills and knowledge, then academic learning is an essential part of developmentally appropriate early childhood programs. Of course, for a program to be developmentally appropriate, such learning goals must also be addressed in ways that fit children's ways of learning. When what you have is a narrowly defined set of specific facts and skills being taught apart from meaningful context and without attention to engaging children's interest, such a distorted form of academic learning is clearly *not* appropriate for young children.

I think DAP makes sense, but the families I serve have different ideas about how their children should be taught. What should I do?

Begin by dropping the jargon when you communicate with families. Don't start by talking about "DAP" or even "developmentally appropriate practice." Instead, have a conversation with families about your learning goals for their child and their goals.

Negotiating differences begins with you as a teacher or administrator clearly understanding your own preferences and where they come from. This might require you to do some serious thinking and reflecting first. Then communicate about your point of view and listen, truly *listen,* to the family's concerns. When you and the family articulate your respective goals, it is likely that you can find common ground. Be open to learning from family members and willing to expand your view of effective, developmentally appropriate practice based on what you learn. In a successful negotiation, families also learn and change. If you just give in to parents' demands, you will lose self-respect and probably effectiveness; if parents just give in to your position, they lose their power in their relationship with you and in their children's lives. In either case, children ultimately lose. The goal is a win-win outcome in which teacher and family learn from each other and come up with a solution that works for both.

I need to get my child ready to succeed in school. Doesn't she need more than DAP in her preschool experience?

According to research evidence, high-quality, developmentally appropriate preschool programs prepare children to succeed in school, especially children living in poverty (Schweinhart & Weikart 1997; Bowman, Donovan, & Burns 2000). A quality early childhood program helps children acquire key knowledge and skills in language, early literacy and mathematics, social and emotional development, and other aspects of school readiness. In fact, if chil-

dren are not making learning and developmental progress toward important outcomes, then the program is not developmentally appropriate.

I've heard that it is "developmentally inappropriate" to put the alphabet up on a preschool classroom wall or to teach children to read before first grade. Are these things true?

The alphabet part of this question has become a DAP urban myth. It originated in the context of 1980s schooling, in which first grade expectations were being thrust on preschoolers. In response, NAEYC's 1987 position statement on developmentally appropriate practice called for not teaching letters in isolation (see Bredekamp 1987). That position statement emphasized teaching letters in the context of meaningful words, such as in children's names or as initial consonants of words children encounter in books or other print materials. From this emphasis, the myth of "no alphabet charts" arose.

To clear up such misunderstandings, which were making many early childhood teachers feel they should avoid literacy teaching, NAEYC developed a joint position statement with the International Reading Association called *Learning to Read and Write: Developmentally Appropriate Practices for Young Children* (IRA & NAEYC 1998) and has produced and disseminated numerous other literacy resources (described on the Association's website: www.naeyc.org). Such publications, as well as the IRA/NAEYC position statement, describe effective learning experiences to help children become readers. The position statement specifically addresses the question of the alphabet's place in a developmentally appropriate classroom. It states that letters should be where children can see them, touch them, and manipulate them in their work and play. Because learning the alphabet is such a strong predictor of reading, DAP classrooms will certainly have an alphabet on the wall at children's eye level.

As for the second part of the question, developmentally appropriate preschool and kindergarten programs teach children the many important early literacy skills that are the foundations of successful reading. With such experiences, some children will become competent readers before first grade; others will not be reading independently but will make very good progress toward this goal. All children should get the learning experiences necessary to enable them to become eager and fluent readers. If children have ground to make up—for whatever reason—additional resources may be needed, and teachers will need to think carefully about what each child needs to move forward.

What are developmentally appropriate ways of teaching phonemic or phonological awareness in preschool?

Phonemic awareness refers to attending to the smallest units of sound that make up the speech stream—phonemes. *Phonological awareness* is a more inclusive term, encompassing attention to larger units of speech such as words and syllables, as well as phonemes. Research shows that children who are adept at phonemic awareness in kindergarten are much more likely to become successful readers (Snow, Burns, & Griffin 1998). Even more striking is the extent to which very low phonemic awareness is correlated with difficulty in learning to read. Without this important skill, the learning of sound/letter relationships (phonics) does not make sense.

So, we know that phonemic awareness is important, but how do we foster its development? Activities that involve playing with language—singing, doing finger plays, playing rhyming and alliteration games, listening to poems, clapping out the syllables of names or words, and reading books such as those by Dr. Seuss—need to be a regular part of the preschool day for all children. Teachers need to be intentional about planning such experiences and choosing books, songs, and materials that promote phonemic and other forms of phonological awareness. At the same time, we should remember that more goes into learning words than just phonological awareness. It is a key skill but by no means the only language skill that is critical for success in reading.

I teach in a public school where there is a prescribed curriculum from kindergarten on. How can I use DAP in my situation?

Developmentally appropriate practice calls for creating a caring community of learners in which everyone feels respected and included; establishing warm, positive relationships with each child; and developing respectful, reciprocal relationships with families. Although some settings, curricula, and school policies make carrying out these principles more of a challenge, in virtually all situations teachers will be able to create a positive classroom environment and respectful relationships with children and families.

Of course, developmentally appropriate practice also means getting to know each learner and adapting the curriculum and teaching practices to ensure that children make continual progress in their learning and development. So whatever the designated curriculum, the teacher needs to adapt it to the children in his or her class—as a group and as individuals—if it is to be developmentally appropriate for them. In some situations, teachers are limited in the flexibility they have to make such adaptations, and having limited flexibility is a disadvantage. But teachers can do some adapting, often more than they might realize—particularly if they become skilled at describing the things they do in their classrooms in terms of the standards or outcomes they are required to meet.

For example, you can explain that the basis for having children work together on a project includes "increased opportunity for language use, extended discourse, and deeper understanding of concepts" and you can detail the aspects of literacy, mathematics, science, and other curriculum domains that they will learn from the project. In other words, you will need to think about how the approaches and learning experiences you want to use with children address the curriculum's prescribed goals and content, and then be able to communicate this link to others.

I teach children with disabilities. Does DAP apply to them?

Children with disabilities are children first. They share most of the same developmental and learning needs and have many of the same strengths as their typically developing peers. We know from decades of research in early childhood special education that children with disabilities benefit most from being served in inclusive settings—that is, places where they would be found if they did not have a disability (Odom 2002; Sandall et al. 2005).

The emphasis that developmentally appropriate practice puts on meeting children where they are and helping them to reach challenging and achievable goals is even more important for children with disabilities. Likewise, the principle of adapting the environment and teaching for individual differences is clearly essential for children with special needs, who will often require more systematic instruction and other modifications or accommodations to achieve their potential. Teachers of children with identified disabilities should be part of a team that includes specialists and families and that develops and implements an individualized education plan (IEP) for the child. The plan, along with the child's participation in the inclusive setting, is important in making sure that the child makes desired progress toward the shared goals of the family and the program.

My program serves children from a variety of cultures, and I'm wondering whether DAP is the best thing for them. Is DAP for all children or just for some children?

As defined by NAEYC, developmentally appropriate practice calls for teachers to pay attention to the social and cultural contexts in which their children live and to take these into account in shaping the learning environment and their interactions with children and families. Whatever children's prior experiences or cultural expectations, teachers help all children to make sense of new experiences. At times, this

situation will require explicit teaching of the rules or skills that the child has not previously encountered. Or it will require the teacher to recognize that children can acquire the same skills and ideas through different experiences and routines. For example, children can gain phonological awareness and knowledge of concepts of print through rhymes and books in English or in Spanish.

At the same time, it is necessary to acknowledge that developmentally appropriate practice (as defined by NAEYC) reflects the individualistic, independence-oriented culture prevalent in many Western societies (in contrast to the emphasis on interdependence that characterizes many non-Western societies). This cultural difference means that contradictions are likely to arise between the views of teachers basing their work on DAP and the cultural views of some families or communities. These contradictions will need to be negotiated in the best interests of children. Most important, the classroom must be a welcoming environment that demonstrates respect and support for all children's cultural and family backgrounds.

I am sometimes daunted by the learning needs of children living in poverty and children who come into my class speaking little English, and I'm wondering whether DAP will enable them to catch up and succeed in school?

This is a good question, and the answer is "yes, but…." In the 2009 DAP position statement, NAEYC challenges the field of early care and education to consider how we can more effectively contribute to closing these achievement gaps. It is a formidable but critical challenge that needs to be tackled early in children's lives. Without intervention, differences in children's opportunities to learn can be staggering. For instance, a child in a professional family hears on average 11 million words a year, while a child in a family receiving public assistance hears an average of just 3 million (Hart & Risley 1995). Most English-language learners also hear far fewer words in English than do their peers from English-speaking homes. Clearly, programs serving low-income children and English language learners need to give special attention to building children's oral language and vocabulary.

In a number of other learning domains, research has also identified skills and knowledge important for school success (see the position statement), and such information is vital in informing the work of early childhood teachers. Teachers need to be knowledgeable about the learning needs of the children they teach and the teaching strategies with proven success in helping English language learners and children from low-income families reach higher levels of achievement.

A key factor for the well-being of children and families living with the many stresses of poverty is that they typically need access to comprehensive services including health, nutrition, and social services. Outside of Head Start, few children and families receive these services, and their absence makes improving learning and development outcomes that much more difficult. Thus, advocating for these services is important for all those concerned about children's well-being. Of course, narrowing achievement gaps cannot be the sole responsibility of teachers, but all of us have a responsibility to do as much as we can to increase excellence and equity in early childhood programs.

How do you improve the literacy skills of young children who haven't had many literacy learning experiences before they come to school?

Some educators suggest that children far behind their peers need drill-and-practice activities, including isolated letter or phonics instruction at the most rudimentary level. But for most of these children, the real basics are extending their language and vocabulary, increasing their awareness of print, and introducing them to the pleasures and purposes of reading and writing. Trying to learn sound/letter connections, for example, without understanding the alphabetic principle is confusing and too abstract for children. We need to begin with the large picture—

the purposes of reading and writing—and show children how literacy functions in daily activities. Children then become interested in finding out how reading and writing work, how letters and sounds come together to form words, and how these words tell a story. Children are motivated to learn and use sound/letter combinations when they write, using their own temporary phonetic—or developmental—spellings. Of critical importance, too, are developing children's oral language and providing interesting curriculum studies that broaden children's background knowledge—both key to reading comprehension.

I've heard DAP is about not hurrying children, about giving them the gift of time. Is that right?

The expression "gift of time" comes from a valid concern of not expecting too much of children too soon. But the response of just giving a child time would often do him a real disservice. Why? It isn't just time that promotes human development, it is also what happens while the time passes—the experiences the child is having with objects and people. When the gift of time takes the form of having a child wait a year to enter school, for example, the child is likely to make less progress out of school than he would in it. Many children who are judged to be "unready" for school actually have not had the same opportunities to learn that other, presumably "more ready" children have had.

So DAP does not mean simply waiting until children are "ready." It means setting developmentally appropriate expectations and understanding that, although there are some biological limitations, children's learning experiences will drive their development. For example, 2-year-olds and many 3-year-olds lack the fine motor skills needed to manipulate a pencil and to form letters, but opportunities to scribble and draw help lay the foundation. Maturation is needed, but so is experience.

Isn't DAP too "easy" for children once they get to kindergarten or the primary grades?

What is developmentally appropriate varies with the age, experience, and abilities of the children. So, in developmentally appropriate kindergarten and first grade classrooms, the expectations and outcomes will not be "too easy" for those 5-, 6-, or 7-year-old children. Rather, the expectations and outcomes of the programs will continue to be achievable but also challenging. For instance, conventional reading—the ability to gain meaning from unfamiliar text—may be an inappropriate expectation for most preschoolers to meet, but it is certainly developmentally appropriate for most first-graders.

High-quality, developmentally appropriate experiences such as those described here will go a long way to preparing all children to succeed. At the same time, because these experiences are developmentally appropriate, every child will live each year of life in the most enjoyable, meaningful, and productive way possible. As Jimmy Hymes put it:

> Every child has a right to his fifth year of life, his fourth year,
> his third year. He has a right to live each year with joy and self-fulfillment.
> No one should ever claim the power to make a child mortgage his today
> for the sake of tomorrow.

References

AAAS (American Association for the Advancement of Science). 2008. *Benchmarks.* Online: www.project2061.org/publications/bsl/online/index.php?home=true.

AAP (American Academy of Pediatrics). 2008. *American Academy of Pediatrics: Dedicated to the health of all children.* Online: www.aap.org.

AAP (American Academy of Pediatrics) & APHA (American Public Health Association). 1992. *Caring for our children—National health and safety performance standards: Guidelines for out-of-home-child care programs.* Washington, DC: APHA.

Access Center. 2008. *Using peer tutoring to facilitate access.* Washington, DC: Author.

Achenback, T.M., & C. Edelbrock. 1991. *National survey of the problems and competencies among four- to sixteen-year-olds.* Monographs of the Society for Research in Child Development, vol. 56, no. 3, serial no. 225. Chicago: University of Chicago Press.

AHA (American Heart Association). 2008. *Exercise (physical activity) and children.* Online: www.americanheart.org/presenter.jhtml?identifier=4596.

Anglin, J.M. 1993. *Vocabulary development: A morphological analysis.* Monographs of the Society for Research in Child Development, vol. 58, no. 10, serial no. 238. Chicago: University of Chicago Press.

Aronson, S.S. 2002. *Model child care health policies.* 4th ed. Elk Grove Village, IL: American Academy of Pediatrics.

Aronson, S.S., & P.M. Spahr. 2002. *Healthy young children: A manual for programs.* 4th ed. Washington, DC: NAEYC.

ASHA (American Speech-Language-Hearing Association). 2008. Learning two languages. *Learning more than one language.* Online: asha.org/public/speech/development/learn.htn.

Asher, S.R., & G.A. Williams. 1987. Helping children without friends in home and school contexts. In *Children's social development: Information for teachers and parents.* Urbana, IL: ERIC Clearinghouse on Elementary and Early Childhood Education.

August, D., & E.E. Garcia. 1988. *Language minority education in the United States.* Springfield, IL: Thomas.

August, D., & T. Shanahan, eds. 2006. *Developing literacy in second-language learners.* Report of the National Literacy Panel on Language-Minority Children and Youth. Mahwah, NJ: Lawrence Erlbaum.

Bagwell, C.L., M.E. Schmidt, A.F. Newcomb, & W.M. Bukowski. 2001. Friendship and peer rejection as predictors of adult adjustment. In *The role of friendship in psychological adjustment,* eds. D.W. Nangle & C.A. Erdley, 25–49. San Francisco: Jossey-Bass.

Banigan, R.L., & C.B. Mervis. 1988. Role of adult input in young children's category evolution: An experimental study. *Journal of Child Language* 15: 35–47.

Barnett, W.S., D. Yarosz, J. Thomas, K. Jung, & D. Blanco. 2007. *Two-way and monolingual English immersion in preschool education: An experimental comparison.* New Brunswick, NJ: National Institute for Early Education Research.

Barton, K.C., & L.S. Levstik. 1996. "Back when God was around and everything": Elementary children's understanding of historical time. *American Educational Research Journal* 33 (2): 419–54.

Beck, I., & M.G. McKeown. 2007. Increasing young low-income children's oral vocabulary repertoires through rich and focused instruction. *Elementary School Journal* 107 (3): 251–71.

Behrmann, M.M., & E.A. Lahm. 1994. Computer applications in early childhood special education. In *Young children: Active learners in a technological age,* eds. J. Wright & D. Shade, 105–20. Washington, DC: NAEYC.

Bergen, D., & D. Mauer. 2000. Symbolic play, phonological awareness, and literacy skills at three age levels. In *Play and literacy in early childhood: Research from multiple perspectives,* eds. K.A. Roskos & J.F. Christie, 45–62. Mahwah, NJ: Lawrence Erlbaum.

Berk, L.E. 2006a. Looking at children in kindergarten. In *K today: Teaching and learning in the kindergarten year,* ed. D.F. Gullo, 11–25. Washington, DC: NAEYC.

Berk, L.E. 2006b. Make-believe play: Wellspring for development of self-regulation. In *Play = learning: How play motivates and enhances children's cognitive and social-emotional growth,* eds. D. Singer, K. Hirsh-Pasek, & R. Golinkoff. New York: Oxford University Press.

Berk, L.E. 2008. *Infants and children: Prenatal through middle childhood.* 6th ed. Boston: Pearson/Allyn & Bacon.

Berk, L.E. 2009. *Child development.* 8th ed. Boston: Pearson/Allyn & Bacon.

Berk, L.E., & A. Winsler. 1995. *Scaffolding children's learning.* Washington, DC: NAEYC.

Bialystok, E. 2001. *Bilingualism in development: Language, literacy, and cognition.* Cambridge: Cambridge University Press.

Biemiller, A. 2004. Teaching vocabulary in the primary grades: Vocabulary instruction needed. In *Vocabulary instruction: Research to practice,* eds. J.F. Baumann & E.J. Kame'enui, 28–40. New York: Guilford.

Biemiller, A., & C. Boote. 2006. An effective method of building vocabulary in primary grades. *Journal of Educational Psychology* 98 (1): 44–62.

Birch, S.H., & G.W. Ladd. 1998. Children's interpersonal behaviors and the teacher-child relationship. *Developmental Psychology* 34 (5): 934–46.

Bjorklund, D.F. 1988. Acquiring a mnemonic: Age and category knowledge effects. *Journal of Experimental Child Psychology* 45: 71–87.

Bjorklund, D.F. 2007. *Why youth is not wasted on the young: Immaturity in human development.* Oxford: Blackwell.

Bjorklund, D.F., W. Schneider, W.S. Cassel, & E. Ashley. 1994. Training and extension of a memory strategy: Evidence for utilization deficiencies in high- and low-IQ children. *Child Development* 65 (3): 951–65.

Blair, C. 2002. School readiness: Integrating cognition and emotion in a neurobiological conceptualization of children's functioning at school entry. *American Psychologist* 57 (2): 111–27.

Blair, C., & R.P. Razza. 2007. Relating effortful control, executive function, and false belief understanding to emerging math and literacy ability in kindergarten. *Child Development* 78 (2): 647–63.

Bloom, L. 1998. Language acquisition in its developmental context. In *Handbook of child psychology, Vol. 2: Cognition, perception, and language*, 5th ed., eds. D. Kuhn & R.S. Siegler, 309–70. New York: John Wiley & Sons.

Bodrova, E., & D.J. Leong. 2003. The importance of being playful. *Educational Leadership* 60 (7): 50–53.

Bodrova, E., & D.J. Leong. 2005a. Promoting student self-regulation in learning. *Education Digest* 71 (2): 54–57.

Bodrova, E., & D.J. Leong. 2005b. Self-regulation: A foundation for early learning. *Principal* 85 (1): 30–35.

Bodrova, E., & D.J. Leong. 2006. Vygotskian perspectives on teaching and learning early literacy. In *Handbook of early literacy research, Vol. 2*, eds. D.K. Dickinson & S.B. Neuman, 243–56. New York: Guilford.

Bodrova, E., & D.J. Leong. 2007. *Tools of the mind: The Vygotskian approach to early childhood education.* 2d ed. Upper Saddle River, NJ: Pearson/Merrill Prentice Hall.

Bodrova, E., & D.J. Leong. 2008. Developing self-regulation in kindergarten: Can we keep all the crickets in the basket? *Young Children* 63 (2): 56–58.

Bono, M.A., & C.A. Stifter. 2003. Maternal attention-directing strategies and infant focused attention during problem solving. *Infancy* 4: 235–56.

Boulton, M.J. 1999. Concurrent and longitudinal relations between children's playground behavior and social preference, victimization, and bullying. *Child Development* 70 (4): 944–54.

Bowie, B.H. 2007. Relational aggression, gender, and the developmental process. *Journal of Child & Adolescent Psychiatric Nursing* 20 (2): 107–15.

Bowman, B.T., S. Donovan, & M.S. Burns. 2000. *Eager to learn: Educating our preschoolers.* Washington, DC: National Academies Press.

Braine, L.G., L. Schauble, S. Kugelmass, & A. Winter. 1993. Representation of depth by children: Spatial strategies and lateral biases. *Developmental Psychology* 29 (3): 466–79.

Bransford, J., A.L. Brown, & R.R. Cocking, eds. 2003. *How people learn: Brain, mind, experience, and school.* A report of the National Research Council. Washington, DC: National Academies Press.

Bredekamp, S., ed. 1987. *Developmentally appropriate practice in early childhood programs serving children from birth through age 8.* Expanded edition. Washington, DC: NAEYC.

Bredekamp, S., & T. Rosegrant. 1992. Reaching potentials through appropriate curriculum: Conceptual frameworks for applying the guidelines. In *Reaching potentials, Vol. 1: Appropriate curriculum and assessment for young children*, eds. S. Bredekamp & T. Rosegrant, 28–42. Washington, DC: NAEYC.

Bredekamp, S., & T. Rosegrant. 1995. Transforming curriculum organization. In *Reaching potentials, Vol. 2: Transforming early childhood curriculum and assessment*, eds. S. Bredekamp & T. Rosegrant, 167–76. Washington, DC: NAEYC.

Brice-Heath, S. 1983. *Ways with words: Language, life, and work in communities and classrooms.* New York: Cambridge University Press.

Bronson, M.B. 1994. The usefulness of an observational measure of children's social and mastery behaviors in early childhood classrooms. *Early Childhood Research Quarterly* 9: 19–43.

Bronson, M.B. 2006. Developing social and emotional competence. In *K today: Teaching and learning in the kindergarten year*, ed. D.F. Gullo, 47–56. Washington, DC: NAEYC.

Brooks, A.M. 1913. The value of outdoor kindergartens. *Journal of Education* 78 (5): 121.

Brooks, P.J., J.B. Hanauere, B. Padowski, & H. Rosman. 2003. The role of selective attention in preschoolers' ruse use in a novel dimensional card sort. *Cognitive Development* 18: 195–215.

Brooks-Gunn, J., P.K. Klebanov, & G.J. Duncan. 1996. Ethnic differences in children's intelligence test scores: Role of economic deprivation, home environment, and maternal characteristics. *Child Development* 67 (2): 396–408.

Brophy, J. 2004. *Motivating students to learn.* 2d ed. Mahwah, NJ: Lawrence Erlbaum.

Brown, S.A., D.H. Arnold, J. Dobbs, & G.L. Doctoroff. 2007. Parenting predictors of relational aggression among Puerto Rican and European American school-age children. *Early Childhood Research Quarterly* 22 (1): 147–59.

Browne, C.A., & J.D. Woolley. 2004. Preschooler's magical explanations for violations of physical, social, and mental laws. *Journal of Cognition and Development* 5: 239–60.

Bruer, J.T. 1999. *The myth of the first three years.* New York: Free Press.

Bukowski, W.M. 2001. Friendship and the worlds of childhood. In *The role of friendship in psychological adjustment*, eds. D.W. Nangle & C.A. Erdley, 93–105. San Francisco: Jossey-Bass.

Burchinal, M., C. Howes, R.C. Pianta, D. Bryant, D. Early, R. Clifford, & O. Barbarin. 2008. Predicting child outcomes at the end of kindergarten from the quality of pre-kindergarten teacher-child interactions and instruction. *Applied Developmental Science* 12 (3): 140–53.

Burhans, K.K., & C.S. Dweck. 1995. Helplessness in early childhood: The role of contingent worth. *Child Development* 66 (6): 1719–38.

Burns, M.S., P. Griffin, & C.E. Snow. 1999. *Starting out right: A guide to promoting children's reading success.* A report of the National Research Council. Washington, DC: National Academies Press.

Burton, C.B. 1987. Children's peer relationships. In *Children's social development: Information for teachers and parents.* Urbana, IL: ERIC Clearinghouse on Elementary and Early Childhood Education.

Bush, G., P. Luu, & M.I. Posner. 2000. Cognitive and emotional influences in the anterior cingulate cortex. *Trends in Cognitive Sciences* 4: 215–22.

Campos, S.J. 1995. The Carpenteria preschool program: A long-term effects study. In *Meeting the challenge of linguistic and cultural diversity in early childhood education*, eds. E.E. Garcia & B. McLaughlin, 34–48. New York: Teachers College Press.

Campos, J.J., D. Mumme, R. Kermoian, & R.G. Campos. 1994. A functionalist perspective on the nature of emotions. In *The development of emotion regulation*, ed. N. Fox, 284–303. Chicago: University of Chicago Press.

Carnegie Corporation of New York. 1998. *Years of promise: A comprehensive learning strategy for America's children.* Online: www.carnegie.org/sub/pubs/execsum.html.

Developmentally Appropriate Practice, 3d Edition

Carpenter, E.M., & D.W. Nangle. 2006. Caught between stages: Relational aggression emerging as a developmental advance in at-risk preschoolers. *Journal of Research in Childhood Education* 21 (2): 177–88.

Case, R. 1998. The development of central conceptual structures. In *Handbook of child psychology, Vol. 2: Cognition, perception, and language*, 5th ed., eds. D. Kuhn & R.S. Siegler, 745–800. New York: John Wiley & Sons.

Case, R., & Y. Okamoto, eds. 1996. *The role of central conceptual structures in the development of children's thought*. Monographs of the Society for Research in Child Development, vol. 61, nos. 1–2, serial no. 246. Chicago: University of Chicago Press.

Casey, B., S. Durston, & J. Fossella. 2001. Evidence for a mechanistic model of cognitive control. *Clinical Neuroscience Research* 1: 267–82.

Caspi, A. 1998. Personality development across the life span. In *Handbook of child psychology, Vol. 3: Social, emotional, and personality development*, 5th ed., ed. N. Eisenberg, 311–88. New York: John Wiley & Sons.

Center on Education Policy. 2008. Instructional time in elementary schools: A closer look at changes for specific subjects. *Arts Education Policy Review* 109 (6): 23–28.

Chalufour, I., & K. Worth. 2003. *Discovering nature with young children*. St. Paul, MN: Redleaf Press.

Chalufour, I., & K. Worth. 2005. *Exploring water with young children*. St. Paul, MN: Redleaf Press.

Chomsky, N. 1968. *Language and mind*. New York: Harcourt, Brace & World.

Chugani, H.T. 1996. Neuroimaging of developmental non-linearity and developmental pathologies. In *Developmental neuroimaging: Mapping the development of brain and behavior*, eds. R.W. Thatcher, G.R. Lyon, J. Rumsey, & N. Krasnegor. San Diego: Academic Press.

Clements, D.H. 2001. Mathematics in the preschool. *Teaching Children Mathematics* 7 (4): 270–75.

Colorín Colorado. 2007. *Reading comprehension strategies for content learning*. Online: www.colorincolorado.org/educators/content/comprehension.

Coplan, R.J., K. Prakash, K. O'Neil, & M. Armer. 2004. Do you "want" to play? Distinguishing between conflicted shyness and social disinterest in early childhood. *Developmental Psychology* 40: 244–58.

Copple, C., I.E. Sigel, & R. Saunders. 1984. *Educating the young thinker: Classroom strategies for cognitive growth*. Hillsdale, NJ: Lawrence Erlbaum.

Cost, Quality, and Child Outcomes Study Team. 1995. *Cost, quality, and child outcomes in child care centers* (Technical Report). Denver: University of Colorado, Center for Research in Economics and Social Policy.

Cowan, N., L.D. Nugent, E.M. Elliott, I. Ponomarev, & J.S. Saults. 1999. The role of attention in the development of short-term memory: Age differences in the verbal span of apprehension. *Child Development* 70 (5): 1082–97.

Cowen, E.L., A. Pedersen, H. Babigian, L.D. Izzo, & M.A. Trost. 1973. Long-term follow-up of early detected vulnerable children. *Journal of Consulting and Clinical Psychology* 41: 438–46.

Coyne, M.D., D.C. Simmons, E.J. Kame'enui, & M. Stoolmiller. 2004. Teaching vocabulary during shared storybook readings: An examination of differential effects. *Exceptionality* 12 (3): 145–62. Hillsdale, NJ: Lawrence Erlbaum.

Craig, G.J., & D. Baucum. 2002. *Human development*. 9th ed. Upper Saddle River, NJ: Prentice Hall.

Cratty, B.J. 1986. *Perceptual and motor development in infants and children*. 3d ed. Englewood Cliffs, NJ: Prentice Hall.

Creasey, G.L., P.A. Jarvis, & L.E. Berk. 1998. Play and social competence. In *Multiple perspectives on play in early childhood education*, eds. O.N. Saracho & B. Spodek, 116–43. Albany, NY: State University of New York.

Crick, N.R., J.F. Casas, & M. Mosher. 1997. Relational and overt aggression in preschool. *Developmental Psychology* 33: 579–88.

Crick, N.R., & K.A. Dodge. 1994. A review and reformulation of social information-processing mechanisms in children's social adjustment. *Psychological Bulletin* 115: 74–101.

CSEFEL (Center on the Social and Emotional Foundations for Early Learning). 2008. *Center on the Social and Emotional Foundations for Early Learning*. Online: www.vanderbilt.edu/csefel/index.html.

Cummins, J. 1994. Knowledge, power, and identity in teaching English as a second language. In *Educating second language children: The whole child, the whole curriculum, the whole community*, ed. F. Genesee, 103–25. Cambridge: Cambridge University Press.

Cunningham, A.E., & K.E. Stanovich. 1998. What reading does for the mind. *American Educator* 22 (1–2): 8–15.

Cutting, L.E., C.W. Koth, E.M. Mahone, & M.B. Denckla. 2003. Evidence for unexpected weaknesses in learning in children with Attention-Deficit/Hyperactivity Disorder without reading disabilities. *Journal of Learning Disabilities* 36 (3): 259–69.

Dana Alliance on Brain Initiatives. 1996. *Delivering results: A progress report on brain research*. Washington, DC: Author.

Dearing, E., H. Kreider, & H.B. Weiss. 2008. Increased family involvement in school predicts improved child-teacher relationships and feelings about school for low-income children. *Marriage & Family Review* 43 (3–4): 226–54.

DeLoache, J.S. 2006. Mindful of SYMBOLS. *Scientific American Mind* 17 (1): 71–75.

Dempster, F.N. 1993. Resistance to interference: Developmental changes in a basic processing mechanis In *Emerging themes in cognitive development: Foundations, Vol. 1*, eds. M.L. Howe & R. Pasnak, 3–27. New York: Springer-Verlag.

Denham, S.A. 1998. *Emotional development in young children*. New York: Guilford.

Denham, S.A., & A.T. Kochanoff. 2002. Parental contributions to preschoolers' understanding of emotion. *Marriage and Family Review* 34: 311–43.

Denham, S.A., & R.P. Weissberg. 2004. Social-emotional learning in early childhood: What we know and where to go from here. In *A blueprint for the promotion of prosocial behavior in early childhood*, eds. E. Chesebrough, P. King, T.P. Gullotta, & M. Bloom, 13–50. New York: Kluwer Academic/Plenum.

Diamond, K.E., S.Y. Hong, & H. Tu. 2008. Context influences preschool children's decisions to include a peer with a physical disability in play. *Exceptionality* 16 (3): 141–55.

Dickinson, D.K. 2001a. Large-group and free-play times: Conversational settings supporting language and literacy development. In *Beginning literacy with language*, eds. D.K. Dickinson & P.O. Tabors, 223–56. Baltimore: Paul H. Brookes.

Developmentally Appropriate Practice, 3d Edition

Dickinson, D.K. 2001b. Putting the pieces together: Impact of preschool on children's language and literacy development in kindergarten. In *Beginning literacy with language*, eds. D.K. Dickinson & P.O. Tabors, 257–88. Baltimore: Paul H. Brookes.

Dickinson, D.K., A. McCabe., & K. Sprague. 2003. Teacher rating of oral language and literacy (TROLL): Individualizing early literacy instruction with a standards-based rating tool. *The Reading Teacher* 56 (6): 554–64.

Dickinson, D.K., & M.W. Smith. 1994. Long-term effects of preschool teachers' book readings on low-income children's vocabulary and story comprehension. *Reading Research Quarterly* 29 (2): 104–22.

Dickinson, D.K., & P.O. Tabors. 2001. *Beginning literacy with language: Young children learning at home and school*. Baltimore: Paul H. Brookes.

Diffily, D., & C. Sassman. 2002. *Project-based learning with young children*. Portsmouth, NH: Heinemann.

Dodge, K.A. 2007. Fast track randomized controlled trial to prevent externalizing psychiatric disorders: Findings from grades 3 to 9. *Journal of the American Academy of Child & Adolescent Psychiatry* 46 (10): 1250–62.

Dodge, K.A. 2008. On the meaning of meaning when being mean: Commentary on Berkowitz's "On the consideration of automatic as well as controlled psychological processes in aggression." *Aggressive Behavior* 34 (2): 133–35.

Dodge, K.A., J.E. Lansford, V.S. Burks, J.E. Bates, G.S. Pettit, R. Fontaine, & J.M. Price. 2003. Peer rejection and social information-processing factors in the development of aggressive behavior problems in children. *Child Development* 74 (2): 374–93.

Douglas-Hall, A., & M. Chau. 2008. *Basic facts about low-income children, birth to age 6*. New York: Columbia University, National Center for Children in Poverty. Online: www.nccp.org/publications/pub_847 html.

Downer, J.T., K. Driscoll, & R.C. Pianta. 2006. Transition from kindergarten to first grade. In *K today: Teaching and learning in the kindergarten year*, ed. D.F. Gullo, 151–60. Washington, DC: NAEYC.

Duda, M., & V. Minick. 2006. Easing the transition to kindergarten: Demonstrating partnership through service learning. *Mentoring & Tutoring: Partnership in Learning* 14 (1): 111–21.

Duncan, G.J., C.J. Dowsett, A. Claessens, K. Magnuson, A.C. Huston, P. Klebanov, L.S. Pagani, L. Feinstein, M. Engel, & J. Brooks-Gunn. 2007. School readiness and later achievement. *Developmental Psychology* 43 (6): 1428–46.

Dunn, J. 1988. *The beginnings of social understanding*. Cambridge, MA: Harvard University Press.

Dunn, J., J.R. Brown, & M. Maguire. 1995. The development of children's moral sensibility: Individual differences and emotion understanding. *Developmental Psychology* 31: 649–59.

Dweck, C. 2002. The development of ability conceptions. In *The development of achievement motivation*, eds. A. Wigfield & J.S. Eccles, 57–88. San Diego: Academic Press.

Early, D.M., O. Barbarin, D. Bryant, M. Burchinal, F. Chang, R. Clifford, G. Crawford, & W. Weaver. 2005. *Pre-kindergarten in eleven states: NCEDL's multi-state study of pre-kindergarten and study of statewide early education programs (SWEEP): Preliminary descriptive report*. New York: Foundation for Child Development. Online: www.fcd-us.org/usr_doc/Prekindergartenin11States.pdf.

Eccles, J., A. Wigfield, R.D. Harold, & P. Blumenfeld. 1993. Age and gender differences in children's self- and task perceptions during elementary school. *Child Development* 64 (3): 830–47.

Eder, R.A., & S.C. Mangelsdorf. 1997. The emotional basis of early personality development: Implications for the emergent self-concept. In *Handbook of personality psychology*, eds. R. Hogan, J. Johnson, & S. Briggs, 209–40. San Diego: Academic Press.

Edwards, C.P., L. Gandini, & G. Forman, eds. 1998. *The hundred languages of children: The Reggio Emilia approach—Advanced reflections*. 2d ed. Greenwich, CT: Ablex.

Eisenberg, N. 1989a. *The development of prosocial moral reasoning in childhood and mid-adolescence*. Paper presented at the biennial meeting of the Society for Research in Child Development, April 27–30, Kansas City, MO.

Eisenberg, N. 1989b. The development of prosocial values. In *Social and moral values: Individual and social perspectives*, eds. N. Eisenberg, J. Reykowski, & E. Staub. Hillsdale, NJ: Lawrence Erlbaum.

Eisenberg, N. 2003. Prosocial behavior, empathy, and sympathy. In *Well-being: Positive development across the life course*, eds. M.H. Bornstein & L. Davidson, 253–65. Mahwah, NJ: Lawrence Erlbaum.

Eisenberg, N., & R.A. Fabes. 1992. Emotion, regulation, and the development of social competence. In *Review of personality and social psychology, Vol. 14: Emotion and social behavior*, ed. M.S. Clark. Newbury Park, CA: Sage Publications.

Eisenberg, N., & R.A. Fabes. 1998. Prosocial development. In *Handbook of child psychology, Vol. 3: Social, emotional, and personality development*, 5th ed., ed., N. Eisenberg, 701–78. New York: John Wiley & Sons.

Eisenberg, N., R.A. Fabes, & S. Losoya. 1997. Emotional responding: Regulation, social correlates, and socialization. In *Emotional development and emotional intelligence: Educational implications*, eds. P. Salovey & D. Sluyter, 129–63. New York: Basic.

Eisenberg, N., R.A. Fabes, & T.L. Spinrad. 2006. Prosocial development. In *Handbook of child psychology, Vol. 3: Social, emotional, and personality development*, 6th ed., N. Eisenberg, 646–718. New York: John Wiley & Sons.

Eisenberg, N., & P.H. Mussen. 1989. *The roots of prosocial behavior in children*. Cambridge: Cambridge University Press.

Elias, C., & L.E. Berk. 2002. Self-regulation in young children: Is there a role for sociodramatic play? *Early Childhood Research Quarterly* 17 (1): 216–38.

Elkind, D. 1981. *Children and adolescents: Interpretive essays on Jean Piaget*. New York: Oxford University Press.

Elkonin, D. 1972. Toward the problem of stages in the mental development of the child. *Soviet Psychology* 10: 225–51.

Ely, R. 2005. Language and literacy in the school years. In *The development of language*, 6th ed., ed. J.B. Gleason, 395–443. Boston: Allyn & Bacon.

Emory, R., M. Caughy, T.R. Harris, & L. Franzini. 2008. Neighborhood social processes and academic achievement in elementary school. *Journal of Community Psychology* 36 (7): 885–98.

Entwisle, D.R., & K.L. Alexander. 1998. Facilitating the transition to first grade: The nature of transition and research on factors affecting it. *Elementary School Journal* 98 (4): 351–64.

Epstein, A.S. 2007. *The intentional teacher: Choosing the best strategies for young children's learning.* Washington, DC: NAEYC.

Erikson, E. 1963. *Childhood and society.* New York: Norton.

Espinosa, L.M. 2007. English language learners as they enter school. In *School readiness and the transition to kindergarten in the era of accountability,* eds. R.C. Pianta, M.J. Cox, & K.L. Snow. Baltimore: Paul H. Brookes.

Espinosa, L.M. 2008. Challenging common myths about young English language learners. *Foundation for Child Development Policy Brief, Advancing PK–3* 8.

Fabes, R.A., N. Eisenberg, L.D. Hanish, & T.L. Spinrad. 2001. Preschoolers' spontaneous emotion vocabulary: Relations to likability. *Early Education and Development* 12: 1127.

Fabes, R.A., N. Eisenberg, M.C. Smith, & B. Murphy. 1996. Getting angry at peers: Associations with liking of the provocateur. *Child Development* 67 (3): 942–56.

Fantuzzo, J., M.A. Perry, & P. McDermott. 2004. Preschool approaches to learning and their relationship to other relevant classroom competencies for low-income children. *School Psychology Quarterly* 19 (3): 212–30.

Farkas, G., & K. Beron. 2004. The detailed age trajectory of oral vocabulary knowledge: Differences by class and race. *Social Science Research* 33: 464–97.

Flavell, J.H. 2000. Development of children's knowledge about the mental world. *International Journal of Behavioral Development* 24: 15–23.

Flavell, J.H., P. Miller, & S. Miller. 2001. *Cognitive development.* 4th ed. Upper Saddle River, NJ: Prentice Hall.

Foley, J.T., R.R. Bryan, & J.A. McCubbin. 2008. Daily physical activity levels of elementary school-aged children with and without mental retardation. *Journal of Developmental & Physical Disabilities* 20 (4): 365–78.

Foorman, B.R., & J. Torgesen. 2001. Critical elements of classroom and small group instruction promote reading success in all children. *Learning Disabilities Research and Practice* 16 (4): 203–12.

Forman, E.A., N. Minick, & C.A. Stone. 1993. *Contexts for learning: Sociocultural dynamics in children's development.* New York: Oxford University Press.

Forman, G. 1994. Different media, different languages. In *Reflections on the Reggio Emilia approach,* eds. L.G. Katz & B. Cesarone, 37–46. Urbana, IL: ERIC Clearinghouse on Elementary and Early Childhood Education.

Foy, J.G., & V. Mann. 2003. Home literacy environment and phonological awareness in preschool children: Differential effects for rhyme and phoneme awareness. *Applied Psycholinguistics* 24: 59–88.

Friedman, S.L., E.K. Scholnick, & R.R. Cocking. 1987. Reflections on reflections: What planning is and how it develops. In *Blueprints for thinking: The role of planning in cognitive development,* eds. S.L. Friedman, E.K. Scholnick, & R.R. Cocking. New York: Cambridge University Press.

Fuchs, D., L.S. Fuchs, K. Karns, L. Yazdian, & S. Powell. 2001. Creating a strong foundation for mathematics learning with kindergarten peer-assisted learning strategies. *Teaching Exceptional Children* 33: 84–87.

Fuchs, L.S., D. Fuchs, S.R. Powell, P.M. Seethaler, P.T. Cirino, & J.M. Fletcher. 2008. Intensive intervention for students with mathematics disabilities: Seven principles of effective practice. *Learning Disability Quarterly* 31 (2): 79–92.

Furman, E. 1980. Early latency: Normal and pathological aspects. In *The course of life, Vol. 2: Latency, adolescence and youth,* eds. S. Greenspan & G. Pollock. Washington, DC: U.S. Department of Health & Human Services, National Institute of Mental Health.

Furman, E. 1987. *The teacher's guide to helping young children grow.* Madison, CT: International Universities Press.

Gabbard, C.P. 2007. *Lifelong motor development.* 5th ed. Boston: Allyn & Bacon.

Gallahue, D.L. 1995. Transforming physical education curriculum. In *Reaching potentials, Vol. 2: Transforming early childhood curriculum and assessment,* eds. S. Bredekamp & T. Rosegrant, 125–44. Washington, DC: NAEYC.

Gartrell, D. 2004. *The power of guidance: Teaching social-emotional skills in early childhood classrooms.* Clifton Park, NY: Thomson Delmar Learning.

Gay, G., & T.C. Howard. 2000. Multicultural teacher education for the 21st century. *Teacher Educator* 36 (1): 1–16.

Gelman, R., & K. Brenneman. 2004. Science learning pathways for young children. *Early Childhood Research Quarterly* 19: 150–58.

Gelman, R., & M. Shatz. 1978. Appropriate speech adjustments: The operation of conversational constraints on talk to two-year-olds. In *Interaction, conversation, and the development of language,* eds. M. Lewis & R.A. Rosenblum, 27–61. New York: John Wiley & Sons.

Gelman, S.A., & J.E. Opfer. 2002. Development of the animate-inanimate distinction. In *Blackwell handbook of childhood cognitive development,* ed. U. Goswami, 151–66. Malden, MA: Blackwell.

George, T.P., & D.P. Hartmann. 1996. Friendship networks of unpopular, average, and popular children. *Child Development* 67 (5): 2301–16.

Golbeck, S.L. 2006. Developing key cognitive skills. In *K today: Teaching and learning in the kindergarten year,* ed. D.F. Gullo, 37–46. Washington, DC: NAEYC.

Goldberg, M.C., D. Maurer, & T.L. Lewis. 2001. Developmental changes in attention: The effects of endogenous cueing and of distracters. *Developmental Science* 4: 209–19.

Golomb, C. 2004. *The child's creation of a pictorial world.* 2d ed. Mahwah, NJ: Lawrence Erlbaum.

Gonzalez-Mena, J. 2008. *Child, family, and community: Family-centered early care and education.* Indianapolis, IN: Prentice Hall.

Gopnik, A., & J.W. Astington. 1988. Children's understanding of representational change and its relation to the understanding of false belief and the appearance-reality distinction. *Child Development* 59 (1): 26–37.

Greenes, C. 1999. Ready to learn: Developing young children's mathematical powers. In *Mathematics in the early years,* ed. J. Copley, 39–47. Reston, VA: National Council of Teachers of Mathematics, and Washington, DC: NAEYC.

Greer, T., & J.J. Lockman. 1998. Using writing instruments: Invariances in young children and adults. *Child Development* 69 (4): 888–902.

Grineski, S. 1993. Children, cooperative learning, and physical education. *Teaching Elementary Physical Education* 4: 10–11, 14.

Grusec, J. 2006. The development of moral behavior and conscience from a socialization perspective. In *Handbook of moral development,* eds. M. Killen & J. Smetana, 243–66. New York: Routledge.

Gullo, D.F. 1994. *Understanding assessment and evaluation in early childhood education.* New York: Teachers College Press.

Gullo, D.F. 2006a. Assessment in kindergarten. In *K today: Teaching and learning in the kindergarten year,* ed. D.F Gullo, 138–47. Washington, DC: NAEYC.

Gullo, D.F., ed. 2006b. *K today: Teaching and learning in the kindergarten year.* Washington, DC: NAEYC.

Gunnar, M.R. 2000. Early adversity and the development of stress reactivity and regulation. In *Minnesota symposia on child psychology, Vol. 31: The effects of adversity on neurobehavioral development,* ed. C.A. Nelson, 163–200. Mahwah, NJ: Lawrence Erlbaum.

Gutierrez-Clellen, V. 1999. Language choice in intervention with bilingual children. *American Journal of Speech-Language Pathology* 8: 291–302.

Haggerty, J., L.R. Sherrod, N. Garmezy, & M. Rutter. 1996. *Stress, risk and resilience in children and adolescents—processes, mechanisms, and interventions.* Cambridge: Cambridge University Press.

Hakuta, K., B. Ferdman, & R. Diaz. 1987. Bilingualism and cognitive development: Three perspectives. In *Advances in applied psycholinguistics: Reading, writing, and language learning, Vol. 2,* ed. S. Rosenberg, 284–319. New York: Cambridge University Press.

Halberstadt, A.G., & K.L. Eaton. 2002. Socialization of emotion expression and understanding in the family. *Marriage and Family Review* 34: 35–62.

Hale-Benson, J. 1986. *Black children: Their roots, culture, and learning styles.* Rev. ed. Baltimore: Johns Hopkins University Press.

Halfon, N., E. Shulman, & M. Hochstein. 2001. Brain development in early childhood. *Policy Briefs* 13: 1–4. Los Angeles: UCLA Center for Healthier Children, Family and Communities, California Policy Research Center.

Halford, G.S., & G. Andrews. 2006. Reasoning and problem solving. In *Handbook of child psychology, Vol. 2: Cognition, perception, and language,* 6th ed., eds. D. Kuhn & R. Siegler. Hoboken, NJ: John Wiley & Sons.

Halgunseth, L.C., J. Ispa, & D. Rudy. 2006. Parental control in Latino families: An integrated review of the literature. *Child Development* 77 (5): 1282–97.

Hampson, S.E. 2008. Mechanisms by which childhood personality traits influence adult well-being. *Current Directions in Psychological Science* 17 (4): 264–68.

Hamre, B.K., & R.C. Pianta. 2001. Early teacher-child relationships and the trajectory of children's school outcomes through eighth grade. *Child Development* 72 (2): 625–38.

Hamre, B.K., & R.C. Pianta. 2005. Can instructional and emotional support in the first grade classroom make a difference for children at risk of school failure? *Child Development* 76 (5): 949–67.

Hanish, L.D., B. Kochenderfer-Ladd, R.A. Fabes, C.L. Martin, & D. Denning. 2004. Bullying among young children: The influence of peers and teachers. In *Bullying in American schools: A social ecological perspective on prevention and intervention,* eds. D.L. Espelage & S.M. Swearer, 141–60. Mahwah, NJ: Lawrence Erlbaum.

Harnishfeger, K.K. 1995. The development of cognitive inhibition: Theories, definitions, and research evidence. In *New perspectives on interference and inhibition in cognition,* eds. F.F. Dempster & C.J. Brainerd, 176–204. San Diego: Academic Press.

Harris, A.C. 1986. *Child development.* St. Paul, MN: West.

Harris, P.L. 2006. Social cognition. In *Handbook of child psychology, Vol. 2: Cognition, perception, and language,* 6th ed., eds. D. Kuhn & R. Siegler. Hoboken, NJ: John Wiley & Sons.

Hart, B., & T.R. Risley. 1995. *Meaningful differences in the everyday experience of young American children.* Baltimore: Paul H. Brookes.

Hart, B., & T.R. Risley. 1999. *The social world of children learning to talk.* Baltimore: Paul H. Brookes.

Hart, B., & T.R. Risley. 2003. The early catastrophe. *Education Review* 17 (1): 110–18.

Harter, S. 1990. Causes, correlates, and the functional role of global self-worth: A life-span perspective. In *Perceptions of competence and incompetence across the life span,* eds. J. Kolligan & R. Sternberg. New Haven, CT: Yale University Press.

Harter, S. 1996. Developmental changes in self-understanding across the 5 to 7 shift. In *The five to seven year shift,* eds. A.J. Sameroff & M.M. Haith, 207–36. Chicago: University of Chicago Press.

Harter, S. 1999. *The cognitive and social construction of the developing self.* New York: Guilford.

Harter, S. 2003. The development of self-representations during childhood and adolescence. In *Handbook of self and identity,* eds. M.R. Leary & J.P. Tangney, 610–42. New York: Guilford.

Harter, S. 2006. The self. In *Handbook of child psychology, Vol. 3: Social, emotional, and personality development,* 6th ed., ed. N. Eisenberg, 505–70. New York: John Wiley & Sons.

Hartup, W.W. 1996. The company they keep: Friendships and their developmental significance. *Child Development* 67 (1): 1–13.

Haywood, K.M., & N. Getchell. 2005. *Life span motor development.* 4th ed. Champaign, IL: Human Kinetics.

Hazen, N.L., B. Black, & F. Fleming-Johnson. 1984. Social acceptance: Strategies children use and how teachers can help children learn them. *Young Children* 39 (6): 26–36.

Helm, J., & L.G. Katz. 2001. *Young investigators: The project approach in the early years.* New York: Teachers College Press.

Heyman, G.D., & S.A. Gelman. 2000. Preschool children's use of trait labels to make inductive inferences. *Journal of Experimental Child Psychology* 77: 1–19.

Hibben, J., & R. Scheer. 1982. Music and movement for special needs children. *Teaching Exceptional Children* 14: 171–76.

Hirsh-Pasek, K., R.M. Golinkoff, L.E. Berk, & D.G. Singer. 2009. *A mandate for playful learning in preschool: Presenting the evidence.* New York: Oxford University Press.

Hoffman, M.L. 1983. Affective and cognitive processes in moral internalization. In *Social cognition and social development: A sociocultural perspective,* eds. E.T. Higgins, D.N. Ridale, & W.W. Hartup, 236–74. Cambridge: Cambridge University Press.

Hoglund, W.L.G., C.E. Lalonde, B.J. Leadbeater. 2008. Social-cognitive competence, peer rejection and neglect, and behavioral and emotional problems in middle childhood. *Social Development* 17 (3): 528–53.

Honig, A.S. 2002. *Secure relationships: Nurturing infant/toddler attachment in early care settings.* Washington, DC: NAEYC.

Horton-Ikard, R. 2006. The influence of culture, class, and linguistic diversity on early language development. *Zero to Three* 27 (1): 6–12.

Howes, C. 1988. Relations between early child care and schooling. *Developmental Psychology* 24 (1): 53–57.

Howes, C. 2000. Social-emotional classroom climate in child care, child-teacher relationships and children's second grade peer relations. *Social Development* 38: 113–32.

Howes, C., & C.C. Matheson. 1992. Sequences in the development of competent play with peers: Social and social pretend play. *Developmental Psychology* 28: 961–74.

Howes, C., C.C. Matheson, & C.E. Hamilton. 1994. Maternal, teacher, and child care history correlates of children's relationships with peers. *Child Development* 65 (1): 264–73.

Howes, C., & S. Ritchie. 2002. *A matter of trust: Connecting teachers and learners in the early childhood classroom*. New York: Teachers College Press.

Howse, R.B., S.D. Calkins, A.D. Anastopoulos, S.R. Keane, & T.L. Shelton. 2003. Regulatory contributors to children's kindergarten achievement. *Early Education and Development* 14 (1): 101–19.

Hubbard, J.A., & J.D. Coie. 1994. Emotional correlates of social competence in children's peer relations. *Merrill-Palmer Quarterly* 40: 1–20.

Hudson, J.A., B. Sosa, & L.R. Shapiro. 1997. Scripts and plans: The development of preschool children's event knowledge and event planning. In *The developmental psychology of planning: Why, how, and when do we plan?*, eds. S.L. Friedman & E. K. Scholnick, 77–102. Mahwah, NJ: Lawrence Erlbaum.

Huttenlocher, P.R. 2002. *Neural plasticity: The effects of environment on the development of the cerebral cortex*. Cambridge, MA: Harvard University Press.

Hyson, M. 2004. *The emotional development of young children: Building an emotion-centered curriculum*. 2d ed. New York: Teachers College Press.

Hyson, M. 2008. *Enthusiastic and engaged learners: Approaches to learning in the early childhood classroom*. New York: Teachers College Press.

Hyson, M., C. Copple, & J. Jones. 2006. Early childhood development and education. In *Handbook of child psychology, Vol. 4: Child psychology in practice*, 6th ed., eds., K.A. Renninger & I. Sigel, 3–47. New York: John Wiley & Sons.

Iaquinta, A. 2006. Guided reading: A research-based response to the challenges of early reading instruction. *Early Childhood Education Journal* 33 (6): 413–18.

IRA (International Reading Association) & NAEYC. 1998. *Learning to read and write: Developmentally appropriate practices for young children*. A joint position statement. Washington, DC: NAEYC.

IRA (International Reading Association) & NCTE (National Council of Teachers of English). 1996. *Standards for the English language arts*. Newark, DE: IRA, and Urbana, IL: NCTE.

Irujo, S. 2007. What does research tell us about teaching reading to English language learners? *The ELL Outlook*. Online: www.readingrockets.org/article/19757.

Irwin, D.M., & S.R. Ambron. 1973. *Moral judgment and role-taking in children ages three to seven*. Paper presented at the biennial meeting of the Society for Research in Child Development, March 29–April 1, Philadelphia, PA.

Isenberg, J.P., & M.R. Jalongo. 2002. *Creative expression and play in early childhood curriculum*. New York: Merrill.

Jalongo, M.R., & J.P. Isenberg. 2006. Creative expression and thought in kindergarten. In *K today: Teaching and learning in the kindergarten year*, ed. D.F. Gullo, 116–26. Washington, DC: NAEYC.

Jones, N.P. 2005. Big jobs: Planning for competence. *Young Children* 60 (2): 86–93.

Juel, C., G. Biancarosa, D. Coker, & R. Deffes. 2003. Walking with Rosie: A cautionary tale of early reading instruction. *Educational Leadership* 60 (7): 12–18.

Kalkowski, P. 2001. *Peer and cross-age tutoring*. Portland, OR: Northwest Regional Educational Laboratory. Online: www.nwrel.org/scpd/sirs/9/c018.html.

Karmiloff-Smith, A., J. Grant, K. Sims, M. Jones, & P. Cuckle. 1996. Rethinking metalinguistic awareness: Representing and accessing knowledge about what counts as a word. *Cognition* 58: 197–219.

Katz, L.G., & S.C. Chard. 2000. *Engaging children's minds: The project approach*. 2d ed. Norwood, NJ: Ablex.

Katz, L.G., & D.E. McClellan. 1997. *Fostering children's social competence: The teacher's role*. Washington, DC: NAEYC.

Kavanaugh, R.D. 2006. Pretend play. In *Handbook of research on the education of young children*, 2d ed., eds. B. Spodek & O.N. Saracho, 269–78. Mahwah, NJ: Lawrence Erlbaum.

Kavanaugh, R.D., & S. Engel. 1998. The development of pretense and narrative in early childhood. In *Multiple perspectives on play in early childhood education*, eds. O.N. Saracho & B. Spodek, 80–99. Albany, NY: State University of New York.

Kendrick, A., R. Kaufmann, & K. Messenger. 1995. *Healthy young children: A manual for programs*. Washington, DC: NAEYC.

Kenny, D.A., T.V. West, A.H.N. Cillessen, J.D. Coie, K.A. Dodge, J.A. Hubbard, & D. Schwartz. 2007. Accuracy in judgments of aggressiveness. *Personality & Social Psychology Bulletin* 33 (9): 1225–36.

Keyser, J. 2006. *From parents to partners: Building a family-centered early childhood program*. St. Paul, MN: Redleaf Press.

Kitayama, S., & H. Markus, eds. 1994. *Emotion and culture*. Washington, DC: American Psychological Association.

Klibanoff, R.S., S.C. Levine, J. Huttenlocher, M. Vasilyeva, & L.V. Hedges. 2006. Preschool children's mathematical knowledge: The effect of teacher "math talk." *Developmental Psychology* 42 (1): 59–69.

Klomek, A.B., A. Sourander, K. Kumpulainen, J. Piha, T. Tamminen, I. Moilanen, F. Almqvist, & M.S. Gould. 2008. Childhood bullying as a risk for later depression and suicidal ideation among Finnish males. *Journal of Affective Disorders* 109 (1–2): 47–55.

Kochanska, G., & N. Aksan. 2007. Conscience in childhood: Past, present, and future. In *Appraising the human developmental sciences: Essays in honor of Merrill-Palmer Quarterly*, ed. G.W. Ladd, 238–49. Detroit, MI: Wayne State University Press.

Kochanska, G., & A. Knaack. 2003. Effortful control as a personality characteristic of young children: Antecedents, correlates, and consequences. *Journal of Personality* 71: 1087–112.

Kochenderfer-Ladd, B. 2003. Identification of aggressive and asocial victims and the stability of their peer victimization. *Merrill-Palmer Quarterly* 49: 401–25.

Kochenderfer-Ladd, B., & M.E. Pelletier. 2008. Teachers' views and beliefs about bullying: Influences on classroom management strategies and students' coping with peer victimization. *Journal of School Psychology* 46 (4): 431–53.

Kochenderfer-Ladd, B., & J.L. Wardrop. 2001. Chronicity and instability of children's peer victimization experiences as predictors of loneliness and social satisfaction trajectories. *Child Development* 72 (1): 134–51.

Koestner, R., C. Franz, & J. Weinberger. 1990. The family origins of empathetic concern: A 26-year longitudinal study. *Journal of Personality and Social Psychology* 58: 709–16.

Kontos, S., & L. Keyes. 1999. An ecobehavioral analysis of early childhood classrooms. *Early Childhood Research Quarterly* 14 (1): 35–50.

Kosanovich, M., K. Ladinsky, L. Nelson, & J. Torgesen. 2006. *Differentiated reading instruction: Small group alternative lesson structures for all students.* Tallahassee, FL: Florida Center for Reading Research.

Kovelman, I., S. Baker, & L.A. Petitto. 2006. *Bilingual and monolingual brains compared: An fMRI study of a "neurological signature" of bilingualism.* Paper presented at the annual meeting of the Society for Neuroscience, October 14–18, Atlanta, GA.

Krackow, E., & P. Gordon. 1998. Are lions and tigers substitutes or associates? Evidence against slot filler accounts of children's early categorization. *Child Development* 69 (2): 347–54.

Krascum, R.M., & S. Andrews. 1998. The effects of theories on children's acquisition of family-resemblance categories. *Child Development* 69 (2): 333–46.

Kuczmarski, R.J., C.L. Ogden, S.S. Guo, L.M. Grummer-Strawn, K.M. Flegal, Z. Mei, R. Wei, L.R. Curtin, A.F. Roche, & C.L. Johnson. 2002. 2000 CDC growth charts for the United States: Methods and development. *Vital Health Statistics* 11 (246). Online: www.cdc.gov/nchs/data/series/sr_11/sr11_246.pdf.

Kuhl, P. 2000. *A new view of language acquisition.* Paper presented at the National Academy of Sciences colloquium, May 19–21, Irvine, CA.

Kuhn, D. 2000. Why development does (and does not) occur: Evidence from the domain of inductive reasoning. In *Mechanisms of cognitive development*, eds. R. Siegler & J. McClelland, 221–49. Mahwah, NJ: Lawrence Erlbaum.

Kuhn, D., & D. Dean, Jr. 2004. Connecting scientific reasoning and causal inference. *Journal of Cognition and Development* 5: 261–88.

Kupersmidt, J., & J.D. Coie. 1990. Preadolescent peer status, aggression, and school adjustment as predictors of externalizing problems in adolescence. *Child Development* 61 (5): 1350–62.

Kusche, C.A., & M.T. Greenberg. In press. PATHS in your classroom: Promoting emotional literacy and alleviating emotional distress. In *Social emotional learning and the elementary school child: A guide for educators*, ed. J. Cohen. New York: Teachers College Press.

Ladd, G.W. 1999. Peer relationships and social competence during early and middle childhood. *Annual Review of Psychology* 50: 333–59.

Ladd, G.W., S.H. Birch, & E.S. Buhs. 1999. Children's social and scholastic lives in kindergarten: Related spheres of influence? *Child Development* 70 (6): 1373–400.

Ladd, G.W., E.S. Buhs, & M. Seid. 2000. Children's initial sentiments about kindergarten: Is school liking an antecedent of early classroom participation and achievement? *Merrill-Palmer Quarterly* 46: 255–79.

Lam, M.S., & A. Pollard. 2006. A conceptual framework for understanding children as agents in the transition from home to kindergarten. *Early Years: Journal of International Research & Development* 26 (2): 123–41.

Land, K.C. 2008. *2008 special focus report: Trends in infancy/early childhood and middle childhood well-being. 1994–2006.* New York: Foundation for Child Development, Child and Youth Well-Being Index (CWI) Project.

Landry, S.H. 2008. Effective early childhood programs: Turning knowledge into action. In *Investing in early childhood development: Evidence to support a movement for educational change*, eds. A.R. Tarlov & M.P. Debbink. New York: Palgrave Macmillan.

Landry, S.H., K.E. Smith, P.R. Swank, & C.L. Miller-Loncar. 2000. Early maternal and child influences on children's later independent cognitive and social functioning. *Child Development* 71 (2): 358–75.

Landy, S. 2002. *Pathways to competence: Encouraging healthy social and emotional development in young children.* Baltimore: Paul H. Brookes.

Lansford, J.E., C. Capanna, K.A. Dodge, G.V. Caprara, J.E. Bates, G.S. Pettit, & C. Pastorelli. 2007. Peer social preference and depressive symptoms of children in Italy and the United States. *International Journal of Behavioral Development* 31 (3): 274–83.

Lansford, J.E., P.S. Malone, K.A. Dodge, J.C. Crozier, G.S. Pettit, & J.E. Bates. 2006. A 12-year prospective study of patterns of social information processing problems and externalizing behaviors. *Journal of Abnormal Child Psychology* 34 (5): 709–18.

Lee, O., R. Deaktor, C. Enders, & J. Lambert. 2008. Impact of a multiyear professional development intervention on science achievement of culturally and linguistically diverse elementary students. *Journal of Research in Science Teaching* 45 (6): 726–47.

Lee, S., M. Sills, & G. Oh. 2002. *Disabilities among children and mothers in low-income families.* Research in brief, IWPR publication #D449. Washington, DC: Institute for Women's Policy Research.

Lee, V.E., & D.T. Burkam. 2002. *Inequality at the starting gate: Social background differences in achievement as children begin school.* New York: Economic Policy Institute.

Leong, D.J., & E. Bodrova. 2005. Why children need play! *Scholastic Parent & Child* 13 (1): 37.

Lin, C.C., C.K. Hsiao, & W.J. Chen. 1999. Development of sustained attention assessed using the continuous performance test among children 6–15 years. *Journal of Abstract Child Psychology* 27 (5): 403–412.

Lindsey, E.W., & M.J. Colwell. 2003. Preschoolers' emotional competence: Links to pretend and physical play. *Child Study Journal* 33: 39–52.

Lonigan, C.J. 2006. Development, assessment, and promotion of preliteracy skills. *Early Education and Development* 17 (1): 91–114.

Lord, R.H., & B. Kozar. 1996. Overuse injuries in young athletes. In *Children and youth in sport: A biopsychological perspective*, eds. F.L. Smoll & R.E. Smith, 281–94. Dubuque, IA: Brown & Benchmark.

Maccoby, E.E., & C.N. Jacklin. 1987. Gender segregation in childhood. In *Advances in child development and behavior, Vol. 20*, ed. E.H. Reese, 239–87. New York: Academic Press.

Mahar, M.T., S.K. Murphy, D.A. Rowe, J. Golden, A.T. Shields, & T.D. Raedeke. 2006. Effects of a classroom-based program on physical activity and on-task behavior. *Medicine & Science in Sports and Exercise* 38 (12): 286–94.

Mahone, E.M., & W. Silverman. 2008. ADHD and executive functions: Lessons learned from research. *Exceptional Parent* 38 (8): 48–51.

Mandler, J.M. 2004. *The foundations of mind: Origins of conceptual thought.* New York: Oxford University Press.

Manross, M.A. 1994. *What children think, feel, and know about the overhand throw.* Master's thesis, Virginia Tech University. Blacksburg, VA.

Manross, M.A. 2000. Learning to throw in physical education class: Part 3. *Teaching Elementary Physical Education* 11 (3): 26–29.

Martin, C.L., & C.A. Fabes. 2001. The stability and consequences of young children's same-sex peer interactions. *Developmental Psychology* 37: 431–46.

Masten, A.S. 2001. Ordinary magic: Resilience processes and development. *American Psychologist* 56: 227–38.

Masten, A.S., & J.D. Coatsworth. 1998. The development of competence in favorable and unfavorable environments: Lessons from research on successful children. *American Psychologist* 53 (2): 205–20.

Matteson, D.M., & D.K. Freeman. 2006. *Assessing and teaching beginning readers: A picture is worth 1000 words.* New York: Richard C. Owen Publishers.

Mayeski, M. 2002. *Creative activities for young children.* 6th ed. Albany, NY: Delmar Learning.

McAfee, O., D.J. Leong, & E. Bodrova. 2004. *Basics of assessment: A primer for early childhood educators.* Washington, DC: NAEYC.

McClelland, M.M., A.C. Acock, & F.J. Morrison. 2006. The impact of kindergarten learning-related skills on academic trajectories at the end of elementary school. *Early Childhood Research Quarterly* 21 (4): 471–90.

McClelland, M.M., F.J. Morrison, & D.L. Holmes. 2000. Children at risk for early academic problems: The role of learning-related social skills. *Early Childhood Research Quarterly* 15 (3): 307–29.

McCune, L. 1993. The development of play as the development of consciousness. In *New directions for child development,* no. 59, eds. M.H. Bornstein & A. O'Reilly, 67–79. San Francisco: Jossey-Bass.

Mechelli, A., J.T. Crinion, U. Noppeney, J. O'Doherty, J. Ashburner, R. Frackowiak, & C.J. Price. 2004. Structural plasticity in the bilingual brain. *Nature* 431: 757.

Mehaffie, K.E., & R.B. McCall. 2002. *Kindergarten readiness: An overview of issues and assessment* (Special Report). Pittsburgh, PA: University of Pittsburgh, Office of Child Development.

Meiers, M. 2004. Reading for pleasure and literacy achievement. *Research Developments* 12. Online: research.acer.edu.au/resdev/vol12/iss12/5.

Metz, K. 1995. Reassessment of developmental constraints on children's science instruction. *Review of Educational Research* 65 (2): 93–127.

Mikami, A., & S. Hinshaw. 2006. Resilient adolescent adjustment among girls: Buffers of childhood peer rejection and Attention-Deficit/Hyperactivity Disorder. *Journal of Abnormal Child Psychology* 34 (6): 823–37.

Mize, J. 1995. Coaching preschool children in social skills: A cognitive-social learning curriculum. In *Teaching social skills to children and youth: Innovative approaches,* 3d ed., eds. G. Carteledge & J.F. Milbum, 237–61. Boston: Allyn & Bacon.

Montie, J.E., Z. Xiang, & L.J. Schweinhart. 2006. Preschool experience in 10 countries: Cognitive and language performance at age 7. *Early Childhood Research Quarterly* 21: 313–31.

Monzó, L.D., & R.S. Rueda. 2001. Professional roles, caring, and scaffolds: Latino teachers' and paraeducators' interactions with Latino students. *American Journal of Education* 109 (4): 438–71.

Morrison, F.J. 2007. *Contemporary perspectives on children's engagement in learning.* Symposium presented at the biennial meeting of the Society for Research in Child Development, March 29–April 1, Boston, MA.

Murphy, L.M.B., C. Laurie-Rose, T.M. Brinkman, & K.A. McNamara. 2007. Sustained attention and social competence in typically developing preschool-aged children. *Early Child Development and Care* 177 (2): 133–49.

Mussen, P., & N. Eisenberg-Berg. 1977. *Roots of caring, sharing, and helping: The development of prosocial behavior in children.* San Francisco: W.H. Freeman.

Myers, S.S., & R.C. Pianta. 2008. Developmental commentary: Individual and contextual influences on student-teacher relationships and children's early problem behaviors. *Journal of Clinical Child & Adolescent Psychology* 37 (3): 600–08.

NAEYC. 1996. Developmentally appropriate practice in early childhood programs serving children from birth through age 8. A position statement of the National Association for the Education of Young Children. In *Developmentally appropriate practice in early childhood programs,* Rev. ed., eds. S. Bredekamp & C. Copple, 3–30. Washington, DC: Author.

NAEYC. 2005a. *NAEYC early childhood program standards and accreditation criteria.* 11 vols. Washington, DC: Author.

NAEYC. 2005b. *Screening and assessment of young English-language learners.* Supplement to the NAEYC and NAECS/SDE joint position statement on early childhood curriculum, assessment, and program evaluation. Washington, DC: Author. Online: www.naeyc.org/dap.

NAEYC & NAECS/SDE (National Association of Early Childhood Specialists in State Departments of Education). 2002. *Early learning standards: Creating the conditions for success.* Joint position statement. Online: www.naeyc.org/dap.

NAEYC & NAECS/SDE (National Association of Early Childhood Specialists in State Departments of Education). 2003. *Early childhood curriculum, assessment, and program evaluation: Building an effective, accountable system in programs for children birth through age 8.* Joint position statement. Online: www.naeyc.org/dap.

NASPE (National Association for Sport and Physical Education). 2000. *Appropriate practices in movement programs for young children ages 3–5.* Reston, VA: Author.

NASPE (National Association for Sport and Physical Education). 2002. *Active start: A statement of physical activity guidelines for children birth to five years.* Online: www.aahperd.org/naspe/template.cfm?template=ns_active.html.

NASPE (National Association for Sport and Physical Education). 2004. *Moving into the future: National standards for physical education.* 2d ed. Reston, VA: Author.

Developmentally Appropriate Practice, 3d Edition

NASPE (National Association for Sport and Physical Education). 2008a. *Appropriate maximum class length for elementary physical education*. Position statement. Reston, VA: Author.

NASPE (National Association for Sport and Physical Education). 2008b. *Comprehensive school physical activity programs*. Position statement. Reston, VA: Author.

National Reading Panel. 2000. *Report of the National Reading Panel: Teaching people to read*. Washington, DC: National Institute of Child Health and Human Development.

National Scientific Council on the Developing Child. 2005. *Excessive stress disrupts the architecture of the developing brain*. Working paper no. 3. Online: www.developingchild. net/pubs/wp/excessive_stress.pdf.

NCES (National Center for Education Statistics). 1997. *The elementary school performance and adjustment of children who enter kindergarten late or repeat kindergarten: Findings from national surveys* (Publication No. 98097). Washington, DC: U.S. Dept. of Education.

NCES (National Center for Education Statistics). 2008. All levels of education. In *Digest of Education Statistics, 2007* (NCES 2008-022). Online: nces.ed.gov/programs/digest/d07/ch_1.asp.

NCTE (National Council of Teachers of English). 2003. *Writing in the early grades, K–2*. Online: www.ncte.org/prog/writing/research/113328.htm.

NCTM (National Council of Teachers of Mathematics). 2000. *Principles and standards for school mathematics*. Position statement. Reston, VA: Author.

NCTM (National Council of Teachers of Mathematics). 2006. *Curriculum focal points for prekindergarten through grade 8 mathematics: A quest for coherence*. Reston, VA: Author.

NEGP (National Education Goals Panel). 1997. *The National Education Goals report: Building a nation of learners*. Washington, DC: U.S. Government Printing Office.

Nelson, C.A. 2002. Neural development and lifelong plasticity. In *Handbook of applied developmental science, Vol. 1*, eds. R.M. Lerner, F. Jacobs, & D. Wertlieb, 31–60. Thousand Oaks, CA: Sage Publications.

Nelson, C.A., K.M. Thomas, & M. de Haan. 2006. Neural bases of cognitive development. In *Handbook of child psychology, Vol. 2: Cognition, perception, and language*, 6th ed., eds. D. Kuhn & R. Siegler, 3–57. Hoboken, NJ: John Wiley & Sons.

Neuman, S.B. 2003. From rhetoric to reality: The case for high-quality compensatory prekindergarten programs. *Phi Delta Kappan* 85 (4): 286–91.

Newcombe, N.S. 2005. *What do we mean when we say modularity?* Master lecture presented at the biennial meeting of the Society for Research in Child Development, April 7–10, Atlanta, GA.

Newcombe, N., & J. Huttenlocher. 1992. Children's early ability to solve perspective taking problems. *Developmental Psychology* 28: 654–64.

Newman, L.S. 1990. Intentional and unintentional memory in young children: Remembering vs. playing. *Journal of Experimental Child Psychology* 50 (2): 243–58.

Newman, R.S. 2008. Adaptive and nonadaptive help seeking with peer harassment: An integrative perspective of coping and self-regulation. *Educational Psychologist* 43 (1): 1–15.

NICHD (National Institute for Child Health and Human Development) Early Child Care Research Network. 2002. The relation of global first-grade classroom environment to structural classroom features and teacher and student behaviors. *Elementary School Journal* 102 (5): 367–87.

NICHD (National Institute for Child Health and Human Development) Early Child Care Research Network. 2006. Childcare effect sizes for the NICHD Study of Early Child Care and Youth Development. *American Psychologist* 61: 99–116.

NICHD (National Institute for Child Health and Human Development) Early Child Care Research Network. 2007. Age of entry to kindergarten and children's academic achievement and socioemotional development. *Early Education and Development* 18 (2): 337–68.

Nielsen, D.C., A.L. Barry, P.T. Staab. 2008. Teachers' reflections of professional change during a literacy-reform initiative. *Teaching & Teacher Education* 24 (5): 1288–303.

Nguyen, S.P., & G.L. Murphy. 2003. An apple is more than just a fruit: Cross-classification in children's concepts. *Child Development* 74 (6): 1783–806.

Odom, S.L., ed. 2002. *Widening the circle: Including children with disabilities in preschool programs*. New York: Teachers College Press.

Ostrov, J.M., D.A. Gentile, & N.R. Crick. 2006. Media exposure, aggression and prosocial behavior during early childhood: A longitudinal study. *Social Development* 15 (4): 612–27.

PE Central. 2009. *PE Central: The premier web site for health and physical education*. Online: www.pecentral.org.

Patterson, D.L., & H. Van Der Mars. 2008. Distant interactions and their effects on children's physical activity levels. *Physical Education & Sport Pedagogy* 13 (3): 277–94.

Penno, J.F., I.A.G. Wilkinson, & D.W. Moore. 2002. Vocabulary acquisition from teacher explanation and repeated listening to stories: Do they overcome the Matthew effect? *Journal of Educational Psychology* 94 (1): 23–33.

Perfetti, C.A., & L. Hart. 2002. The lexical quality hypothesis. *Studies in written language and literacy, Vol. 11: Precursors of functional literacy*, eds. L. Verhoeven, D. Elbro, & P. Reitsma. Philadelphia: John Benjamins.

Perner, J., B. Lang, & D. Kloo. 2002. Theory of mind and self-control: More than a common problem of inhibition. *Child Development* 73 (3): 752–67.

Perry, B.D., L. Hogan, & S. Marlin. 2000. Curiosity, pleasure and play: A neurodevelopmental perspective. *HAAEYC Advocate*. Online: www.ChildTrauma.org/ctamaterials/Curiosity.asp.

Peth-Pierce, R. 2000. *A good beginning: Sending America's children to school with the social emotional competence they need to succeed*. Child Mental Health Foundations and Agencies Network (FAN) Monograph. Bethesda, MD: National Institute of Mental Health, Office of Communications and Public Liaison.

Pettit, G.S. 2004. Violent children in developmental perspective. *Current Directions in Psychological Science* 13: 194–97.

Piaget, J. 1930. *The child's conception of the world*. New York: Harcourt, Brace & World.

Piaget, J. 1932/1965. *The moral judgement of the child*. New York: Free Press.

Piaget, J. 1951. *Play, dreams, and imitation in childhood*. New York: Norton.

Piaget, J. 1952. *The origins of intelligence in children*. New York: International Universities Press.

Piaget, J. 1962. *Play, dreams and imitation in childhood*. New York: Norton.

Piaget, J., & B. Inhelder. 1969. *The psychology of the child*. New York: Basic.

Pianta, R.C., J. Belsky, N. Vandergrift, R. Houts, & F.J. Morrison. 2008. Classroom effects on children's achievement trajectories in elementary school. *American Educational Research Journal* 45 (2): 365–97.

Pianta, R.C., & M. Kraft-Sayre. 2003. *Successful kindergarten transition: Your guide to connecting children, families, and schools*. Baltimore: Paul H. Brookes.

Pianta, R.C., B. Hamre, & M.W. Stuhlman. 2003. Relationships between teachers and children. In *Comprehensive handbook of psychology, Vol. 7: Educational psychology*, eds. W. Reynolds & G. Miller, 199–234. Hoboken, NJ: John Wiley & Sons.

Pianta, R.C., & M.W. Stuhlman. 2004. Teacher-child relationships and children's success in the first years of school. *School Psychology Review* 33 (3): 444–58.

Pica, R. 2004. *Experiences in movement: Birth to age eight*. 3d ed. Clifton Park, NY: Delmar Learning.

Pre-K Now. 2008a. *Pre-K across the country fact sheet*. Online: www.preknow.org/advocate/factsheets/snapshot.cfm.

Pre-K Now. 2008b. *Pre-K and Latinos fact sheet*. Online: www.preknow.org/policy/factsheets/latinos.cfm.

Purvis, K.L., & R. Tannock. 1997. Language ability in children with attention deficit hyperactivity disorder, reading disabilities, and normal controls. *Journal of Abnormal Child Psychology* 25: 133–44.

Quillian, L., & M.E. Campbell. 2003. Beyond black and white: The present and future of multiracial friendship segregation. *American Sociological Review* 68: 540–66.

Radelet, M.A., S.M. Lephart, E.N. Rubinstein, & J.B. Myers. 2002. Survey of the injury rate for children in community sports. *Pediatrics* 110 (3): e28.

Raine, A., K.A. Dodge, R. Loeber, L. Gatzke-Kopp, D. Lynam, C. Reynolds, M. Stouthamer-Loeber, & J. Liu. 2006. The reactive-proactive aggression questionnaire: Differential correlates of reactive and proactive aggression in adolescent boys. *Aggressive Behavior* 32 (2): 159–71.

RAND Reading Study Group. 2002. *Reading for understanding: Toward an R&D program in reading comprehension*. Santa Monica, CA: RAND Education, Science & Technology Policy Institute.

Raver, C.C. 2002. *Emotions matter: Making the case for the role of young children's emotional development for early school readiness*. Ann Arbor, MI: Society for Research in Child Development.

Raver, C.C., & J. Knitzer. 2002. *Ready to enter: What research tells policymakers about strategies to promote social and emotional school readiness among three- and four-year-old children*. New York: Columbia University, National Center for Children in Poverty.

Ray, A., B. Bowman, & J. Robbins. 2006. *Preparing early childhood teachers to successfully educate all children*. Foundation for Child Development Policy Report. Online: www.fcd-us.org/resources/resources_show. htm?doc_id=463599.

Reggio Emilia Department of Early Education. 1987. *The hundred languages of children: Narrative of the possible* (Exhibit Catalog). Reggio Emilia, region of Emilia Romagna, Italy: Author.

Restrepo, M.A., & K. Kruth. 2003. Grammatical characteristics of a bilingual student with specific language impairment. *Communications Disorders Quarterly* 21: 66–76.

Rhodes, M., B. Enz, & M. LaCount. 2006. Leaps and bounds: Preparing parents for kindergarten. *Young Children* 61 (1): 50–51.

Ridderinkhof, K., M.W. van der Molen, G. Band, & T. Bashore. 1997. Sources of interference from irrelevant information: A developmental study. *Journal of Experimental Child Psychology* 65: 315–41.

Ridley, S.M., R.A. McWilliam, & C.S. Oates. 2000. Observed engagement as an indicator of child care program quality. *Early Education and Development* 11 (2): 133–46.

Rigby, K. 2004. Bullying in childhood. In *Blackwell handbook of childhood social development*, eds. P.K. Smith & C.H. Hart, 549–69. Malden, MA: Blackwell.

Rimm-Kaufman, S.E., K.M. La Paro, J.T. Downer, & R.C. Pianta. 2005. The contribution of classroom setting and quality of instruction to children's behavior in kindergarten classrooms. *Elementary School Journal* 105 (4): 377–94.

Rimm-Kaufman, S.E., R.C. Pianta, & M. Cox. 2001. Teachers' judgments of problems in the transition to school. *Early Childhood Research Quarterly* 15: 147–66.

Roberton, M.A. 1984. Changing motor patterns during childhood. In *Motor development during childhood and adolescence*, ed. J.R. Thomas, 48–90. Minneapolis, MN: Burgess.

Rogoff, B. 2003. *The cultural nature of human development*. Oxford: Oxford University Press.

Rogoff, B., M. Sellers, S. Pirotta, N. Fox, & S. White. 1975. Age of assignment of roles and responsibilities to children. *Human Development* 18: 353–69.

Rohrbeck, C.A., M.D. Ginsburgh-Block, J.W. Fantuzzo, & T.R. Miller. 2003. Peer-assisted learning interventions with elementary school students: A meta-analytic review. *Journal of Educational Psychology* 95 (2): 240–57.

Roseberry-McKibbin, C., & A. Brice. 2005. *What's "normal," what's not: Acquiring English as a second language*. American Speech-Language-Hearing Association. Online: www.readingrockets.org/article/5126.

Rosengren, K.S., & A.K. Hickling. 2000. The development of children's thinking about possible events and plausible mechanisms. In *Imagining the impossible*, eds. K.S. Rosengren, C.N. Johnson, & P.L. Harris, 75–98. Cambridge: Cambridge University Press.

Rothbart, M.K., & J.E. Bates. 2006. Temperament. In *Handbook of child psychology, Vol. 3: Social, emotional, and personality development*, 6th ed., ed. N. Eisenberg, 99–166. New York: John Wiley & Sons.

Rubin, K.H., W. Bukowski, & J. Parker. 2006. Peer interactions, relationships, and groups. In *Handbook of child psychology, Vol. 3: Social, emotional, and personality development*, 6th ed., ed. N. Eisenberg, 571–645. New York: John Wiley & Sons.

Rubin, K.H., K.B. Burgess, & P.D. Hastings. 2002. Stability and social-behavioral consequences of toddlers' inhibited temperament and parenting behaviors. *Child Development* 73 (2): 483–95.

Rubin, K.H., & R.J. Coplan. 1998. Social and nonsocial play in childhood: An individual differences perspective. In *Multiple perspectives on play in early childhood*, eds. O.N. Saracho & B. Spodek, 144–70. Albany, NY: State University of New York Press.

Rueda, M.R., J. Fan, B.D. McCandliss, J.D. Halparin, D.B. Gruber, L.P. Lercari, & M.I. Posner. 2004. Development of attentional networks in childhood. *Neuropsychologia* 42 (8): 1029–40.

Ruff, D. 2002. Variation in human body size and shape. *Annual Review of Anthropology* 31: 211–32.

Ruff, H.A., & M.C. Capozzoli. 2003. Development of attention and distractibility in the first 4 years of life. *Developmental Psychology* 39: 877–90.

Ruffman, T. 1999. Children's understanding of logical inconsistency. *Child Development* 70 (4): 872–86.

Rushton, S., & A. Juola-Rushton. 2008. Classroom learning environment, brain research and the No Child Left Behind initiative: 6 years later. *Early Childhood Education Journal* 36 (1): 87–92.

Ryan, R.M., & E.L. Deci. 2000. Self-determination theory and the facilitation of intrinsic motivation, social development, and well-being. *American Psychologist* 55: 68–78.

Saarni, C. 1999. *The development of emotional competence.* New York: Guilford.

Saarni, C., J.J. Campos, L. Camras, & D. Witherington. 2006. Emotional development: Action, communication, and understanding. In *Handbook of child psychology, Vol. 3: Social, emotional, and personality development,* 6th ed., ed. N. Eisenberg, 226–99. New York: John Wiley & Sons.

Sameroff, A., & S.C. McDonough. 1994. Educational implications of developmental transitions. *Phi Delta Kappan* 76 (3): 188–93.

San Francisco, A.R., E. Mo, M. Carlo, D. August, & C.E. Snow. 2006. The influences of language of literacy instruction and vocabulary on the spelling of Spanish-English bilinguals. *Reading and Writing* 19: 627–42.

Sandall, S., M.L. Hemmeter, B.J. Smith, & M.E. McLean, eds. 2005. *DEC recommended practices: A comprehensive guide for practical application in early intervention/early childhood special education.* Longmont, CO: Sopris West, and Missoula, MT: Division for Early Childhood, Council for Exceptional Children.

Sanders, S.W. 2002. *Active for life: Developmentally appropriate movement programs for young children.* Washington, DC: NAEYC.

Sanders, S.W. 2006. Physical education in kindergarten. In *K today: Teaching and learning in the kindergarten year,* ed. D.F. Gullo, 127–37. Washington, DC: NAEYC.

Sarama, J., & D.H. Clements. 2006. Mathematics in kindergarten. In *K today: Teaching and learning in the kindergarten year,* ed. D.F. Gullo, 85–94. Washington, DC: NAEYC.

Schneider, W. 2002. Memory development in childhood. In *Blackwell handbook of childhood cognitive development,* ed. U. Goswami, 236–56. Malden, MA: Blackwell.

Scholnick, E.K. 1995. Knowing and constructing plans. *SRCD Newsletter* (Fall): 1–2, 17.

Schultz, D., C.E. Izard, B.P. Ackerman, & E. Youngstrom. 2001. Emotion knowledge in economically disadvantaged children: Self-regulatory antecendents and relations to social difficulties and withdrawal. *Development and Psychopathology* 13: 53–67.

Schunk, D.H. 1994. Self-regulation of self-efficacy and attributions in academic settings. In *Self-regulation of learning and performance: Issues and educational implications,* eds. D.H. Schunk & B.J. Zimmerman, 75–100. Hillsdale, NJ: Lawrence Erlbaum.

Schwanenflugel, P.J., R.L. Henderson, & W.V. Fabricius. 1998. Developing organization of mental verbs and theory of mind in middle childhood: Evidence from extensions. *Developmental Psychology* 34: 514–24.

Schweinhart, L.J., & D.P. Weikart. 1997. *Lasting differences: The High/Scope preschool curriculum comparison study through age 23.* Monographs of the High/Scope Educational Research Foundation, vol. 12. Ypsilanti, MI: High/Scope Press.

Seefeldt, C. 2005. *How to work with standards in early childhood classrooms.* New York: Teachers College Press.

Seifert, K. 1993. Cognitive development and early childhood education. In *Handbook of research on the education of young children,* ed. B. Spodek, 9–23. New York: Macmillan.

Shonkoff, J.P., & D.A. Phillips, eds. 2000. *From neurons to neighborhoods: The science of early child development.* A report of the National Research Council. Washington, DC: National Academies Press.

Shuy, R.W., & J. Staton. 1982. Assessing oral language ability in children. In *The language of children reared in poverty: Implications for evaluation and intervention,* eds. L. Feagans & D.C. Farran, 181–95. New York: Academic Press.

Siegler, R., J.S. DeLoache, & N. Eisenberg. 2006. *How children develop.* 2d ed. New York: Worth Publishers.

Silver, R.B., J.R. Measelle, J.M. Armstrong, & M.J. Essex. 2005. Trajectories of classroom externalizing behavior: Contributions of child characteristics, family characteristics, and the teacher-child relationship during the school transition. *Journal of School Psychology* 43 (1): 39–60.

Slack, Jill. 2008. Organizing for effective reading instruction. *SEDL Letter* 19 (2): 7–11. Southwest Educational Development Laboratory (SEDL). Online: www.reading rockets.org/article/25695.

Smith, C.B. 1997. Vocabulary instruction and reading comprehension. *ERIC Digest,* ED412506. Bloomington, IN: ERIC Clearinghouse on Reading English and Communication.

Snider, V.E., & R. Roehl. 2007. Teachers' beliefs about pedagogy and related issues. *Psychology in the Schools* 44 (8): 873–86.

Snow, C.E. 2005. From literacy to learning. *Harvard Education Letter* (July/August). Online: www.edletter.org/current/snow.shtml.

Snow, C.E., M.S. Burns, & P. Griffin. 1998. *Preventing reading difficulties in young children.* Washington, DC: National Academies Press.

Snyder, J., M. Brooker, M.R. Patrick, A. Snyder, L. Schrepferman, & M. Stoolmiller. 2003. Observed peer victimization during early elementary school: Continuity, growth, and relation to risk for child antisocial and depressive behavior. *Child Development* 74 (6): 1881–98.

Sobel, D.M. 2006. How fantasy benefits young children's understanding of pretense. *Developmental Science* 9: 63–75.

Souto-Manning, M., & J. Dice. 2007. Reflective teaching in the early years: A case for mentoring diverse educators. *Early Childhood Education Journal* 34 (6): 425–30.

Spada, N., & P.M. Lightbown. 2008. Form-focused instruction: Isolated or integrated? *Tesol Quarterly* 42 (2): 181–207.

Sroufe, L.A. 1995. *Emotional development: The organization of emotional life in the early years.* Cambridge: Cambridge University Press.

Sroufe, L.A., E. Carlson, & S. Shulman. 1993. Individuals in relationships: Development from infancy through adolescence. In *Studying lives through time: Personality and development*, eds. D.C. Funder, R.D. Parke, C. Tomlinson-Keasey, & K. Widaman, 315–42. Washington, DC: American Psychological Association.

Stahl, S.A., & M.M. Fairbanks. 1986. The effects of vocabulary instruction: A model-based meta-analysis. *Review of Educational Research* 56: 72–110.

Starfield, B. 1992. Child and adolescent health status measures. In *The future of children*, ed. R.E. Behrman. Los Angeles: Center for the Future of Children of the David and Lucile Packard Foundation.

Stearns, E., K.A. Dodge, & M. Nicholson. 2008. Peer contextual influences on the growth of authority-acceptance problems in early elementary school. *Merrill-Palmer Quarterly* 54 (2): 208–31.

Sternberg, R.J. 2002. Intelligence is not just inside the head: The theory of successful intelligence. In *Improving academic achievement*, ed. J. Aronson, 227–44. San Diego: Academic Press.

Sternberg, R.J., & E.L. Grikorenko. 2004. Why we need to explore development in its cultural context. *Merrill-Palmer Quarterly* 50: 369–86.

Strayer, J., & W. Roberts. 2004. Children's anger, emotional expressiveness, and parenting practices. *Social Development* 13: 229–54.

Striano, T., M. Tomasello, & P. Rochat. 2001. Social and object support for early symbolic play. *Developmental Science* 4: 442–55.

Strickland, D.S. 2002. Bridging the gap for African American children. In *Love to read: Essays in developing and enhancing early literacy skills of African American children*, ed. B. Bowman, 63–71. Washington, DC: National Black Child Development Institute.

Strickland, D.S. 2006. Language and literacy in kindergarten. In *K today: Teaching and learning in the kindergarten year*, ed. D.F. Gullo, 73–84. Washington, DC: NAEYC.

Strickland, D.S., & J.A. Schickedanz. 2004. *Learning about print in preschool: Working with letters, words, and beginning links with phonemic awareness*. Newark, DE: International Reading Association.

Subbotsky, E.V. 2004. Magical thinking in judgments of causation: Can anomalous phenomena affect ontological causal beliefs in children and adults? *British Journal of Developmental Psychology* 22: 123–52.

Sulzby, E., & W.H. Teale. 2003. The development of the young child and the emergence of literacy. In *Handbook of research on teaching the English language arts*, 2d ed., ed. J. Flood. Mahwah, NJ: Lawrence Erlbaum.

Sylvester, R. 1995. *A celebration of neurons: An educator's guide to the human brain*. Alexandria, VA: Association for Supervision and Curriculum Development.

Tabors, P.O. 2008. *One child, two languages: A guide for early childhood educators of children learning English as a second language*. 2d ed. Baltimore: Paul H. Brookes.

Tager-Flusberg, H. 2005. Putting words together: Morphology and syntax in the preschool years. In *The development of language*, 5th ed., ed. J.B. Gleason, 148–90. Boston: Allyn & Bacon.

Templeton, S., & D. Bear. 1992. *Development of orthographic knowledge and the foundations of literacy*. Hillsdale, NJ: Lawrence Erlbaum.

Thatcher, R.W., G.R. Lyon, J. Rumsey, & J. Krasnegor. 1996. *Developmental neuroimaging*. San Diego: Academic Press.

Thelen, E., & L.B. Smith. 1998. Dynamic systems theories. In *Handbook of child psychology, Vol. 1: Theoretical models of human development*, 5th ed., ed. R.M. Lerner, 563–634. New York: John Wiley & Sons.

Thomas, W., & V. Collier. 2002. *A national study of school effectiveness for language minority students' long-term academic achievement*. Santa Cruz, CA: Center for Research on Education, Diversity & Excellence.

Thompson, R.A. 2006. The development of the person: Social understanding, relationships, self, conscience. In *Handbook of child psychology, Vol. 3: Social, emotional, and personality development*, 6th ed., ed. N. Eisenberg, 24–98. New York: John Wiley & Sons.

Thompson, R.A., S. Meyer, & M. McGinley. 2006. Understanding values in relationship: The development of conscience. In *Handbook of moral development*, eds. M. Killen & J. Smetana, 267–97. Mahwah, NJ: Lawrence Erlbaum.

Thornton, S., & R. Vukelich. 1988. Effects of children's understanding of time concepts on historical understanding. *Theory and Research in Social Education* 16: 69–82.

Tobin, J., D. Wu, & D. Davidson. 1989. *Preschool in three cultures: Japan, China, and the United States*. New Haven, CT: Yale University Press.

Toomela, A. 2002. Drawing as a verbally mediated activity: A study of relationships between verbal, motor, visuospatial skills and drawing in children. *International Journal of Behavioral Development* 26: 234–47.

Tremblay, R.E. 2000. The development of aggressive behaviour during childhood: What have we learned in the past century? *International Journal of Behavioural Development* 24: 129–41.

Tremblay, R.E., R.O. Pihl, F. Vitaro, & P.L. Dobhin. 1994. Predicting early onset of male antisocial behavior from preschool behavior. *Archives of General Psychiatry* 51 (9): 732.

Tyminski, A.M., M. Weilbacher, N. Lenburg, & C. Brown. 2008. Ladybug lengths: Beginning measurement. *Teaching Children Mathematics* 15 (1): 34–37.

U.S. Census Bureau. 2003. *Language use and English-speaking ability: 2000* (Census 2000 Brief). By H.B. Shin & R. Bruno. Online: www.census.gov/prod/2003pubs/c2kbr-29.pdf.

U.S. Dept. of Education. 2001. *To assure the free appropriate public education of all children with disabilities: Twenty-third annual report to Congress on the implementation of the Individuals with Disabilities Education Act*. Washington, DC: Author.

U.S. Dept. of Health and Human Services & U.S. Dept. of Agriculture. 2005. *The dietary guidelines for Americans, 2005*. 6th ed. Washington, DC: Authors.

Utley, C.A., & S.L. Mortweet. 1997. Peer-mediated instruction and interventions. *Focus on Exceptional Children* 29 (5): 1–23.

Valdes, G. 1996. *Con respeto: Bridging the distances between culturally diverse families and schools. An ethnographic portrait*. New York: Teachers College Press.

Vaughn, B.E., T.N. Colvin, M.R. Azria, L. Caya, & L. Krzysik. 2001. Dyadic analyses of friendship in a sample of preschool-age children attending Head Start: Correspondence between measures and implications for social competence. *Child Development* 72 (3): 862–78.

Verscheuren, K., A. Marcoen, & V. Schoefs. 1996. The internal working model of the self, attachment, and competence in five-year-olds. *Child Development* 67 (5): 2493–511.

Vieillevoye, S., & N. Nader-Grosbois. 2008. Self-regulation during pretend play in children with intellectual disability and in normally developing children. *Research in Developmental Disabilities* 29 (3): 256–72.

Vygotsky, L. 1978. *Mind in society: The development of higher psychological processes*. Cambridge, MA: Harvard University Press.

Wahlstrom, K.L., & K.S. Louis. 2008. How teachers experience principal leadership: The roles of professional community, trust, efficacy, and shared responsibility. *Educational Administration Quarterly* 44 (4): 458–95.

Wasik, B.A. 2001. Phonemic awareness and young children. *Childhood Education* 77 (3): 128–33.

Webster-Stratton, C., M.J. Reid, & M. Hammond. 2001. Preventing conduct problems, promoting social competence: A parent and teacher training partnership in Head Start. *Journal of Child Clinical Psychology* 30: 283–302.

Weissbourd, R. 1996. The feel-good trap. *The New Republic* (19 & 26 August): 12–14.

Wellman, H.M., D. Cross, & J. Watson. 2001. Meta-analysis of theory-of-mind development: The truth about false belief. *Child Development* 72 (3): 655–84.

Werner, E., & R. Smith. 2001. *Journeys from childhood to midlife: Risk, resilience, and recovery*. Ithaca, NY: Cornell University Press.

Werner, R.S., K.W. Cassidy, & M. Juliano. 2006. The role of social-cognitive abilities in preschoolers' aggressive behaviour. *British Journal of Developmental Psychology* 24 (4): 775–99.

White, S.H. 1965. Evidence for a hierarchical arrangement of learning processes. In *Advances in child development and behavior*, eds. L.P. Lipsitt & C.C. Spiker, 187–220. New York: Academic Press.

White, S.H. 1970. Some general outlines of the matrix of developmental changes between five and seven years. *Bulletin of the Orton Society* 20: 41–57.

White, T.G., M.F. Graves, & W.H. Slater. 1990. Growth of reading vocabulary in diverse elementary schools: Decoding and word meaning. *Journal of Educational Psychology* 82: 281–90.

Whitehurst, G.J. 1999. The role of inside-out skills in reading readiness of children from low-income families. In *From prereaders to readers: The role of phonological processing skills in at risk and typically developing children*, chaired by C. Lonigan. Symposium conducted at the biennial meeting of the Society for Research in Child Development, April 15–18, Albuquerque, NM.

Whitin, P. 2001. Kindness in a jar. *Young Children* 56 (5): 18–22.

Whiting, B.B., & C.P. Edwards. 1988. *Children of different worlds: The formation of social behavior*. Cambridge, MA: Harvard University Press.

Williams, K., K.I. Haywood, & M. Painter. 1996. Environmental versus biological influences on gender differences in the overarm throw for force: Dominant and nondominant arm throws. *Women in Sport and Physical Activity Journal* 5: 29–48.

Wilson, H.K., R.C. Pianta, & M.W. Stuhlman. 2007. Typical classroom experiences in first grade: The role of classroom climate and functional risk in the development of social competencies. *Elementary School Journal* 108 (2): 81–96.

Wood, C. 2007. *Yardsticks: Children in the classroom, ages 4–14*. 3d ed. Turner Falls, MA: Northeast Foundation for Children.

Wood-Ramsey, J., & P.H. Miller. 1988. The facilitation of selective attention in preschoolers. *Child Development* 59 (6): 1497–503.

Worth, K., & S. Grollman. 2003. *Worms, shadows and whirlpools: Science in the early childhood classroom*. Portsmouth, NH: Heinemann.

Yang, O.S. 2000. Guiding children's verbal plan and evaluation during free play: An application of Vygotsky's genetic epistemology to the early childhood classroom. *Early Childhood Education Journal* 28 (1): 3–10.

Yu, S., & E. Hannum. 2007. Food for thought: Poverty, family nutritional environment, and children's educational performance in rural China. *Sociological Perspectives* 50 (1): 53–77.

Zehr, M.A. 2007. Interactivity seen as key. *Education Week's Digital Directions* 1: 29.

Zero to Three. 2008. *Caring for infants and toddlers in groups: Developmentally appropriate practice*. 2d ed. Washington, DC: Author.

Zill, N., & J. West. 2001. *Entering kindergarten: Findings from the condition of education, 2000*. Washington, DC: U.S. Dept. of Education, National Center for Education Statistics.

Zins, J., M. Bloodworth, R. Weissberg, & H. Walberg. 2004. The scientific base linking social and emotional learning to school success. In *Building academic success on social and emotional learning: What does the research say?*, eds. J. Zins, R. Weissberg, M. Wang, & H.J. Walberg, 1–22. New York: Teachers College Press.

Zuckerman, G. 2003. The learning activity in the first years of schooling: The developmental path toward reflection. In *Vygotsky's educational theory in cultural context*, eds. A. Kozulin, B. Gindis, V.S. Ageev, & S.K. Miller, 177–99. Cambridge: Cambridge University Press.

Index

Developmentally Appropriate Practice, 3d Edition

join us
to build better futures for all young children...

naeyc®
National Association for the Education of Young Children

NAEYC delivers **VALUE** to our members through

PROFESSIONAL DEVELOPMENT Attend the NAEYC Annual Conference & Expo, the largest conference of early childhood educators in the world, and the National Institute for Early Childhood Professional Development. Receive NAEYC's researched-based publications with the latest information on early childhood education.

ADVOCACY NAEYC is the voice of the early childhood profession in Washington, D.C., and state and local Affiliates advocate for early childhood education issues in your community.

NETWORKING NAEYC's members have access to great networking opportunities to make friends and build professional relationships through the many NAEYC Interest Forums and Web-based NAEYC Online Communities.

SERVICE Join today to receive discounts with your membership. Members are our top priority, and the NAEYC staff is ready to serve you. Call the NAEYC Customer Service Center at 800-424-2460 or e-mail membership@naeyc.org.

Two easy ways to join!
Visit www.naeyc.org • Call 800-424-2460

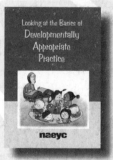